Knowing Asia, Being Asian

This book studies the various representations of Asia in Bengali literary periodicals between the 1860s and 1940s. It looks at how these periodicals tried to analyse the political situation in Asia in the context of world politics and how Indian nationalistic ideas and associations impacted their vision.

The volume highlights the influences of cosmopolitanism, universalism and nationalism which contributed towards a common vision of a united and powerful Asia and how these ideas were put into practice. It analyses travel accounts by men and women and examines how women became the focus of the didactic efforts of all writers for a horizontal dissemination of Asian consciousness. The author also provides a discussion on Asian art and culture, past and present connections between Asian countries and the resurgence of 19th-century Buddhism in the consciousness of the Bengalis.

Rich in archival material, *Knowing Asia, Being Asian* will be useful for scholars and researchers of history, Asian studies, modern India, cultural studies, media studies, journalism, publishing, post-colonial studies, travel writings, women and gender studies, political studies and social anthropology.

Sarvani Gooptu is Professor of Asian Literary and Cultural Studies at Netaji Institute for Asian Studies, Kolkata, India. Previously she worked in the History Department at Calcutta Girls' College, Calcutta University, as Associate Professor and Head (1997–2016). Her main areas of research are nationalism and culture in the colonial and post-colonial periods. Among her publications are *The Actress in the Public Theatres of Calcutta* (2015), *The Music of Nationhood: Dwijendralal Roy of Bengal* (2018) and two co-edited volumes *On Modern Indian Sensibilities: Culture, Politics, History* with Ishita Banerjee-Dube, (2018) and *The Regional Great Game in the Indian Ocean and India's Evolving Maritime Strategy* (2020) with Vivek Mishra. She has published extensively in national and international journals on diverse topics like minority communities of Calcutta; biographical works on leading Indian men and women; Asia in Bengali journals and literature; India's relations with China, Japan and Burma; women's travel narratives; Buddhist pilgrimages in the past and present in Asia and Gandhi and Bengal. She is Council Member for 21 years at Netaji Research Bureau and is also Council member and Secretary of Indian Association of Asian and Pacific Studies.

Knowing Asia, Being Asian

Cosmopolitanism and Nationalism in Bengali Periodicals, 1860–1940

Sarvani Gooptu

Routledge
Taylor & Francis Group
NEW YORK AND LONDON

First published 2022
by Routledge
2 Park Square, Milton Park, Abingdon, Oxon OX14 4RN

and by Routledge
605 Third Avenue, New York, NY 10158

Routledge is an imprint of the Taylor & Francis Group, an informa business

British Library Cataloguing-in-Publication Data
A catalogue record for this book is available from the British Library

Library of Congress Cataloging-in-Publication Data
A catalog record has been requested for this book

ISBN: 978-0-367-63977-8 (hbk)
ISBN: 978-1-032-15363-6 (pbk)
ISBN: 978-1-003-24378-6 (ebk)

DOI: 10.4324/9781003243786

Typeset in Sabon
by Deanta Global Publishing Services, Chennai, India

To
My father, Nirendra Nath Dutta (1928–2019), whom I miss a lot
And
Pradeep, Subhalakshmi and Siddhesh with love

Contents

Acknowledgements

This book is the result of a long journey that started when I went hunting in the old Bengali periodicals for sources on Dwijendralal Roy, and then later on the actresses of the Bengali theatre. A nebulous idea about Asian consciousness got concrete shape when my friends Professors Rajasri Basu (whom we lost tragically), Suchandra Ghosh, Lipi Ghosh and Anasua Basu Raychaudhuri requested me to present my ideas at a conference. I thank them for their confidence in me. I owe a huge intellectual debt to Professor Sugata Bose, whose lectures and writings on Asian Connections have inspired me over the years. Thank you for always helping me in every way, especially for reading the manuscript despite your busy schedule. This project was financed by the Education Department, West Bengal Government, and I thank them for the grant and Professor Suranjan Das, Director, NIAS, for supporting my proposal.

I owe more than I can ever repay to Professor Gautam Bhadra, who literally taught me how to research and write, and his review of my article on Japan in the volume *On Modern Indian Sensibilities* dedicated to him helped me immensely. The support of my dear friends Professors R. Mahalakshmi and Rakesh Batabyal of Jawaharlal Nehru University gave me the confidence to transform the articles I presented at conferences there into a larger research. Also, the input that I received at conferences held in Seoul National University, Hebrew University and Manipal University helped me tremendously. I thank my friend Dr Susmita Mukherjee for correcting parts of the draft, for listening patiently to my ramblings and for always offering academic and friendly support.

My mother Bijaya Dutta has been my role model in academics and music and I must acknowledge her for teaching me to have faith in all circumstances. I look forward to her delight on this offering though we will miss my father Nirendranath Dutta's presence sorely.

Krishnamashi, Smt. Krishna Bose, teacher, writer, parliamentarian and lifelong researcher on Netaji, has been my favourite aunt and friend for a long time with whom I shared all my jokes and new researches and who to my regret will not be able to launch this book as she has the previous ones. I dedicate this book to her in the memory of her love. I also acknowledge the kindness that Professor Sugata Bose, Sumantra Bose and my friends at Netaji Research Bureau, specially Raka Sen and my Rabindra Sangeet Guru Pramita Mullick, have always shown me. I thank the staff there for their constant help, specially Monohar and Sujata.

Netaji Institute for Asian Studies is the most wonderful place to work in, thanks to the best boss anyone can have, Professor Suranjan Das, and I thank him and my young friends and colleagues, Anup Sekhar Chakraborty, Vivek Mishra, Sandip Halder and the supportive staff there, specially Sraboni, Gourango, Nilotpal, Anuradha, Mita, Arpita and Tarak. I must also thank research assistants, Paulomi Mallick and Priti Singh for their help during my research work.

I take this opportunity to express my gratitude to all my teachers, colleagues and friends who have supported, guided and encouraged me in my research, specially to my teachers, Professors Sekhar Bandopadhyay, Binay Bhushan Chaudhuri, Arun Bandopadhyay, Bharati Ray and Hari Vasudevan (whose untimely passing saddened me). I'm grateful to my friends, Professors Ishita Banerjee-Dube, Choi Chatterjee, Samita Sen, Nandini Bhattacharya, Sipra Mukherjee, Nayeem Anis, Purna Chowdhury (for help with a chapter title), Susmita Sinha, Dinky Dutt and Nandita Palchoudhuri for always being there for me. I am grateful to Professors Tansen Sen and Seema Alavi for their support and advice at various points in my career.

I'm very grateful to Kamalika Mukherjee of Centre for Studies in Social Sciences (Archives) without whose help this work would have been impossible to achieve. I thank all the staff at National Library, Nehru Memorial Library, British Library and Calcutta Club Library for their help during my research.

My heartfelt thanks go to Shashank Sinha, Anvitaa Bajaj and Antara Ray Chaudhary at Routledge for being so supportive these past years.

I thank my friends and family who have kept me motivated and cheerful with their advice, messages and pictures during the dreadful pandemic while I completed the book – Aindrila Bose, Nabanita Gooptu, Arun and Anupama Jhunjhunwala, Raja and Rakhi Mookherjee, Udit and Sanjukta Mitra, Susmita Dasgupta, Chandrani Chakraborty, Paramita Gupta, Sramana Chatterjee, Debisree Dutta, Ballari Bagchi, Sounak Chattopadhyay, Maitreyee Bandopadhyay, Mahua Chakraborty, friends at Rotary Clubs (Calcutta and Inner City), my very dear friends of Carmel Convent and Lady Brabourne College, Bhowanipur Baikali Association, IAAPS and all my cousins at Dutta Bari Worldwide.

My deepest appreciation and love go to my sisters Indrani Bose, Sakti Kunz, Raja Duggumali Dutta and Sohini Gooptu and my brothers Suvendranath Dutta, Indranath Bose, Brian Kunz and Adheep Gooptu who have always supported me in all my ventures and demands.

My special thanks go to Abon Gooptu, for his immense help in typing parts of the manuscript and bibliography, Subhalakshmi Gooptu, for hunting out books online and keeping me aware of the latest academic trends, and Siddhesh Gooptu, for technical help at all times. My love and good wishes to the babies of the family – Aniruddha, Frances, Neel and Tara Bose, Arunendro and Rajendro Dutta, Ahon Gooptu and my respects to Ma and Baba, Arundhati and Ajit Gooptu.

And finally my children, Subhalakshmi and Siddhesh, whose achievements I'm very proud of, and Pradeep, friend, husband and confidant – thank you for being mine.

Introduction

With the start of the process of decolonisation in Asia, a realisation dawned in the minds of Asians that it was important to acknowledge Asian ties or the 'call of Asiatic blood', as Burmese nationalist leader Ba Maw described it so eloquently. It was also felt by most commentators in this period that despite this alleged commonality, there was a lack of detailed information about the different countries that constituted Asia. In the welcome address in the Asian Relations Conference held in the historic Purana Qila in Delhi in 1947, Sir Shri Ram, industrialist, educationist and the Chairman of the Reception Committee, made a prophetic remark when he said that there was a contrast between the 'fairly free intercourse' between India and her neighbouring countries ten or even twenty centuries ago, in spite of the then prevailing difficulties of transport, delays and risks, and the almost 'total absence of any intercourse between us in recent times' in spite of the far better means of transport and other facilities.[1]

This 'invisible, but nonetheless effective barrier' that Sri Ram regretfully talked about in 1947 became the matter of course strangely enough, post-independence, and we moved away from the free intercourse with people that was discussed and popularised amongst the educated public through a method that was educative yet entertaining throughout the late 19th and early 20th centuries. Intellectuals were always aware that Asian connections were of utmost importance if there was any hope for survival of the people of the East. The easiest way to interact with a large number of people on a regular basis was the vernacular periodical which from the 19th century had turned out to be a medium of creating conscious public opinion. My argument in this book is that Indian intellectuals, far from collaborating with the colonizer's powers, as they are sometimes accused of, effectively appropriated western practices, techniques, ideas and philosophies and turned them in their own favour, against exploitative imperial rule. They assimilated the techniques of pedagogy through entertainment and used that technique to create a veritable treasure trove of periodicals through which serious discussions and analysis of literature, religion, ethics, biographical studies, history, archaeology, anthropology, translations, physical sciences, home science, medicine, cultural practices, politics, and nationalism took place. In this book, I have used as my main source the literary periodicals (*sahitya patrika*) which contain articles on Asia, and which were owned and edited by Bengalis in Calcutta or elsewhere. The awareness about the need to discuss other Asian countries and to travel to them for different reasons and then write about people the travellers encountered fascinated me. Inward-looking nationalism as the highest virtue was not the only way nationalism was looked at even at the time when it was the highest order of things. Today despite the triumph of globalisation, we still interact culturally only with the west and we have barricaded our minds against the east. We are blind and deaf to Asia. Reading these periodicals from the 1860s right up to the 1940s, I realised that many writers in them were exhorting people to fight against that amnesia about past Asian interactions that had overtaken them in the preceding centuries. The process of revival of memories of ties with Asian countries continued for a century and a half, but faded from public memory gradually. With the declaration of the 20th century as the Asian century we have to again rediscover Asian interactions.

There are some who believe that the ancient Asian interactions were not conducive to healthy interaction between Asian countries because of the excessive nationalistic jargon that plagued it. It is my contention that this is a partial truth. One cannot brush aside, on those grounds, a whole progressive intellectual movement by individuals holding varied beliefs and philosophies, not connected by associations, caste, sex or political affiliations. That is why the use of a multitude of periodical articles written by many people who were often not very well known or belonging to any identifiable political strand, yet who spoke in a common language, had a common motive, had a common vision for the improvement of their fellowmen which was not inward-looking, seems to be a logical way to prove that a society had many strands of influences working simultaneously over a considerable period – in this case cosmopolitanism, universalism and nationalism in the period 1860–1940 towards a vision of a united and powerful Asia through explorations of historical memory and travel.

By using the recommendation of Jaspers, to use 'the whole history of mankind to furnish us with standards by which to measure the meaning of what is happening at the present time',[2] I have located 531 articles on Asia from 37 periodicals, with an intention to 'measure the encounters between civilizations to understand the present', as Toynbee suggested.[3] The fact that from the first issues these Bengali periodicals that emerged from the middle of the 19th century showed a commitment to Asia along with the expected interest in England and Europe has to do with both cosmopolitan and nationalist ideas existing without any contradiction in a large number of Bengali intellectuals. Knowing about Asia and exploring what being Asian might mean for Indians became an important focus for the vernacular press who fancied themselves as public educators or the other way around, those who had something important to say started a periodical. Newspapers and literary periodicals were considered the best means of training the readers to form opinions on all contemporary matters as well as past history, which cast long shadows on the present. Taking advantage of the innovations of printing and education that were introduced in the 19th century, Indians turned the tables on the British Raj and later the British government by moulding public opinion. It is my contention that the vernacular periodicals of the period not only wrote about patriotism and nationalism but also prevented being blindsided by it through its cosmopolitanism. These lines which in retrospect seem clear, in that period when so many new ideas were converging and so many paths were emerging to different goals, were rather fuzzy.

What was this 'Asia'? In the writings of Orientalist scholars in the second half of the 18th century, Asia was considered as a whole despite their imperialist biases. As Tony Ballantyne has shown in his work *Orientalism and Race*, a number of Scottish scholars, trained in Edinburgh, used the experience of their service under the British empire in India and South-East Asia 'to write histories of Asian societies . . . against the backdrop of the universalist development of civilization'.[4] Using comparative philology and anthropology, scholars like William Robertson, Alexander Hamilton, Francis

Buchanan, William Marsden, Stamford Raffles and John Crawford tried to establish connections and linkages between India and South-East Asia. There was, of course, no question about their identity as imperialists and in the use of the term 'Further India', Ballantyne saw the reality of the British looking upon both the mainland and the island South-East Asia as frontiers of their Indian empire. Generally, Asia has been seen as a contrast to Europe. But as another historian Michael Edwards in 1962 pointed out, imperialism was the diffuser of western civilisation and no matter what the motive of this diffusion was, this 'baggage of imperialism' led to a desire among colonists to re-acquire the success of power which the western countries had demonstrated in Asia. 'The men who beat the West at its own game', Edwards wrote, 'were western style national leaders, who used the west's own weapons against itself'.[5] Rene Grousset had gone further in 1946, when he wrote in *Sum of History*, that 'conquest or penetration of Asia by Europe has produced, as a kind of counterstroke, the invasion of Europe by Asiatic art, and to some extent by the ideas which inspired this art'.[6]

Using similar terminologies, Asians identified themselves through the double other. One, as Asians versus Europeans, by using differences of Oriental and Occidental values and ideals; and second, trying to locate themselves within Asia by using the prism of similarity–dissimilarity with other Asian nationalities. As Pramatha Chaudhuri, using an alias, Birbal writes satirically in an article called 'Us and You' in *Bharati*, 'Europe and Asia are different and precisely because of that, Asia exists, otherwise there would have been no us but only you'.[7] It might also have been an ironical statement, if Chaudhuri was aware that it was precisely how Europe was conceptualised in opposition to Asia as historian Denys Hay has shown.[8] Almost all the writers in the journals attempting to identify Asia in a comparative manner talked about the passivity of the east compared to the energy of the west. This was undoubtedly the prevailing notion till Japan changed the equation leading to newer standards of comparison. It is not as if western viewpoint was totally linear and there were always those who attempted to understand Asia with 'a view to mutual respect and benefit' by not dwell(ing) upon the points of similarity'. whether they originate in imitation of one of the parties by the other or from a mere convergence due to other causes.' To Jean Herbert, cooperation is hardly worthwhile unless 'each party contributes what its partners do not possess' so that there is justifiable contribution to 'the building of the "universe"as opposed to the multiverse'"'[9] Mutual respect among the Asian people can come only through careful remembrance in which aggression of all sorts has been sifted out and as Dick Wilson pointed out that for Asia today re-understanding past linkages is the only way the constituent nations can recover from the 'wounds of Western imperialism' through a reiteration of 'the idea of an Asian community, an Asian coherence', as 'a favourite medicine to stifle the pain'.[10]

Cosmopolitan ideas and Asian sensibilities among some prominent Indians

Ideas of universalism and cosmopolitanism came simultaneously with the education implemented by the colonial government. This was possible partly because of the conversation of the English-educated Indians with, what Charles E. Trevelyan, the avid Anglicist along with Macaulay and Duff during the education debate in 1835 called, the 'best and wisest Englishmen through the medium of their works' rather than through 'personal contact'.[11] For him it was gratifying that Indians could thereby form higher ideas about England, but what actually happened was the release of the Indian mind from the shackles of colonial domination at least to some extent. There was also a simultaneous quest for reaching out beyond Britain into Europe for expansion of knowledge. Ram Mohan Roy, considered to be a standard of appeal by protagonists of both sides of the debate, was one of many who due to a knowledge of many languages could have a broader conception of history and a consciousness about India in Asia. Roy, in analysing the advantages and disadvantages of 'settlement in India by Europeans', expressed his Asia consciousness and also laid the foundation of a viewpoint assiduously believed in by his later compatriots, when he writes that Indians with the help of European settlers 'may succeed sooner or later in enlightening and civilizing the surrounding nations of Asia'.[12] He substituted Asia for India in his memorial to the King in Council against the Press Ordinance of 1823, when he wrote about good governance of Asian princes in their submission to the 'judgement of their subjects'.[13] His awareness of the countries of Asia is expressed brilliantly in the satirical work, 'A Dialogue between a Missionary and Three Chinese Converts', where Roy shows how the three converts while initially appearing to be inconsistent about their own religious and philosophical concepts ultimately proved to the smug missionaries how much they knew about not only Chinese knowledge but also had tolerance regarding different world philosophical systems.[14] Keshab Chandra Sen under Roy's influence and guidance of Debendranath Tagore became a Brahmo missionary travelling to Ceylon with Tagore, his son Satyendranath and a friend Kalikamal Ganguly. Sen's travelogue of that voyage written as Diary entries[15] was the beginning of a spiritual journey through the *Bharatbarshiya Brahmo Samaj* against Tagore's *Adi Brahmo Samaj* and then moved ahead to establish *Nababidhan* or New Dispensation, the universal religion combining world religions.

Another world figure Swami Vivekananda, represented Asia in the west, which he visited twice – 1893–1897 and 1899–1902 – and was able to establish connections with many intellectuals in Europe, England and America. On his way to and from the west, he travelled through many parts of Asia. An interesting travelogue has been compiled by Swami Sambuddhananda, General Secretary of Swami Vivekananda Centenary Committee, as *Swami Vivekananda on Himself*,[16] which appears to be in the Swami's voice but which is really a collection of stories told to his disciples. It is interesting to read his 'observations' on the cities he is passing through from his departure point Bombay. At Colombo he only recalls the 'gigantic *murti* (image) of the Lord Buddha in a reclining posture, entering Nirvana', while Penang which he called 'only a strip of land along the sea in the body of the Malay Peninsula' passed like a blur before he reached Singapore. He describes the rare plants he saw at the botanical gardens and adversely compares their mangosteen to the 'nonpareil mango'.[17] Hong Kong which came next in the itinerary brought for him a feel of China, and he describes the 'Chinese boats that one sees as soon as the steamer casts anchor'. He also describes the boatmen, their families and the little Chinese babies. It is interesting he refers to the Chinese babies who dangle their feet from the backpack of their mothers as John Chinaman'.[18] The case of John Chinaman that is referred to in the words attributed to Swami Vivekananda may have been a example of association of ideas by the disciple writer to whom allegedly the travelogue was quoted. It is obvious this refers to a later reference which became popular among the Bengalis ever since Rabindranath Tagore published a translation article in *Bangadarshan*. This was a book by G.L. Dickinson, a professor of English at Oxford, who anonymously wrote 'Letters of John Chinaman' during his visit to China. It greatly excited the attention of both Tagore and Kakuzo Okakura, the cultural leaders of India and Japan, respectively, as vindication of their common belief of the greatness of eastern values against the superiority myth of Europeans. This reference may or may not have been made by Swami Vivekananda but is proof of a widely used phrase for referring to Chinese by Bengalis in the early 20th century. Neither Tagore nor Okakura, along with many others like Sister Nivedita, realised that the essay was by an Englishman. Incidentally, Tagore's translation of this essay as 'Chinaman's Letters' in *Bangadarshan*, despite its supposed symbolism, led to an attack on his writing style by the editor of *Rangalay*, Panchkadi Bandopadhyay, and thus probably became a discussion item in every Bengali household.[19]

Vivekananda appears to have been unimpressed by Canton which he describes as the 'dirtiest town' he saw, though Hong Kong was 'beautiful'.[20] Nagasaki in Japan appeared to be one of the greatest cities and the Japanese were to Vivekananda 'one of the cleanliest peoples on earth' and 'Japan is the land of the picturesque!' with its neat houses with Japanese-style gardens.[21] He travelled through Japan by road to visit Osaka, Kyoto and Tokyo and compared Tokyo to Calcutta saying that it was twice the size with nearly double the population. Vivekananda found everything in Japan interesting and praised them as a great nation retaining their individuality despite a fine assimilation of European art and knowledge'.[22] When the Swami's American disciple Mrs Mac Leod visited Japan, she met Okakura and Hori San, who then accompanied her to India in 1901 and met the Swami at the Belur monastery. Okakura Kakuzo who greatly admired Vivekananda invited him to Japan for a lecture tour and even advanced money for his travel but poor health had made this journey impossible.

Even if one can sense the cosmopolitan spirit in many families of the time, I will only refer to some Bengali families, who represented the temperament of the time as well as expressed it to others through their writing, specifically in the leading Bengali periodicals where I have identified Asia consciousness: the Tagores, who were associated with many periodicals including *Bharati*, *Sahitya*, *Balak* and *Bangadarshan*; Ramananda Chattopadhyay, who was the first to represent Bengali diaspora outside Bengal and reigned over *Pradip, Dasi, Prabashi* and *Modern Review*; Upendrakishore Raychowdhury and his family associated with children's magazines *Sakha* and *Sandesh*, as well as introducing advanced printing technology in their journalistic ventures; and the Roys of Krishnanagar, whose contribution to Bengali literature and journalism was immense. The importance of women's magazines like *Bamabodhini Patrika, Mahila, Bangalakshmi, Bharat Mahila and Antahpur* and women editors like Swarnakumari Debi, Sarala Debi, Gyanadanandini Debi, Hemantakumari Chaudhuri, Sarajubala Debi and Kumudini Mitra has been dealt with later.

As Edward Thompson said in *Rabindranath Tagore: Poet and Dramatist*, 'in no other family, than the Tagores, could all the varied impulses of the time have been felt so strongly and fully. These impulses had come from many men'.[23] The Tagores of Jorasanko and Pathuriaghata as one of the cultural and social leaders of Bengal followed Dwarakanath Tagore in his universalist vision rare in his time, leading to his ostracism even by his own family. Yet, his wholehearted support, including financial, for modern medical education, steam communication, fight for free press, coinciding with his deep admiration for the British, gained him many admirers as well. The diaries he kept on his travel to Europe and description of Ceylon, Cairo and Alexandria make interesting reading.[24] His son Devendranath Tagore's autobiography shows an adventurous spirit in both his travels and his explorations in spirituality. In the context of my book, I found his chapter on a visit to Burma very charming. In 1850, while intending to travel to Allahabad, he jumped on a sea-bound steamer and reached Moulmein where he stayed as guest of a 'Mudaliar of Madras, who was a high government official and a real gentleman'. Tagore took a keen interest in the roads and markets he saw, food they eat and also savoured their distinct culture, the 'phungis' he met on the way and who he thought were 'similar to the Dandi sect of Benaras', and enjoyed sightseeing on elephant back.[25] In the same year, he also travelled to Ceylon, accompanied by his son Satyendranath and his disciple Keshab Chandra Sen. All the Tagores believed in what Rabindranath so succinctly put, in establishing relationships between men of different countries, since those were the only ones which survived.[26] Rabindranath Tagore's articulation of the ideas trending in Bengal is the easiest to trace since so much of what he said or wrote has been meticulously documented. Beyond that, his writing was normative because he wanted to convey what he and others of his time considered as ideal and should be conveyed to the public. The contributions of Jyotirindranath Tagore, his sister Swarnakumari Debi, niece Sarala Ghoshal/Chowdhurani in essays and of Abanindranath and Gaganendranath Tagore in paintings, Sourindra Mohon Tagore in music and Satyendranath Tagore in philosophy and Buddhism created a new culture for Bengalis which was connected to Asia and the world.

An important point to note was that these families were like nodal points through which creativity and culture radiated out. Many personalities were also in close association with them. Another family closely connected with the Tagores and the journalistic world were the Raychowdhurys or Rays as they later called themselves. Although today their names are synonymous with children's literature and films, it was another family all of whose members brought the world to the public: different aspects of it – art, technology, humour, poetry and stories all of which contributed to creation of a new youth who for the first time became a world citizen. The house in which they lived, 13 Cornwallis Street, was considered of historic importance since it housed many important personalities of the time like Upendrakishore's father-in-law Dwarakanath Ganguly (Brahmo leader and founder editor of *Sanjivani* and *Abalabandhab* patrikas), his stepmother-in-law Dr Kadambini Ganguly, first woman graduate of Calcutta University, leading Brahmo leaders of the time as well as seat of institutions like Calcutta Training academy (where Rabindranath started his schooling) and National School of Nabagopal Mitra.[27] Also, Upendrakishore who contributed articles to *Sakha* and then started *Sandesh* in 1913 for children was ably helped by his sons, Sukumar and Subinoy, and his daughters, Sukhalata and Punyalata, in contributing to 'creativity and modernity'[28] in Bengal. Later Satyajit Ray, Sukumar Ray's son, revived *Sandesh*, and achieved world renown with his stories, novels and films.

The sons of Dewan Kartikeya Chandra Roy were also culturally connected to many well-known Bengali personalities in their childhood in Krishnanagar, a culturally rich town of Bengal. Later Dewan's sons, notably Gyanendralal and Harendralal, settled in Calcutta regularly writing and editing literary periodicals like *Bangabasi*, *Pataka* and *Nabaprabha*. The youngest of seven brothers, Dwijendralal Roy, was not only a talented poet, dramatist and musician but also took the initiative to organise the publication of the periodical *Bharatvarsha*,[29]another site of many articles on Asia developed after Roy's death by Jaladhar Sen. If there was any subtle tug of war in cultural leadership among Bengal's leading towns, the Bengali diaspora in other Indian cities and towns, particularly Allahabad, were well represented through Ramananda Chattopadhyay's efforts in bringing them into focus through his periodicals. After 1908, Chattopadhyay settled in Calcutta and took a centre stage along with his daughters Sita and Shanta and his sons Kedarnath and Ashoke in taking literary and political journalism to its height.

Othering the self in Asia

Othering the self implies an urgency to not only find similarities but also to discover within the self those areas of backwardness which made colonisation so easy and overcoming it so difficult. With identification of the ailments possibility of change would follow. What is interesting is that in this agenda of improvement, the idea of the self is broadened to include other similar people, identified as Easterners or Asians, dissimilar with each other but broadly similar in comparison with the Occidentals who separated themselves by their aggressive actions. There was a realisation that because of the lack of information, people in India knew less about their neighbours than their western counterparts. In the period that I have looked into, roughly from the 1860s to the 1940s, every periodical or journal has in every issue at least one article where there is information on some part of Asia – predicated on providing knowledge so as to identify the relationship of that country with India (or sometimes Bengal) through highlighting similarities and dissimilarities. There is thus a twofold othering of self – one the obvious other, the colonial power, and the other 'other', the Asian countries, which initially appears to be outwardly at least the other but gradually reveals itself to be a part of the self. There is always a focus while othering the self on modes of improvement of the self. This whole process of identifying the Asian countries as 'other' since they appear different from our country (the reason it was claimed was due to our lack of knowledge rather than anything intrinsic to that country) and then showing how they are similar because they are a part of Asia like us, can be identified in all the articles.

Obviously, China and Japan are the favourites and majority of the articles are on them. However, though the claim to be close to these powerful actors is expected, it is the constantly changing position with regard to that closeness, in accordance with the changing political climate, which makes interesting reading for us. Even more fascinating is the position of the intellectuals vis-à-vis the lesser important actors – countries of South and South-East Asia. They are actually referred to as Asia while China and Japan like India are referred to by name. The attitude towards the 'Asian' countries – Java, Bali, Sumatra, Malaya, Burma, Sri Lanka, Shyamdesh or Thailand (to use the names which the journals use) is more personal compared to East Asia verging on condescension at times. There are also cameos of some other Asian countries like Borneo, Philippines, Turkey, Cambodia, Arabia and Afghanistan.

Judging from the number of articles written in the periodicals over the latter half of 19th century and the first half of the 20th century, *Japan* wins hands down, followed by China and then the rest of Asia. In the minds of the Indians, apart from India and the West, two other powers which stood alone in splendour were Japan and China. The rest of Asia stood 'apart' from them and comprised of South, South-East and West Asia.[30] I have noticed from the articles that were written in the period that India did not stand alone in that fascination. Even the West was grappling with the phenomena that were Japan and China as is evident from the large number of books on these countries as symbolising the East. The distinction that I make, though with some trepidation, is that these writings on Asia in the pre-1904–1905 period were motivated by a desire to understand the emerging Asian culture and from 1905 became a means to self-discovery. Japan henceforth was able to achieve iconic status in the world as an Asian power destroying the myth of western invincibility by defeating Russia in war, reach an apogee of power through self-modernisation, aspire to provide leadership to the rest of Asia through a united pan-Asian inspiration and then ruin the hold that she had established over the countries of Asia and definitely the Indian intellectuals by its aggressive actions in East Asia. The Asia wide impact and excitement of the outcome of Russo–Japanese war can be symbolically seen in the pause between two popular plays at the Minerva Theatre in Calcutta on 30 October 1904, for a screening of a Bioscope on the war.[31] Majority of the articles however still focussed on a fascination for hunting out the 'secret of Japan's success', though Rabindranath Tagore alone tried to convince the world of the pitfall of excessive nationalism and braved inordinate hostility in the two east Asian countries. This search for the values which brought success to Japan by which she was able to transform herself from just another backward Asiatic country to a powerful nation towards whom both the western and eastern countries expressed awe was explored in various ways following different strategies by the writers, many of whom were students in Japan or were travelling there for various reasons. The destruction of the myth of the lethargic and mystic East present in the western rhetoric began to inspire confidence and hope in the other Asiatic nations to probe shared Eastern values and re-examine their past and present assets and resources. In India's case, these ideas were always associated with a reassessment of the colonial situation when it was discussed that if 'tiny' Japan could rise above its apparently insurmountable past problems of lack of resources and openness in all spheres, India too could 'improve' herself despite her colonial subordination through adopting Japan's secret formula of success. Analysts in the western and eastern countries were engrossed in probing and analysing this 'secret' which helped Japan's rise. I have discussed these points elsewhere in more detail.[32] As is quite well known, Rabindranath Tagore's initial euphoria faced a setback soon afterwards and his indictment of Japanese aggression was a marked change. The tone of admiration that had become associated in any discussion on Japan began to change in the second decade with Japan's territorial ambitions on Korea, for some at least though many others continued to admire the west-like might of a non-western country. Rabindranath Tagore who was alarmed by Japan's aggression on China as a result of ambitions in Korea, called it 'creating a painful incongruence in the Japanese spirit of selflessness by a display of pride and power'.[33] Occupation of Korea in 1910 and the First World War worried Tagore so much that in his lecture tours he faced the ire of the Japanese students while campaigning against the ideology of aggressive nationalism in which he saw the roots of the World War. *Nationalism*[34] was published in 1917 which was an open indictment against 'the political civilization which has sprung up from the soil of Europe and is overrunning the whole world' since it is 'scientific, and not human'. As Rabindranath said in the speech to the Indian community in Japan in April 1925:

> it was here that I first saw the Nation, in all its naked ugliness, whose spirit we Orientals have borrowed from the West . . . I heartily deplored the fact that she

> (Japan), with her code of honour, her ideal of perfection and her belief in the need for grace in everyday life, could yet become infected with this epidemic of selfishness and with the boastfulness of egotism.[35]

Associations with Japan now had to be more aggressively cultural. Internationalism rather than nationalism was stressed. Tagore's missionary travels abroad were partly aided by the climate of internationalism prevailing after the end of the First World War and formation of the League of Nations and partly by the positive developments in Asia like the establishment of the republic of Turkey by Kamal Ataturk (1923), whom Tagore admired and the anti-imperialist struggle in Indonesia (1926).[36] Again in 1938, *Bharatvarsha* in its editorial said that Tagore, who did not approve of the famous Japanese poet Noguchi writing to him to justify the Japanese attack on China, warned Noguchi that Japan was oblivious of the fact that 'China has much greater moral strength than Japan and they should in the near future erase the painful memories and recreate a pure Asia'.[37] Some other important articles on Japan by Jyotirindranath Tagore, Jadunath Sarkar, Girindra Chandra Mukhopadhyay, P.C. Sorcar, Benoy Kumar Sarkar, Manmathanath Ghosh, etc., have been discussed later. Subhas Chandra Bose neatly summed up the history of Indian sentiment towards Japan when he wrote,

> Japan was the first country which prevented the people of an alien continent from committing aggression in the Asian continent. Japan's victory over Russia in 1905 was the first harbinger of Asian resurgence . . . Therefore, Indians feel that the existence of a strong Japan is essential for the reconstruction of Asia. It is true that India's views on Japan underwent some change following the Chinese affair . . . India and Japan have in the past been bound by deep cultural ties . . . (which) have been interrupted because of British domination of India . . . . once India is free these ties will be revived and strengthened.[38]

Second on the list of favourites, as far as the number of articles on countries goes, is *China*. The urge to know and discuss the qualities and values that made China great has been an important part of the intellectual history of India from the latter half of the 19th century and this is connected to cosmopolitan and nationalist ideas emerging among the educated elite. China was an important element in this discussion, being a strong Asian country like Japan, and because India identified spiritual and material connectivity with her in the past and in the present. In the evolution of a 'new Asia awakening to a consciousness of unity', Tagore felt the need to apply an 'eastern outlook' to analyse the qualities of Asians, though he does not believe that these values are only applicable to Asians. He talks about universal human ideals which must be perfected by maintaining the distinctiveness of each country but accepting the truth that there are great qualities in all. But the 'eastern outlook' is distinct because 'in the East, we are conscious through all individual things of the infinity which embraces them'. If people in India became aware of Japan with her modernisation, China apparently was always in their minds. As an author in *Bamabodhini Patrika* in 1893 writes, the name of China as one of world's most ancient civilizations is familiar. 'When the present civilised England was still the land of naked aborigines, and the rest of the Europe was in awe of Greek and Roman civilization, Chinese and Indian civilizations were at their glorious peak'.

There was in the past at least some shared glory between the two ancient civilisations, despite the loss of freedom in India and the degeneration of the society in China, while Japan in the present was successfully engaging with the powerful west. So not only is there a focus on the ancientness of China, its policy of isolation was referred to as an expression of dignity, and importance of family and national values sustained over the ages.

Most of these initial writings at least were based on western journals and books which created problems of their own. The comment that American journalist Emily Hahn, who spent many years in Shanghai and wrote 52 books, writes about these writings in the context of her discussion on William Hickey's *Memoirs* is also applicable to these Bengali writers who write about China. She says, 'Hickey met and talked with only a very few Chinese . . . He took for gospel all he was told by the other foreigners, and naturally embraced their prejudices'.[39] The Bengali writers while talking about Chinese customs and traditions embraced prejudices twice – once from the accounts of the westerners which they based their writings on, when they did not travel to China themselves of course, and then the second time when they interpreted what they read according to their own prejudices – weighing Chinese 'peculiarities' or 'similarities' against their own customs and traditions.[40] Yet, their interest in China and desire to make the Chinese understand despite the differences in customs and traditions stayed intact the entire period. Travellers to China and those residing there for any length of time wrote important series on their experience of life there and analysed the position of China vis-à-vis India and the world.[41]

The story of Burma or Brahmadesha[42] that I am going to describe in this book is the view of the Bengalis living, working or travelling there based on their writing in the periodicals – their affinity with the land they live in as an extension of their homeland, as part of a common Asia and a part of the enslaved empire. This Burma was of course the creation of the colonial policies of the British who, according to Thant Myint-U, ushered in a modern Burmese era from 1886 when monarchy was abolished and royalty banished from the kingdom. The policy that the British used in Burma was the total abandonment of the erstwhile ruling classes and displacement in the Irrawaddy, Brahmaputra and Salween river basins of the prevailing Mandalay authority by an 'aggressive British Indian state'.[43] By implication, this aggressive policy required a huge administrative support staff as well as private players to help in the regeneration of the country's development with the displacement of the centre of gravity from Mandalay to Rangoon. It is in this sphere that the Indians played an important role as an important minority group in Burma's economic, social, cultural and political life. Many modern historians writing on Indians in Burma discuss the origins of migration and settlements of Indians in Burma and point out that Indian immigrants who came from Chittagong and Calcutta as well as from other parts of the country were mainly sent by the British government but a large number also went privately in search of livelihood.[44] Many of them settled in Rangoon as well in other areas of Burma with their families, but there were also a large number of people who formed a floating migrant population since they settled there for shorter periods of time – travelling on work as well as for tourism. There are also a large number of writers who analyse the contemporary political condition of Burma in a sympathetic manner and try to link their condition of subjection to the Indian situation under colonial rule in the hope of creating empathy between the populations of the two countries suffering under British imperialism. These articles by people not necessarily present in Rangoon provide an imaginative view of Burma as well as the details that are provided by the Indian diaspora population in Burma.

In the late 19th century when Burma was effectively linked with India by the common British imperial rule, it seemed imperative for those who were in Rangoon to 'familiarize the readers (back home in India) with Burma which now has a full settlement of Indians, though hardly any one visited it in the past . . . After all her fate is closely tied up with that of India, since the British are masters of both countries', as Mrinalini Raha says in *Antahpur* in 1902,[45] or Girindranath Sarkar, who in *Prabashi*, describes the life and culture of Bengalis in Burma[46] or another Rangoon resident, Pushpalata Debi's travels in Malaya in *Mahila* in 1903 show.[47] These people who were writing about Burma when they go on work or are visiting relatives describe Burma for tourists. There is a sense of belonging to Burma, not just due to territorial proximity but because as easterners they share values and are fellow sufferers under the same coloniser. But by the same yardstick, there is a sense of superiority among Bengalis towards Burma, a condescension born due to the fact that much of the industry, agriculture, railways, and public works are built by Indians as partners of the colonisers. It is the very same reason which made the Bengalis targets of the nascent nationalism developing in the second and third decades of the 20th century in Burma. What sympathy there appears to be present in the journals was obviously lacking in practical lives, since there was hardly any intermingling with local people and hardly any understanding of the sensibilities of the Burmese. Comparison between Calcutta and Rangoon was more a reality to them, though one must admit that a similar approach is also seen in the writing of some Burmese as well.[48] Burma or more specifically Rangoon under British rule was the site of a number of conferences in the 20th century, not only political and economic but also cultural and there is evidence of many Indians travelling to Burma by road or sea to attend them. Perhaps that's why when Sarala Debi Chaudhurani was invited to give the presidential address at the Burma Provincial Hindu Conference in 1928, she wasn't at all worried. As she says in her article that was published in *Bharatvarsha* in 1931 that, 'this was hardly a sea voyage, this is simply going to the other end of India, only one end of Greater India'.[49] Rediscovery of Buddhism among the intellectuals since the mid-19th century had created for the Bengalis an imaginative space outside the reality of their own degraded existence under colonialism which belonged to a glorious past where India's contribution to the Asiatic religious world was at par with any world power. Travelling to visit Buddhist religious sites became an important 'pilgrimage' for the intellectual Buddhists who analysed and admired the tenets of Buddhism but rarely converted. Appreciation of art and architecture was also connected with this enterprise as was discovery of Buddhist literary texts in different parts of Asia and writing about the journeys to the different Buddhist sites. In travelogues to Buddhist sites, one sees this nationalistic strain where there is mention of India being the original homeland of this pure religion but it is sad that she had lost her grip on a continuous history of glory. The articles almost always start with a background of how Buddhism was spread from India to that particular country. As far as Burma was concerned, there were descriptions of their dramas and *poye* dances in many articles as well as food.[50] Rabindranath Tagore played an important role in this sphere when he travelled to Burma three times in 1916, 1924 and 1927 since he was already a world-renowned figure whose deep appreciation of Burmese culture had a great impact in popularising Burmese culture. Besides Shwe Dagon and other pagodas, what struck all those writing on Burma were its people and their lifestyle. Not simply those living in Burma but even those visiting it for a short period mention what they call 'women's freedom in Burma', sometimes approvingly, and at others disapprovingly.

Thailand or Shyam, too, by virtue of familiarity due to its close proximity with India was discussed in many articles. Interest in Thai life and interest in the royal family takes precedence over political discussions, though the fact that Thailand was never colonised is mentioned in all the articles. Narendra Dev, the famous poet, residing in Santiniketan, wrote a series on Thailand (1924 in *Bharatvarsha*). This series coincided with Tagore's visit to Thailand, but it is not clear whether Narendra Dev travelled to the places he writes about. The essays include a large range of pictures of people and places. While discussing the people of Thailand, Dev seems to make sweeping and general statements. At times, pride of an independent country, resisting western influence comes out in his statements and at other times his generalisations appear strange in such an erudite writer.[51] Like others, Dev describes customs, food and dress and compares them with India, and like all travellers to Thailand, practices in Buddhism and pilgrimages play an important role.[52]

Sri Lanka, or Singhal or Ceylon as the country was variously referred to in the articles, offers a varied interest because of being so close to India yet having differences in natural and human resources. The earliest writings on the country by travellers and analysts refer to connectivity with India, stressing on comparative development while always referring to natural beauty and dedication to Buddhism. The Buddhist reformer Anagarika Dharmapala's visits to India and particularly Calcutta obviously revived an interest in Sinhalese Buddhism in the late 19th and early 20th centuries. Comparing Calcutta's magnificence to that of Colombo in 1884, Ta Pra Cha (pseudonym) writes in his 'Travel to Singhal' in *Nabajiban* that Colombo's importance is because it is a port where ships from all countries halt, yet 'it can hardly compare with the magnificence of Chowringhee, though Singhal is more well to do than Bengal'.[53]

The interest in Korea started around the 1890s, when China and Japan squabbled over its control, and peaked in 1911, when Japan annexed it. In 1895, an article on Korean women in *Bamabodhini Patrika* starts with the sentence, that the readers must be aware that for some time Korea is the bone of contention between China and Japan and though for centuries people did not have much idea about Korea, the present war has brought the country within everyone's mental horizon of the world so that people want to know details about the country. [54]. Then the author describes the lives of Korean women in comparison with Chinese and Japanese women. Articles on Manchuria, its past and present history as well as life in Manchuria became popular in the 1930s in the wake of Japanese aggression. Bharat Chandra Basu, who is a regular contributor to *Bharatvarsha* writing descriptive essays about countries of the west and east, writes about Manchuria in 1932.

Java, Bali, Sumatra and Borneo excited the attention of many writers talking about connections in the past, but was also intriguing in the present possibly because it was under a different set of colonisers. It got special attention after Rabindranath Tagore's 'pilgrimage' to these countries, which was followed by many newspapers and journals and his memoirs (Letters from a Traveller to Java) were first published together with his travels in Europe as *Jatri* or Traveller in 1929 and then separately in 1960.[55] Suniti Kumar Chattopadhyay's articles on Java (1929) hinted that Java fared better under Dutch rule than India under the British. Regarding the ancient period, Chattopadhyay remained true to his Greater India loyalties when he published the series of travel writing, accompanying Tagore to Java, Bali and Sumatra as *Dvipamoy*

Bharat or Island India or Insulindia. Similarly, Narendra Dev writing about the Islands of Eastern India, in *Bharatvarsha* in 1924, also believed that Dutch colonialism was a benevolent one. He also described in this set of articles – the life of people in the three cities of Batavia, Shyamranga (Semearang) and Surbaya – the way of living, their character, the beauty of their women, places of interest, art and performances, dress and ornaments, their homes and hospitality, social customs and religious beliefs and food. Unlike Chattopadhyay, Dev probably did not see first-hand what he described. But it is difficult to understand whether he is simply quoting a book on Indonesian music or whether he is talking from experience when he writes in one place that 'though the Javanese were very inclined towards musical performances, there was a sad note prevalent in their music which might indicate a melancholic strain in their mental makeup'. His admiration for the Dutch administration is obviously an implicit criticism of the British rule in India. Dev also writes about Sumatra from 'where the Dutch dominate the islands of Eastern Indian seas with ease'. Dev provides an anthropological study of Borneo with its six racial groups, Kayak, Keniah, Klementan, Murat, Punan and Dayak, whose dress and lifestyle he describes in *Bharatvarsha*. He describes the customs of the different tribes, like the ear piercing of the Kayak and Keniah beauties (he adds a picture as well), the various customs and superstitions regarding the birth and death of children, or flattening of heads of the newborns among the Klementans who are not named till they are 3 or 4 years old. Dev also describes the courtship rituals of the Keniah and Kayak youths, providing information which he knows will amaze his readers. Another article on the forest people of Borneo by Hemanta Chattopadhyay starts saying it is important that one reads about Borneo since 'most people of the civilized world think that the people who live in the forests of Borneo are fearful looking primitive people and are still cannibals'. But he continues to refer to them as 'uncivilized' or 'half civilized', even if they are not 'fearful looking and cannibalistic'. The essay contains a number of pictures of the tribal people. He describes the dress and ornaments 'of the half-civilized people' as 'sophisticated and of an artistic standard generally not expected from the 'uncivilized'. It is not clear whether the article is based on a personal visit or whether he has based his knowledge on books by intrepid western travellers. That he was aware of westerners' accounts is evident, since he mentions misconceptions of the western travellers and their analyses of trade in Borneo under British rule.

Much before Bali became known to Bengalis due to Tagore's visit, Nagendra Chandra Som in *Prabashi* wrote about the religion and worship customs of Bali in 1902, but Suniti Chattopadhyay writing in 1930 highlighted a view popular among some academics that the Dutch authorities jointly with the Balinese people were more interested in Bali's past history and culture than British authorities in their colonies. Chattopadhaya claims to have noticed that in Bali there was a consciousness about their past culture, religion, literature and art, an attachment towards past traditions but instead of relying only on 'blind sentiment' alone, they have strengthened and perfected their knowledge of their past history with the help of 'their King' and the 'Dutch authorities,' thereby implying a lack of endeavour in both the Indians and their colonial rulers. Rabindranath Tagore's visit to Bali and the presence of his entourage at a royal occasion and the descriptions of Balidvipa created interest in its study and two articles in *Bichitra* on Bali came out in 1928. The Philippines, on the other hand, occupies a much lesser space in the writings in the Bengali periodicals, though Narendra Dev followed up his discussion on South-East Asia, which he referred to as

Eastern Indian islands by describing the Philippines in two articles of *Bharatvarsha*. He describes the country as

> comprising as many as three hundred islands in the Pacific Ocean to the south of the China sea and original tribes as belonging to at least eighty different races who were pale, yellow, dark, black and white skinned (gour, peet, shyam, krishna, or svetombo) . . . There was a mixture of Indonesians who entered the island and original Negritos (Andamanese and Papuans mainly and not Kafri) and rise of Igorot, Tinguian, Bagobo, and Mandayara races . . . Besides Indonesians, people from Borneo, Sumatra and Malaya as well Chinese and Spanish adventurers came and settled here making the racial distinctiveness even more difficult to maintain.[56]

Dev's description of the indigenous people is unique since nowhere in his articles does the Greater India pride emerge, though he is writing in its heyday.

Very few articles exist on Cambodia, and one article by Hemanta Chattopadhyay is an informative piece and not a travelogue. Chattopadhyay's article starts with the geographical description of the land and the largest river Mekong which provides water and livelihood to the people, then he goes only to say that Cambodians could not prevent colonisation since in the present day

> it is only a shadow of her former glorious self, whereas in the 12th century, under Jayavarman, Cambodia's borders spread from the Bay of Bengal to the China sea . . . with great effort the Hindu kingdoms have been retained in Sumatra and Java, in Cambodia only memories remain . . . It was to resist the onslaught from the Mongolian migrants from China and settlers from Shyamdesh and Annam that Cambodians appealed to the French. It was with their help that the capital at Ankor was recovered and the jungles around it were cleared.[57]

Chattopadhyay describes in detail the life of the people of Cambodia, their dress, food and culture and concludes that though they have adopted the practice of opium-smoking from the Chinese and Annamese, it has not yet become a national vice.

Asiatic Turkey, on the other hand, was of sufficient interest throughout the period, but mainly regarding women's position in society and later the consolidation of a modern Turkey by Mustafa Kemal Pasha. From the late 19th century, Turkey remained of interest as a comparative analogy for status of Indian women as Hemendranath Datta's article in 1908 *Bharat Mahila*[58] showed the same pattern was visible when 20 years later a comparative picture was drawn regarding the status of Turkish women before and under the Republic by Monomohan Ghosh in *Bichitra*.[59] In a number of articles in the late 1920s, there is expression of admiration for the rise of a new and progressive Turkey having overcome its manifold problems. *Bangabani* in 1924 highlights the Turkish achievement in separating politics from religion following the establishment of the Republic. Kamal Pasha's meteoric rise to power excited response in many of the writings in the journals. The editor of the journal *Basumati*, Hemendra Prasad Ghosh wrote a two-issue series on the victory of Turkey,[60] outlining Kamal's rise and using reports in foreign newspapers to provide an insight into his activities and an analysis of the significance of Turkey's rise to power in the contemporary world.[61] This being the general trend in writing about Turkey in these periodicals, *Pracharak*[62] stands out in its lavishness of writing on Turkey. In 1900, in its second year, *Pracharak* published articles on the Sultan of Turkey by Munshi Saiyid Fazle Haq[63] and more interestingly an elegy or *marsiya* which they called *Shokochhash* in Bengali on the Lion of Plevna, Osman Nuri Pasha (Turkish commander of the siege of Plevna by the Russo Rumanian army in 1877–1888) who despite his loss became a legendary hero. This elegy was written by Gholam Maula after the death of the war hero. Another poem was written on the silver jubilee of the rule of the Amirul Momenin, Kalifatul Moslemin Ghazi Abdul Hamid Khan of Turkey by Ismail Hossain Sirazi, which was read at a celebration of the occasion at Serazganj.[64] Bipin Chandra Pal called these writings (especially the periodical *Sadharani* with its powerful political message) an expression of 'our new patriotism which had a universal outlook'.[65]

Persian society and status of women was always of interest in comparative analysis with India, and *Bamabodhini Patrika* carried articles in 1870 and 1887. Later too in the context of changing status of women and their participation in an international women's meet in 1930, Sita Debi wrote an article on women in Persia in *Bangalakshmi*. When in 1932, an invitation was extended by Reza Shah Pahlavi to Rabindranath Tagore to visit Persia, Tagore decided to go in order to revive the ancient ties between India and Persia and immortalised his experience in *Parashya Jatri*.[66]

On the other hand, the other country, which lies astride two continents, Arabia, though imaginatively excites Bengalis in their stories, songs and poetry, does not find too much place in the periodicals. There is a long poem on Arabia by Munshi Ismail Hossain Shirazi in *Pracharak*,[67] Narendra Dev's descriptive article on Arabia for *Bharatvarsha* in 1923 and ten years later two articles on Aden, the port city, and on Cairo, the capital of Egypt, were written by Nityananda Bandopadhyay. There are also some translations of Arabian stories in the children's magazines.

With the establishment of British colonial control over the Malayan Straits and Singapore after the 1820s, the Bengali periodicals reflected an interest, when Nibaran Chandra Mukhopadhay wrote on the spread of Hindu religion in islands of Malaya for *Bharati* in 1882 followed by a similar article tracing Hindu language and literature by Ganapati Roy in 1911. The articles by Bijon Raj Chattopadhyay in 1923 on Malaya and Thailand, Subimal Chandra Sarkar's 'travel to Malaya' in 1930 and Keshab Chandra Gupta's 'Traveller to Malaya' in 1936 are much more graphic and contemporary.

Vietnam or Indo-China was introduced to Bengali readers by a translation from a French travelogue by Jyotirindranath Tagore in *Bharati* in 1909 after which there are no more articles till Phanindranath Bose writes on Hindu colonisation in Champa during the heyday of Greater India movement in 1926.

The Bengal scholar of Tibetan language and culture, Sarat Chandra Das's intrepid journey to Tibet in 1879 and 1881–1882, first published in 1902 as *Journey to Lhasa and Central Tibet* and the romantic story of an Indian spy for the British, masquerading as a school headmaster in Darjeeling and while on the mission of gathering intelligence in Tibet falling in love with the place and its language and philosophy, greatly impacted the Bengali readers.[68] A Bengali version was published a year earlier as 'On the way to Tibet' in *Navya Bharat* in 1901.

Cosmopolitanism and nationalism in Asia consciousness

Cosmopolitanism is the ideology that all human beings belong to a single community, based on a shared morality, a shared economic relationship or a political structure that encompasses different nations. In this case, it was more a concept which highlighted mutual respect as a means of inner growth. It was closely associated with the ideas of nationalism that were being developed in India at the turn of the century, the experiments that were thought of and acted upon. This cosmopolitanism was less a political project or practice but more a philosophy or world view or even an attitude or a disposition as Vertovec and Cohen (2002) in *Conceiving Cosmopolitanism* pointed out or even better a cosmopolitan outlook as Ulrich Beck pointed out.[69] The word 'cosmopolitanism' is commonly used of late, although it continues to escape an easy definition. Philosophers and sociologists find it difficult to define. There are different ways of being cosmopolitan but what most cosmopolitans share is a disposition of openness to the world around them. It is also one common theme connecting a vast majority of conceptions of cosmopolitanism through its history: from Diogenes to Kant (1983), Nussbaum (1996) to Derrida (2000). Vertovec and Cohen (2002) in *Conceiving Cosmopolitanism* talked about a concept that has the potential to be socially and politically transformative. In their view, there are six characterisations of cosmopolitanism as a sociocultural condition – a kind of philosophy or world view; a political project towards building transnational institutions; a political project for recognising multiple identities; an attitudinal or dispositional orientation; and a mode of practice or competence.

Ulrich Beck pointed out in *Cosmopolitan Sociology: Outline of a Paradigm Shift* that in recent times cosmopolitanism has changed its form, from a 'merely controversial idea and ideal; in however a distorted form, it has left the realm of philosophical castles in the air and has entered reality'. He feels that this world 'that has become cosmopolitan urgently demands a new standpoint, the cosmopolitan outlook, from which we can grasp the social and political realities in which we live and act'.[70] According to him, 'methodological nationalism' which 'equates modern society with society organised in territorially limited nation states' and 'assumes that the nation, state and society are the "natural" social and political forms of the modern world' leads to humanity being divided into a limited number of nations, organised into nation states which 'on the outside, set boundaries to distinguish themselves from other nation states'. Making a distinction between cosmopolitanism in a normative philosophical sense and cosmopolitisation as a social scientific research programme, Beck feels that instead of cosmopolitanism in Immanuel Kant's philosophical sense of 'a task, a conscious and voluntary choice, clearly the affair of an elite, a top down issue' (Kant 1983, 1996), what is needed today is a movement 'horizontally through the main fields of communication, interaction and social and political practices'.[71]

Brown and Held[72] discussed the origins of contemporary cosmopolitan thought through the ages from Diogenes' view of being a universal citizen, a kosmopolites who are all part of a fraternity of mankind and not merely defined by his cosmos but rather by positive duties of hospitality and brotherly love, as if they were common citizens or Zeno 'calling for a cosmopolitan utopia that reached beyond the confines of traditional political association – not only a new sense of cosmopolitan citizenship and common brotherly love, but a worldwide political order that could embrace all of humanity under a form of universal law'[73]. The ideas of the Stoics too spanning half a millennium appeal to the same sentiment, especially those who believed that human beings share a similar capacity for reason and that this universal trait bestowed a moral worth upon any individual who wished to exercise it. Cicero who spoke about 'bond of connection' which is reason and speech, which 'associate men together and unite them into a sort of natural fraternity' and Aurelius who talked about 'intellectual capacity and reason as common to all'.[74] The accusation against cosmopolitanism that it ignores the value of local obligation and community is not valid for all cosmopolitan arguments as Seneca's view shows, which says that all humans inhabit two communities – local and determined by place of birth and one that represents a community of human kind.

In the last few decades, historians have brought new dimensions to words like cosmopolitanism, universalism or even connections and circulation. While circulation was looked at from the point of view of imperial history with regard to movements of labour, knowledge, information and administrative processes, there was also discussion about not only vernacular nationalism but connections and linkages between nationalists of different nations. Journalism and literature always played an important role in both imperial links and nationalist linkages. Homi Bhaba spoke about vernacular cosmopolitanism in 2000 while Kwame Anthony Appiah in *Cosmopolitanism: Ethics in a World of Strangers* spoke of two strands that intertwine in the notion of cosmopolitanism. One is the idea that we have obligations to others, not only those who are our kith and kin or even those with whom we have 'formal ties of a shared citizenship' and the other is that we 'take seriously the value not just of human life but of particular human lives' in their 'practices and beliefs that lend them significance'. In Appiah's view the cosmopolitan individual knows that 'people are different', 'and there is much to learn from our differences'. Despite occasional clash of these ideas of 'universal concern and respect for legitimate difference' it must be remembered that 'cosmopolitanism is the name not of the solution but of the challenge'.[75] Apprehensive of both 'steely' loyalists and the 'noisiest foes', Appiah wishes to defend a 'partial cosmopolitanism'.

There was awareness and research on the Asia consciousness of the intellectuals during the colonial period in the aftermath of decolonisation followed by historians looking at the role of non-state actors in forging interactions through travel and commerce by land and sea. Within the realm of connectivity, themes about war and aggression and the role of pan-Asianism also began to be addressed. In *A Hundred Horizons*, Sugata Bose shows keeping the global arena in mind, 'the peoples of the Indian ocean made their own history . . . and the oceanic space supplied a key venue for articulating different universalisms from the one Europe claimed monopoly'.[76] This making of their own history came, as Bayly and Harper had written, from the revolution occurring in the 'minds of Asians' which 'was greater even than the political and economic revolutions on the ground'.[77] Writing on Tagore's Asian voyages some years later, Sugata Bose speaks of a time when 'universalism, cosmopolitanism and internationalism are words and concepts jostling for interpretive space in new global, interregional and transnational histories'. He believes that 'both notions of universalism with a difference' and 'cosmopolitanism springing from vernacular roots' are different from those views which 'see detached reason as its only source' and display a 'visceral distaste for patriotism, confusing it with the narrowest forms of particularism', and proclaiming 'a high moral ground' for 'colourless cosmopolitanism', 'colourful patriotism is deemed to be seductive but devoid of any ethical content'. For Bose, connecting Rabindranath Tagore to 'this version of cosmopolitanism' would be to denude him 'of much of his poetry and music and all of his passion and moral philosophy'.[78] Even though Tagore was critical of an unalloyed nation worshipping, yet he never abandoned his 'basic anti-nationalist stance'. Bose contends that the cosmopolitanism that prevailed in the colonised world was one in which patriotism was 'perfectly compatible with a cosmopolitan attitude that transcended the lines of particular cultural differences'.[79] Kris Manjapra refers to the word 'aspirational cosmopolitanism' to denote the 'conversations across lines of difference' which 'provisionally created shared public worlds', when moving through 'cosmopolitan thought zones'.[80] A recent book by Tansen Sen describes the connected history of the world with a focus on China and India, where he describes 'connections and circulations' in the past and present and wades through the present complicated national identities inhibiting connections, to discuss role of 'individuals, wider linkages and impact of India–China interactions'. His intention is to demonstrate that India–China exchanges were connected and integrated into broader circulations of ideas, people and objects within and beyond the Asian continent.[81] Sen further explored the India–China interaction along with Brian Tsui and a host of other scholars in a broad perspective of time, history and imagination to go 'beyond pan-Asiatist, anti-colonialist interactions between intellectuals and political activists and the celebration of "brotherly" relations in the 1950s' in order to examine the 'engagement of China with South Asia and vice versa in more ambiguous terms'.[82]

Ashis Nandi's article in *A New Cosmopolitanism: Towards a Dialogue of Asian Civilizations* finds three layers within the discourse on discovery of Asia. 'Asia', he says,

> is a geographical, not cultural entity. Though many Asians have defined their continent culturally during the last 150 years, that definition can be read as an artefact of Asian reactions to Western colonialism rather than as an autonomous search for larger cultural similarities.

This he refers to as

> a psychological defence against the internalized imperial fantasy of the continent as a location of ancient civilizations that had once been great and were now decadent, decrepit and senile . . . shaped by imperial metaphor of the body, built on European folk imageries of stages of life as taken over and remodelled by nineteenth-century biology and social evolutionism.

Nandy finds 'outside the realm of these definitions and self-definitions, an Asia which does not probably even see itself as Asia. That Asia has known the West for two millennia and interacted with it seriously for over six hundred years'. Nandy finds a third Asia from the 18th century when a confident west seeks to resolve the contest for world domination among the European nations on the soil of Asia.[83] An inevitable clash of civilisations occurred since almost all colonised nations reacted to the presence of the colonisers but the contact was not inevitably an 'unmitigated disaster' since those countries became 'truly multi-civilizational' and despite the western centrality, dialogues emerged between Asian nations.[84] Though Nandy is theorising about the present in the Asian context, the hypothesis of the west as the 'third participant' in any dialogue or even monologue among the Asian nations may be noticed in the period that this book talks about. In fact, the colonial presence being all-pervasive, the 'unrecognised' element is debatable. Two other points that Nandy makes in this article are also important in this discussion: that of the emerging new politics of knowledge and cultures and a hierarchical, unequal and oppressive mode of dialogue.[85]

Carolien Stolte's dissertation on 'Orienting India: Interwar Internationalism in an Asian Inflection (19171–937)' has brilliantly and in detail looked at what she calls India's 'international moment', when, as a review of her dissertation, Michele Louro quotes her: 'impetus for international associations, mobilizations, and networks reached an unprecedented height beginning in the 1920s and gradually declining in the later 1930s'. Though she uses different sources, the summary of her chapters shows a very similar trajectory that comes across in the vernacular periodicals that I am working on, which confirms my idea that a large number of intellectuals across India were thinking in a similar way where nationalistic ideas with international spirit were preparing the basis of new nationalism which Asian Relations Conference based itself on. Stolte considered Asian Relations Conference as the endpoint of 'two decades of Asian cooperation' due to the twin factors of Cold War politics and contentious governmental interests which undid non-governmental solidarities.[86]In a joint article by Stolte and Harald Fischer-Tine, various concepts of Asia and pan-Asian designs through 'appropriations of the concept of Asianism' have been provided to establish a 'distinct anti-colonial, identity and the tensions due to conflict between various nationalisms in Asia' and the 'macro-nationalistic Pan Asianism'.[87]

Birendra Prasad though focussing mainly on the national movement in India focussed on India's 'Asian Consciousness', even though 'as a subject country all the thought and energy of nationalist India were directed towards the achievement of its own freedom'. This keen interest according to Prasad led to a 'spirit of fellow-feeling with Asian nations' and prompted Indian leaders to encourage Indians to consider India as a 'part of the wide Asian World', in order to eliminate 'the common enemy, i.e. Western Imperialism'.[88] Through a detailed discussion on Keshab Chandra Sen, the Brahmo leader, Prasad has shown how Sen 'impressed upon the people of India that they must get into the habit of looking at India as a part of the wide Asian world',[89] and it is Keshab Chandra Sen who in Prasad's view should have the credit of being hailed as the 'prophet of pan-Asianism'.[90]

Though research on travel literature has taken off hugely in the last few decades, books on Indians travelling to the west is more common and there are very few on Bengalis travelling abroad, except Rabindranath Tagore. Narayan Sen's article on two early Bengalis travelling to China[91] and Simonti Sen's *Travels to Europe: Self and Other in Bengali Travel Narratives, 1870–1910,* establish a new genre of research. Quoting Swami Vivekananda, 'we have to travel, we have to go to foreign lands . . . if we have to really constitute ourselves as a nation, we have to mingle freely with other nations', Simonti Sen underlines the importance of travel despite scriptural injunctions against it, and travelogues as 'one of the forms of modern self-expression'. It is no wonder she argues that the '*sahityapatras* (Bengali literary journals) maintained regular spaces in their magazines for serialised presentation of such narratives to cater to public demand'.[92] Very recently, Jayati Gupta's *Travel Culture, Travel Writing and Bengali Women, 1870–1940* explores the intersections of power, indigeneity and the representations of the 'self' and the 'other' in these writings by women.[93] Ramchandra Guha's 'Travelling with Rabindranath', both literally and metaphorically, stresses the importance of Tagore's travels as expression of his widening mental horizon leading to his uncompromising stress on universalism in the face of the burgeoning nationalist passions within his homeland.[94]

Satadru Sen, in his book *Benoy Kumar Sarkar: Restoring the Nation to the World,* brilliantly underlines 'three broad cultural and political projects' which were important in the intellectual writing of the time. One was the project of 'opposing rather than reinforcing oriental narratives of difference', second was 'imperative of restoring the nation to the world', and third was to 'produce the Indian as a fundamentally new creature'.[95] However, Sen has not included the articles by Sarkar in the Bengali periodicals, nor his travel writings in his important work.

No contradiction with nationalism

Fighting for freedom against imperial rule came to be of paramount importance in large parts of Asia from the beginning of the 20th century and for half a century before the ground work was being laid. Despite nationalism being the obsession of all colonised people, other prevailing trends did not necessarily contradict or impede it. At times doubts were raised and accusations of being anti-nationalist were thrown at anyone who dared to be different. Like Dwijendralal Roy who was accused of being anti-national for experimenting with western music in his songs[96] or Upendra kishore Raychowdhury who was labelled an 'illicit cosmopolitan' by O.C. Ganguly, a leading advocate and patron of the Bengal school of art, when the former, who invented improved methods of half-tone reproductions, 'argued that there was no necessary contradiction between patriotism and a critical receptivity to external values and methods'.[97] Of course, Asian consciousness, as we shall see throughout this book, meant different things to different people, but in most cases there appears no contradiction with anti-colonial nationalism and a delicate balance was invariably maintained. As I show in my conclusion, the three nationalist cosmopolitans Rabindranath Tagore, Subhas Chandra Bose and Jawaharlal Nehru tried to give a permanent institutional basis to the idea of Asian consciousness since there was no conflict of interest in their convictions. While Rabindranath Tagore wanted a universalist consciousness to override excessive nationalism, Subhas Chandra Bose never loses sight of his pledge to India's freedom even when he lauds Asian consciousness to mean a country's 'desire to help other Asiatic nations to achieve their liberation'[98] and Nehru, who as the only one who got the concrete chance to, shaped the foreign policy of the free Indian state to include a strong Asian consciousness. Though Bose's strong opposition to British imperialism took an experimental path away in 1941, from the non-violent strategy of Mahatma Gandhi trending in India and upheld by Bose's compatriot Nehru, Bose's idea of true and false internationalism is intriguing and relevant here. According to him, it was because India had been committed from the medieval times to false internationalism that she was subjugated by an alien imperialist power. 'But we have', Bose wrote, 'learned through sorrow, suffering and humiliation to distinguish now between false internationalism and the true. We know now that internationalism is true, which does not ignore nationalism, but is rooted in it'.[99] Though Bose uses the term internationalism and not cosmopolitanism, it seems to be what Appiah was talking about in another context when he points out that a 'Cosmopolitan Patriot' could 'celebrate the variety of human cultures,' '*rooted*' (italics mine) loyal to one local society (or a few) that they count as home, '*liberal*' – convinced of the value of the individual and '*patriotic*' celebrating the institutions of the state (or states) within which they live.[100] Or when a cosmopolitan patriot can

> entertain the possibility of a world in which everyone is a rooted cosmopolitan, attached to a home of her own, with its own cultural particularities, but taking pleasure from the presence of the other, different, places that are home to other, different people.[101]

In the colonial phase, of course, this would have to be the ideal independent state of the patriot's dream. Sheldon Pollock's idea of how vernacular cosmopolitanism from the early medieval period in India destroyed old cosmopolitan cultural practices and finally leads to new cosmopolitanism also echoes Bose's logic[102]

Dynamic role of *Sahitya Patras* in Bengali society

Writing a history of vernacular press in India is imperative today, but it is a formidable proposition given their large number in different Indian languages. In the case of Bengal, some accounts deal with the history of the journals in the initial phase but a full survey of the *Sahitya Patrika* from whose wombs almost all the major thoughts, ideas, creative literature emerged is still an ongoing process. The best history of periodicals in the period 1816–1868 is by Brajendranath Bandopadhyay till date and makes interesting reading because of the anecdotal style he has used instead of the simply listing them chronologically. Interestingly, he has not made the distinction between newspapers and magazines or journals that we are used to now. There was possibly not that much difference between them since they are all referred to as *Samayik Patra* or *Patrika* in the plural. In the 19th century at least, the difference was more in the sense of time or frequency of production. Those which were monthly or bimonthly were more like the periodicals of later period or today's magazines since they dealt more with issues than daily news and analysis of events rather than simple presentation of events. Some of the dailies (newspapers of today or even in the sense that English language newspapers were then), on the other hand, though ultimately dealing with daily news, often at the time of inception, were monthly or more rarely weekly and gradually increasing frequency of production publishing triweekly before becoming dailies.

In the Introduction I have limited myself to discussing some of the historiography on the vernacular press in India. In the next chapter, however, I have tried to trace the beginnings of some of the Bengali periodicals which contain articles on Asia in the latter half of the 19th and first half of the 20th centuries as well as introduce the editors and writers. Here I address and acknowledge some of the stalwart historians of the Bengali press without whose efforts at documentation much of this rich archive would be lost. Brajendranath Bandopadhyay (Banerjee) has written an exhaustive and definitive history of Bengali periodicals from 1818 to 1868 and I have used this book to trace the early beginnings.[103] Unfortunately, for me this history ends at a time when most of the periodicals I have used to trace articles on Asia start; so for the major part of the periodicals in the late 19th and 20th centuries I have had to search for other sources. Some of the periodicals or their editors/owners/writers have been referred to in other works,[104] but there are many for which I could not find any material other than that provided by the excellent guide of the collection at Centre for Studies in Social Sciences. P.N. Bose and H.W.B. Moreno's *A Hundred Years of the Bengali Press* is an interesting read because of the anecdotes surrounding the publication of the Bengali periodicals which however ends in 1920.[105] Margarita Barns' *The Indian Press: A History of the Growth of Public Opinion in India*, written in 1940, deals mainly with the role of Indian newspapers in forming a public opinion against colonial rule[106] and, like Banerjee, she stresses the importance of the different press acts in moulding the growth of the media in India.

An extensive study of the history of pan-India press from its inception to the 1950s has been made by J. Natarajan where the major vernacular newspapers in the whole country are discussed. His focus is mainly on the impact of the political analysis and their impact in nationalism and on the newspapers as well in the context of the repressive press laws. He paints detailed pen-pictures of the *Mirat-ul-Akbar* and *Amrita Bazar Patrika* in this context. His stress is mainly on the English language newspapers and journals, though he quantifies through detailed lists of vernacular newspapers in different states over the whole colonial period and post-independence as well.[107] Literary journals are beyond the scheme of his study.

In India, the history of press began with the arrival of the Europeans. Printing press was brought for the first time to India by the Portuguese, and the English East India Company set up a printing press in India in 1684 in Bombay. James Augustus Hickey published the first newspaper in India entitled *The Bengal Gazette* or Calcutta General Advertiser (it was also the first newspaper printed in Asia) in the year 1780, although this newspaper was seized in 1782 on the ground of criticising the government. The *Calcutta Gazette* was first published on 4 March 1784; and in 1818 the *Calcutta Journal*, a new newspaper, launched by James Silk Buckingham, started. The *Bengal Journal* (1785; Founders: Thomas Jones and William Duane; weekly journal), *The Oriental Magazine of Calcutta* or *Calcutta Amusement* (1785), *The Calcutta Chronicle* (1786), *The Madras Courier* (1788), *The Bombay Herald* (1789) were some of the earlier newspapers published in India. Raja Ram Mohan Roy united with both the Indian and European editors to force Lord William Bentinck to liberalise the existing press laws and established *Brahmenical Magazine* in English, *Sambad Kaumudi* in Bangla and the *Mirat-ul-Akbar* in Persian. Apprehending a French invasion of India and engaged in the struggle for supremacy in India, Governor-General Lord Wellesley imposed censorship on all newspapers in 1799 and in 1807, it was extended to cover other publications as well. In 1818, Lord Hastings relaxed some of the restrictions. In 1823, the Licencing Regulation Act was imposed by John Adams, the acting Governor-General, who goes down in history as an oppressor of free press in India. This act provided that every printer and publisher had to obtain a licence for starting a press or for using it and a penalty of Rs. 400 for each publication without permission, with a rigorous punishment was imposed. Magistrates were authorised to seal the press and the Governor-General could revoke the licence too. Many vernaculars like Raja Ram Mohan Roy's *Mirat ul-Akbar* had to stop publication under the provisions of this act. Although a liberal attitude towards press was adopted by William Bentinck (1828–1835) and considerable freedom was given to Indian press, the 1823 Act was not revoked. That was later by the Governor General Metcalfe during 1835–1836. For this liberal policy towards Indian press, he is known as the Liberator of Indian Press. An interesting book *Liberator of the Indian Press* was written by Chandicharan Sen in 1887, which described in detail the whole process.[108] The panic created by the Revolt of 1857 brought a new act called The Licensing Act by which, in addition to the already existing registration procedure laid down by Metcalfe Act, licensing restrictions were imposed and at the same time government reserved the right to stop publication and circulation of any newspaper, book or printed matter. The act's duration was limited to one year and it was an emergency measure and was withdrawn. But the Press and Registration of Books Act of 1867 was continued with amendments in 1914, 1952 and 1953.

All the histories of the press in India discuss the role of the newspapers and periodical magazines as a tool of mass agitation and Barns talks about how the Indian Press helped in the growth of public opinion in India. Bandopadhyay shows through an analysis of the impact, that the vernacular periodicals in the period 1818–1868 had on the Bengali society and on the government officials who reacted to the criticism of the government policies and actions published as translated reports in the government records, (as *Report of Native newspapers*), how important the press had become. Bandopadhyay shows that not only the metropolis but also every mofussil town saw mushrooming of weekly and monthly periodicals, which tried to keep Bengalis abreast of all occurrences in the country and the world. Undoubtedly, *Bibidhartha Sangraha*, *Tattvabodhini Patrika*, *Bamabodhini Patrika*, *Bharati* and others were popular among readers young and old, but the government's ire was against not these literary journals but those which published what they considered inflammatory articles or criticised governmental policies. Natarajan in his book discusses that when the Vernacular Press Act was passed, there were 35 vernacular papers in Bengal, including the *Amrita Bazar Patrika* edited by Sisir Kumar Ghosh, who refused to comply with Sir Ashley Eden's demand that he should submit his paper to the government for final approval. Ghosh refused to compromise his commitment to honest journalism and it is possible that the Vernacular Press Act may have been precipitated by this incident. Sir Ashley remarked in a speech that 45 seditious writings published in 15 different vernacular papers had been scrutinised before the Act was finalised.

The main blow to the freedom of the vernacular periodicals was dealt by the Vernacular Press Act of 1878 by which the District Magistrate was entrusted with the power to call upon the printer and publisher of any vernacular newspaper to enter into an undertaking with the government to ensure that they didn't publish anything which may incite the public feeling or create disaffection towards the government or that may create enmity based on caste, religion or race. Publishers had to deposit the security and in case of infringement of the provision of the act, the security could be forfeited. If the offence recurred, even the press equipment could be seized. All the proof sheets of contents of newspapers and magazines were to be submitted to police rather than judiciary before publication. Decision of the Magistrate in such cases was considered final and no appeal could be made against such action in the court of law. If the vernacular language newspaper could submit the proof to a government censor, then it could get exemption from the application of the act. The most criticised feature of the act was that there was no provision for appeal and there was discrimination between European language newspapers and the local language ones. To escape from the provisions of the Vernacular Press Act, the *Amrita Bazar Patrika* transformed itself overnight into an English language newspaper from the original Bengali. Publication of Iswar Chandra Vidyasagar's *Som Prakash* was suspended and after getting reassurance of allegiance towards the government in writing, it reappeared in 1880. *Dacca Prakash*, *Halisahar Patrika*, *Sulabh Samachar*, *Bharat Mihir*, *Sadharani and Bharat Sanskarak*, etc. were said to have been leading the seditious movement against the government and under the provisions of the act, many of the papers were fined and the editors were jailed. All the native associations and prominent leaders of Bengal and India irrespective of religion, caste and creed condemned the Vernacular Press Act, 1878, and demanded its immediate withdrawal. The entire Vernacular Press Act of 1878 was repealed by Lord Ripon in 1882.

During boycott and Swadeshi movement held in protest of the decision of the government to partition Bengal during 1905, the government in order to suppress anti-government activities and repress the rising militant trends imposed restrictions in the form of Newspapers Act of 1908. The District Magistrate was empowered to confiscate printing press or other related material in case he found the newspaper publishing anti-government material, though the editors and printers of the confiscated newspaper had the right to appeal to the High Court within 15 days of forfeiture of the press. The powerful influence of the popular journals like *Kesari*, *Jugantar* and *Bandematram* on the local youth and attempted assassinations in Bengal by militant nationalists led to the Indian Press Act of 1910 which revived the extreme repressive provisions of the Vernacular Press Act of 1878. It was only in 1921, following the recommendations of the Sapru Committee, that the 1908 and 1910 Acts were repealed. Even after that the government tried to use emergency powers to suppress the nationalist movement by controlling the Indian Press through the Act of 1931, which was later amplified into the Criminal Amendment Act of 1932 to include all activities which undermined governmental authority.

Rabindranath Tagore's discussion on the importance of periodicals for impressionable youth in the late 19th century is probably the most well-read commendation given to them. In his Reminiscences of his Life, *Jibonsmriti*, Tagore writes about three important periodicals that held sway in his youth. The first was *Bibidhartha Sangraha* edited by Rajendralal Mitra, which held children captive because of the varied content and illustrations in the magazine. In his inimitable style Tagore describes in his autobiography how he would clutch the 'square bound volumes' which he borrowed from his third brother's bookcase and lie flat on the wooden bed in their common bedroom during holiday afternoons and devour stories about narwhal whales and the amusing stories of the Qazi's judgement, and novels like *Krishnakumari*.[109]

On *Bangadarshan* by the novelist Bankim Chandra Chattopadhyay, Rabindranath Tagore wrote in *Jibonsmriti* that 'it took the Bengali heart by storm. It was bad enough that we had to wait till the next monthly number was out, but to be kept waiting further till my elders were done with it was intolerable'.[110] The undulations of his tumultous relationship with the first successful Bengali novelist Bankim Chandra, was closely connected with the different periodicals of the time. As Tagore himself pointed out, Bankim Chandra's imposing looks and behaviour, his imperious contempt for small talk made it impossible for a young aspiring writer to approach him, so despite being a contributor to the Bankim edited *Bangadarshan*, Tagore maintained a prudent distance. He however followed closely the conflict that Bankim Chandra embarked on with Sasadhar Tarkachuramoni through his religious discourse in *Prachar* after the Bangadarshan phase. However, Tagore also recalls coming into conflict with Bankim Chandra which saw face off articles exchanged between them in *Bharati* and *Prachar*. It was finally ended by Bankim Chandra who sent Tagore a letter of forgiveness which 'plucked out the thorn from the flesh of the debate'.[111]

Benoy Ghosh in his book on *Bengali Society in the Periodicals* starts his introduction with a story when the publishers of *Samvad Prabhakar*, inspired by Iswar Chandra Gupta, satirist and poet, came to visit the famous Bengali novelist Bankim Chandra Chatterjee, who asked them whether the admirers of Iswar Chandra Gupta were avid readers of the daily. Chatterjee, incidentally, that day was hosting not only Gosaidas of *Samvad Prabhakar* but also Rajkrishna Mukherjee, who was the government-appointed translator of Bengali periodicals for the *Report of Native newspapers* file. Chatterjee, who admired Ishwar Chandra Gupta as not only the teacher of all the famous men of Bengali literature of the day but also as the only person who 'had the fearlessness to speak the truth about anyone', asked Gosaidas whether the demand for the newspaper was only for news or also for its literary merit. The reply that Gosaidas gave Chatterjee is of relevance here. 'On the first of every month Gupta sends a poem to be published in the monthly edition . . .. Hundreds of people would cue up from the morning at the Prabhakar office of the magazine to pick up a copy'.[112] The literary element of these journals was the most important element which attracted the reading public. Bangadarshan edited by Bankim Chandra and then his elder brother Sanjib Chandra Chatterjee also had that reputation.

Haraprasad Sastri, essayist and commentator on Bengali literature and history, describes Bankim Chandra's role in making *Bangadarshan* one of the most highly valued monthlies which continued even after Chatterjee formally handed over the baton to his brother Sanjib Chandra. Sastri describes how his association with the periodical started when he approached the Chatterjees at their home to offer his prize-winning essay 'On the Highest Ideal of Women's Character as Set Forth in Ancient Sanskrit Writers', which he had written during his Bachelor's degree in Sanskrit, on the invitation of the Brahmo leader Acharya Keshab Chandra Sen and funded by Raja Holkar. It had been previously rejected by *Aryadarshan*'s editor, Jogendra Nath Bandopadhyay. A fruitful relationship evolved between Sastri and *Bangadarshan* from where a number of his articles came out. *Bangadarshan* in the 1870s as Sastri points out was doing very well and had a large number of subscribers who were all willing to donate large amounts for its continued publication.[113] The reason for its continued success was that it remained true to its motto, 'Knowledge filtered down' and in this task of dissemination of knowledge Bangadarshan succeeded more than many other periodicals. It was in *Bangadarshan* that Bankim Chandra had been able to, through simple language and simple style, percolate deep scientific philosophy and the tenets of patriotism and nationalism to the ordinary reader.[114]

Haraprasad Shastri describes the impact of *Narayan*, the periodical started by Chittaranjan Das, as extraordinary, since even those who never read Bengali read *Narayan.*' According to Shastri, it was Das' innermost belief that Narayan, (the God), in the form of *Narayan* (the periodical) would save the country and that is what *Narayan* tried to achieve. Even the section of the Bengali population, like the 'barristers and the England returned' who turned their noses up against Bengali language did not hesitate to read *Narayan*. The reason for that, of course, was its supremo Chittaranjan Das. In another way, according to Sastri, *Narayan* played an important role. It broke through the barriers of convention even in academic disciplines. That of course brought a lot of criticism on its head. but the editor's courage and the fact that the criticism was diffused helped amateur writers survive against disciplinarian academicians.[115] Sastri humorously discusses the naming of *Narayan* as unique too. Initially, he writes, 'periodicals had "darshan" as suffix – *Bangadarshan, Aryadarshan*, etc., then came feminine names like *Tarangini, Jyotsna, Jahnabi, Janmabhumi*, etc. But *Narayan* was unique because of its divine provenance'.[116] Sastri however goes on to say that unlike what most people thought, *Narayan* was not a religious magazine, its main focus was national regeneration. Das got his political mentor Bipin Chandra Pal to write *Nutone Puratone* (In the Old and New) on Hindu revivalism, which in the poetic words of Sastri 'first sowed seed in the final days of *Bangadarshan*, showed signs of first leaves in *Prachar*, and further branches and leaves in Akshoy Dutta's *Nabajiban*' and finally flowered in full fearless bloom in Das' *Narayan*. In Sastri's analysis, this article proclaimed a protest against those Indians who emboldened with western education rejected their own traditions and philosophies.[117]

As Hemendra Kumar Roy pointed out in an article in *Bharati*, on its 40th anniversary, there were two reasons, besides the fact of its illustrious editors and support from the Tagore family, why the periodical had continued its existence while so many other good periodicals had perished. One was 'its continued commitment of holding up a mirror to the contemporary age' and the other was that from it, 'the reader could sift through the large amount of writing and identify good literature'.[118]

Rabindranath Tagore remembers how *Bangadarshan* had stolen the heart of every Bengali and it was a difficult prospect indeed waiting for its arrival every month and waiting agonisingly for all the grown-ups to finish reading.

> Today anyone can read Bishabrishka, Chandrasekhar etc (famous novels of Bankim Chandra Chatterjee) at one go anytime one wants, but then for us it was a wait full of want, desire, expectation, a short reading experience made long and fulfilling because we savoured every episode in our leisure moments, with satisfaction and dissatisfaction, satiation and curiosity intermingling with each other making the whole reading experience unique in a way people can't imagine now.[119]

A similar story is echoed by Suniti Kumar Chatterjee, linguist and educationist, who recalled the debt that all students during his youth owed to the literary periodicals when he writes about *Prabashi* how they would at the beginning of each month rush to the Calcutta University Institute library for the latest edition of the periodical *Prabashi* which had become 'a national institution for expression of political, literary and cultural history in Bengali'.[120] – just as Chattopadhyay's *The Modern Review* was for the readers in English.[121] Though Chatterjee used Tagore's love for *Bangadarshan* as a reference for learning Bengali, Tagore had also mentioned in that context, *Abodhbandhu*, as having inculcated in him love for poetry since they first introduced Biharilal Chakraborty's romantic poems to Bengalis and the tragic romance of *Paul et Virginie* (Paul and Virginia), from a translation of the 18th-century novel by Jacques Henri Bernadin de Saint Pierre by Krishnakamal Bhattacharya.

Sometimes it was the content of a periodical in the context of a particular event or an ideology which made it sought after. Sahana Devi, a singer and devotee of Sri Aurobindo, recalls in her memoirs about her maternal uncle Chittaranjan Das' household where she grew up referring to many periodicals which played an important role in their lives. During the Swadeshi movement in 1905, she refers to *Sandhya,* edited by Brahma Bandhab Upadhyay, theologian, journalist and freedom fighter, which published fiery anti-British articles in protest against the partition of Bengal: 'The fire that spewed from his pen was reflected in the hearts of the readers who scrambled for copies of his journal'. This naturally attracted retaliation from the British government who charged him with sedition. Represented by Chittaranjan Das, the firebrand Upadhyay decided to fight the British in court but within a short time succumbed to an illness and died.[122] Sahana Debi also refers to the great popularity of the journal edited by Aurobindo Ghosh, *Bande Mataram*, saying that, 'people went mad trying to collect a copy of *Bande Mataram* to read Ghosh's articles there'. She also describes how the British government who arrested Aurobindo for sedition for editing the *Bande Mataram* could not prosecute him for lack of evidence. So, they decided to call in Bipin Chandra Pal for questioning. Prior to appearing before the British, Pal went to C.R. Das for advice who told him that he had three options. If he admitted that Ghosh was the editor, then Ghosh would be jailed and the periodical would close down, severely hampering the freedom struggle; the second option was to say that Ghosh was not the editor, which would be a blatant lie and liable to perjury; and the third option was to deny to speak about the matter in court, which would result in jail time for Pal since he would be obstructing justice. Bipin Chandra Pal went to court the next day and acted on the third option for which he was jailed for six months.[123] Sahana Devi's memoirs paint an intimate pen-picture of the man C.R. Das and his activities in the service of the country. In that context, she brings in the important periodicals that Das was associated with – the monthly *Narayan* where he published articles on religion and ethics and the daily newspaper *Forward*, which contained his spirited expression of discontent against the British rule, especially during the arrest of his close confidant and fellow freedom fighter Subhas Chandra Bose.[124] Finally, I must also refer to a brilliant satirical/humorous anonymous critique of the leading Indo-English as well the Bengali Press which came out in *The Indian World*, edited by Prithwis Chandra Roy, in 1906, though the Bengali literary journals do not fall under the purview of his study.[125]

That the vernacular periodicals had the duty of educating the public was hardly ever doubted and the Walter Lippmann and John Dewey debate in the 1920s on the role of journalism in modern democracy would have appeared strange to these Bengali journalists and publishers. To Lippmann, the journalist fulfilled the role of the mediator, or translator, between the general public and policymaking elites and the complex facts of the modern society were to be filtered to the public who was located at the bottom of the power chain. But he denigrated the opinion of not only the readers but also the powerful publishers whom he distrusted. Dewey, on the other hand, believed that not only was the public capable of understanding the issues created or responded to by the elite, but also that it was in the public forum that decisions should be made after discussion and debate. When issues were thoroughly vetted, the best ideas would bubble to the surface. There is no doubting the importance that journalism played in disseminating the predominant ideas of the day. Ram Mohan Roy had so many years ago added a caveat to this when he wrote in the prospectus of *Mirat-ul-Akbar* or the 'Mirror of Intelligence', the first Indian Persian paper of note, the following words:

> some gentlemen of this nation publish in the English language, the news of this and other countries for the improvement of the Public at large; . . . but as the English language is not understood in all parts of India, those unacquainted with it must either have recourse to others in their enquiries after information, or remain totally uninformed. On this account, I, humblest of the human race, am desirous of publishing a Weekly Newspaper, written in the Persian language, which is understood by all the respectable part of the Native Community, and am ready to distribute it to all who may be so inclined.

He also clearly spelt out his social and political motives in starting the newspaper where he wanted to not only 'lay before the Public such articles of Intelligence as may increase their experience, and tend to their social improvement'; but also communicate to the Rulers a knowledge of the real situation of their subjects', and make the subjects acquainted with the established laws and conditions of their Rulers'. The aim of this interaction was to enable the rulers to 'more readily find an opportunity of granting relief to the people; and the people may be put in possession of the means of obtaining protection and redress from their rulers'.[126]

That pedagogy was considered to be the real motive of the periodicals was attested to when a memorial against the Press Ordinance passed by the Acting Governor-General in Council in 1823 was sent to the Supreme Court in Calcutta by six Bengalis – (Chunder Coomar Tagore, Dwarkanath Tagore, Ram Mohan Roy, Hurchunder Ghose, Gowree Churn Bonnerjee and Prasanna Kumar Tagore) in which they wrote that the four native newspapers (two Bengali and two Persian) were the result of 'free discussion among the Natives and inducing them to reflect and inquire after knowledge, (which has) . . . already served greatly to improve their minds and ameliorating their condition'.[127]

Knowing Asia, Being Asian aims to discuss most of the articles which expressed an Asia consciousness through various lenses. In Chapter 1, I provide a summary of the important periodicals that published these articles, how they were started and who the main authors were. Chapters 2 and 3 mainly deal with travel accounts by men and women and I discuss how women became the focus of the didactic efforts of all writers for a horizontal dissemination of Asian consciousness. As a corollary to women's knowledge, education of children for the development of an ideal nation meant engaging them with knowledge beyond the classroom (Chapter 4). A mixture of entertainment and knowledge was brought forth by the children's magazines to bring the faintly familiar knowledge about Asia within the grasp of the young adults. Cultural connections in the past and present were the smoothest means by which Asia could be brought close to Indians and I take a look in Chapter 5 how through discussion on Asian art and culture past and present connections between Asian countries were explored. In Chapter 6, I show how Buddhism from the 19th century re-entered the consciousness of the Bengalis and how they evolved a new pilgrimage in Asian countries in their quest for an unconquered past and a faith untainted with existing decadence. In Chapter 7, I look at how these periodicals tried to analyse the political situation in Asia in the context of world politics and how Indian nationalistic ideas and associations impacted their vision. In Chapter 8, I try to see how the pan-Asian ideas of unity conflicted with the nationalist agendas of those very same countries leading to disillusionment. Finally, I discuss three Indian leaders who tried to implement their dreams of Asian consciousness and hopes of Asian unity into practice through an international university, a national government in exile based in Asia and a conference uniting heads and scholars of different countries of Asia.

Notes

1 Shri Ram, Welcome Address, *Asian Relations: Report of the Proceedings and Documentation of the First Asian Relations Conference New Delhi, March–April 1947*, Delhi: Asian Relations Organisation, 1948, pp. 16–17.
2 Karl Jaspers, *The Origin and Goal of History*, London: Yale University Press, 1953 (1965 ed.), Introduction, p. xiii.
3 Sisir Kumar Ghosh, ed., *Arnold Toynbee, Faith of a Historian*, Bombay: Bharatiya Vidya Bhawan, 1967, pp. 24–25.
4 Tony Ballantyne, *Orientalism and Race: Aryanism in the British Empire*, New York: Palgrave Macmillan, 2002, pp. 33–35.
5 Michael Edwardes, *Asia in the European Age, 1498–1955*, Bombay: Asia Publishing House, 1990 (Indian ed.), p. 13.
6 Rene Grousset, *Sum of History*, Essex: Town Bridge Publication, 1951 (1946), p. 90.
7 Birbal, Amra O Tomra, *Bharati*, 26(4), 1902, pp. 405–408.

8 Denys Hay, *Europe: The Emergence of an Idea*, Edinburgh: Edinburgh University Press, 1968.
9 Jean Herbert, *An Introduction to Asia*, London: George Allen & Unwin Ltd., 1965, p. 12.
10 Dick Wilson, *Asia Awakens: A Continent in Transition*, London: Weidenfeld and Nicolson, 1970, p. 2.
11 Charles E. Trevelyan, *On the Education of the People of India*, London: Longman, Orme, Brown, Green and Longmans, 1838, p. 47.
12 Rammohan Roy, *Selected Works of Raja Rammohan Roy*, Delhi: Publications Division, 1958, p. 83.
13 J.K. Majumdar, ed., *Indian Speeches and Documents on British Rule 1821–1918*, Calcutta: Longmans, Green and Co. Ltd, 1937, pp. 19–20.
14 Rammohan Roy, 'A Dialogue between a Missionary and Three Chinese Converts', in Kalidas Nag and Debajyoti Burman, eds., *English Works of Raja Rammohan Roy, Part IV,* Calcutta: Sadharon Brahmo Samaj, 1947, pp. 75–79.
15 Keshab Chandra Sen, *Acharya Keshab Chandra – Biography*, Calcutta: Mangalganj Mission Press, 1891, pp. 69–114.
16 Swami Sambuddhananda, Swami *Vivekananda on Himself,* Calcutta: Swami Vivekananda Centenary, 1959.
17 Ibid., p. 128.
18 Swami Sambuddhananda, *Swami Vivekananda on Himself*, op. cit., p. 129.
19 Prasanta Kumar Pal, *Rabijibani*, vols 1–9, Calcutta: Ananda Publishers, 2002 (2nd ed).
20 Ibid., p. 130.
21 Ibid., p. 131.
22 Ibid.
23 Edward Thompson, *Rabindranath Tagore: Poet and Dramatist,* London: Oxford University Press, 1926, p. 18.
24 Kissory Chand Mittra, *Memoir of Dwarakanath Tagore,* Calcutta: Parul, 2011 (originally read at the 27th Hare Anniversary meeting held at the Town Hall on the 1st of June 1870).
25 Devendranath Tagore, *The Autobiography of Maharshi Devendranath Tagore*, translation by Satyendranath Tagore and Indira Devi, London: Macmillan and Co., 1914, pp. 184–190.
26 Rabindranath Tagore, *Greater India* (authorised translation), Madras: S. Ganesan, 1921, pp. 15–16.
27 Hemanta Kumar Adya, *Sukumar Ray: Jibonkatha,* Calcutta: Pustak Bipani, 1990, pp. 3–4.
28 Chandak Sengupta, *Creativity and Modernity in Colonial India*, Delhi: Oxford University Press, 2016.
29 Sarvani Gooptu, *The Music of Nationhood: Dwijendralal Roy of Bengal*, Delhi: Primus Books, 2018.
30 I owe this suggestion to Professor Gautam Bhadra.
31 Sankar Bhattacharya, *Bangla Rangalayer Itihasher Upadan,* Calcutta: W.B. Natya Academy, 1994, p. 157.
32 Sarvani Gooptu, 'Japan and Asian Destiny: India's Intellectual Journey through Contemporary Periodicals, 1880s–1930s', in Ishita Banerjee-Dube and Sarvani Gooptu, eds., *On Modern Indian Sensibilities: Culture, Politics, History,* London: Routledge, 2018, pp. 198–216.
33 Rabindranath Tagore, *Japan Jatri*, Calcutta: Visva Bharati Publications, 2013 (1919), p. 91.
34 Tagore, *Nationalism*, Calcutta: Rupa and Company, 1992 (1917), p. 24.
35 Rabindranath Tagore, To the Indian Community in Japan, *Japan Jatri,* op. cit., p. 118.
36 Sabyasachi Bhattacharya, *Rabindranath Tagore: An Interpretation*, Delhi: Penguin/Viking, 2011, p. 133.
37 Japan O Rabindranath, Samayiki, *Bharatvarsha*, 26(1), 1938, pp. 790–1.
38 Subhas Chandra Bose, *Chalo Delhi: Writings and Speeches 1943–1945*, in Sisir Kumar Bose and Sugata Bose, eds., *Netaji Collected Works,* vol. 12, Ranikhet: Permanent Black, 2007, pp. 18–19.
39 Emily Hahn, *China Only Yesterday, 1850–1950: A Century of Change*, London: Weidenfeld and Nicholson, 1963, p. 2.

40 See the series on Chinese women in Raj Mohon Bose, Chiner Sabhyata, Sahitya o Naridharma, *Mahila,* 12(5), 1906, pp. 127–131; 12(6), 1907, 150–155.
41 Ramlal Sarkar's series on different aspects of China in *Prabashi* (1904–1906) and *Navya Bharat* , Kedarnath Bandopadhyay's Letters and Memories from China in *Bharati* and *Bichitra,* Kshitish Chandra Bandopadhyay in *Bharatvarsha,* Jamini Kanta Sen in *Bharatvarsha,* Ashutosh Roy in *Bharati* among others.
42 Presented some of these ideas at conferences in Jadavpur University, Kolkata, and at Indian History Congress, Kannur session.
43 Thant Myint-U, *The Making of Modern Burma,* Cambridge: Cambridge University Press, 2001, pp. 3–11.
44 Uma Shankar Singh, Indians in Burma I, pp. 98–99 and Parimal Kumar Das, Indians in Burma II, p. 117 in I.J. Bahadur Singh, ed., *Indians in South East Asia,* Delhi: Sterling Publishers, 1982.
45 Mrinalini Raha, Brahmadesher Kotha, *Antahpur,* 5(8), 1902, pp. 161–164.
46 Girindranath Sarkar, Brahmadeshe Bangali, *Prabashi,* 1(8/9), 1901, pp. 347–350.
47 Pushpabala Debi, Malay Rajya, *Mahila,* 9(3), 1903, pp. 71–72.
48 Aung San Suu Kyi, *Burma and India Some Aspects of Intellectual Life under Colonialism,* Shimla: IIAS, 1990 and Thant Myint-U, *Where China Meets India: Burma and the New Crossroads of Asia,* London: Faber and Faber, 2011.
49 Sarala Debi Chaudhurani, Burma Jatra, *Bharatvarsha,* 19(1)(5), 1931, p. 773.
50 Brahmadeshiya Natok o Natokabhnoy, *Bharati,* 2(7), 1877, pp. 306–314; Paresh Chandra Sen, Machchagirir Padamule, *Bharatvarsha,* I(5), 1927, p. 785.
51 Narendra Dev, Shyambhoomi, *Bharatvarsha,* 12(1)(5), 1924, pp. 761–773; 12(1)(6), 1927, pp. 901–910.
52 Paresh Chandra Sen, Machchagirir Padamule, *Bharabarsha,* 15(1)(5), 1927, pp. 781–793; Sri Pad Darshan, Bharatvarsha, 15(2)(2), 1927, pp. 238–249.
53 Ta Pra Cha, Singhal Yatra, *Nabajiban,* 1(2), 1884, p. 89.
54 Anon., Korea Prodesher Mahila, *Bamabodhini Patrika,* 5(3) (361), 1895, pp. 313–314.
55 Rabindranath Tagore, *Java Jatrir Patra,* Calcutta: Visva Bharati Publishers, 1960.
56 Narendra Dev, Philippine, *Bharatvarsha,* 12(1)(3), 1924, pp. 444–460; 13(1)(4), 1924, pp. 901–910.
57 Hemanta Chattopadhyay, British Borneor Aranyabashider Kotha, *Bharatvarsha,* 15(1)(1), 1927, pp. 933–941, Borneo Dvipbashider Kotha, *Bharatvarsha,* 15(1)(2), 1927, pp. 315–326.
58 Hemendranath Dutta, Turashker Ramani, *Bharat Mahila,* 4(8), 1908, pp. 171–174.
59 Monomohan Ghosh, Turk Shadharon Tantre Narir Mukti, *Bichitra,* 2(2)(5), 1928, 722–732.
60 Hemendra Prasad Ghosh, Turkir Joy, *Mashik Basumati,* 1(2)(1), 1922, pp. 81–87; 1(2)(2), 1922, pp. 257–263.
61 Hemendra Prasad Ghosh, Turkir Punarabhyudoy O Bartoman Samashya, *Mashik Basumati,* 1(2)(3), 1922, pp. 295–300).
62 Different from *Islam Pracharak (1891–93),* edited by Md Reyazzudin Ahmed. *Pracharak* was edited by Madhu Mian.
63 Fazle Haq, Turashker Sultan, *Pracharak,* 2(5), pp. 124–127; 2(6), 1900, pp. 141–144; 2(9), 1900, pp. 239–241.
64 Ismail Hussain Sirazi, Roupya Jubilee, *Pracharak,* 2(10), 1900, pp. 254–261.
65 Bipin Chandra Pal, *Memories of My Life and Times,* Calcutta: Modern Book Agency, 1932.
66 Rabindranath Tagore, *Parashya Jatri,* Calcutta: Visva Bharati Publications, 1963 (previously published in *Prabashi* and *Bichitra* between 1932 and 1933).
67 Munshi Ismail Hossain Shirazi, Arab, *Pracharak,* 2(12), 1900, pp. 293–301.
68 Birendra Nath Ghosh, Sarat Chandra Das, *Bharatvarsha,* 17(2)(1), 1929, pp. 158–162.
69 Ulrich Beck, 'Cosmopolitan Sociology: Outline of a Paradigm Shift', in Maria Rovisco and Magdalena Nowicka, eds., *The Ashgate Research Companion to Cosmopolitanism,* Surrey: Ashgate Publishing Ltd., 2011, p. 17.
70 Ibid.
71 Ibid., pp. 18–20.
72 Garette Wallace Brown and David Held, *The Cosmopolitanism Reader,* Cambridge: Polity Press, 2010.
73 Ibid., Introduction, p. 4.

74 Ibid., p. 5.
75 Kwame Anthony Appiah, *Cosmopolitanism: Ethics in a World of Strangers*, New York: W.W. Norton, 2006, Introduction, p. xv.
76 Sugata Bose, *A Hundred Horizons: The Indian Ocean in the Age of Global Empire*, Cambridge: Harvard University Press, 2006, p. 273.
77 Christopher Bayly and Tim Harper, *Forgotten Armies: Britain's Asian Empire and the War with Japan*, London: Penguin Books, 2004.
78 See details of Colourful Cosmopolitanism in Sugata Bose, 'Different Universalisms, Colourful Cosmopolitanisms: The Global Imagination of the Colonized Sugata Bose', in Kris Manjapra, ed., *Cosmopolitan Thought Zones: South Asia and the Global Circulation of Ideas*, London: Palgrave Macmillan, 2010, pp. 97–111.
79 Sugata Bose, 'Rabindranath Tagore and Asian Universalism', in *Tagore's Asian Voyages: Selected Speeches and Writings on Rabindranath Tagore,* Nalanda – Srivijaya Centre, Institute of Southeast Asian Studies, Singapore, 201, pp. 10–11, http://research.gold.ac.uk/20908/23/Rabindranath%20Tagore%20and%20Asian%20Universalism.pdf, accessed on 30.07.19.
80 Kris Manjapra, 'Introduction', in Sugata Bose and Kris Manjapra, eds., *Cosmopolitan Thought Zones: South Asia and the Global Circulation of Ideas*, op. cit., p. 1.
81 Tansen Sen, *India, China and the World: A Connected History,* Delhi: Oxford University Press, 2018, pp. 25–26.
82 Tansen Sen and Brian Tsui, eds., *Beyond Pan-Asianism: Connecting China and India, 1840s and 1960s*, Delhi: Oxford University Press, 2021, pp. 1–2.
83 Ashis Nandy, 'A New Cosmopolitanism: Towards a Dialogue of Asian Civilizations', in Kuan-Hsing Chen, ed., *Trajectories: Inter-Asia Cultural Studies*, London: Routledge, 1998, p. 142.
84 Ibid., p. 144.
85 Ibid. p. 145.
86 Michele L. Louro, Asianist Projects in India 1917–1937, Review of Carolien Stolte's Dissertation, Orienting India: Interwar Period in an Asian Inflection, 1917–1937, http://dissertationreviews.org/archives/8419, accessed on 03.02.2020.
87 Carolien Stolte and Harald Fischer-Tine, 'Imagining Asia in India: Nationalism and Internationalism (ca 1905–1940)', *Comparative Studies in Society and History*, 54(1), 2012, pp. 65–92.
88 Birendra Prasad, *Indian Nationalism and Asia (1900–1947),* Delhi: B.R. Publishing Corporation, 1979 (1952), p. 23.
89 Ibid., p. 27.
90 Ibid., p. 29.
91 Narayan C. Sen, 'China as Viewed by Two Early Bengali Travellers: The Travel Accounts of Indumadhav Mullick and Benoy Kumar Sarkar', *China Report*, 43(4), 2007, pp. 465–484.
92 Simonti Sen, *Travels to Europe: Self and Other in Bengali Travel Narratives, 1870–1910,* Delhi: Orient Longman, 2005, p. 1.
93 Jayati Gupta, *Travel Culture, Travel Writing and Bengali Women, 1870–1940*, London: Routledge, 2021.
94 Ramachandra Guha, 'Travelling with Tagore', in *Democrats and Dissenters*, Delhi Penguin Books, 2017, pp. 300–338.
95 Satadru Sen, *Benoy Kumar Sarkar, Restoring the Nation to the World*, Delhi: Routledge India, 2015, p. 3.
96 Sarvani Gooptu, *The Idea of Nationhood: Dwijendralal Roy of Bengal*, op. cit., p. 207.
97 Sumit Sarkar, *Modern Times: India 1880s to 1950s,* Ranikhet: Permanent Black, 2014, p. 427.
98 Subhas Chandra Bose, *Chalo Delhi: Writngs and Speeches 1943–1945*, in Sisir Kumar Bose and Sugata Bose, eds., *Netaji Collected Works*, vol. 12, Ranikhet: Permanent Black, 2007, p. 43.
99 Subhas Chandra Bose, 'Netaji at the Assembly of Greater East Asia Nations', *Chalo Delhi*, op. cit., p. 150.
100 Kwame Anthony Appiah, 'Cosmopolitan Patriots', in Pheng Cheah and Bruce Robbins, eds., *Cosmopolitics: Thinking and Feeling beyond the Nation*, Minneapolis: University of Minnesota Press, 1998, pp. 91–114(106).

101 Kwame Anthony Appiah, 'Against National Culture', in Laura Garcia-Moreno and Peter C. Pfeiffer, eds., *Text and Nation: Cross-Disciplinary Essays on Cultural and National Identities*, Columbia: Camdin House, 1996, p. 175.
102 Sheldon Pollock, 'Cosmopolitan and Vernacular in History', in Brekenridge, Carol A., Pollock, Sheldon, Bhaba, Homi K., Chakraborty, Dipesh, eds., *Cosmopolitanism*, Durham/London: Duke University Press, 2002, pp. 15–53.
103 Brojendra Nath Bandopadhyay, *Bangla Samayik Patra (1818–1868)*, Calcutta: Bangiya Sahitya Parishad, 1935.
104 Benoy Ghosh, *Samayikpatre Banglar Samajchitra, Part I: Sanvad Prabhakar*, Calcutta: Prakash Bhavan, 2015 (1962); Chandak Sengoopta, *The Rays before Satyajit: Creativity and Modernity in Colonial India*, Oxford University Press, 2016; Anikendra Sen, Devangshu Datta, Nilanjana S. Roy, eds., *Patriots, Poets and Prisoners: Ramananda Chatterjee's The Modern Review*, Noida: Harper Collins India, 2016.
105 P.N. Bose and H.W.B. Moreno, *A Hundred Years of the Bengali Press: Being a History of the Bengali Newspapers from Their Inception to the Present Day*, Calcutta: Central Press, 1920.
106 Margarita Barns, *The Indian Press: A History of the Growth of Public Opinion in India*, London: George Alen & Unwin Ltd, 1940.
107 J. Natarajan, *History of Indian Journalism: Part II of the Report of the Press Commission*, Delhi: Publications Division GOI-M.I&B, 2017(1955), https://archive.org/details/historyofindianj00nata, accessed on 12.07.20.
108 Chandicharan Sen, *Mudrajantrer Swadhinata Pradata – Liberator of the Indian Press*, Calcutta: Victoria Press, 1887.
109 Rabindranath Tagore, Jibonsmriti, *Rabindra Rachanabali (Collected Works)*, Vol IX, Calcutta: Visva Bharati, 2008 (1989), p. 452.
110 Rabindranath Tagore, 'Jibonsmriti', op. cit., pp. 452–453.
111 Ibid., p. 506.
112 Benoy Ghosh, *Samayikpatre Banglar Samajchitra, Part I: Sanvad Prabhakar*, Calcutta: Prakash Bhavan, 2015 (1962), p. 10.
113 Sukumar Sen, ed., *Haraprasad Sastri, Rachana Samagra* (Collected Works 1853–1931), Calcutta: W.B. State School Book Society, 1981, Vol II, pp. 15–23.
114 Ibid., pp. 29–30.
115 Haraprasad Sastri, Chittaranjan Prasanga, *Rachana Samagra* (Collected Works 1853–1931), Sukumar Sen, ed., op. cit., pp. 162–164.
116 Ibid., p. 168.
117 Ibid., pp. 170–171.
118 Hemendra Kumar Roy, Bharatir Itihas, *Bharati*, 40(1), 1916, p. 127.
119 Rabindranath Tagore, *Jibonsmriti*, op. cit., p. 453.
120 Prabashi's role in moulding the youthful minds mentioned in Kshitimohon Sen's Preface in Shanta Nag, *Bharat Muktisadhak Ramananda Chattopadhyay O Ardhashatabir Bangla*, Calcutta: Firma KLM, 2000(reprint). She also mentions in her book the responsibility that Rabindranath Tagore and his students and teachers of Visva Bharati undertook to collect and translate important essays from foreign periodicals for *Prabashi*.
121 Suniti Kumar Chatterjee, *Ogranthito Suniti Kumar (Unpublished Works of Suniti Kumar)*, BaridBaran Ghosh, ed., Calcutta: Deep Prakashani, 2009, pp. 222–223.
122 Sahana Debi, *Smritir Kheya*, Calcutta: Prima Publications, 1960, p. 59.
123 Ibid., pp. 61–62.
124 Ibid., pp. 92–97, 111–113.
125 Anti-Humbug, 'The Indo-English Newspaper Press', *The Indian World*, 4(1), 1906, pp. 204–206.
126 Rammohan Roy, Prospectus of the 'Mirat-ul-Akhbar' or the 'Mirror of Intelligence' (no. 1, 1822), the first Indian Persian paper of note, said to be owned and edited by Raja Rammohan Roy, J.K. Majumdar, ed., *Indian Speeches and Documents on British Rule 1821–1918*, Calcutta: Longmans, Green and Co., 1937, pp. 3–4.
127 J.K. Majumdar, ed., *Indian Speeches and Documents on British Rule 1821–1918*, op. cit., p. 9.

1 Othering the self through *Sahitya Patrikas*

The history of nationalism in India has shown us that like many nationalisms that existed along with the large framework of anti-colonial nationalism, there were also many 'others' besides the colonial government. Identifying the other was an important element in self-identification as well. The process of self-discovery is never uncomplicated or straightforward and for those who had discovered themselves and their country through the medium of western education with the 'west as catalyst', in the words of Tapan Raychaudhuri,[1] the path of othering was hazy. It required strong self-conviction to understand the self in the context of the relationship with the other and then to set forth on the task of othering – setting the self as different from the other. This self-analysis through the medium of vernacular literature and periodicals was a unique feature of nationalism which, according to the spirited nationalist Bipin Chandra Pal, provided a new 'depth and reality' to the old patriotism leading to growth of a 'strong messianic hope and aspiration'.[2] I feel compelled to point out that though Pal distinguishes as 'old style politics' the pre-1905 anti-colonial movement since it was conducted in English and 'which left no mark on vernacular literature', the evidence of political articles in vernacular newspapers and journals from the mid-19th century belies that claim.

Despite the dilemma regarding the 'benefits' and the 'drawbacks' of the west among the educated elite of Bengal, there was a general acceptance of the view that the west was dominant because of its access to modern knowledge. One of the benefits of colonial rule was the beginning of arrival of world news through books and the press. No matter what the objective of the government, and despite the legendary war between any press and government control, with the start of the vernacular press which followed on the heels of the English language press, freedom to express opinions and influence the reading public became the new norm. Literary journals such as these could actually bypass the punitive repression acts that were more easily used against the openly nationalistic press. Another benefit of the new access to international news and knowledge system was an opening of the mind of the Bengali to the world. The easiest and the first connections made were with the west because their world was easier to access. But, surprisingly soon Asia became a focus – knowing about Asia and writing about it.

This chapter tries to surf through the immense amount of data to locate this focus from the large number of *Samayik Patra/Patrika* or periodicals published in Bengali. I have tried in brief to locate the start of the journals, identify the editors as well as the writers who wrote about Asia. This large intellectual group, most of whom were skilled writers as well, subtly influenced and trained the contemporary social mindset

DOI: 10.4324/9781003243786-1

by bringing the world to the Bengali home and percolating through the latest cosmopolitan and nationalistic trends in a simple, comprehensible and attractive manner. But it is impossible for the most part to gauge the reaction of the readership since very few of the journals have a Letters to the Editor section. Reactions to articles can be gauged only through reports by other journals, but that too is more the reaction of the editor than the readers. Though there was no real watershed which differentiated the focus of the articles from the standpoint of cosmopolitanism and/or nationalism, I believe that in Bengal at least, patriotic nationalism, though in a state of flux in the second half of the 19th century, was more conducive to combining cosmopolitan ideas with universalist ideas than with the nationalist ideas that came in the 20th century and which were concretised through institutions and movements.

The very fact of time difference in the publication of the two types, i.e. one providing news daily and other published weekly, biweekly or monthly, makes a difference in the content. Since the journals do not provide daily news, they focus on summaries, notes, miscellanies while at the same time providing analytical featured essays on politics, social issues and inspirational and motivational features. Introspection as well as awareness of the outside world was noticeable from the beginning. The fact that the publications were by educated men or women who were also socially committed led to the richness of content. Some of the journals with professed literary focus as *sahityapatra* really means were generally led by or were associated with accomplished and established litterateurs. Others were organs of different associations and *sabhas* with commitment to the associated issues. It was a whole world within the intellectual world of the Bengalis who not only took pride in knowledge for themselves but desired to expand the horizon to include the rest of the country, Asia and the world. Communications through the written word of books and periodicals as well as physical travel played an important role in this journalistic world.

As I have written elsewhere, 'vernacular literary periodicals reached out to all sections of the Bengali society, including women and children, with the dual aim in mind – education and entertainment not only focussed on Indian heritage but knowledge about other civilizations as well'.[3] In fact, Rabindranath Tagore testifies to the fact when he writes that his enjoyment of reading periodicals in his childhood proves that children do not really need magazines which are aimed at 'childhood' only. He always believed that every kind of information should be handed over to all, irrespective of age and sex and their minds would select what they 'understood and what they didn't'.[4] Tagore considered of greatest importance in the formation of a large educated middle class

> not journals which focussed on specialized and in depth discussions on science or archaeology or even large numbers of stories, poems and inane travelogues, but rather middle ranking magazines which were comfort reading for the common people. Rather like *Chamber's Journal, Castle's Magazine, Strand Magazine* of England majority of which cater to the ordinary folks. They use their wealth of knowledge to provide their countrymen their basic needs. It is this basic need, like food and clothing that is the greatest need of people.[5]

Bibidhartha Sangraha that he used to read in his childhood, according to Tagore, was one such periodical which was the need of the hour.

Here I will only take a quick glance at the periodicals that were published in the second half of the 19th century and some major ones in the 20th century which contain articles published on Asia, concentrating mainly on identifying authors and editors as far as possible. These periodicals are in their own microcosmic way a reflection of the social milieu it started in, whether in the metropolis or whether it was in the important district towns and each of them carries a story which again collectively form a larger picture of urban and social history. The distinction that Tagore makes about periodicals in the late 19th century and the period when he was writing *Jibonsmriti*, regarding content of the periodicals, is also applicable to my mind with slight modifications when looking at writings on Asia. In the former period which I have identified as 1850–1900, the periodicals brought varied information from other countries for the knowledge and entertainment of their readers with less nationalistic mission necessitating urgent pedagogy. I distinguish here between the two periods since it is striking how much awareness there existed in the society regarding the world outside the home where a conscious positioning of the nation does not yet occur. From the turn of the century, information about the rise of Japanese military power, Japan–China clashes over territorial ambitions and the rise of nationalistic ideas within Bengal culminating in anti-Partition of Bengal movement had created a consciousness of the self in Bengal vis-à-vis the colonial government as well as a position as Asian vis-à-vis an Asian power who had captured the world's imagination. Having said that, I must also add the caveat that these differentiations between loving one's own country and touring others in imagination or reality to understand other societies as well as taking a nationalistic stand as a world citizen should not be laboured too much because the sense of patriotism and nationalism in the period, if taken in the sense of an emotion, was very blurred. Also, since these are written testimonies by many people, the range of emotions and its scope too was vast. If one article could qualify as representing one particular type of nationalism, another would in the very same journal refute or go beyond it. What is certain is that while in the 19th century the quest for spreading knowledge about the lesser known parts of the continent of Asia was more dominant, from the beginning of the 20th century claiming a position started.

Understanding Asia through vernacular periodicals: the editors and writers identified

19th century

Newspapers started in January 1780 when James Hickey published *Hickey's Bengal Gazette*, the first newspaper in India.[6] Along with other English newspapers in the late 18th century like *Bengal Journal* and *Indian World* (William Duane), *Madras Gazette* and *Calcutta Journal* (1818) by James Silk Buckingham (1818–1819), Bengali news publications were *Digdarshan*, a monthly, and *Samachar Darpan*, a weekly, published by the Serampore missionaries, *Bengal Gazetti* (1818) by Ganga Kishor Bhattacharya, *Sangbad Kaumudi* (1821 by Raja Ram Mohan Roy) and *Sangbad Timir Nashak* (1823).[7] By 1830, there were 16 Bengali newspapers and periodicals published daily, weekly and biweekly. One was monthly – *Tattvabodhini Patrika* (1843) established to propagate principles of Brahmo religion and was edited by Akshay Kumar Dutta. It held a high place for the high quality of its writings and circulated 700 copies a month according to James Long in 1855.[8] The other Bengali journals of the period were *Samachar Chandrika* (1822, published by Bhabani Charan Bandopadhyay, first as a weekly and then daily by 1829), *Bibidhartha Sangraha* (1851), *Masik Patrika*

(1854), *Som Prakash* (1858), *Sulabh Samachar* (1870 by Keshav Chandra Sen) and *Bangadarshan* (1872 by Bankim Chandra Chattopadhyay). From this period onwards, a large number of periodicals started publication dealing with various aspects of Indian life and I will only refer to the ones I have used in this study, i.e. those with a focus on educating the Bengali readers about Asia and India's linkages with other Asian countries.[9] Many of the journals that I have referred to started publication from outside Calcutta, but most of them shifted to Calcutta, once the journal gained popularity or to avoid printing and distribution difficulties in the district towns.

Sangbad Prabhakar, one of India's most important newspapers which also continued for a long period, was started in 1831 as a weekly and its editor was Iswar Chandra Vidyasagar. Within three years, it turned into a triweekly and from 1839 became a daily newspaper. In 1835, a newspaper *Sangbad Purnachandra* started as a monthly and nine years later it became a daily. It continued to publish for 73 years. In 1843, *Tattvabodhini Patrika,* a monthly was started as an organ of the Brahmo Samaj. Most of the social reform activities like women's education, religious reformation and science education were strongly supported in this journal. It was a very important periodical for the propagation of science and modern thought in Bengali. The first editor of the periodical was Akshoy Kumar Dutta from 1843 to 1855 followed by Iswar Chandra Vidyasagar in 1856. Many members of the Tagore family like Satyendranath, Dwijendranath, Rabindranath, Kshitindranath, Kshemendranath Tagore were its editors. The last editors were Kshitindranath Tagore and Banawarilal Chaudhury in the 1930s. Another newspaper which started as a biweekly in 1839 was *Sangbad Bhaskar* which ten years later became triweekly. Other than Debendranath Tagore's visit to China, these journals did not show much Asia consciousness.

In 1851, Rajendralal Mitra started *Bibidhartha Sangraha* which was taken over after ten years by Kaliprasanna Sinha. It was the first illustrated magazine and its popularity is testified by Tagore in *Jibonsmriti.* In that year, a Vernacular Literary Committee (a translations committee) had been set up in Calcutta under the leadership of Ishwar Chandra Vidyasagar, Radhakanta Deb, Rajendralal Mitra, Hajson Pratt (ICS inspector of Schools in Nadia and who set up the Bidhannagar public library), Archdeacon of Calcutta, Seaton Kerr, Reverend Long and Robinson. Its aim was

> to publish translations of such works as are not included in the design of the Tract of Christian Knowledge societies on the one hand, or of the school Book and Asiatic societies on the other and likewise to provide a sound and useful vernacular Domestic literature for Bengal.

In the tradition of *Penny Magazine*, the first periodical with pictures with the intention of providing, as the advertisement said, the people of Bengal with knowledge – moral and uplifting – written for young and old, the journal used simple language and for greater comprehension was accompanied by pictures. The 16-page periodical's subscription was fixed at 1 rupee annually.[10] *Bibidhartha Sangraha* however did not provide pleasure to everyone as was evident during the editorship of Kaliprasanna Sinha who criticised in his editorial the interment of Reverend Long by the Indigo planters in 1861. The retribution of the colonial government was swift and definite – the periodical, in Brojendranath Bandopadhyay's words, 'died an untimely death'.[11] In 1858, *Som Prakash* was published as a weekly newspaper on political and cultural subjects from Calcutta with Dwarkanath Vidyabhushan as editor and supported by Iswar Chandra Vidyasagar. *Somprakash* became a key element in the growth of nationalistic press in Bengal and majority of its pages were translated for government review. It faced the government's wrath under the Vernacular Press Regulation Act in 1878 and went underground for two years. *Rahasya Sandharbha*, started in 1862 by Rajendralal Mitra, was aimed at spreading modern knowledge and had a number of articles on natural sciences.

In 1863, a revolution of sorts took place when *Bamabodhini Patrika* was started with the aim to kindle the minds of women, as the name suggested. Umesh Chandra Dutta was the editor of this magazine which became an important vehicle of analysis of social status of contemporary women. The most important issues discussed in this journal were debates on women's education and the editorial board of the periodical was comprised of liberal advocates of women's education. That this journal was important is justified by the very fact of its continuity for 60 years when most periodicals had a very short life. Dutta, one of the key figures of the Sadharan Brahmo Samaj under Keshav Chandra Sen's leadership, was a staunch supporter of education for women and also wrote two books on the subject – *Bamarachanabali* (*Women's Writings*) and *Strilokdiger bidyar abasykata* (*The Need for Female Education*). After Dutta, the editorship was continued by Ashutosh Ghosh (1904–1905) and for a longer time by Santosh Kumar Dutta (1908–1923). In the earlier years of *Bamabodhini Patrika*, the names of the authors were not mentioned and only in the second decade of the 20th century do we occasionally find authors mentioned. *Bamabodhini Patrika*'s dedication in imparting education also included knowledge about other Asian countries as the many articles show. Many of the articles in the early phase do not contain the writer's name or else, it was the editor who did most of the writing. A scrutiny of *Bamabodhini*'s articles in the first phase shows that along with lessons in ethics and values, an attempt to educate Indians on how women live in other Asian countries is visible. I have discussed these writings in another chapter, but it is important to note that women's lives in China, Japan, Persia, Sri Lanka and Burma were discussed in the period 1867–1895. The periodical was the organ of the Bamabodhini Sabha. As the introduction pointed out:

> it was divine grace that the attention of the country had fallen on their women. Just like men, women's education was vital not only to end their miserable condition but for the future well-being and development of the country. Efforts are being made in this regard and the benevolent government has been forthcoming in this regard, yet the beneficiaries are only a few girls. Unless education's rays break through the darkness of the age the wellbeing of all cannot be achieved. There are some pitfalls in the path of women's education. They do not have the time, inspiration nor tutor's support for effective learning. Thus, unless a way is found by which knowledge can be spread among many through easy comprehensible means, the disabilities of learning will persist. Nowadays quite a few books in Bengali are being published but they are not of much use . . . One has to aim for education to free women from all follies and superstitious beliefs.[12]

Bandopadhyay reminisces that initially 1000 copies were printed and from the first annual subscription by a woman called Bhuvanmohihni Basu it began to be welcomed in Calcutta and the suburbs. Its popularity attracted the patronage of Acharya Keshab Chandra Sen who wanted to undertake its responsibility. However, since his work led him to stay outside Calcutta for long periods, it was decided that he would be helped by an editorial team of Kshetramohon Dutta and Basanta Kumar Dutta. *Bamabodhini Patrika* had 500–600 loyal subscribers but it repeatedly suffered and would have stopped totally had it not been for the selfless support of some benefactors from time to time like Pyarichand Mitra, Shibchandra Deb, Swarnamoyee Debi and others.[13]

In the same year as this important periodical, 1863, another one came out from Calcutta, called *Abodhbandhu*, edited by a famous poet of Bengal, Biharilal Chakraborty, as a monthly. In fact, this periodical was started three years earlier by the homeopath Jogendranath Ghosh, but it folded up soon. *Abodhbandhu* mainly aimed at biographies and literature-based articles. In 1871, *Mashik Prakashika* started as a monthly. It was a literary magazine. Manomohan Bose started *Madhyastha* in 1873 as a monthly and *Sadharani* was also started in the same year by Akshaychandra Sarkar and contained articles on political, municipal and rural issues.

In 1874, *Aryadarshan* was started in Calcutta as a monthly by Jogendranath Bandopadhyay who aimed at propagating 'modern knowledge'. Bandopadhyay, a Sanskrit scholar, close to Ishwar Chandra Vidyasagar, Aurobindo Ghosh and Swami Vivekananda, strongly believed in importance of creating a role model for the Indian youth. He was considered to be a pioneer in writing inspirational biographies and encouraging the youth for revolutionary activities. *Aryadarshan* was distinguished by its high-quality printing and production, which attracted leading writers to publish their work in it. It dealt with different aspects of Indian history, biographies of Mill and others, inspirational articles of patriotic characters like Rana Pratap, articles on scientific inventions and quite a few articles on theatre. There are a number of travelogues published over the years, but the destination for them was not Asia but Europe and England and a translation of an Irish traveller sojourn in Peking where he is referred to as 'our traveller' or 'representative of the British Raj'.[14] In another article describing 'Travels of a Bengali to Europe' in 1885, the writer is travelling to France for 'tourism and commerce studies'. Travelling with his brother, the author who is not named describes the journey on board the ship and the time spent in Colombo, visiting a Buddhist monastery and a museum. His focus on Hindu gods at the monastery 'who are paying homage to Buddha', his awe at the gigantic Buddha image at the monastery, the golden images in the museum and his recalling the conquest of Sri Lanka by Bijoy in 543 BC and the importance of Ramayana in the lives of the Sinhalese reveal his Indian biases.[15] *Aryadarshan*'s seven-episode article on musical travels in China was by Sri Sourindro. This was an interesting set of articles and I have dealt with it in detail in the next chapter.

Another journal started in the same year, 1874, was *Bandhab* edited by Kaliprasanna Ghosh whose periodical was inspired by *Bangadarshan*. *Bhramar*, a short-lived monthly edited by Sanjib Chandra Chattopadhyay, too was started in the same year. Though most of the articles were on literature, an important one dealt with Bengali readership. Another periodical in the same year was another short-lived monthly, *Darshak*, under the editorship of Avinash Chandra Niyogi, which contained among other articles, reviews of books and descriptions of plays in Bengal. In 1874, Rajnarayan Bose started *Samadarshi,* the Liberal monthly.

The year 1875 was another landmark for women when a monthly *Banga Mahila* was started under the editorship of Bhuban Mohan Sarkar. This was an important document in the fields of studies on women's education and gender question raised by the liberal pedagogues in 19th-century Bengal. This periodical was published by the Board of Principals of Chorbagan Balika Bidyalaya on Muktaram Babu Street, a school for women's formal education, and an acting board to conduct examinations in *Zenana* schools established by Pyari Charan Sarkar in 1863. After Pyaricharan's death in 1875, Bhuban Mohon took charge of the school himself. Issues related to women from both the liberal and conservative perspectives were featured in the pages of this periodical.

From 1877, *Bharati* was started and became hugely popular among the literary journals in the late 19th century with a number of articles on Asia over the 1880s and the 1890s. This periodical is a landmark both in the evolution of Bengali literature and in the rise of prominent women writers and editors. It was published from the Tagore family of Jorasanko and was often acknowledged as a Tagore family magazine. Rabindranath recalls in *Jibonsmriti* that the plan to start a periodical was devised by his elder brother Jyotirindranath with the eldest among them Dwijendranath Tagore becoming the editor in 1877. Rabindranath despite his tender age (16 years) was closely involved in the editorial board and contributed his first set of poems *Kobi Kahini* that year.[16] When Swarnakumari Debi took the responsibility of its publication from Dwijendranath Tagore in 1884, it became the second Bengali periodical to be edited by a woman, the first being *Anathini* by Thakomoni Debi (1875). It also became the first well-organised, widely circulated and well-acclaimed monthly in the Bengali language. The periodical was not established to support the women's cause, but Swarnakumari turned it into a women's magazine. When the publication of *Bharati* ceased in 1926, it set a record of the first longest surviving Bengali monthly. Its editors were Dwijendranath Tagore (1877–1884), Swarnakumari Debi (1884–1895, 1908–1915), Hiranmayi Debi (1895–1898), Sarala Debi (1895–1898, 1903–1908, 1924–1926), Rabindranath Tagore (1898–1903) and Sourindramohan Mukhopadhyay jointly with Manilal Gangopadhyay (1915–1924). The periodical started publishing in 1877 and in 1894 another periodical *Balak* (started in 1885) edited by Jnanadanandini Debi Tagore with Rabindranath Tagore as the executive editor merged with it and continued as *Bharati O Balak* for six years. Just like *Bamabodhini Patrika*, many of the articles here did not accompany the names of the authors, probably from a desire to maintain uninterrupted reading but unlike the former, a contents list provided details of authorship.

In the 1980s, articles on China, Japan and South-East Asia appeared in *Bharati* along with Kailash Chandra Sinha's article on Hiuen Tsang's visit to Bengal (1880). Editorials on Chinese military strength (1880) and Japan's recent development and its causes (1881), as well as articles on the opium trade and its impact on society (1881) were published. In 1882, Dwijendranath Tagore also wrote three articles on Fa Hien's pilgrimage, while Nibaran Chandra Mukhopadhyay, a Brahmo reformer based on government service in Bhagalpore, wrote on the spread of Hindu religion in Malay Islands (1882), obviously based on European academic researches. Haricharan Mukhopadhyay analysed the British in Burma (1885) just two months after the Declaration by Viceroy Lord Dufferin that Burma would be an integral part of British India, discussing their process of occupation and the role of the ruling dynasty there. Dinendra Kumar Roy, who later won fame as the creator of detective Robert Blake, had his first articles published in *Bharati*. An obvious cosmopolitan, since he based his Robert Blake on Sexton Blake of comic strips, he translated into Bengali the book on Japan by M. Aime from Mrs Cashel's English translation in 1896. Before that in 1893, he wrote two articles on internal affairs in Thailand with an intimate look at the royal dynasty.

One year after *Bharati*, in 1878, *Paricharika* started as a monthly with Girish Chandra Sen as its editor. Sen was a religious scholar and translated the Quran into Bengali. He became a Brahmo under the influence of Keshab Chandra Sen and Bijoy Krishna Goswami and carried on missionary work spreading Brahmoism in different parts of India and Burma. *Paricharika* was intended for educating Bengali women in the scientific method of child-rearing and housekeeping. Protap Chunder Mozoomdar, another Brahmo, interested in the comparative study of religions took over the editorship from 1878. From 1892, *Paricharika* came into its own with a woman editor Mohini Devi who was the daughter-in-law of Keshab Chandra Sen followed by Sucharu Debi during the Swadeshi movement period. This periodical continued to publish till 1906 and was revived by Nirupama Debi, the princess of Coochbehar, from 1916 for nine years. In 1882, a couple of periodicals started – one was *Bijnan Darpan*, a monthly on science under the editorship of Pranadananda Kabibhusan and Bireswar Pande. Another periodical started publishing once in two months under the aegis of the Shribati Chittaranjani Sahitya Sabha. In both, there are discussions on imperial ideologies on the Bengalis that the British were propagating, namely race theory and effeminacy of Bengalis relating to food. In 1883, *Nabajiban* was started as a monthly in Calcutta by Akshoy Chandra Sarkar on literature, history and religion. In the second year, i.e. 1884, a travelogue by Ta. Pra. Cha (probably Taraprasad Chattopadhyay) on travel to Sri Lanka, 'Singhal Yatra', was published in *Nabajiban* in six episodes. *Navyabharat* also started in 1883 as a monthly with Deviprasanna Roychowdhury as the editor. In the second year of this periodical, Kailash Chandra Singha, the author of *Rajamala*, wrote a rebuttal of the royal genealogy that Chattopadhyay had mentioned in the travelogue.

In 1884, *Prachar* was started by Umacharan Bandopadhyay and Rakhal Chandra Bandopadhyay took over from 1886. This periodical aimed at liberating the society from superstitions and ritual dependence. It claimed to have women as its main reading target. In 1884 itself, *Alochana* was started as a monthly in Calcutta by Gagan Chandra Hom, under the inspiration of Bipin Chandra Pal. Its articles mainly covered contemporary religious and social reforms. In 1886, Amritalal Banerjee started *Shilpa Pushpanjali* as a monthly in Calcutta and its articles were mostly on literature and art.

The year 1887 saw *Anusandhan*, which was started by Durgadas Lahiri who wanted to expose the corruption in all public institutions. He stated in the first volume of the periodical, 'it would fight against and expose before the public all types of corruption in Government, the political parties and in various institutions'. The periodical was published as a fortnightly up to its eighth year and then turned into a weekly. In its fifth year, an article was written anonymously (probably by Lahiri himself) on the lifestyle of the Chinese to indicate the similarities between 'the two great countries which saw the light of civilization very early'. He describes the 'Chinese way of life as static and who believe that their country is at the centre of the world, whereas we know that China is situated at the southeast corner of Asia and it is India which occupies the real central spot'.[17] The essay is a descriptive one about the geography, natural resources and the dynastic history of the rulers, as well as food habits, economic activities, descriptions of dress and homes from western accounts. Another article in the same issue discussed the wedding practices of the Chinese. The writer claims that they were very similar to the Indian customs, age of marriage, the fear of dying without an heir to mourn.[18] In 1894, following the travels of an Englishman to China (name not mentioned), Charu Chandra Mitra wrote 'Perambulations through China' describing important tourist spots and characteristics of their lives and appearance.[19] In 1887, *Gan o Golpo* was started as a fortnightly by Motilal Bose, and made a significant contribution to literature. *Daridraranjan* was started as a monthly from Calcutta by Radhanath Mitra in 1889.

Sahitya was started by Suresh Chandra Samajpati as a monthly from Calcutta in 1890 who had already the previous year published *Sahitya Kalpadrum*. *Sahitya* led the field in its articles on Bengali literature and continued till 1924, under Samajpati and later Panchkadi Bandopadhyay. It published a number of articles on Asia. Nagendra Nath Gupta, who was a prolific writer of stories and biographies and contributed to *Bharati* and *Balak* and while in Sind, Karachi and Lahore edited *Sind Times*, *Phoenix* and *The Tribune*,[20] wrote an article on Chinese saints in the third volume. Dinendra Kumar Roy's article on Persian royal family and two articles – one by Sarat Chandra Das on Japanese literature and another 'Letters from Japan' by an anonymous author 'Paribrajak' or Traveller – were published in 1897. In 1891, *Sadhana* was started by Sudhindranath Tagore and many literary figures of Bengal contributed to this magazine. In 1892, Rukmini Kumar Chakraborty published his travelogue to Sri Lanka – 'Singhal Bhraman' in *Sadhana*. *Purnima* saw a full series on Brahmadesher Bibaran (Descriptions of Burma) by an anonymous writer in 1895, and Ananda Gopal Ghosh's 'Travels in China' also came out the same year.

The year 1892 was an important year since Ramananda Chattopadhyay, one of the most important figures of Bengali journalism, started *Dasi*, which was published from Dashashram, a home for the poor. *Anushilan* was published in 1892 as a mouthpiece of an association called Bandhab Samity, and it mainly published articles on Hindu nationalism. From the second year, the name was changed to *Anushilan o Purohit* and the editor was Mahendranath Bidyanidhi. This journal had a number of articles on theatre and travel within the country. *Purnima* was published on every full moon from Hooghly under an editorial board followed by Satindra Deb Ray from 1897. In the same year, *Pradip* was inaugurated by Ramananda Chattopadhyay; in 1899, it published an article on Bali by Akshoy Kumar Maitreya, the noted historian on Bengal, and also another article on Japan by the editor himself. *Punya* was started by Prajnasundari Debi in 1897 in which articles on Sri Lanka and Japan were published in 1899.

Aitihasik Chitra started as a monthly journal of history in 1898 by Akshay Chandra Maitreya at Rajshahi with the introduction by Rabindranath Tagore and cover design by Upendrakishore Raychowdhury, but the Rajshahi edition was short-lived after which it was continued by Nikhilnath Ray from 1904 and then Jogesh Chandra Gupta from 1909. This journal, which simplified archaeology for non-academic readers, had many specialists writing for it and aimed at rediscovery of Indian heritage. *Anjali* started in Chittagong in the same year, 1898, by Rajeswar Gupta and it contained articles on literature and aimed at children's education and moral upgradation.

The monthly *Antahpur* based in Calcutta was also started in 1898 by Hemantakumari Chaudhuri under the editorship of Banalata Devi. Born and brought up in Lahore, Chaudhuri was already an active advocate of women's improvement through literary and social endeavours. In 1885, she started an association, Banita Budhi Bikasini Sabha, for the intellectual development of fellow women and a Hindi monthly magazine *Sugrihini* for spread of knowledge about Hindi literature among Indian women. It is not known precisely when she shifted to Bengal to make *Antahpur* possible, but in 1903 she was the headmistress of a college in Sylhet before returning to north India as principal of Victoria College in Patiala. In 1928, Chaudhuri became the Commissioner of Dehradoon municipality. *Antahpur* was special since from the beginning it was declared to be a magazine for women by women. The editors of the periodical were all women. After the death of Banalata Debi in 1900, Hemantakumari Chaudhuri and Kumudini Mitra took up the reins. The year 1900 also saw another periodical, *Arati*, starting in Mymensingh in East Bengal as a monthly by Umesh Chandra Bidyaratna. It was an important periodical dealing with agriculture and economic issues as well as fiction and poetry. It included articles on social and economic conditions of Bengal as well as on literature. In 1906, an article of this periodical dealt with the rise of Asia and was written with a penname of Sri Swadeshi, in acknowledgement of the movement going on in Bengal then. *Pracharak* edited by Madhu Mian in 1899 aimed at propagating the humanitarian aspects in Islam.

20th century

At the turn of the century, Japan's successful transformation into a modern nation also brought forth a number of new publications and many articles on Asia. Most prominent among them in the first decade of the 20th century was *Prabashi*, which started its publication under Ramananda Chatterjee in 1901 in Allahabad. Chatterjee, having failed in his short-lived ventures with *Pradip* and *Dasi*, brought out the monthly *Prabashi* on his own. Chintamoni Ghosh, the owner of the Indian Press at Allahabad, helped him in the venture. Ramananda taught in a local college but resigned in 1906. Then he simultaneously started an English monthly, *The Modern Review*,[21] also from Allahabad. Within two years, the British Government ordered him to leave Allahabad, finding some fault with the English journal, which was propagating Swadeshi ideals. Ramananda finally settled in Calcutta in 1908 and continued to publish both the journals from the city. Ramananda edited both almost until his death. *Prabashi*'s fame remains almost unsurpassed by any other Bengali periodical. Well edited and well produced, it contained multicoloured prints of paintings from the second year. *Prabashi* regularly published articles on art and artists and by religiously publishing the works of the Bengal School of Art, Ramananda helped much in popularising Abanindranath Tagore, Nandalal Bose and others, whose pictures accompanied each issue. Rabindranath's writings were published in *Prabashi* almost regularly from 1907, until his death. Though creative writing was its forte, articles on history, art, archaeology, sociology, education, literature and literary theories, scientific topics and travelogues were published regularly. With Ramakanta Ray's 'Letters from a domicile in Japan', the flood burst, followed by Girindranath Sarkar and Narendranath Bhattacharya on Burma, Nagendra Chandra Som on Bali and then from 1904, Ramlal Sarkar's majestic collection of articles on China. Over three years, nine articles were published followed by articles on Japan by Akshoy Kumar Majumdar, Brojo Sundar Sanyal and Suresh Chandra Bandopadhyay in the period 1904–1909. Rabindranath Tagore's 'Thoughts on Universalism' came out in 1909. The year 1906 also saw an interesting article by Mrinalini Raha who was domiciled in Burma and wrote about her experiences there. The same year an anonymous writer in *Arati* also spoke about the rise of Asia.

Bharat Mahila had started around 1904 but only from the fourth year do we see articles on Asia, most of them by Sarajubala Dutta, the editor. Hemendranath Dutta's article on the women of Turkey came out in 1908. Between 1910 and 1912, articles on Japan were published by Ganapati Roy, Rabindranath Sen and Kalimohon Ghosh, as well as articles on China and Turkey. But the most memorable today is the travel series by Hariprabha Takeda on her visit to meet her husband Uemon Takeda's family in Japan in 1912–1913. In the meantime, *Bharati* continued her journey on Asia at the turn of the century with writings on Indians in Japan by Dharmananda Mahabharati and Ashutosh Deb. *Bharati* is also unique in the poems that were published on Japan and China, and the 1903 poem on the brave Japanese soldier by Swarnakumari Debi, the editor herself, was excellent.

An important event in the history of Asian articles in literary journals occurred in the second decade of the 20th century: the birth of *Bharatvarsha* under the inspiration of the nationalist poet-dramatist and song writer Dwijendralal Roy, who sought through the literary journal to spread the universal values that he held so dear and who tried to disseminate those values through his creative writing as well.[22] It is often pointed out that Roy aimed this journal to be a challenge to the Tagore household-guided *Bharati*, which held sway over the magazine world. According to his biographers, Roy was very protective of the new venture, attempting to channelise it to his concepts of what was morally important for the new Bengali youth, rejecting articles and paintings by very eminent writers and artists as not suitable to his ideal journal, but unfortunately due to a delay and Roy's untimely death, the journal could only be published four months after the Bengali New Year, under the editorship of Jaladhar Sen. From Satyaranjan Roy's 'Tales of Brahmadesha', the Asian journey started for *Bharatvarsha* and Ashutosh Roy and Hemendra Prasad Ghosh's articles on the war front were published in the second decade.

In the aftermath of the Korean annexation by Japan in 1910, *Bharati* published 16 articles on Japan by Jadunath Sarkar during 1910–1914. This Jadunath Sarkar was not the famous historian on medieval India, but who studied and worked in Japan during 1906–1914 and contributed 29 articles in *Bharati* alone. That the focus in 1910–1911 was on Japan is visible from other articles in *Bharati* as well. Besides Sarkar, Ganapati Roy, Surendranath Bhattacharya, Suresh Chandra Bandopadhyay and Satyendranath Dutta wrote articles on Japan. Satyendranath Dutta and Santosh Kumar Bose wrote on Chinese poetry, Sudhangshu on travel in China and Jnendranath Chakraborty wrote a two-series essay on letters from a Chinese woman. Jyotirindranath Tagore also wrote a five-series article on the Islands of Java. Ganapati Roy wrote on Malaya, Kalachand Dalal on Burmese monasteries and Burmese women and Kalipada Mitra on the Buddhist art of Central Asia.

A new journal called *Grihastha* came out in 1909 and from 1913, Ramlal Sarkar and Upendranath Maitreya wrote articles on China. But *Grihastha*'s best contributions came from Benoy Kumar Sarkar's travelogues to Japan in the period 1915–1916 and a translation of a Chinese poem in 1917. *Manashi* started its publications from 1909 and the first issue was Brojendranath Bandopadhyay's essay on Chinese marriages. Between 1908 and 1913, there were eight articles on Japan by Manmatha Nath Ghosh and Ganapati Roy. In 1919, *Manashi* merged with *Marmabani* and published Sitanath Bhatta's 'Autobiography of a Bengali Imprisoned by Turks in the Kut War', rewritten by Krishna Behari Roy, and Purna Chandra Mitra wrote an essay on Mesopotamia. The Japan focus in *Prabashi* was continued in this decade by Suresh Chandra Bandopadhyay in his articles on Japanese religion, Ronin, and Mikado Mitsuhito and Hemlata Debi in her writings on the saints of Japan and Manilal Gangopadhyay in his translation of a Japanese story. There were articles on Thailand by Jyotirindranath Tagore, travel in China by Ashutosh Roy, Buddhist viharas in Sri Lanka by Hemada Kanta Chowdhury and the tribes on the borders of China and Burma by Ramlal Sarkar. Japan was on Rabindranath Tagore's radar as well in this decade as his Japaner Kotha revealed in *Sabuj Patra* in 1917.

Bangabani was started from 1921 and Rabindranath Tagore's address in Rangoon was published in 1924 and Kalidas Nag's 'Letters from the East' came out in the same year as did Sarat Mukherjee's 'Young Turks'. A year before that R. Kimura's four-part article on Japan's social practices came out in *Bangabani*. *Bharatvarsha*'s main articles on Asia came out in the 1930s, but in this decade too there were some important articles. Rabindranath's 'Chin o Japan' was published in 1924, along with Narendra Dev's articles on Thailand, the Philippines and Islands on the eastern Indian sea, Ganesh Chandra Maitra's 'Picture of Life in Domicile in Burma', Hemanta Chattopadhyay's articles on the tribes of British Borneo in 1927 and Cambodia. Paresh Chandra Sen's travels into unfamiliar Burma on his pilgrimage to Sri Pad are interesting to read and were published in 1927, while Kumar Munindra Dev Ray's trip with his group into Sri Lanka in Singhal Dvipa was published in two parts in 1928.

Bichitra started publishing from 1927, and in the second year Dhirendranath Chowdhury wrote 'Bali the Land of Temples' followed by Surendranath Kar in 'Tales of Bali'. In 1927–1928, Prabhat Kumar Mukhopadhyay (of Rabindranath Tagore biography fame) and Sudhamoyee Debi published a nine-part series on Hindu literature in China. He was employed as the librarian of Santiniketan and learnt Chinese and Tibetan from Sylvain Levi and conducted research in that area. Monomohan Ghosh wrote on the role of women in the Turkish Republic in 1928, and Himangshu Kumar Bose wrote two articles in 1929 – 'Dance Forms among the Lamas of Tibet' and 'Natural Beauty of Burma'. In *Manashi o Marmabani*, Phanindranath Bose published an article 'Hindu Kingdom of Thailand' or Shyamdesha in 1920 and in the same year Gour Hari Sen published an article 'Future of Japan', while Kinnaresh Roy described his adventures among the 'Phungis in Mog Land'. Another article – 'Lamas of Tibet' – was written by Nalini Kanta Majumdar in 1924 and Abani Kumar De wrote two articles – 'Japan's Robin Hood' and 'China's Foreign Policy Problems' – in 1926 and 1927, respectively. *Prabashi* in the 1920s included a number of brilliant articles on Asian travel, like those of Suniti Kumar Chatterjee's 'Javadviper Pothe' and 'Dvipamoy Bharat' when he was accompanying Rabindranath Tagore on his trip to Java, Bali and Sumatra in the period 1927–1930. There were in this decade also a number of analytical articles on the politics and society of different countries of Asia, like that of Paresh Chandra Sharma on Thailand, Bijoy Kumar Bhowmick on Bagdad, Hemendralal Roy on Thailand, Suresh Chandra Das on Nepal and the dance forms of Java, Phanindra Nath Bose's academic work under the aegis of Greater India Society on the Hindu colonisation of Champa, Kalidas Nag's brilliant essay 'Brihattara Bharat (Greater India)', Haripada Ghoshal's essay 'Confucius', an analysis of Manindra Bhushan Gupta's contribution as a visiting art lecturer at Sri Lanka by Gyanendra Mohon Das in 1926 and Satish Ranjan Khastagir's article on a Bengali living in Sri Lanka. *Masik Basumati* had a number of articles on Asia in the 1920s. There was an anonymous article 'Wonderous Chinese Wall' in 1922, and Hemendra Prasad Ghosh, who was also the editor of the magazine, wrote three articles on Turkey in the same year. Sarojnath Ghosh wrote two articles on Japanese dancers and another on China in 1923 and 1927, respectively. Harisadhan Ghoshal in 1927 wrote an article 'Indian Ideas in China'.

Bangalakshmi (edited by Hemlata Debi), which started in around 1924, ventured into Asia with Sita Debi's 'Women of Persia' in 1930 and Subimal Chandra Sarkar's 'On the Way to Malaya' in the same year. *Bangasree* (edited by Sachchidananda Bhattacharya) in its third year (1940) published the popular Bengali humourist and writer of short stories Sibram Chakraborty's article 'Japan: The Land of Fish', and another great Bengali novelist Bibhuti Bhushan Bandopadhyay's articles on the countries of Micronesia, Java, the forests and rivers of Asia, Middle East, in the section *Bichitra Jagat*, were published between 1935 and 1941.

The majority of the articles on Asia came out in *Bharatvarsha* in the 1930s. Two of the finest articles on travel in Asia is by Sarala Debi Chowdhurani published in three parts: 'Burma Yatra', 'Rangoon' and 'Shwe Dagon' in 1931, and the rare travelogue by the historian Ramesh Chandra Majumdar on his trip to Champarajya. R.C. Majumdar's fame in this era is generally limited to his Indianisation thesis through the Greater India Society and later in the history textbooks. But here a personal history of travel, its trials, discomforts as well as intense pleasure is visible in his 'Prabasher Patra' published in *Bharatvarsha* in 1931. Bharat Kumar Bose published journalistic articles on the politics and society of Manchuria and Iraq in 1932, Hemendralal Roy wrote a three-part article on Afghanistan in 1933–1934, Keshab Chandra Gupta wrote a six-part article on a traveller to Malaya, Himangshu Bhushan Sarkar wrote a history-based article on the Indic influences on Insulindia. In 1937, Girindra Chandra Mukhopadhyay's 'Story of China' and a six-part article on Japan were published. In 1937 came the magician P.C. Sorcar's series on his travel to Japan in a four-part article as well as Narendra Dev's analysis of Japan's impact in the East and West. Then came the Kshitish Chandra Bandopadhyay's adventures 'In the Hands of the Dacoits in China' in 1938 and 'A Bengali Traveller in Philippines' in the same year. Jamini Kanta Sen's analysis of Chinese art also came out in 1938 as well as Gajanand Bajpei's article on the famous Japanese industrialist Mitsui.

Bichitra (1927) edited by Upendranath Gangopadhyay had a number of publications on Asia in the 1930s. Kedarnath Bandopadhyay's 'Reminiscences of China' was published in 1933 followed by Manilal Sen Sharma who wrote on the art of Manindra Bhushan Gupta who had been sent from Santiniketan to Colombo to teach in the art college. In 1933 itself, Rabindranarayan Ghosh wrote an analytical piece 'Understanding the East'. Santidev Ghosh, a student and then a teacher at Visva Bharati, Santiniketan, published 'Rabindranath in Sri Lanka' in 1934 followed by Bibhuti Bhushan Bandopadhyay's descriptions of different countries, although he never visited any of them after a couple of years. *Bichitra* published his article on Borneo Islands in 1936 and then 'Travels to Tibet and Sikkim for Twelve Days' by Sailakumar Mukhopadhaya during 1935–1936. P.C. Sorcar wrote another two-part article on his experiences in Japan in 1936–1937 and in 1930, *Prabashi* published articles by Pannalal Bose on Dafadar Hariarayan Basu's role in the China war, and by Manindra Bhushan Gupta who artistically paints a pen picture of Sri Lanka. *Masik Basumati* contained a number of articles on Asia: Swami Jagadishwarananda's 'Tales from Sri Lanka' in three parts in 1933, Aparna Debi's 'What I Saw in Japan' in the same year, Jamini Kanta Sen's 'Indian Treasures in Chinese Paintings' in 1935, Swami Sadananda's 'Gods and Goddesses of Greater India' in 1935 and Girindranath Sarkar's 'Sarat Chandra in Burma' in 1937.

What really stands out are the magazines designated for children. They concentrated on enhancing the education level of children beyond the school texts or at least supplementing them entertainingly. The best of them was of course *Sandesh* by the Ray Chowdhury family who later dropped the Chowdhury. But even before *Sandesh* came *Sakha*, in 1885, by Pramadacharan Sen, who himself was a writer of children's literature, and after his death the editorship was taken over by Sibnath Sastri. Upendrakishore Raychowdhury wrote 'Tales of China' in 1886 and Biharilal Gupta also wrote on the same subject in 1887, in *Sakha*.

Sandesh was started in 1913, with U. Raychowdhury writing the 'Japanese Gods' in 1913, 'Chinese Tales' in 1915 and translation of a Japanese story 'Frog's Visit to the Sea' in 1915. Kuladaranjan Ray in 1915 wrote 'Rustom and Sohrab' and 'Story of China'. In the same year, Mukul Chandra De who accompanied Rabindranath Tagore on his travels to the East wrote a two-part article 'Tales from Japan' and 'Fujiyama' in 1910. There were more translations from Japanese and Chinese stories by unnamed writers which were very popular among children. Punyalata Chakraborty's translation of an Arab tale was published in 1919 and then Jyotirmoyee Debi's 'Dushtu Gemunu', translation of a Sri Lankan tale, came out in 1920, along with articles on Chinese wall, and translations of Chinese stories by Kuladaranjan Ray. Ray also published in 1920 more translations from Turkish folktales.

Ramdhanu started publishing in 1928 under the editorship of Bireshwar Bhattacharya, and Prabhat Kumar Mukhopadhyay's famous 'Kajir Bichar' was published in the first year along with Nripendra Chandra Bandopadhyay's 'Tales of Burma' in three parts. Then Bimal Sen's 'The Student Community in China' came out followed by some anonymously written articles 'Rise of Japan' and 'Turkey's Mustapha Kemal Pasha'. Kshitindra Narayan Bhattacharya's articles on 'Children of Japan' and 'Then and Now in Persia' were published in 1929. Bhattacharya had become editor then and was already famous for his science articles for children. In 1931, Biraj Kumar Bandopadhyay's 'The Amazing Wall' was published and the next year came Manoranjan Bhattacharya's 'Shyam Desh' and 'Java'. In 1933, Dhirendra Lal Dhar's 'Balidvip' and Shanti Aich's 'A Tale of Japan' were published. The editor's 'Desert Lands of Central Asia' came out in 1935 along with Satya Gopal's 'The Adventures of Dr. Chiranjeev'. In 1936 came Jagatmohon Sen's 'Japan! Japan!' and in 1937 came Kalidas Roy's 'Stories of Japan'. In 1938, Karuna Mukhopadhyay's 'Mih Thun Poye' and Dhirendralal Dhar's 'At the Nanking Front' were published. Another children's magazine *Rangmashal* was started by the master of children's adventure stories Hemendra Kumar Roy in 1937; it published translation of Chinese stories by Bibhas Roychowdhury.

The famous and not so famous writers

It is easy to understand the attraction that the literary periodicals had for the readers since majority of the famous novels were first published in them, but these periodicals were also famous for important essays by famous and not so famous men and women on the burning issues of the time. Bharati Ray has shown in two volumes how women's issues in *Bamabodhini Patrika* and *Prabashi* played a crucial role in developing the awareness of the community regarding women's education and social emancipation.[23] The role of the periodicals in formation of public opinion on many other issues, most important of which was the anti-colonial national movement, has been discussed in all accounts of the independence movement. While in most cases the issues that were discussed in the articles were more important than the person who wrote it, in other cases it was the very fact that a famous personality was expressing his/her unique view that clinched the matter for the reader. Paresh Chandra Sen, while travelling through inhospitable terrains on horseback to a fair in Machchagiri in upper Burma in 1927, was surprised and gratified to be recognised as a writer of *Bharatvarsha* by a Bengali businessman Rajani Kanta Kochu of Salin who warmly treated him and offered rest and home-cooked meal[24] while others like Bankim Chandra Chattopadhyay, Rabindranath Tagore, Sarala Debi Chowdhurani, Upendrakishore Raychowdhury, Sukumar Ray and Ramananda Chattopadhyay contributed to the Bengali periodical movement, not simply by publishing creative writing and essays but also actively contributing as editors and publishers. There were yet others too who contributed in different ways to popularise their views regarding important issues of the time. Bibhuti Bhushan Bandopadhyay, one of the greatest writers in Bengali penning 16 novels and 200 short stories, many of which were published in the journals, also contributed to the knowledge of Asia in the journals through his translations. Jyotirindra Nath Tagore must also be mentioned along with his more famous younger brother since he translated many articles on Asia from French and English as well as writing three articles on Java in 1910. Amulyacharan Vidyabhushan writing in *Bharati* in 1920 was a scholar extraordinaire who from very humble beginnings became a scholar of ancient Indian religion and culture, writing well over 17 books, and who had command over many languages. Ashutosh Deb, who wrote about the Indian diaspora in Japan, in *Bharati* in 1902, was a publisher who started life in his father's publishing company BMR and later set up Deb Sahitya Kutir, famed for a number of publications for children. Deb was also famous for his dictionary which was used by Bengali students (Students' Favourite Dictionary) for decades. Benoy Kumar Sarkar (1887–1949) was a social scientist, professor and nationalist. He founded several institutes in Calcutta, including the Bengali Institute of Sociology, Bengali Asia Academy, Bengali Dante Society and Bengali Institute of American Culture. Sarkar travelled extensively and left travelogues on his stay in Japan, published in *Grihastha*. P.C. Sorcar was a well-loved magician. The stories of his travels are interesting as everywhere he was recognised and feted and well received by his fellow magicians and the media.

Many of the writers were domiciled in different Asian countries acquainting their fellow countrymen with the land they were residing in. Keshab Chandra Gupta resided in Malaya and Ganesh Chandra Maitra stayed and wrote about Burma, although as I have pointed out elsewhere, Bengalis in Burma lived in a bubble, only associating with other Bengalis or at the most other Indians. They appear to be unconscious about local people and sentiment or worse make condescending and scathing remarks about them.[25] Jadunath Sarkar (not to be confused with the famous historian), who studied and worked in Japan, was a prolific writer contributing on all aspects of Japanese history, economy, society and culture. Kedarnath Bandopadhyay lived and worked in China at the turn of the century but appears in his memoirs to be an admirer of Japanese people. Ramlal Sarkar, on the other hand, is a prolific writer on all aspects of Chinese history, politics and life. Most of his contributions have appeared in *Prabashi*, although he has also written in *Navyabharat*. His fictional writing *Child Theft in China* is well known.

Greater India Society set up in Calcutta gave a great fillip to interest in South-East Asia riding the nationalist wave, in which many scholars, French and German, were feted as collaborators and mentors in the search for the roots of Indian contribution to the civilisational growth in those countries. Majority of the famous names among the scholars were contributors in English and only some of their writings were translated for the Bengali periodicals. Original writing by some of these academics or articles based on their works are found occasionally and I have dealt with them in a later chapter. Greater India theory stalwarts who wrote in Bengali were Rabindranath Tagore (venerated as the High Priest or Purodha) but whose writings were hardly unalloyed championing of the Indic civilisational triumph unlike some of the others – R.C. Majumdar, Himangshu Bhushan Sarkar, Bijon Raj Chatterjee, Prabhat Kumar Mukhopadhyay and Shudhamoyee Debi. Suniti Kumar Chatterjee, Kalidas Nag, Ramananda Chattopadhyay, painters and writers on art, Nandalal Bose, Mukul Chandra De, Manindra Bhushan Gupta, Jamini Kanta Sen were all fellow pilgrims to 'Greater India' as close associates and followers of Tagore and connected to Santiniketan, but they were much more inclined to Tagore's universalism than others.

The speciality of these literary periodicals in my opinion was that the literary quantum was never compromised in presenting information in the news stories in the best journalistic style. This could be because the components of featured writing by academics or litterateurs and features by professional journalists which are such distinct elements in today's journalism was far more blurred than in these periodicals. Dinendra Kumar Roy was a novelist, Aurobindo Ghosh's Bengali tutor and an editor of a monthly detective magazine *Nandan Kanan*. He wrote 217 detective books as well as other social novels and articles on Thailand. Narendra Dev was a famous poet, based in Santiniketan, whose articles on Annam, Island India, Shyambhumi, the Philippines, Japan, pirates in the China Sea as well as many countries of the west make excellent reading. Hemanta Chattopadhyay (British Borneo, Cambodia), Bharat Kumar Basu (Manchuria Iraq), Hemendralal Roy, Girindra Chandra Mukherjee (Japan), Nitya Narayan Bandopadhyay (West Asia), Ashutosh Roy (China), Hemendra Prasad Ghosh, editor of *Masik Basumati* (Turkey) were more journalists in today's sense focused on informative pieces of different countries and issues. An element of pride for the Bengalis was expressed in the articles on Bengalis as war heroes and Hemendra Prasad Ghosh, Ashutosh Roy, Nibaran Chandra Mitra, among others contributed travelogues on participation in wartime. Also interesting are articles written by Indians settled abroad like Kalachand Dalal (Burma), Panchanan Bhowmick (a revolutionary who settled in Burma and organised the Bengal branch of the Jugantar party in Rangoon[26]).

Out of 531 articles that I have consulted in this book, only 35 are written by women, including editorials. While it seems strange to have such few women contributors when a large number of the articles are directed at and addressed to women readers and over such a long period of 90 years when many books by women writers were being regularly published, one may speculate that it was because it was still a taboo to write in such a public forum. Here are some writers who may not be professionals or even regular contributors but their writings specially on travel capture the interest of the reader as examples of women's achievements and also because of the intimacy that they seem to establish with the reader –Himangshubala Debi, Pramila Devi, Sukumari Roychowdhury and Bimala Dasgupta, who wrote about their travels to the west, Aparna Debi and Sarala Debi Chowdhurani. Some of these contributors were already famous in India for having come from famous families or else have made a name through some extraordinary achievement, for example Sarala. Sarala Debi Chowdhurani nee Ghoshal, whose articles on travel to Rangoon are some of the best travel writings, was born to an accomplished mother, Swarnakumari Debi, writer, poet and editor of *Bharati* and had spent her childhood with her maternal family, the Tagores of Jorasanko. Her free spirits were nurtured by the family giving her permission to travel and work outside her hometown as well as participate in public and political life, including editing *Bharati.* Sarala Deb is considered to be one of the early feminists of India, being much more than simply a writer of travelogues and editor of *Bharati.*[27] She was thinker, writer, a social activist and a staunch anti-colonial nationalist, close and loyal to both Tagore and Gandhi. Others like Sita Devi or Shanta Devi started out writing in the periodicals and then became famous fiction writers whose books were serially first published in the journals. These two women were incidentally part of the periodical family, being daughters of the legendary Ramananda Chattopadhyay, of *Prabashi* and *The Modern Review* fame. Shanta Devi was married to Kalidas Nag who was one of the stalwarts of the Greater India Society and a close associate of Rabindranath Tagore. Both the sisters wrote autobiographies *Punyasmriti* (Sita Debi) and *Purbasmriti* (Shanta Debi), which are not only literary gems but also of great value as sources of knowledge of the contemporary Bengali society. Sita Debi lived in Rangoon for some time after her marriage. Mrinalini Raha and Pushpalata Debi stayed in South-East Asia and travelled extensively, trying to acquaint the countrymen with the lands which were their homes now. Hariprabha Takeda's 'Travel to Japan' which was submitted to the editor of *Bharat Mahila* in a diary form successfully created a bond between the traveller and the reader till today. The credit for this must go to the editor Sarajubala Dutta, who added a short bionote providing the reader with the reasons for the travel and this created an intimacy lasting over a century. The importance of women editors in inspiring confidence in other women to write for publication cannot be overstated. Just as Swarnakumari Debi, Sarala Devi Chowdhurani and Hiranmoyee Devi were synonymous with *Bharati*, Gyanadanandini Devi with *Balak*, others too played leading roles as editors of influential periodicals – like Hemlata Devi with *Bangalakshmi*, Prajnasundari Devi with *Punya*, Sarajubala Dutta with *Bharat Mahila*, Banalata Devi and Hemantakumari Chaudhuri with *Antahpur* and Kumudini Mitra with both *Antahpur* and *Suprabhat.*[28]

Notes

1 Tapan Raychaudhuri, *Perceptions, Emotions and Sensibilities: Essays in India's Colonial and Post-colonial Experiences*, Delhi: Oxford University Press, 1999, p. 3.
2 Bipin Chandra Pal, *The Spirit of Indian Nationalism*, London: Hind Nationalist Agency, 1910, p. 16.
3 Sarvani Gooptu, 'Locating *Bharat* in Asia: Cosmopolitanism and Nationalism in Vernacular Periodicals', in Pallab Sengupta, ed., *India's Vernacular Journalism: A Journey of Two Centuries*, Calcutta: Setu Prakashani, 2019, pp. 94–113.
4 Rabindranath Tagore, 'Jibonsmriti' (Memories of My Life', *Rabindra Rachanabali (Collected Works)*, Vol. IX, Calcutta: Visva Bharati, 2008 (1989), p. 452.
5 Ibid.
6 Andrew Otis, *Hicky's Bengal Gazette: The Untold Story of India's First Newspaper*, Chennai: Tranquebar, 2018.
7 Hiranmay Karlekar, 'Vernacular Journalism, the Bengal Renaissance and the Beginning of the Independence Movement', in Pallab Sengupta, ed., *India's Vernacular Journalism: A Journey of Two Centuries*, Calcutta: SEtu Prakashani, 2019, pp. 34–40.
8 J. Long, *A Descriptive Catalogue of Bengali Works*, Calcutta: Sanders, Cones and Co., 1855, p. 65, https://archive.org/details/adescriptivecat00longgoog/page/n4/mode/2up, accessed on 22.11.2018.

9 For details of the major journals, see Abhijit Bhattacharya, *A Guide to Hitesh Ranjan Sanyal Memorial Collection*, Calcutta: Centre for Studies in Social Sciences, 1998, https://www.cssscal.org/pdf/archive/guide.pdf, accessed on 22.11.2018.

10 Brojendra Nath Bandopadhyay, *Bangla Samayik Patra (1818–1868)*, Calcutta: Bangiya Sahitya Parishad, 1935, pp. 123–124.

11 Ibid., p. 125.

12 Quoted in Brojendra Nath Bandopadhyay, op. cit., p. 188.

13 Ibid., pp. 190–191.

14 *Aryadarshan*, 5(12), 1878, pp. 570–576.

15 Anon., Bangabashir Europe Yatra: Kolkata hoite Brindisi hoiya France, *Aryadarshan*, 11(4), 1885, pp. 185–192.

16 Rabindranath Tagore, Jibonsmriti, *Rabindra Rachanabali*, vol. 9, Calcutta: Visva Bharati, 2008 (1989), p. 466.

17 Anon., Chindiger Aachar Byabohar, *Anusandhan*, 5(23) 1891, p. 524.

18 Anon., Chinidiger Bibaha Paddhati, *Anusandhan*, 5(23), 1891, p. 546.

19 Charu Chandra Mitra, Chin Paribhraman, *Anusandhan*, 8(30), 1894, pp. 796–799.

20 Nagendranath Gupta, *Reflections and Reminiscences*, Delhi: Hind Kitabs, 1947.

21 For some important articles of *The Modern Review*, see Anikendra Sen, Devangshu Dutta and Nilanjana S. Ray, eds., *Patriots, Poets and Prisoners: Selections from Ramananda Chatterjee's The Modern Review (1907–1947)*, Noida: Harper Collins India, 2016.

22 Sarvani Gooptu, *The Music of Nationhood: Dwijendralal Roy of Bengal*, Delhi: Primus Books, 2018.

23 Bharati Ray, ed., *Prabashi te Naari (1901–1947)*, Calcutta: Ananda Publishers, 2016.

24 Paresh Chandra Sen, Machhagirir Paadamoole, ***Bharatvarsha***, 15(1)(5), 1927, p. 782.

25 See Sarvani Gooptu, 'Importance of Cultural Linkages through Popular Interactions: Written Testimonies in Vernacular Periodicals in the Colonial Period', in Rakhahari Chatterji and Anasua Basu Raychaudhury, eds., *Reimaging BIMSTEC: Strengthening Regional Solidarity across the Bay of Bengal* Delhi: Observer Research Foundation, 2021 and 'Forging New Friendships through Oceanic Travels: Cosmopolitan and Nationalistic Ideas in Bengali Journals (late 19th and 20th Centuries)', in Suranjan Das and Anita Sengupta, eds., *Contiguity Connectivity and Access: The Importance of the Bay of Bengal Region in India's Foreign Policy*, Delhi: KW publishers, 2021.

26 Susmita Mukherjee, 'The Bengali Revolutionaries in Burma, 1923–1933', *Proceedings of the Indian History Congress*, vol. 61, 2000, pp. 1104–1117, www.jstor.org/stable/44144425, accessed on 28.07.2020.

27 Bharati Ray, *Early Feminists of Colonial India: Sarala Devi Chaudhurani and Rokeya Sakhawat Hossain*, Delhi: Oxford University Press, 2002.

28 For more details on women editors, see Shovarani Bhattacharya, *Mahila Sampadito Bangla Samayik Sahitya Patrika (Prak Swadhinata Parba)*, 2000, Digital Library of India Item 2015.266991, accessed on 6.05.2020.

2 Travelling in Asian lands

A male gaze

Travel accounts have been an important source of history since ancient times. These accounts of foreign travellers into India whether they were made from religious/pilgrimage or commercial motives have provided information for construction of Indian historical accounts. Indian history writing has more or less documented and incorporated these accounts. What is as yet awaiting completion is the documentation of accounts by Indian travellers and writers on the Asian lands.[1] My endeavour is in this regard. With the rise and spread of education among the Bengalis, awareness of foreign lands and reading about travels in them became an exciting pastime. Bengali literature and magazines are replete with translations of real-life adventure stories by men and women travelling to distant lands. The first popular travel writings in the Bengali magazines were by travellers to western countries but gradually from the late 19th century, the focus came to be Asia.

Colonialism, despite its oppressive and motivated administrative policies, brought distant areas close through establishment of communications links. People not only travelled on pilgrimages within the country but went on secular travels abroad as well. Commercial travelling to different Asian countries was perhaps not new, but what was new was the documentation in the form of articles and essays in the different journals. This coincided with the educative mission that had been initiated through the Bengali literary magazines regarding Asia – the commonalities and differences. The photographs of places of tourist and religious interest, architectural monuments and people were used profusely to attract the attention of the reader along with a comparative style where similarity or dissimilarity with Indian culture and history was used. What was even more striking in this show of commonality of Asian cultures was highlighting the basic dissimilarity with the west, despite apparent familiarity through English literature and language. This stress on Asian solidarity hinted at initially and then openly stated in the 20th century writing was motivated by a belief that it could be a means of empowerment against colonialism.

In general, in these travelogues, two aspects are important. One was the straightforward travel story where the traveller is describing the places he visits, routes he takes and then inspires his fellowmen to follow suit. The other aspect in these essays is more complex and nuanced and must be gleaned through inferences. Description of places of interest as well as customs, dresses and culture as well as notes on political, social and cultural values of the places visited reflects an Indian vision, and makes these articles valuable to understand the psyche of the society the writer belongs to as well as the national and local context in relation to the places visited and the time when the visit occurs. One challenging aspect for the researcher besides the mindset of the visitor is to ascertain how

DOI: 10.4324/9781003243786-2

much of these 'travelogues' is from personal experience and how much is from the books they read. There is actually a blurring of these boundaries, since the mindset is formed by their reading. In specialised journals like women's journals and children's magazines, the possible interests of the readers are kept in mind by the writers and I have dealt with this more extensively in later chapters. Here I only look at the travelling men.

Discussions on western travellers and translations of their travelogues

Descriptions of travels by the intrepid western travellers fascinated Bengali readers ever since the books in English became available to them. So, when opportunity came to pass it on to the less fortunate who had less access, the editors invariably included translations of travelogues and academic articles in Bengali journals. It is interesting that though all the travel writing is not by well-known writers, most of the translation is. Jyotirindranath Tagore translated the travel of French writer Felicien Challaye[2] to Japan as well as Lafcadio Hearn's ideas via Challaye's writings[3] which were published in *Bharati* in 1908. Tagore's choice of Challaye for translation is significant since the travelogue and essay are written by a westerner but with 'eastern eyes'. This eastern view was later adopted by his younger brother Rabindranath while writing 'Traveller to Japan'. In 1910, in *Prabashi*, Jyotirindranath also translated the visit of Siam by the Grand Duke Boris Vladimirovich of Russia who was allegedly sent on a world tour by his father to turn his mind away from his *mesalliances* at home. He came to Thailand for eight days as guest of King Chulalongkorn in 1902. Following the reportage in *Le Review*, Jyotirindranath Tagore published a three-episode article 'Travels in Siam Kingdom'.[4] Tagore's choice of this voyage for translation is interesting since his aim is obviously to describe Siam or Thailand since the Grand Duke travelled to many countries of Asia, including Egypt, India, Ceylon, Indo China and Japan as well as America during this grand tour. It appears as if Tagore himself is a part of the Grand Duke's entourage. The Grand Duke sailed from Singapore on Singora with the Russian flag flying high and reached Bangkok where two sons of King Chulalongkorn received him. The article describes the hospitality of the Thai king as well as grace and gravity of the Queen Savang Vadhana and then goes on to describe the dress and demeanour of Siamese women and children.[5] The third issue of the article entirely consists of elephant hunting in Bang Pa In, 'considered to be the Versailles of Thailand'.[6] A similar choice can also be seen in another translation by Jyotirindranath, when he translates the Singhal or Sri Lankan part of Pierre Loti (pseudonym of Louis Marie Julien Vivand) officer and novelist's L'inde sans les Anglais or India without the English for *Sahitya* in 1904.[7]

Another famous writer Bibhuti Bhusan Bandopadhyay whose novels set in exotic locales or adventure stories to distant lands have been loved by readers of all ages was probably initiated into these imaginative meanderings through the essays he wrote in the periodicals where he translates the writings of European travellers. In *Bangasri*, in the period 1935–1945, many of these descriptive essays and translations of travelogues were published under a specialised selection called Bichitra Jagat. For example, in 1935, Bandopadhyay wrote 'Morubhumir Desh Arabia'[8] (In Arabia, the Land of Deserts) where he translates the writing of Daniel van der Meulen who was the Dutch consul at Yemen and explorer of Hadramut. In 1936, in *Bichitra*, Bibhuti Bhushan Bandopadhyay speaks about the travels of John Hulse by bicycle or on foot, in the villages of Dutch East India Company-controlled Borneo.[9]

In the same journal in 1936, Prabhat Chattopadhyay published a translation of the account of travels of the Austrian-American explorer and botanist/geographer Joseph Rock to the Muli kingdom at Tibetan- Chinese border region.[10] Suresh Chandra Bose writes about an American globetrotter Hippolite Martinet, who travelled in Burma on foot, and describes him as a unique and ideal traveller since he is humble, unencumbered by family ties yet able to withstand great hardship.[11] Reference has been made to a person with same descriptions and same name who was travelling on foot in Baghdad by an aviator D'Arcy Grieg who was faced with this apparition in tattered clothes and shoes, apparently hiking across Arabia. What is interesting and common in the two descriptions of Bose and Grieg about Martinet is the calling card he carried with him. A picture of the card bearing the inscription, 'H. Martinet, American globetrotter' has been provided in a Bengali article, while Grieg writes that Martinet sold 'signed postcards of himself'.[12] Bose also mentions that Martinet travelled across Burma staying in people's houses for one or two days on an average. He spent two days in the author's house and discussed his travels. Martinet was intrigued to know that Bose had travelled extensively in Burma and had written a travelogue called '*Bichitra Bhuban*' (the Amazing world). Bose spoke warmly about the 'jocular traveller' to whom he had come quite close.[13]

Another translation, 'The exploits of the Chinese pirates', traces an exciting adventure of two Norwegian sailors who were kidnapped and ransomed by Chinese pirates off the China Sea. The story follows the narrative of the first officer Westerhalme who along with Captain Harland was kidnapped when their ship *Botnia* became grounded near Hacao.[14] Dinendra Kumar Roy who wrote this was the assistant editor of the magazine and later became a famous detective novelist, creating the character of Robert Blake, a detective based in Baker Street with an assistant Smith for his Bengali readers. Translations of the writings of Sven Hadin and Aurel Stein are found in most of the journals – not only for the young readers but for adults too by some of the best writers of the time. As travelogues in children's literature show writing about places which are difficult to visit like mountains, deserts are the most popular which is why translated travelogues of these intrepid travellers are most welcomed in the popular journals.

Tales of the road

Himangshu Kumar Bose's article 'The Natural Beauty of Burma' is interesting because it enumerates the 'real reasons' why one should travel to Burma. As he points out, it is passé to go for work to Burma. He expresses a disdain for Indian tourist spots for much the same reason, and says that when one feels annoyed at only 'hearing Hindi being spoken all around in the tourist spots in northern India', Burma made a 'refreshing change' with its 'beautiful nature, unknown language, the attractive looks, interesting clothes and hospitable nature of the local men and women.' He concludes that 'unexpected pleasure' can only come from 'the unknown'.[15]

An anonymous writer, calling himself Ta Pra Cha (probably the first letters of his name, here it could be Taraprasad Chattopadhyay from the list of writers provided in the contents page) in *Nabajiban*, 1884, writes a travelogue describing a trip to Sri Lanka a year after he set sail in the winter of 1883. In his detailed and well-researched travelogue, he writes that a first-class passenger to Singhal (Sri Lanka) has to pay Rs. 180 return fare which was valid for six months. This ticket included meals made on board but the rule was if one carried a servant along, then the traveller would have to provide for his own meals though the servant's travel was free, which Cha did. The reason for that, of course, was Cha's mother feared that community meals would mean caste contamination.[16] Fear of losing caste was however not the monopoly of the middle classes alone, but a reality even among labouring classes which impacted the indenture system as well. The fear was considerably more in women who have traditionally been the anchor of caste rules leading to refusal of women to leave their homestead and accompany their men on indenture ships, leading to greater exploitation of the few women who did travel with their men.

Closer home, Sailakumar Mukhopadhyay describes his 12-day tour of Sikkim and Tibet with his attorney friends with interesting details. The article describes the preparations for the trek which would start from Kalimpong in Bengal to Gangtok in Sikkim and then Karponang, Changu, Nathula, Champitang and Yatung in Tibet. They had to apply in advance for a frontier pass from the authorities to travel in Tibet which had many stipulations, including a directive that one could not publish any article in any newspaper or journal about the travel without the government's approval or in such a way that may hurt the sentiments of the Tibetans. Besides tinned food, they carried medicines, firearms with permission and an emergency medical set from Bengal Chemicals. As Mukhopadhyay writes:

> since one cannot get the fullest pleasure of a trip without pictures and memory is notoriously treacherous, we carried with us Rolleiflex (Rolliflex) and movex (movie) cameras along with raincoats, hill sticks, hot bag, glare glass, thermos flask, binocular and stoves as compulsory baggage for our trip.[17]

Besides descriptions of preparation for travel, the favourite for the writers was the journey by rail or water. In an article dated 1892, Rukmini Kanta Chakraborty's description of travel by rail to Candy is detailed and interesting to read.

> After lunch we left for Candy by train around 3. The trains here do not use coal because there are no coal mines and use wood instead . . . I was so impressed by their friendly attitude that I began to think that all the people of the country were polite and simple . . . The changing scenery was breath-taking, after miles of coconut trees and betel forests on both sides from Pangohala station, small hills greeted us . . . what a beautiful sight – mountains on all sides, interspersed with small fruit orchards and rice fields descending from mountains and disappearing into the horizon on the plains. I now realise the truth of the verses by Michael Madhusudan Dutta who wrote, 'O beautiful Lanke, you are the world's desire, the abode of happiness'.[18]

Many travellers at different times describe journey by train in Japan. In a series of letters published in *Mahila* in 1903, Satya Sundar Deb describes his travel in the following words:

> I boarded the train for Osaka at Kobe. The Japanese railway system is beautiful. The coaches are not like ours and there are connecting doors so that one can easily travel from one coach to another. Every passenger has a specified attendant who will provide what is asked for by the passenger.[19]

A more famous traveller in Japan, Benoy Kumar Sarkar was equally fascinated by the Japanese railway and he too mentions the presence of an attendant who looked after all the needs of the passengers. In one such journey from Tokyo to Hokkeido, he wrote:

> like the Americans the Japanese too provide sleepers for their passengers. But what the American trains do not have are personal attendants in each car who look after all the needs of the passengers including making beds, cleaning compartments, doing laundry and even cleaning shoes. Another unique thing in Japanese trains is that the passengers are provided with mosquito nets and slippers . . . Not all the coaches in Japanese railway have dining cars. They bring their own food, even in the first and second classes. Most of the passengers also generally wear national garments and not western clothes Even in the restrooms at the station I noticed that though there were chairs and tables the local people prefer to spread rugs for sitting and eating . . . In India though majority of the passengers in trains and steamers are Indians, the rail company prefers to look after the comfort of the few white men and women travellers and make arrangements accordingly. . . . That is why travelling by train or steamer is tough for the Indians. But though the Japanese learnt the benefits of the railway system from India they were able to adapt the western technological advances to suit their own comforts.[20]

Travel by ship was fascinating for most travellers. Ashutosh Roy who was travelling as a commissariat officer to the Basra war front in 1915, during the Second World War, has a lyrical description about his journey by sea. 'On all sides there was only an infinite expanse of water . . . orchestrating an unending musical and dance performance' and much more in that vein.[21] He describes the various ports which the ship, SS Arunkola, touches – Aden on the third day where he is intrigued to see flying fish and seals, Muscat and Bushire on the fifth day and finally on the sixth day entered the Shat el Arab, river front, marked by 'date trees standing guard like soldiers on duty'.[22] Premadananda Sen describes his journey to Rangoon in the following words. 'We boarded the ship *Ludhiana* at Kadamtala Ghat of Calcutta to go to Burma . . . after the first night fall when we woke up we had reached the mudpoint, where Bhagirathi flows into the ocean'. Sen also describes his first view of the Arakan mountains and then Elephant Point which marked the first view of Rangoon.

> We could soon see the large red building of Bombay Burma Trading Corporation Limited with a white elephant flag flying on top, signalling the unity of islands of British Burma. The white elephant not available anywhere else in the world was the Burmese king Thibaw's symbol, but now it has been appropriated by the wood manufacturers and merchants.[23]

One of the best travelogues is by the famous philologist, Suniti Kumar Chattopadhyay, who accompanied Rabindranath Tagore in his travels in South-East Asia and wrote 'Javadviper Pathe' and 'Dvipamoy Bharat' published in *Prabashi* in the period 1929–1931. His writings not only provide a lively picture of the region and its people (quite literally as well, through the accompanying sketches by Surendranath Kar) but is also an interesting document of how a nationalist enterprise interwove a universalist focus at every step. On the way to Java, his description of the co-passengers and crew on the *Amboise* demonstrate his cosmopolitan mindset as well as his nationalist concerns:

> The ship is quite large, around 15 tonnes and there are almost five hundred people in its first, second and third classes. Besides, there are two open decks covered in canvas to keep the sun and water away where there are around 100 people travelling as deck or fourth class passengers. Around three to four hundred Annami and French soldiers are travelling by ship. The ship is full and seems to be the meeting point of people from different races. There are besides the French (the ship is a French one travelling from Marseilles to Tongking's Hyphong port over a period of five weeks), Indians (Tamils of Pondicherry as well as Hindu, Christian and Muslims Tamils, Moplah Muslims, Malayali Telegus from Malabar, Bengali Hindus), Annamis from Tongking who colour their teeth black and from Cochin China who keep their teeth a natural white, about sixty–seventy Arabs, Algerians, people from Aden. Most of the French, white, dark and Creole from the French colonies of Madagascar, Spice islands work in the engine room, while the Kafris and Chinese work in the kitchens . . . There are so many different races who have varied languages, varied mentality, varied customs, yet they all work harmoniously together. If one makes up their mind to live with civility and accommodate respect for others along with self-pride and not allow religious bigotry and racial pride to cloud their judgement, then camaraderie is never hampered. The ship was a living proof of that theory.[24]

He gives a detailed description of how all the different food preparation went on by chefs and sous-chefs from different races working in unison without discord, with French being the connecting language between them. His nationalist concern is revealed when he concludes this description of the voyage by pointing out that

> if only our countrymen could see this miniature world where mutual tolerance bred harmony and camaraderie they could contrast it with the hell that had been created in India by the machinations of some selfish and communal minded individuals within the Hindus and Muslims, they would be ashamed of themselves.[25]

In 1936, Keshab Chandra Gupta travelling to Malaya with his brother Anil describes his journey by the *Karapara Royal* mail steamship and refers to the presence of Bengalis in the crew. He talked about Banerjee who was an assistant of the Chief Engineer Wells and the ship doctor who was also a Bengali, Dr Pal.[26] Asking the question of why Indians cannot move out of the stalemate of studying in college and taking up government services, he answers himself that it requires great stamina to choose an occupation outside the beaten track. In admiration, he describes the work of some Bengali Muslims from Chittagong he discovers working in the Engine room as firemen and khalasi (lascars). Gupta felt that it was a terrible job that these men had, firing up the boilers. In the ship Karapara, there were many boilers running and almost every minute one had to open up the hatches and shovel in coal. It was a fearsome job standing and working in front of the fiery boilers. The men had a bucket filled with water in front of them and every time they shovelled in coal they drank from the mug to cool down.[27]

A year later in 1937, the famous Bengali magician P.C. Sorcar describes the journey on *Sirdhana* which was carrying 800 Englishmen and Indians along with 1,400 tons of cargo to Japan.[28] Like many others, Sorcar refers to the sea sickness and the English food as the twin burdens the passengers had to bear on the journey.

The ports of call

The ports that the ships touch on the way provide excitement and relief during the long voyages since sometimes the passengers alight for a few hours or even days and enjoy the change of scenario and getting a taste of a new country. Most ships make a stop at Rangoon and Penang which are considered to be wonderful halts for most. Keshab Chandra Gupta describes both places on his way to Malaya. 'The flow of humanity in Rangoon reminds me of the many races meeting at the Indian National Congress sessions and the international meetings of the League of Nations in Geneva'.[29] P.C. Sorcar on his way to Japan, recalls the roar of joy that came from the passengers when they glimpsed the first view of Penang/ or Georgetown/ or Prince of Wales island as it was variously called, an important port and city of the English occupied Malayan Strait Settlements. Sorcar found its natural beauty remarkable and described how its main roads were lined with beautiful trees. Besides the beauty of course, Georgetown was considered to be the most healthy city in Malaya. Like all travellers from Bengal, Sorcar noted the tiniest similarities with Calcutta and proudly pointed them out. 'Similar to the Calcutta Lift,' he wrote, 'a new electric railway line carried tourists to the hills.' He also mentions the railway line called the Federated Malay States railway by which one could travel to Singapore in the south and Bangkok in the north. 'It was a quaint railway system – it had no rail lines, no trains and no platforms . . . passengers had to travel by steamer for 25 minutes and then get on a train.'[30]

Sorcar describes the tourist spots in Penang, waterfalls, botanical gardens, Ayer itam temple, Snake temple, cable railway and reservoir, etc.[31]

Singapore was another layover that is described in detail by many. P.C. Sorcar was pleased that his magician's craft was acknowledged in Singapore when he was invited to perform at the Malayan Magic circle. He speaks of the large number of Indians who came to the show and wanted to be acquainted and 'the president of the association Mr Gilroy greeted (him) . . . graciously as a fellow member of the English magicians' society and the eastern representative of the Leicester Magic circle'.[32] Describing Singapore, Sorcar writes:

> that, like Penang, Singapore is a foremost port of English Malaya. The harbour has so many ships stationed, that it looks like a veritable forest and I have never seen so many ships in one place anywhere else. The ships belonging to different nations flying their nation's flags and people of various countries have made Singapore a cosmopolitan town.[33]

He then describes his visit to see the first rubber tree which was planted at the botanical gardens and which then became the main asset of the whole of Malaya. He also visited 'Tyersall', the palace of the Sultan of Johor, Raffles' museum and library, Singapore zoo, the mosque of Malaya, Chinese temple and Chetti-run Hindu temple. Sorcar was interested in the Chetti temple where during the main festival Thaipusam, many Indian yogis walk on fire and fakirs on glass pieces and nails. Sorcar particularly mentions this custom because he wanted to tell his readers that as a magician he had performed and written about this feat.

> Fire walking or walking barefoot on fire is a famous act of Indian magicians. But the act can be performed in two ways, one by strategy and the other through ability. The former is very simple, one only needs to soak one's feet in a medicinal solution, many magicians have done it before me and I too have received accolades for performing this trick. The second is a spiritual pursuit which needs strong faith and will. I have tried this method too but it is extremely difficult for most. Speaking to the yogis here I realised that most of them have achieved the second method of withstanding fire after years and years of faith and practice. .[34]

Sorcar also describes the life and living in Singapore as 'disciplined, orderly, cosmopolitan' and due to free trade much cheaper compared to Calcutta.

Sorcar describes more stops on the way to Japan – Hong Kong, Shanghai and Canton. More than descriptions of the cities, Sorcar writes about how his magic skills were appreciated. He says that the people in Canton appreciated the sleights of hand or machines less than the black arts tricks with skulls. They preferred games with the name ghost, like ghostly rain of money, ghostly room, ghostly spider or ghostly food etc and gave Sorcar a new name- 'Tay long fat soh kah' or the Magic emperor Sorcar.[35] Before reaching Japan, Sorcar's final port of call was Shanghai for which he uses a cosmopolitan language to describe it.

> The most interesting thing about this city is that it appears at first sight to be a French town but . . . after travelling a little it appears to be a Chinese town, with the bad smell of rotting fish that Chinese seem to enjoy and nothing but Chinese script and Chinese men is visible. On reaching King Edward VII Avenue, it feels as if one is in the white part of Calcutta because there are mostly Punjabi policemen and Englishmen to be seen here. Further away the town seems like America's New York, with its high-rise building of 20–40 floors and its red-faced American owners. In the Japanese section, they live in their Japanese style houses going about their work silently. It is as if the city is a mixture of all nations. My interpreter called it a 'league of nations'.[36]

Places and people

In many of the travelogues, places of tourist attraction are highlighted and attractive pictures provided. The articles encourage visitors to travel to these places. To that end, the easiest travel routes are discussed in detail. Not only physical descriptions, the travelogues are attempts to understand the people. This is a time when work and business interests were encouraging people to travel to Asian lands. There has been a shift from only pilgrimage-based travel and sightseeing or exploring to more focused travel. Most of the people who were travelling visited many places on the way to their destination. This could be partly because the route unlike today's travels was never direct but went via many towns and ports. And partly for most travellers, it could be the only time they would be visiting an area so naturally they wanted to make the most out of their visit.

Satya Sundar Deb, son of Trailokyanath Deb, writer of the 'Brahmo Samaj in the Past' (*Atiter Brahmo Samaj*), was sent to Japan to study the manufacture of porcelain. He wrote about his experience there in letters to his father and youngest sister. Trailokyanath handed over some of his son's letters to be printed in *Mahila*. Deb writes in one letter that on arrival in Japan he went to a hotel with two Japanese painters and there he witnessed Japanese hospitality for the first time.

> I cannot describe how polite they were – more so than any other race in the world . . .and we are no match in hospitality. If you go to a shop to buy something, the shopkeeper bows at everything the buyer says and tries to satisfy him in every way. Is it any wonder that the Japanese are so developed? . . .[37]

Ashutosh Roy describing his experiences as the Commissariat officer of the British army in Basra talks less about his professional activities and more about the local life he came across. Roy described the *mahella* boats which travel on the rivers and are owned by almost all well-to-do families and the presence of coffee shops on all important roads, much like the Indian tea shops. The only difference, according to him was that unlike Indian teashops where the customers crowd during morning and evening, here coffee aficionados loll in the *kawakhanas* the whole day. It surprised Roy, how the Armenians and Arabs sat so patiently without moving in one place for such prolonged periods . . . They hardly went home even to have lunch, they just bought some oven (tandoor) made bread (khabuj) from the market and some meat and combined it with coffee, which was very strong and drunk in small cups with a piece of sugar. It was dark black and very bitter and the cup only holds only two dessert spoons (i.e. 2 fluid drachmas) of coffee.[38]

During their stay at Basra, he describes his encounters with the two types of Arabs: the Bedouin (Baddu Arabs who were violent in nature) and the Kurdi Arab who were good looking and strong, but not as violent as the Baddus. He saw similarity between the language of the Kurdi Arabs and Indians. . .. The Armenians, he described as goodlooking and superior in dress and food, but complex in nature which is why they were looked upon with suspicion by the Turks who mistreated them at every instance. It was the Armenians who acted as interpreters for the British army.[39]

Roy then moves with the white Norfolk regiment to Kurna ('of Bible fame where the Garden of Paradise was supposed to be') under General Fry. On arrival they were greeted with Turkish fire, so had to settle to stay on their boats in mid-stream on the Tigris–Euphrates before the defeat of the Turks who dispersed towards Amara leaving the British army to move towards 'a tower visible among the trees in the distance' which they came to know 'was a Armenian saint Ezra's Tomb and one of their main pilgrim centres'.[40]

Benoy Kumar Sarkar during his visit to Japan in 1915 does a tour of Tokyo and nearby places. His description of these places has a unique feel not only in the detailed analysis he does but also in the meticulous research that it accompanies. Like many other Bengali visitors, he is moved by nationalistic feeling in the similarities he draws between India and Japan and the interest he takes in all connections between the two countries in the past. But what is most noticeable is how he places Japan within Asia, imbued with the eastern spirit despite her modernisation along western lines. He also draws out those elements of development in Japan that make her stand out in comparison to not only India but to all other Asian nations but is quick to assert that they are elements that are indigenous or organic to Japan and are not western imports. The westernisation that seems apparent to a non-discerning person specially a westerner is only on the surface and is not '*swadeshi*' to Japan, it is artificial. In the essay where he is describing his sightseeing in 'An Independent Asian Capital – Tokyo', Sarkar, anticipating language problems, writes down names of the places he wants to visit on chits of paper in English and Japanese. He is amazed that even rickshaw pullers could read thanks to their universal education policy but he is sad that this tourist's ploy would not have worked in India. Also he refers to the system of large maps being hung in public places, in a western style, so that people would be aware of the progress of the ongoing war. All passerbys glanced at the maps and kept abreast of the world situation. Such a scene occurring in India would be a matter of dream, Sarkar felt.[41]

Sarkar's tourist eyes are different from others as is evident from his descriptions. He first visits the monuments of the modern world – the departmental stores – Maruzen and Co. which contain a fabulous display of books, and then Mitsukoshi which, in his words, can compare with any departmental store in England or America in décor, interior furnishing, workers' discipline, escalators which till then Sarkar had only seen in western countries, as well as other marvels like efficient fire prevention devices, passenger elevators and mail chutes to convey the cash collected from customers to the main cashier's desk. In Sarkar's eyes the Japanese look unpromising, unintelligent and un-industrious, even unprepossessing in appearance, yet they are now driving ships and running large shops. Sarkar concludes that, 'no Indian has the ability to perform their own jobs well and over think so much that they are plunged in negativity which destroys the ability to perform.'[42]

Sarkar then appointed a tourist guide for a city tour. He was amused to hear that the guide had learnt English from the tourists he had taken round the city and they were famous men like the Gaikwar of Baroda and the Sinhalese Buddhist preacher Dharmapala. Sarkar was fascinated by the description of the umbrellas that the Japanese used. According to Sarkar's guide, there were mainly two types of indigenous umbrellas that the Japanese used. One was to protect oneself from the sun and the other from rains. Both the types were made of paper, only one used in rain was soaked in oil Sarkar admired that high quality of paper production by the Japanese which was also very durable and paper walls, papers ropes and paper umbrellas were the speciality there.[43]

Sarkar in his travels was always trying to discover a 'Japanese Japan' where he found similarities with India rather than the westernised Japan which was confined to the Ginza district, 'the Chowringhee of Tokyo'. Elsewhere was 'Swadeshi Japan' in the

> small houses, tiny lanes, wooden houses, paper walls, wooden shoes, paper roofs, push carts, women carrying their children on their backs, mat covered shops, rice and fish hotels which are visible everywhere . . . Even under the influence of the west in the past fifty years traditional Japan has not died.[44]

He discovered the same traditions of 'medieval Japan, Asian Japan and Japanese Japan' in the vegetable market and the handicrafts and industrial art shops. Sarkar considers his gaze in this regard far superior to that of the foreign tourists who are thrilled with all Japanese metalworks. But Sarkar feels that for an Indian who has seen the arts and crafts of Kasi, Moradabad, Murshidabad and Tanjore will be much less impressed by all the displayed wares. As he writes, 'what catches the eye are the lacquer ware and the embroidery on silk'.[45] The pearl industry according to Sarkar is indigenous to Asia and Japan is no exception. The most famous pearl shop in Tokyo is Mikimato Pearl store which he visits not just to see the pearl items there but to learn about pearl culture or 'harnessing the mollusc for the service of man'. A biologist at Tokyo University, Dr Mitsukuri advised Mikimato to start pearl culture and that is what Sarkar went to study.[46] Sarkar also travelled outside Tokyo which he describes in two other articles in the same journal *Grihastha* in 1915. One was 'Half Japan in One Week',[47] where he talked about his journey to Nikko mountain and the Matsushima Islands and the other is 'Manchester of Asia'.[48]

Hemendralal Roy wrote about his travels to Thailand in *Prabashi* in 1924. He gave details about how to reach Thailand via Singapore and Kuala Lampur, wrote about similarities between India and Thailand, descriptions of the settlers and Indian influence in architecture. He ends with a note of admiration that an Asian state so close to India was prospering on its own.[49] Subimal Chandra Sarkar, in *Malayer Pathe* (On the Way to Malaya), describes the awe and wonder he felt to see the beauty of the Penang with its coconut and betel nut trees. In fact, he starts the essay by saying that 'Penang means betel nut and I realised that the name was justified when the mists cleared as the ship entered the port and the beauty of the island was revealed'.[50] The essay is accompanied by pictures of the trees and Chinese temples on the sides of the mountains. He informs his readers that there is a lot to see in Penang and one way to do so would be to travel by train which he calls 'steam trams' which climb the mountains. It takes only half an hour by train to reach the highest point of Malaya which is Buki Bendera. From there one can get a full view of the island. 'It would not be an exaggeration to call this green piece of land surrounded by blue sea as a piece of Heaven on earth'.[51] However, Sarkar feels that the roadways in Penang are so good that any tourist who can organise a car or bring one can travel across Malaya through 3,500 miles of motorable roads and reach Singapore from Penang comfortably. Sarkar is appreciative of the scenic beauty of the place he's visiting, but in certain statements the prejudices of his time and race are visible. When he steps foot in Penang his first impression is that he has 'landed in a yellow kingdom. It appeared that all the shops-markets, business and industries were all in the hands of the Chinese and in fact as I soon realised this country is under Chinese hegemonic control'. There is an interesting mixture of regret for lack of dynamism of the Indian settlers in Malaya and admiration as well as disdain for the Chinese success when he says that 'both Chinese and Indians came to Malaya as labourers. Indians have remained "coolies" while Chinese through their industry and expertise have become competitors of the British'.[52]

The magician P.C. Sorcar's final destination was Japan – Kobe, Osaka and Tokyo. He not only travelled all over Japan and visited all the tourist sites, his performance was also deeply appreciated and the newspapers hailed him as 'Houdini of India'.[53] A Japanese magician Gasho Ishikawa also writes about Sorcar's visit to Japan and his success there. Ishikawa wrote that on June 1937,the 24 year old Indian magician, visited the shores of Japan with his special magic show. He gave successful magic performances in Kobe on June 20th at the India club, attended by the Prince of Mysore, Mr & Mrs Saxena (World Trade Commissioner), Mr & Mrs Inamdar, Dr. Godbole (delegates to the World Education Conference), members of the India club, the Indian Social Society, the President, Indian National Committee and Indian Trade Association in addition to all the Indian residents of Kobe and Osaka. It was a very successful show and lavish reports were published in all the Japanese newspapers. He later gave shows in Kobe under the joint auspices of the Kansai Japan–India society and the Federation of Buddhist Associations. Sorcar also performed in Tokyo under the arrangement of Late Rash Behari Bose and others. Ananda Mohan Sahay of India lodge organised his Japan tour, which received very good receptions from both the press and public in Japan. (Sorcar in his travelogue also mentions these patrons. [54]) But the real hit according to Ishikawa was on June 15, 1937, when Sorcar visited Nakaza Theatre, Osaka, where Japan's number one (Lady) Illusionist Ten Katsu was giving her full stage show, since she received Sorcar most enthusiastically and gave various letters of introduction to the important persons. This news of Sorcar and Ten Katsu appreciating each other's shows was published throughout the world through the United Press news agency.[55]Ishikawa was able to give this detailed account because he was the manager of Ten Katsu's company then.

Sorcar himself was not unaware of his fame as a magician and throughout the travelogue he skilfully conveys to his readers that he is not an ordinary tourist. When on arrival at Hong Kong, all Indian travellers had to visit the Thomas Cook company office since there was a tie up with Indian banks and letters from home had to be picked up there. Sorcar faced a problem almost immediately because of the English spelling of his name. The situation could be resolved only when he produced a letter from the Governor of Bengal, with its official seal with his name inscribed. Its effect was immediate since the official, out of fear of the official seal, became very cordial. Sorcar also informs his readers that another reason for the official's softened attitude was because the *Morning Post* had carried an article about the life of an Indian magician. When he realised that he was face to face with a celebrity, the official became 'effusive, praising Indian magic and hoping for a pass for a show at the Queens theatre that night'.[56]

Sorcar in the course of his travelogue describes all the Indians he met during his sojourn and warmly refers to their hospitality – Sahay, Rashbehari Bose, Sati Devi who was Sahay's wife and C.R. Das's daughter and describes how they were supportive of all the students who stay at the two hotels – Asia Lodge in Tokyo by Bose and India Lodge in Kobe by Sahay.

> The benefit that these lodges had for the Indian students in Japan was incalculable, since initially Indians invariably fell ill after eating Japanese food, especially rice and fish . . . In the lodge food was made with Indian rice and Indian spices and oils (haldi, ghee and mustard oil), under the direction of Sati Debi . . . Mr Sahay also made sure that the students who stayed at the Lodge got the best opportunity regarding application for jobs in Japanese companies or securing positions in different Japanese universities.[57]

Sorcar also met Raja Mahendra Pratap at the Sahay's Voice of India office and was very impressed by 'the believer in universal brotherhood' a man 'who had rejected his life of luxury to follow his ideals (of World Federation) and had become a pauper in the process.'[58]

After Kobe, Sorcar travelled through different cities of Japan, Moji, Shimonoseki, Osaka, Takarazuka, Nagoya, Kioto, Yokohama, Nara, Fuji and then arrived at the capital Tokyo. He concluded that Japan was the epitome of beauty in the world. It was as if the Creator had been pleased to endow the tiny island with the entire world's bouquet of beauty.

Not only that, Japan which was smaller than Bengal in land area, had achieved so much. There is a however a subtle irony when he points out that though more unique than India it is less authentic. 'The trees here are full of flowers and fruits but the flowers have no smell, there are dogs but they don't bark, children don't cry . . . there are beautiful birds everywhere but they don't sing. Amazing!'

Sorcar was thrilled to meet the veteran Japanese magician Ten Katsu as corroborated by Ishikawa, since though she had more or less retired from performance and it was her daughter who performed most of the tricks yet the audience came from far and wide to watch her. Ten Katsu was charming to Sorcar, spending time with him and showing him all her magician tools. Sorcar was thrilled that in an interview to the press, she described Sorcar as 'the greatest of all the magicians who visited Japan from India'. It gave him great pleasure that she showed him all her magician's tools.[59]

In 1935, Kshitish Chandra Bandopadhyay, a self-professed globetrotter went on a tour of China on a bicycle which he described in a travelogue in *Bharatvarsha* (1937). It appears that the focus of his travels was to go where few men dare to venture, so though passing through large towns was necessary for gathering resources, they appeared uninteresting and uninspiring. His description of his stay in Peking in this article is strangely myopic and unlike other travellers his observations are scattered and vague. He writes:

> There is not much to see in Peking other than a few temples and an ancient palace. Of the temples the Lama temple is famous. I was intrigued to see at the entrance of the Buddhist temples some letters which appeared to me as Devanagari but I could only decipher a few letters. On top of the Peking mountain I noted the presence of a temple where the goddess deity had many hands. I could not make out who the goddess was. Most Chinese are Buddhists or Confucians but almost all of them worship goddesses like the Hindus.

Bandopadhyay had stopped in Peking to get a permission to travel into Outer Mongolia but then decided to go through Inner Mongolia via Kalgan which was the entry gate into Mongolia. 'I proceeded to Kalgan on my bicycle on very poor roads which were full of stones and very mountainous. Most of the roads in China were in this state and in some areas there were no roads at all'.[60] It was at this point when his bicycle was hit by a bullet. He fell unconscious and when he came to, he discovered that he was in a tiny room on a mountain lying on a hospital bed and next to him standing on guard was a uniformed Chinese soldier. Realising that he was not among dacoits, he demanded to be taken to meet their leader. When he was taken to the Captain's room, he noticed that behind the captain's desk were pictures of Lenin and Stalin. He writes:

> Realizing that my captors were Communists I felt a glimmer of hope that I might be able to escape death after all. The Captain indicated that I should sit in the chair before him. Then he asked me in English if I was from India and what the purpose of my visit was and if I could prove that I was not a government spy.

Bandopadhyay showed him his identity papers and a letter from Mahatma Gandhi appreciating his feat of travelling through China on a bicycle. Bandopadhyay was relieved that the reaction to the letter was most gratifying since the Captain immediately set him free saying that he had deep respect for the Mahatma. He also came to know that the man was highly educated and it was his disillusionment with the present government of China that had led him to becoming a revolutionary.[61]

Bandopadhyay then made a fresh start on a new bicycle towards Manchuria and Korea. The next set of articles written by him was based on his travels in the Philippines. Horrors awaited him when the ship carrying him from Yokohama landed amidst a storm on sea at the port of Manila. Though Bandopadhyay had a valid visa, he was not allowed to disembark but was sent to a prison on a small island. After a meagre and unappetising meal and a disturbed night's sleep, he was produced in the immigration office. The passport officer gave him permission to enter Manila, but the official wanted a bribe which he had to reluctantly pay since the only domiciled Indian he knew at Manila, Dr Dhirendranath Roy, refused to pay his bail. It was the Sikh community which came to his rescue providing him lodging and food at the local Gurdwara during his stay. Bandopadhyay's mission made him quite a few fans in Manila and some students came to meet him and take him sightseeing. Some local journalists also came to visit him to question him about his project as well as ask questions about the Mahatma and the Poet Tagore, who were well known among the educated elite. 'It is because of these two sons of Bharat', he wrote, 'that all other Indians get respect abroad'.[62] After a few days' stay in Manila, the writer moved towards a tiny valley Baguio where he spent a pleasant time making new friends. Bandopadhyay has praises for the educational and administrative changes introduced by the Americans 'ending a 400-year-old oppressive rule by the Spanish . . . with improvements in education and infrastructure, along with self-rule'.[63]

Tourism with a difference: in search of God and other things

Traditionally, the only reasons when travel was approved and encouraged in India was when it concerned physical and spiritual well-being, i.e. change of air and for pilgrimage. When Bengalis started travelling to the west with the onset of colonial rule, it was for neither. But with the travel to the other countries of Asia, and the prospect of visiting Buddhist monuments, a renewed interest in pilgrimage, albeit with a difference, was seen among the Bengali travellers. I have discussed this in detail in Chapter 6. In this section, I look at travelogues which were slightly different from descriptions of tourist spots or people they met in the countries they were touring in.

Paresh Chandra Sen, posted in Burma as a schoolteacher, embarks, with his student Mong Ba Han, on a journey into a remote part of the country, not usually traversed by tourists for a double purpose of adventure and visiting a tribal fair at Saindhotoya at the foothills of Machhagiri or the Arakan mountains and a Buddhist pilgrim spot there. A picture accompanies the text showing them astride two white Shan horses, Chetak (named after Rana Pratap's horse from 'the annals of Indian history') and Bandula, white animals which denoted good fortune and safe travel according to Ba Han. Sen describes the journey and writes about the different people he meets on the way.

> We travelled unencumbered by luggage and were hardly worried about food or rest. Ba Han said that in all villages of Burma there were Fungi chang (Buddhist monastic establishments) where all sorts of people, monks, sadhus, merchants, tourists and even thieves and dacoits found food and shelter. Also, in the fertile and fecund Suvarnabhoomi, the people, from the prosperous and potbellied

> merchants called Seths to the poor farmers, all were famed for their hospitality so we had no worries.[64]

On the way he reaches a village where Sen made a rest stop. The village of Thangayin was surrounded by a bamboo fence with a guard at the only entrance. Next to the main gate there was a small room where a large jar of water was kept for thirsty travellers. Sen found that to be a wonderful custom. He wrote, that 'it was said that King Piyadasi Athoka (Ashoka) had ordered for the building of 65,000 temples and drinking water rooms in his empire and today every village in Burma has these water rooms'.[65]He continued on his voyage and in Palin he describes the Emerald Lake which was dug in 1234 AD where many varieties of plants and animals were farmed. Sen found in the town along Palin river, almost a hundred irrigation canals which were said to have been constructed by labourers from Assam, Manipur, Kamrup and Shyamrajya (Thailand) who were brought as prisoners by the Burmese kings.[66] He also visited a silk and khadi (*unthanu*) handloom centre at Sinbu-Joun. 'It is a large centre. We do not know if Mahatma Gandhi came here or how he inspired the people of this remote place in Burma, but all the people here, rich, poor, educated and illiterate, wear *khadi*'.[67]

Another travel writer has a unique style. The name has been withheld and the author calls himself Shou or Sourindra. Whether 'Sangeet Pathik' (Musical Traveller) could be the work of Sourindra Mohon Tagore, the noted musicologist who not only wrote on music theory but also edited an encyclopaedia on world music, is pure speculation on my part. As stated by the author in the preface:

> the intention of the writer is to describe the development, decline, and changes in music in the different countries that he witnessed during his travels. It is not that he will not comment on the places he visits, the people he meets or describe their political or economic condition, but he will concentrate more on the music systems of those countries and compare them to the Indian as well as convey the tunes through the Bengali notation system.[68]

What is not clear from the travelogue is whether the whole journey that is described is an imaginative musical journey or a real one. Why it could be Sourindro Mohan Tagore is because his 'Hindu Music' first published in *Hindoo Patriot* in 1874 and later included in his magnum opus *Hindu Music from Various Authors*[69] (1875) is an analytical work on the relation of Indian music with that of other countries from writings of music scholars of different countries. So, Tagore had in his hand, so to speak, analytical details of Chinese music and its connections with Indian classical. Tagore was also recipient of the Knight of the First Class of the Imperial order of the 'Paou Seng' or the Precious Star, China, among many other honours as the introduction of the book shows.

The first two issues of the serialised essay describe how the traveller fell into difficulties and somehow managed to reach a country he did not know the name of. When he came to his senses, he found himself on the outskirts of a town with people who could neither understand him nor he them. They kept laughing at his distressed appearance not understanding that he was in need of food and shelter. Just when the situation seemed dismal, he saw a rider approaching in western clothes. Realising that he would be able to make himself understood to the Englishman, the writer stood in front of the approaching horse. To his surprise, the man who got off his horse greeted him warmly and asked him when he had arrived. The distressed traveller was overwhelmed by the Englishman's hospitality who then handed him a letter which to his surprise held the crest of his esteemed elder brother. It was amazing to him that he who had forsaken the sanctuary of his brother's loving home and embarked on a world voyage and landed up in this land after travelling through difficult terrains and suffering from starvation for many days, he had re-established connections with his family in this bizarre manner.[70] There are no further biographical details in the articles, so one cannot really guess who he is. He then came to know from the Englishman in whose company he travelled into the city that he had landed in Chua Chu, in China, which was in his words 'a civilization which was the most ancient, a country whose people battled traditionalism and superstitions to maintain their ancient culture and independence', and the people who, 'despite revolutionary changes' had been able to maintain their age old social and political conventions. It was a land with similarities and dissimilarities with his own, a 'land of Confucius and Fo (with whom some find similarities with our great god Shiva), a country whose people despite their many faults, shortcomings, and their cruel behaviour towards me,[71] possessed excellent qualities.' What was admirable to the writer was not only their legendary ability to work hard, but whose 'patriotism was their only wealth, respect for parents only religion and whose good behaviour was the only devotion'.[72]

After recuperating at the home of his rescuer, the writer then embarked on his quest for culture in the land. Realising that the best way to understand a country was through mastering their language, Sourindro started on the difficult task of learning Chinese. In the third issue of the article, the writer describes the process through which pictorial depiction of words was transformed into a scientific and complex language.[73] In this issue he refers to himself as Sourindra and says that depending on the number of marks, there are eighteen groups into which words are divided and the Chinese system was 'so perfect and systematic that it could have become a world script, all the different languages of the world could have used this script.' His real mission was of course, learning Chinese music and making it comprehensible for Indians.[74]

Analysing the works of Sir William Jones, Marshman, Barrow, Guignes and Freret, and De Pauw regarding the origins of the Chinese, Sourindro writes that he found out from his researches that the race which at first seemed so strange initially 'created a magical mist before his eyes were actually originated from the Indian race.' He subscribed this theory to William Jones who claimed that 'they originated from Indians as Chinas' . . . living in the periphery of the society since they were not a part of the Aryan civilization. Gradually they left the place of their origin and travelled beyond the Himalayas. According to Sourindro, 'Marshman followed Jones to point out similarities between the Chinese script and Devnagari, to prove their Hindu origin.'[75]

But Sourindro also acknowledges that this view is not acceptable to many others. He then paraphrases from John Barrow's *Travels in China* (published in 1804): that the Chinese were never Hindus. Jones' views are unacceptable and full of flaws. The outward appearance of the Chinese, their social structure, their language shows that they never considered themselves to be Hindus. The real difference was that the Hindus were slaves of religion, they could sacrifice their lives for it, but the Chinese by nature are not really religious minded. The Hindus are divided into many sects but the Chinese do not accept differences within their race. Sourindro writes that Barrow claimed that it was 'strange why Marshman's head was turned on reading

Canghe's dictionary of Devnagari words in Chinese, because if one reads the ancient poetry of the two countries- the Hindu *Ramayana* and the Chinese *Shi King* one can realise that there are no similarities in the languages.' There were others too according to Sourindro who wrote about Chinese origin. The famous French scholars, M. De Guignes and M. Freret, considered the Chinese to be of Egyptian origin. The first Roman Catholics to come to China claimed Jewish origin for the Chinese. The French scholar M. de Pauw refuted all these theories and said that the Chinese came from the highlands of Tatar country and belonged to the same race.[76]Sourindro says that one cannot judge which scholar is correct but says that Herodotus' view that there are similarities between the Chinese and the Scythians may be true because one can see similarities in the beliefs. The Chinese have faith in the Scythian dragons and snakes. Also, many Chinese towns appear like Tatar camps with their mud walls, as if still protecting the citizens from marauding tribes or ferocious tigers which proves connections with the Tatars. Sourindro concludes that the deep respect that the Chinese had for their forefathers and the faith in their old traditions led them to reject Aryan customs and practices and leave the territory under Aryan control. These traditions the Chinese have maintained till the present times. Their mistrust of foreigners is another relic from that past. Some people try to deny the connections by citing the differences in appearance, but this is hardly acceptable if one considers the Adivasi tribes still living today. The hill people of Santhali origin, in Manipur, Assam, Bhutan and Himalayan regions are very similar in appearance to the Chinese.[77]

Another travelogue by the editor of *Mahila* called Amader Bhraman Brittanto (Our travels), written by Girish Chandra Sen, stands out for documentation of the spread of Brahmoism in different parts of India and Burma.[78] This article also provides a picture of the Bengali Brahmo community in Rangoon. Sen refers to Pushpamala Debi, a resident of Rangoon whose travelogues were serially published in the same magazine in 1903 and which I have discussed later as well as the prayer services he attended in different Brahmo households like that of Purna Chandra Sen, the famous barrister domiciled there.[79] The writer further mentions the service and lecture held at the Rangoon Brahmo Samaj as well as in the Bengal club in Rangoon.

Comparison with India and Indians

All the travelogues compare what they see with India and the people they encounter with Indians. Since I am unable to discuss all the instances, I only provide a few cameos. Paresh Chandra Sen during his travels enjoyed some Burmese cultural performances which he described in the article.

> We watched a play and, in the audience, which comprised of men and women I noticed a group of young women . . . with long hair reaching down to their feet. I had read *Thakurmar Jhuli* (Grandmother's Tales) in my childhood where the merchant's son travels with a fleet of seven ships in search of princess *Keshavati* whose hair touched her feet. I wonder if his fleet had docked at the port of these Burmese Keshavatis.[80]

On reaching Siddhatoya, Sen enjoyed the hospitality of Ba Thu, Ba Han's brother. Sen wrote that he was touched by the thoughtfulness of the family because of the food issues he had. Ba Thu had arranged that his food would be cooked by a Manipuri Brahmin because, in Sen's words, 'though the Burmese were followers of the religion which says that non-violence was of greatest value, they eat all the food that a Hindu shuns like meats from cows and pigs without batting an eyelid.'[81]

Subimal Chandra Sarkar describes the Malayans as mainly of Mongoloid origin with high cheekbones and skin colour varying from fair to dark. There was mixture of racial blood of Philippines, Indo-China, Thailand, Sumatra through colonization or population movements. Sarkar considered Malayans to be sophisticated and leisure loving, and from his visit to a Malaya village he says that, 'most houses have beautiful gardens in front and the houses are raised on stilts.' The Malayans according to him have very good dress sense . . . and unlike the Muslim women in our country, Malayan women are not segregated behind the veil. But it is unfortunate that the general health of the Malayans is poor due to the ravaging malarial disease. 'Most people have a pasty complexion and suffer like Bengalis from indigestion and liver damage.' The majority of Malayans are farmers producing mainly rice, bananas and coconuts. They are less inclined towards industries like Indians. Sarkar concludes that 'the country is prospering with Chinese and Indian workers and one can hardly see Malayans in the cities.'[82]

Benoy Kumar Sarkar, in describing the city of Tokyo, feels a connect with India, at times Tokyo resembles Poona and at times Bengal. Once while entering a Japanese hotel, Sarkar felt as if he was entering a hotel in Gowalando (a small town in Bengal). A maid took him to a small cottage with low tiled roof in which the walls and floors were of wood and paper. Sarkar felt as if he was in a dreamland. Taking off his shoes Sarkar sat down on cushions, crosslegged which he knew was considered a little vulgar by the Japanese who kneel on a cushion. 'It was raining outside and there was no lamp inside the room. The rain pattered on the tiled roof and drained onto the ground. Sitting on the mat and looking around I wondered at how such a peaceful place could exist in a capital city. Is Japan really competing with Europe and American cities, London or New York? It felt as if I was in a rural hut in East Bengal.'[83]

P.C. Sorcar in his *Travelling to Japan* compared Singapore's trade district with Clive Street of Calcutta and the railway system with that of Indian railways. He also compares the policemen in Hong Kong with those in India. Majority of policemen in Hong Kong are Punjabis who are the greatest friends of Indians. In behaviour they are similar to the Punjabi Taxi drivers of Calcutta whereas policemen in Calcutta are unfriendly. In Hong Kong they are so friendly that they even organised a felicitation ceremony followed by a sumptuous dinner for him.[84]

Most Indians travelling abroad were deprived from tasting all the local delicacies by their food inhibitions. Some express their distaste for the local cuisine blatantly, while others express their inability to savour them as their own drawbacks. Sorcar describes humorously the difficulties he faced when he was cordially invited to dinner at his friend Chung Sih Fuh's house.

> My new friend organised a veritable banquet of fried cockroach, frog soup, pork and snake soup-chow chow most of which I could not eat. I could eat only rice, boiled duck eggs and prawn fries. Realising that my friend was very hurt at my refusal to taste the delicacies, I said that I was inhibited by my yogic practices. I was just thankful that he didn't question why I was permitted to eat prawn and not the rest.[85]

Sorcar realised during his stay in Japan that one of the real reasons why Japan was so successful was because they were able to forget differences among themselves and make all Japanese their own. Otherwise how could a country, as small as Bengal, become the world's most powerful nation. They inspired the ideal of humanity within themselves which according to Sorcar, Bengalis could not achieve. 'We have,' he writes, 'created barriers amongst ourselves over trifles and small ambitions and have become self-defeating.– Isn't it time that they become Bengal's and India's ideal in culture, art and patriotism? Or will they always be considered "uncivilized" and "young".'[86]

Colonial collaborator, patriotic nationalist or a universalist observer?

Wartime travels are strikingly different since these writers are part of the British Indian army or its extended constituents and they are all proud of their association with a profession for which Bengalis were hardly ever thought to be fit. Ashutosh Roy on his trip to Basra (1915 – written in 1919) tried to make his article attractive by calling it the 'Autobiography of a War Prisoner',[87] but in reality, the description reveals his pride in being a part of a victorious side and doesn't write about being a prisoner. Hemendra Prasad Ghosh's 'On the Battle-field', in *Bharatvarsha*[88], is even more interesting because he is describing a war front in France which he visits for 'a lifetime-experience' and though he describes in detail about the battlefield, new war methods, Indian soldiers on the battlefield specially one from Punjab with whom he has a conversation, Ghosh cannot really be called a war correspondent since it is obvious that his travel to France is for some other purpose and his visit to the war front is incidental and accidental.

When the travelogue is by a soldier, it was probably very well received since Bengali soldiers were far and in between which made travel writing by them a rare commodity. It also had a feel-good factor and went some way to fight the stigma that Bengalis considered themselves to possess which was lack of courage which made them poor soldiers. Durgadas Bandopadhyay,[89] a soldier of the British army, travelled from his post at Hansi in Punjab to Burma in 1853 at a time when, in his words, Burma was literally a '*moger muluk*', a foreign land where very few Bengalis travelled by ship to. Bandopadhyay convinced his wailing mother that travel to Burma would not only further him in his career and satisfy his lust for seeing new lands but also that it was a safe time to travel there since there was no war going on there.[90] Bandopadhyay in his travel narrative recalls the fuss that the high-caste Hindu soldiers made on board the ship to Burma since they claimed that 'the water was contaminated. In order to prevent a mutiny, the British government arranged for large new drums to be brought onto the ship with water from the Bhagirathi'.[91] Since he is writing this travelogue from memory, many years after his actual travel, he describes those attributes of the people that struck him as special. But there is a derisive attitude as if he did not enjoy his assignment in a land whose people he did not feel connected to. While describing the dresses he refers to the tattoos that he noticed on their bodies 'which made them seem to be wearing a blue dress from far, even when they were actually naked'.[92] He was very scathing when he described the food habits of the Burmese people.

> Their food is rather terrible, they rot their fish into a paste called *napi* and though it has an awful smell . . . the Mogs consider it a delicacy. They use *napi* as a seasoning for all their cooking which involves the use of leaves of all fruit trees,

> boiled and salted. There is nothing that the Mogs will not eat, no bird whose flesh they do not eat and no land or sea animal which does not end up on their table . . . Our regiment at one time faced an epidemic by which two to four horses died every day. From the morning we would notice almost two hundred hungry Mogs, waiting with large axes to pick up the dead horses that were thrown out from the stables. Once when an elephant died, they cut it up and distributed it among each other . . . They are very fond of rice and . . . each morning I would see whole families sit around a meal consisting of rice and boiled leaves.[93]

Kedarnath Bandopadhyay, right after his voyage to China during the Boxer rebellion, had written in two articles in *Bharati* in 1903, but instead of details about China he seems advocating women's education for India.[94] Many years later, in 'Memories of China' published in *Bichitra*, Bandopadhyay is more forthcoming about his stay and actually reveals a subtle anti-colonial perspective in the ironical way he refers to the presence of the Indian army in China in 1900, but his sympathy for the predicament of the Chinese is overshadowed by his admiration for the patriotism of the Japanese. 'It is in the imminent contest between China and Japan that my memories have become fresh', Bandopadhyay writes in 1933.

> It was so long ago – almost thirty years have passed since the start of the Russo-Japanese war in February 1900 when we reached Tientsin in northern China. All the white people of the world were determined in 1900 to campaign against China since the latter could not stand the presence (he uses the Bengali proverb of not being able to stand the smell of) of foreigners in their country. They were showing their disgust of the missionary presence and their teachings. The Chinese are a very conservative race and like to live steeped within their traditional ideas and practices. They can't stand interference by outsiders since they do not believe that others might know better than them . . . they don't realise that for great men spreading knowledge and removing darkness is imperative. When does a patient ever consent to a surgery? One has to force it on him for his improvement. Not able to prevent the interference, the evil men had resorted to violence. In retaliation all the white races became red with anger and led a campaign to China to perform the surgery. In that context, good people like us too were called upon. Our intention was not to give up our lives on this campaign but rather to save ourselves so that we may return home intact. So, we called upon different gods – Ram, Allah, Durga or Kali and sent them petitions before stepping forth. The fear in our voices probably reached the gods because when we reached, we saw that large numbers of Chinese had been dispatched to Heaven, thereby major part of the exercise was complete and . . . only strategies and policies were being discussed to score points against each other.[95]

'We entered the well decorated homes that had been abandoned by the fleeing Chinese and ensconced ourselves in their comfortable beds'. This statement shows sensitivity to the systematic defilement of Chinese 'enclosed, sanctified spaces' that later historians like Julia Lovell talk about. Lovell writes that, 'Privates played hockey around the dynasty's most sacred temples, picked over the private apartments of the emperor and empress, and lolled about on the imperial throne. Captured on Kodak re-loadables, their sacrilegious actions thrilled audiences at home'.[96] This 'thrill' is definitely tinged with sadness in Bandopadhyay's writing at least, where the excesses of the 'foreign soldiers' of which he was a part of, is written with irony,

> We were the officials of the king's race, no effort was left unturned to provide our rations and even comforts . . . so that homesickness did not make inroads into our minds . . . we took to visiting clubs and tennis courts. The 'off-time' also coincided with weekly tea-parties and war-camp became a luxury resort. The only problem was with followers and servants. . . So we had to employ Chinese boys . . . the other interesting thing was even those Indians who found reading a great chore, became poets here, as they sent letters back home on mail day on the special Chinese parchment . . . But of course, good days never last long. The Russo-Japanese war jolted everyone from their slumber.[97]

He writes about Okumura, a young boy, he had mentioned even in his 1903 article. The youth came to visit him with his mother at the onset of war, requesting him to write a letter in his favour so that his government would allow him to fight in the war. Though the author along with his friend, Suresh Chandra Majumdar, tried to dissuade him saying that his shop was excuse enough to avoid joining up, the boy's mother pointed out that she had another younger son to help out in the shop and that shouldn't stop her son from serving his country. Bandopadhyay was astounded at the attitude of the boy and his mother and wrote his petition so that Okumura could join the army. His friend Suresh pointed out satirically that unlike the Bengalis, the Japanese ambition was not to be a Rs 25 salary clerk and avoid military service. They have a country of their own serving which is their heart's desire. . . Bandopadhyay was stunned by the joy Okumura showed when he was handed his petition that he be allowed to fight for his country. Bandopadhyay felt regret at seeing his joy realising that Indians don't know what country means. They fight over a small piece of land and are willing to hand over large fortunes to preserve it and yet this 19 year old boy is handing over his young head to his country that too with his mother's support. Bandopadhyay wondered of it was a dream or was he reading fiction?[98]

Banerjee suffered terribly from guilt at having helped to send a young boy to his death, though he expresses great admiration for the way the Japanese were able to win over the Russians. He mused that when Japanese fight wars, they do it for victory, not to return home safely, they do not believe in saving themselves in combat. Honourable retreat is anathema to them. This was probably considered as foolish by the greatest generals but it was this that won them the war against the Russians . . . Bandopadhyay had been so worried about young Okamura's safety that he was relieved when one day after a few months he received a picture postcard from Okamura with the inscription saying 'oh how great is the victory of Japan'.[99]

On the other hand, Charu Chandra Bandopadhyay, in *Chin Deshe* (In China) in *Bharati* in 1905,[100]betrays his sympathies for China, when he writes how he accompanied the English army as a senior clerk of the Commissariat 'when the countries of east and the west out of their pride as civilized nations blew the trumpets of war against China.' He was excited that he, the homebound Bengali was travelling to a far land to witness battle at first hand.[101] This journey becomes for him important not simply as a means of seeing a new country (with expenses paid) but also as an individual protest against the British imperial policy of stigmatising the Bengalis as wanting in courage and martial spirit.

> It is unfortunate that the English government has deprived the Bengali of the right to fight in war and have drummed into our ears for hundred years, the slanderous accusation of cowardice which has made us discredit our own abilities. I tested myself repeatedly by eagerly facing the battlefield and was reassured that though the sounds of battle thunder made me anxious, my heart stayed calm.[102]

Bandopadhyay was a part of the British Army but the very fact that he was 'kept away' from the battlefield due to a conspiracy on the part of the British gave him a sense of freedom to explore China and the Chinese.

> My only companion was a Chinese man Liang Fu, whom the English had employed as a spy. Ever since I came to know who he really was I was annoyed with his treachery which led him to sell out his country's secrets to a foreign nation. After all Bengalis have been making reparations for their treachery for more than a century. Liang Fu always tried to engage me in conversation and the more questions he asked me the more I would clam up. His small beady eyes would then light up like that of a wild cat and he would seem ferocious.[103]

The author then goes on to with the tale of how he noticed Liang Fu writing in Chinese in his room every day and then burning the sheets before going out. He was suspicious of him, so would try to follow him when he went out. But the Chinese man was too wily for him and would always manage to escape. One evening he found that Liang had left the papers on the table, probably by mistake and with the little Chinese that he knew Bandopadhyay could distinguish some words like Tish, love and autumn festival. He was mystified but was sure that there was something wrong. When the war ended with the Russians occupying Manchuria, the other foreign powers declared peace, making movement of soldiers outside the camp easier. Bandopadhyay had been feeling homesick and one day he got a letter from home informing him that his young wife had contracted plague and had died. Unable to share his grief with the other soldiers, Bandopadhyay took to taking long walks in the town to visit the Buddhist temples. One day he came upon an altercation between some Chinese and Europeans and one young Chinese girl gave him shelter and saved him from the wrath of the Europeans. When asked what her name was, she replied it was Tish. Then he realised that she was Liang's sister and she asked him to stay away from the camp during the autumn festival celebrations. Mystified Bandopadhyay returned to the camp determined to find out why. When the day of the festival dawned and he was debating whether to go the Camp officer to tell him to investigate Liang, he found Tish in the camp moving about surreptitiously. Asked what she was up to, she told him having fallen in love with him, she had come to save his life. Liang and she were Boxer patriots and planned to blow up the camp. They had placed dynamite in every room and had planned to blow themselves up as well. Bandopadhyay refused to let her do so and snatched the matches away from her. While he was debating what story to tell the commandant so that Tish might be saved, the Commander arrived to inform him that Liang had been caught red-handed trying to blow up the camp. Bandopadhyay then risked the wrath of Tish by making up the story that she had come to know of the plan and come to warn them, thereby making her a saviour. The Commandant was very pleased and agreed to let her go. Bandopadhyay then pacified Tish by deciding to marry her and bring her to India. He ends with the entreaty to his readers not to be angry with him for finding a life partner now that he had lost his wife.[104] This article was later published as a collection of stories called *Dhoopchhaya*, but it is difficult to understand if this essay is a fully or even partially imaginative one or not.

The story that Bandopadhyay writes may be part fictional and part true, but it captures the essence of the Boxer Uprising. It also traces the change in the mindset of the writer from a young man wanting adventure in a foreign land via a career in the army to sympathising with patriotic feelings of the Chinese siblings, fighting for deliverance from the 'foreign devils'. He is also unconsciously rallying sympathy between the people of two exploited peoples – Indians and Chinese, though he is a part of the team which has come to deliver the imprisoned westerners from the very people who he is ultimately siding with. There is in the end no sense of treachery for his masters since they are alien and he is able to wholeheartedly accept the Chinese woman as his wife out of a sense of respect that she was able to openly show her patriotism where he could not. The whole story turns around the main narrative that he had begun with – that of being a part of a powerful army going to save 8 powerful nations from the siege that the Boxers had laid on the Legation Quarters where 11 nations (America, Austria-Hungary, Belgium, Great Britain, France, Germany, Holland, Italy, Japan, Russia and Spain) were encircled. The fact that the Indian soldiers who formed the part of the eight-nation relief team were successful in lifting the siege was in the end less important for Bandopadhyay than expressing Asian solidarity with the Chinese rebels or at least one of them. Peter Fleming in his 1959 account of *The Siege at Peking*, points out that the desire to

> put an end to the spoliation of their country by the *yang kuei-tzu*, the foreign devils, the barbarians from without, was the ultimate cause for the 'peasants of North China', taking up 'their swords and spears and muskets'. Their Manchu rulers, being oppressive, extortionate and inept, were themselves alien; but the Boxer catchword was 'Protect the Ch'ing dynasty. Exterminate the Foreigners'. It was to this slogan that the masses rallied.[105]

It was this anti-foreigner sentiment that possibly appealed to Indians. Though these Bengalis were a minority in the British army, Anand Yang points out that these soldiers' tales may be surprising but not 'startling because the largest group of people from India who spent any extended period of time in China in the nineteenth century were military men' fighting in the two Anglo-Chinese wars (1839–1842, 1856–1860) and in the multinational force mobilised against the Boxers in 1900–1901.[106]

Another campaign of the British during the First World War which had a number of Bengalis participating was the Mesopotamia campaign of 1915. Mesopotamia became a focus in the Middle Eastern theatre of the First World War when the Allies represented by the British empire, troops from Britain, Australia, and vast majority from British India fought against the Central Powers – Germany, Austria-Hungary, Bulgaria and mostly the Ottoman Empire. The Anglo-Persian Oil company founded in 1908, following the discovery of an oilfield in Iran, had obtained exclusive rights to petroleum deposits throughout the Persian empire with some exceptions. In 1914, just before the war, the British government had contracted with the Company for oil for the Navy. Shortly after the European war started, the British sent a military force to protect Abadan, the site of one of the world's earliest oil refineries. British operational planning included landing troops in the Shatt-al-Arab. The reinforced

6th Poona Division, formed in 1903, following the Kitchener reforms in the Indian Army, led by Major General Barrett and then Major General Townshend, landed at Mesopotamia in November 1914 at Fao Landing. After a string of early successes, the 6th Division was delivered a setback at the Battle of Ctesiphono in November 1915. The Division then withdrew to Kut where Townshend made the decision to hold the city. After a lengthy siege by the Ottomans, Townshend surrendered in April 1916. A total of 10,061 troops and 3,238 followers were taken captive. Following the surrender, the garrisoned force conducted a forced march back to Anatolia. The suffering of the enlisted soldiers was particularly egregious and over 4,000 were taken captive.[107] Ashutosh Roy's *Autobiography of a War Prisoner* describes this incident.[108] Roy starts his travelogue with the caveat that it took him three years since his return from the terrible campaign to gather courage to reminisce about that time. He left for Bombay via Jhansi from Lucknow with a Treasurer and 23 camp followers by SS Arunkola of the British India Steam Navigation company, and crossing Aden, Muscat and Bushire finally docked in Basra. Giving a background to his story of Basra, Roy writes:

> Muscat is located near a mountain and there is a British army camp located in this healthy spot which is famous for its dates and the sweet dish *halwa*. On the sixth day we entered the mouth of Shatt al Arab river . . . The Anglo Persian Oil company is located here . . . and the first clashes with the Turks took place here. Initially our soldiers were not very successful here but when the armed Cruisers stormed in with cannons, then the Turks scattered like sheared grain. From there the Turks were chased into Basra from where they reassembled in Ahwaz and prepared for battle with Arab forces. On their retreat to Basra the Turks had sunk the two steamers in the hope of impeding the advancing British army.[109]

In Roy's descriptions, there is a distinct flavour of pride in being a part of a victorious imperialistic power. This is most evident during the descriptions of the battle with the Turks. But unlike the case of the Chinese, the Turkish soldiers don't seem to warrant much sympathy in Roy's writing, rather there is a belief in the inevitability of their defeat. He describes the war strategy of the Turks as being as ineffective as the Chinese strategy of 'holding up their round Buddha hats for protection against cannons' and the British success in 'winning over the local Arabs to help in the clearing of the river of debris left by the Turks to hamper the progress of the British war ships'.[110] Roy continues:

> Just 8/9 days before our arrival at Basra, heavy fighting between the English and the Turks took place at Saheba where the destiny of Mesopotamia was decided. If the outcome of the battle had been the other way round and the Turks had won instead of the English, the latter would probably have had to abandon their hopes of holding Mesopotamia. But what a glorious game the god of fortune played. The Turks lost so heavily in this battle that their future battles in different parts of Mesopotamia were also doomed. Our soldiers showed their bravery and unprecedented courage in the battle of Saheba which is praiseworthy and a matter of pride for us. To stand in waist-deep water for 4/5 hours in the face of a veritable rain of shelling in order to force the enemy back takes infinite fortitude and unbelievable courage.[111]

Comments like these enrich the description revealing his awareness of nuances of local politics as well as international ramifications. On their arrival at the occupied Turkish camp, Roy describes how the Turks, when they fled it, left everything intact making it easy for the British army to settle down there. Most of the Turks had fled from Basra but they soon heard rumours that a few dozens were moving around brazenly in the town hiding among the local Arabs, Armenians and Jews. The rich Armenians soon started making friendly overtures to the British commanders and started inviting the General to their homes. It is possible of course that this friendliness may have been genuine since it was obvious that they were most disgusted with the Turkish oppression and were willing to welcome the British with open arms.[112]

In the third part of the article, Roy describes how mines were identified in the Shatt al-Arab River and how the British troops were ordered to destroy them. Roy says that they had no idea about mines or how they were to be defused but they enthusiastically reached the river edge to learn how to. The ships were all removed from the region where the mine had been detected and they were instructed to shoot at a spot from the water's edge. They couldn't make out where the mine was but suddenly a loud bang was heard and the mud-filled water rose up almost twenty feet. A shout went out when they realised the mine had been destroyed.[113]

Roy is filled with pride of belonging to the 6th Division stationed at Ashar, though he claimed that he had no idea that the 6th Division would take the lead in the Mesopotamia war or that its name would remain carved in the history of the world. After almost one and half month halt at Ashar, they were ordered to move to Kurna under the leadership of General Fry. The author sailed with a full white regiment – the Norfolk Regiment who were guarded in front and at the back by two cruisers. The war ships looked very elegant, snow-white in colour, yet inside they carried the most fearful firearms and cannons. They were also accompanied by some other smaller war-supply carriers and an aeroplane flew low above us to provide information about the enemy sighting. The Arab women and children who had lined up along the river to watch the movement of troops were frightened by the monster-like plane and ran away to the shelter of their villages. It was an amazing sight. Roy felt as if he had been transported into the world of Arabian novels where *jins* and demons could carry away humans from their safe havens. They reached Kurna on the third day and were faced with Turkish shelling. Roy writes that 'this was not the hollow cannon firing for honoured guests, this was a purposeful presence of the god of death Yama'. While the shelling continued, an observation post was set up on the banks of the Tigris river. Gradually the shelling stopped for the day and the ships lowered their anchor midstream of the Tigris–Euphrates river. The next morning the Turkish *marhaba* was resumed with more ferocity. Finally, the British retaliated from the cruiser. Unlike the Turkish attacks this one found their mark and created mayhem in the Turkish camp. The British army became aware of the complete devastation of the soldiers in the enemy camp when within a few hours the white flag was hoisted. Then the British troops moved in mahellas (boats) towards the Turkish army and brought back hundreds of prisoners. A total of 700 Arab and Turks were taken prisoners that day by the British.[114]

The travelogue claims to be an autobiography of a prisoner of war possibly supposed to describe the retreat of the British army to Anatolia but is really the story of a victorious campaign where the British army, Roy included, overcomes difficulty to pursue the Turks to Amara. The three-part article ends with the British army pursuing the fleeing Turkish army by river made hazardous by the mines they placed in the waters and finally their halt at Ezra's tomb. It is tragic that this fascinating series was not continued by *Bharatvarsha*.

More of an autobiography of a war prisoner is the memoir of Sitanath Bhatta which was published in *Manasi o Marmabani*, rewritten by Krishna Behari Roy.[115] Roy follows the adventures of Sitanath Bhatta, employed in the Supply and Transport Department of the Indian Government, who was sent to Mesopotamia as a clerk during the siege of Kut-al- Amara. The siege of Kut-al-Amara took place between 7th December 1915 and 29th April 1916, when the British Indian garrison was besieged at Kut followed by the surrender of the 6th Poona battalion. One follows his experiences on the battlefield of Kut, the trials and tribulations of the English and Indian soldiers under Turkish attack from three sides. Bhatta refers to both Major General Patrick Hehir, heading the medical facilities, and Lieutenant Colonel Gerard Leachman, but not by name. Bhatta's description of the battle takes a loyalist line, as a British soldier and was soon captured by the Ottoman forces who in his eyes were devils incarnate.

> they (the Turkish soldiers) stationed themselves at a distance of ten miles from the English camp and targeted us with firearms at a furious pace. The melodious clash of the British war drums and the deep sounds of the war bugles echoed in the desert lands, the waters of the Tigris river and the distant horizon . . . All around us the well-equipped soldiers desperately tried to fulfil their duties. The incessant raining of British and Turkish armaments covered the skies . . . The food stuff that had been carried for the expedition was gradually being depleted and by February it was all gone and the camp faced starvation. On three sides the English camp was surrounded by the enemy and the only way the supplies could be brought in was by the river behind us. Those supplies which were airdropped every two to three days were hardly adequate for forty thousand brave soldiers. An attempt was made to send one ship with supplies to the camp but unfortunately it got grounded on a silted bank and could not proceed. . . . I was impressed by the English courage, commitment and tolerance which I perceived at first hand. From March every person at the camp was given a ration of three ounces of *atta* and some horse meat. With that meagre food in their bellies, the Englishmen showed their mettle in war. Every other war-supply was plentiful and the lack of food ultimately was the reason of defeat. On 28th April when the supplies finished the commander raised the flag declaring an armistice.[116]

On 30th April, the camp was invaded by Turkish soldiers who looted all the property of the soldiers of the English camp, including those of Bhatta who had to leave the camp dressed in pyjamas, shirt and socks and shoes. They were taken to Chamran prison on foot which was 70 miles away through the desert sands. Bhatta has described the journey to Chamran very evocatively where he describes how the lack of food, water and sleep kept slowing the prisoners down and the Turkish soldiers kept using hunters or the rifle-butt to hurry the straggling men along.

> I saw another interesting punishment in Turkey which shocked me, they would force the prisoner to take off his shoes and cane the bare soles. Many of us could not bear the pain of their torture nor the walk through the difficult terrain, and became ill. Some of us were taken to a hospital, but this was nothing like an English hospital, not even like the Calcutta Medical College, Campbell School

> or the Sambhu Nath Pandit hospital. All the patients, no matter what they suffered from were taken to a *hamam* for bathing. Then only a privileged few were given dry clothes to wear so one can surmise from this what the medical treatment would be like or how many patients would be able to join the human race on being released from that hospital. Having spent two and half years with the Turkish people I have realised only too well that their hearts are harder than stone, and they are without any kindness or compassion. They are very mercenary and treat people without money inhumanly . . . It is as if, barbarianism is their ornament and harsh torture their innate nature.[117]

Bhatta describes how he and his Indian compatriots paid their way out with money they had managed to hide in their clothes and reached Chamran prison camp finally. They stayed there for six days and then were transferred to Res-el-Am which was 700 miles away. From Chamran, the British and Indian officers were given a transport cart, though Bhatta being a subordinate clerk had to walk. They reached Res-el-Am on 3rd July where they stayed for six months. They were then transported by rail to Constantinople where he claims the Turkish soldiers submitted them to unspeakable torture.

> I broke into tears at times from the humiliation the soldiers inflicted on us with their satirical comments and abuses. I tried to keep my thoughts above my present situation by recalling sweet memories of time spent with my family . . .. In Constantinople we lived in half starvation and in tattered clothing. I didn't expect any better since the British officers too looked like Digambara sadhus wearing only a loincloth . . .. Mesopotamia is a beautiful city but we were too weak and starved to appreciate any of its beauty . . . In October 1918, we were transferred to another camp where we were given clothes and food by the British government through the consulate at Aleppo . . . thereby saving our lives. Finally, in November we were freed and sent to Egypt from where we came via Suez to Bombay. From Bombay I was able to send a telegram in the name of my son announcing my return to my country. For two and a half years I lived in different cities and war zones, and came into close contact with three strong independent nationalities – English, German and Turkish. Having studied their character and nature closely I have come to the following conclusion. The English are innately kind, compassionate and benevolent and they are by nature fair-minded. They cannot abide the preying on the weak but the other two nationalities do not have any of these good qualities. From the beginning of the war to the end, all the stories of atrocities perpetrated by the Turks and Germans that have been published in the newspapers were considered by many to be untrue or at least exaggerated. I can say strongly that the atrocities on the Belgians by the Germans and on the Armenians by the Turkish were all true just as the newspapers reported. We were eyewitness to the innocent Armenians who were sent to the gallows and some Indian soldiers rescued the infants who were hidden by the condemned men and women and were looking after them. However, the British government had not yet granted permission to bring the young Armenian children to India by the time I left Egypt so their future is still uncertain.[118]

These travel accounts by the soldiers, no matter where their sympathies lay, occupy an important position in understanding the Indian mind.

Appreciation of the dissimilar and engaging with the similar

Through the travel writings, one comes across two kinds of appreciation of the different countries visited. There is first of all a sense of wonder at all novelties and this is more evident in the writing in the first two decades of the 20th century. Appreciation of dissimilarity in dress, food, customs and cultural practices gradually change to stressing of connections. With the popularisation of the idea of Asian solidarity, the linkages and similarities began to be stressed. There is reflection of this not only in the magazine articles but also in Bengali literature. In Bibhuti Bhushan Bandopadhyay's novel *Moroner Donka Baje* (The Death Knell), two young men Bimal and Sureshwar, on their way to Singapore in search of livelihood, divert to Shanghai to offer their services during the Japanese invasion there.[119] This is in fact an imaginative redressing of what was considered to be the greatest drawback of Bengalis – courage and daring in travel and combat. Travelling to Asian lands had captured the imagination of Bengalis, though the actual number of Bengalis staying in other Asian countries was less compared to other Indians. There are references in the travelogues of meeting with ex-patriot Indians in the different countries and a serialised writing in *Modern Review* by Banarasidas[120] calls for linking the diaspora of the different Asian countries. There was also a sense of pride in sharing a common continental heritage with the two great nations of the 20th century: China and Japan. This initial pride soon turned to shock and dismay at the aggressive imperialistic ambitions of Japan in the 1940s and this finds expression in Bandopadhyay's novel. The sympathy expressed at the cold war machinery of the Japanese against the helpless Chinese evokes the repeated comparison with India as the great civilisation at the mercy of the ruthless coloniser.[121] But earlier in the century, it was Japan and China which evoked admiration as two great Asian powers who had developed greatly in comparison to the other Asian countries.

A close reading of the articles in the Bengali periodicals shows another interesting trend. When there are descriptions of the different countries of South-East and South Asia, there is both a detachment and an underlying condescension. Even when there is appreciation, especially of cultural artefacts or styles, there appears to be an involuntary expression of pride that much of it is borrowed from India, however different it may seem. Sometimes there are open comparisons to show the difference,[122] and at other times the similarities are highlighted to distinguish Asians from Europeans.[123] The situation is startlingly different when articles are on East Asia. There is an admiration where Japan is concerned, but the admiration is restrained and formal; in the case of China, there is sympathy and love for an ancient civilisation. In travel writing, admiration is expressed for the discipline and order of the Japanese way of life. At the turn of the century, a well-written account of travel to Japan, China and Java was by the Raja of Kapurthala, Jagatjit Singh in 1903, who unhesitatingly gave his favourable opinion regarding Japan as 'interesting', 'delightful' and the people possessing 'a charm of appearance and manner' while denigrating China and Java as un-praiseworthy. He described the Chinese as devoid of 'national ideals' and 'indifferent to the course of present events', while Javanese were, in his words, 'absolutely apathetic'.[124] In contrast to this royal dismissal of China and Java, the articles in the Bengali journals are kinder, focusing less on the 'material' and more on the spiritual strengths of each country. Tagore spoke about the great powers of concentration of the Japanese when he wrote about his visit there. He linked it to the influence of Buddhism as the term *Dhyani Japan* indicated. He was impressed by the discipline and patience of the people not only during the lectures organised for him but even in day-to-day life in various institutions, at the theatre and even in parks.[125] I would like to say in conclusion that the tradition which Bengalis are famous for today – that of travelling with family or friends every year to different places within the country and outside – has no doubt been fostered from the beginning of the 20th century by these travelogues and travel stories. The motives of the previous era are more or less lost now, but the imagination of the middle-class Bengali that had been fired by the descriptions of the lands and peoples of other parts of Asia still persist. They will be visible in every destination of Asia travelling on a shoestring budget quite like the pilgrims of yore.

Notes

1 In recent times, some travelogues of men and women travelling eastwards are being translated and documented. See among others, Anand A. Yang, ed., *Thirteen Months in China: A Subaltern Indian and the Colonial World,* Trans. by Yang, Kamal Sheel and Ranjana Sheel, New Delhi: Oxford University Press, 2017, Michel O'Sullivan's, 'Vernacular Capitalism and Intellectual History in a Gujarati Account of China, 1860–68 on the Travelogue of Damodar Ishwardas', *Journal of Asian Studies,* 2021, Translations of five travelogues on Japan by Jayati Gupta in *Travel Culture, Travel Writing and Bengali Women 1870–1940*, Oxon: Routledge, 2021, and Sarvani Gooptu, ed., *Wandering Women: Travel Writings in Bengali Periodicals 1900–1940,* Translations by Indrani Bose and Sarvani Gooptu (Forthcoming).

2 Jyotirindranath Tagore, Adhunik Japan: Felician Shaal er Phorashi Hoite *Bharati,* 32(1) (2) (3) (4) (5) (6), 1908.

3 Jyotirindranath Tagore, Lafcadio Hearn er Japan Chitra: Felicia Shaal er Phorashi hoite, *Bharati*, 32(7) (8) (9) (10), 1908.

4 Jyotindranath Tagore, Russiar Grand Duke Boris er shahit Shyam Rajye Bhraman, *Prabashi*, 10(4), 1910, pp. 345–348; Shyam Rajye Bhraman, *Prabashi*, 10(5), 1910, pp. 445–447; 10(6), 1910, pp. 546–549.

5 Jyotindranath Tagore, Shyam Rajye Bhraman, *Prabashi*, 10(4), 1910, pp. 445–446.

6 Jyotindranath Tagore, Shyam Rajye Bhraman, *Prabashi*, 10(6), 1910, p. 546.

7 Jyotirindranath Tagore, Engraj Barjito Bharat, *Sahitya*, 15(4), 1904, pp. 219–226; 15(5), pp. 285–291; 15(6), pp. 339–345; 15(8), pp. 478–482; 15(10), pp. 620–623.

8 Bibhuti Bhusan Bandopadhyay, Morubhumir desh Arabe, *Bangasri*, 2(5), 1935, pp. 659–65.

9 Bibhuti Bhushan Bandopadhyay, Vishwa Prakriti, Borneo Dviper Palli Anchale, *Bichitra*, 10(1)(2), 1936, pp. 163–168.

10 Prabhat Chattopadhyay, Tibbot o Chiner Shimanay, *Bangasri*, 2(2), 1936, pp. 630–637.

11 Suresh Chandra Bose, Brahmadeshe Padabroje Bhu Pradakshinkari Mr. Martini, *Bharatvarsha*, 10(1)(5), 1922, pp. 779–781.

12 D'Arcy Greig, *My Golden Flying Years: From 1918 over France, Through Iraq in the 1920s, to the Schneider Trophy Race of 1927*, Norman Franks, ed., London: Grub Street Publishing, 2011.

13 Suresh Chandra Bose, Brahmadeshe Padabroje Bhu Pradakshinkari Mr. Martin, *Bharatvarsha,* op. cit.

14 Dinendra Kumar Roy, Chiner Jaladashyuder Bombetegiri, *Masik Basumati*, 9(1)(3), 1930, pp. 524–533.

15 Himangshu Kumar Bose, Bibidha Sangraha, Brahmadesher prakitik Shoundorjyo, *Bichitra,* 2(2)(6), 1929, pp. 554–557.

16 Ta Pra Cha., Singhal Yatra, *Nabajiban,* 1(1), 1884, pp. 26–30.

17 Sailakumar Mukhopadhyay, Sikkim O Tibbote Baro din, *Bichitra,* 10(1)(4), 1936, pp. 548–553.

18 Rukmini Kanta Chakraborty, Singhal Bhraman, *Sadhana*, v. 2, pp. 48–49.

19 Satya Sundar Deb, Japan Prabashir Patra, *Mahila*, 9(3), 1903, p. 75.

20 Benoy Kumar Sarkar, Ek Shoptahe Ardha Japan, *Grihastha,* 8(8)(2), 1915, pp. 178–179.

21 Ashutosh Roy, Juddha bandir Atma Kahini, *Bharatvarsha*, 7(1)(6), 1919, p. 784.
22 Ibid.
23 Premadananda Sen, Brahma Prabashir Patra, *Bharati*, 31, 1907, pp. 432–433.
24 Suniti Kumar Chattopadhyay, Javadviper Pothe, *Prabashi*, 27(1)(6), p. 833.
25 Ibid., p. 834.
26 Keshab Chandra Gupta, Malay-Jatri, *Bharatvarsha*, 24(2)(1), 1936, p. 85.
27 Ibid., p. 87.
28 P.C. Sorcar, Japaner Pothe, *Bharatvarsha*, 25(1)(4), 1937, pp. 582–584.
29 Keshab Chandra Gupta, Malay-Jatri, op. cit., p. 88.
30 Ibid., pp. 585–586.
31 Ibid., p. 586.
32 Magician P.C. Sorcar, Japaner Pothe, op. cit., p. 587.
33 Ibid., p. 588.
34 Ibid., pp. 588–589.
35 Ibid., pp. 697–698.
36 P.C. Sorcar, Japaner Pothe, *Bharatvarsha*, 25(2)(1), 1937, pp. 62–63.
37 Satya Sundar Deb, ibid.
38 Ashutosh Roy, Juddha bandir Atma Kahini, *Bharatvarsha,* 7(2)(2), 1919, p. 195.
39 Ibid., pp. 196–197.
40 Ashutosh Roy, Juddha bandir Atma Kahini, *Bharatvarsha,* 7(2)(4), 1919, p. 514.
41 Benoy Kumar Sarkar, Swadhin Ashiar Rajdhani, *Grihastha,* 7(7)(3), 1915, p. 217.
42 Ibid., pp. 218–219.
43 Ibid., p. 220.
44 Ibid., p. 230.
45 Ibid., pp. 232–233.
46 Ibid., pp. 234–235.
47 Benoy Kumar Sarkar, Ek saptahe ardha Japan, *Grihastha,* 7(7)(2), 1915, pp. 167–189.
48 Benoy Kumar Sarkar, Nabin Asiar Janmadata: Asiar Manchester, *Grihastha*, 7(7)(5), 1915, pp. 411–425.
49 Hemendralal Roy, Shyamrajya, *Prabashi*, 24(2)(1), 1924, pp. 64–73.
50 Subimal Chandra Sarkar, Malayer Pothe, *Bangalakshmi*, 6(5), 1930, p. 351.
51 Ibid., pp. 351–355.
52 Subimal Chandra Sarkar, Malayer Pathe, *Bangalakshmi*, 6(5), 1930, p. 354.
53 P.C. Sorcar, Japaner Pothe, *Bharatvarsha*, 26(1)(1), 1937, pp. 62–69.
54 Ibid., p. 66.
55 Gasho Ishikawa, Sorcar in Japan, The International Library of the Great P.C. Sorcar, 2019, www.pcsorcarmagician.com/article4.php, accessed on 20.05.19.
56 P.C. Sorcar, Japaner Pothe, *Bharatvarsha*, 25(1)(5), 1937, pp. 692–698.
57 Ibid., pp. 66–67.
58 Ibid., p. 67.
59 P.C. Sorcar, Japaner Pothe, *Bharatvarsha*, 26(1)(5), 1938, pp. 678–679.
60 Kshitish Chandra Bandopadhyay, Cheena Doshyuderhaate, *Bharatvarsha*, 26 (1)(2), 1938, pp. 261–262.
61 Kshitish Chandra Bandopadhyay, Cheena Doshyuderhaate, op cit., pp. 264–65.
62 Kshitish Chandra Bandopadhyay, Philippine e Bangali Porjyotok, *Bharatvarsha,* 26(1)(5), 1938, pp. 747–751.
63 Kshitish Chandra Bandopadhyay, Philippine e Bangali Porjyotok, *Bharatvarsha,* 26(2)(3), 1938, pp. 452–453.
64 Paresh Chandra Sen, Machhagirir paadamoole, *Bharatvarsha,* 15(1)(5), 1927, p. 782.
65 Ibid., p. 783.
66 Ibid., p. 785.
67 Ibid.
68 Sri Shou/Sri Sourindra.. (name withheld, possibly Sourindra Mohun Tagore), Sangeet Pathik., *Aryadarshan,* 1(1), 1874, p. 51.
69 Sourindro Mohun Tagore, *Hindu Music from Various Authors*, Calcutta: I.C. Bose and Company, 1882 (2nd ed.), https://archive.org/details/cu31924022411650, accessed on 20.10.19.
70 Sri Shou., Sangeet Pathik., op. cit., 1(3), p. 139.

71 They kept laughing at him when he regained his consciousness. Ibid., p. 135.
72 Ibid., p. 140.
73 Sri Shou., Sangeet Pathik., op. cit., 1(4), pp. 192–199.
74 Details of this are in Chapter 4.
75 Ibid., p. 435.
76 Ibid., p. 436.
77 Ibid., p. 439.
78 Anonymous (possibly editor Girish Chandra Sen), Amader Bhraman Brittanto: Tangu o Fiyu nagar, *Mahila,* 13(1), 1907, pp. 19–20.
79 Anonymous (Girish Chandra Sen), Amader Bhraman Brittanto: Rangoon nagar, *Mahila,* 13(4), 1907, pp. 106–107.
80 Paresh Chandra Sen, Machchagirir Padamule, *Bharatvarsha*, 15(1)(5), 1927, p. 785.
81 Paresh Chandra Sen, op cit., p. 788.
82 Subimal Chandra Sarkar, Malayer Pathe, *Bangalakshmi*, 6(5), 1337 BS (1930), p. 355.
83 Benoy Kumar Sarkar, op cit., pp. 226–227.
84 P.C. Sorcar, Japaner Pothe *Bharatvarsha*, 26(1)(5), 1938, p. 696.
85 Ibid.
86 P.C. Sircar, op cit., 26(1)(1), pp. 72–73.
87 Ashutosh Roy, Juddhabandir Atmakahini, *Bharatvarsha*, 7(1)(6), 1919, pp. 782–785.
88 Hemendra Prasad Ghosh, Juddha Kshetre, *Bharatvarsha*, 7(2)(1), 1919, pp. 53–60.
89 Durgadas Bandopadhayay, Amar Jiboncharit, *Janmabhumi*, 1(7), 1(8), 1891, pp. 365–371; 462–471.
90 Durgadas Bandopadhayay, Amar Jiboncharit, *Janmabhumi,* 1(8), 1891, p. 464.
91 Ibid., p. 465.
92 Ibid., pp. 467–468.
93 Ibid., p. 468.
94 Kedarnath Bandopadhyay, Chin Prabashir Patra (1&2), *Bharati,* 27(12), 28(1), 1903–1904, pp. 1186–1193; pp. 46–61.
95 Kedarnath Bandopadhyay, Chiner Smriti, *Bichitra*, 6(2)(6), 1933, p. 732.
96 Julia Lovell, *The Opium War: Drugs, Dreams and the Making of China*, London: Picador, 2011, p. 279.
97 Ibid., p. 733.
98 Ibid., pp. 735–736.
99 Ibid., p. 737.
100 Charu Chandra Bandopadhyay, Chin Deshe, *Bharati*, pp. 310–316.
101 Ibid.
102 Ibid.
103 Ibid.
104 Ibid., pp. 310–316.
105 Peter Fleming, *The Siege at Peking*, London: Rupert Hart-Davis, 1959, pp. 23–24.
106 Anand A. Yang, 'China in the Popular Imagination: Images of Chin in North India at the Turn of the Twentieth Century', in Tansen Sen and Brian Tsui, eds., *Beyond Pan-Asianism: Connecting China and India, 1840s and 1960s,* Delhi: Oxford University Press, 2021, p. 189.
107 F.W. Perry, *Order of Battle of Divisions Part 5B, Indian Army Divisions*, Newport: Ray Westlake Military Books, 1993, p. 78.
108 Ashutosh Roy, Juddhabandir atmakahini, 3 parts *Bharatvarsha,* 7(1)(6), 1919, pp. 782–785; 7(2)(2), 1919, pp. 194–197; 7(2)(4), 1919, pp. 509–514.
109 Ashutosh Roy, Juddhabandir atmakahini, *Bharatvarsha,* 7(1)(6), 1919, p. 784.
110 Ibid., p. 784.
111 Ibid., p. 785.
112 Ashutosh Roy, Juddhabandir atmakahini, *Bharatvarsha,* 7(2)(2), 1919, p. 194.
113 Ashutosh Roy, Juddhabandir atmakahini, *Bharatvarsha,* 7(2)(4), 1919, p. 509.
114 Ibid., pp. 510–513.
115 Krishna Behari Roy, Kut juddhe Turkihoste Bandi Bangalir Atmakahini, *Manashi o Marmabani,* 11(2) (2), 1919, pp. 121–125.
116 Krishna Behari Roy, op. cit., pp. 121–122.
117 Ibid., p. 123.

118 Ibid., pp. 124–125.
119 Bibhuti Bhusan Bandopadhyay, Moroner Donka Baje, *Bibhuti Racanabali,* Vol. 9, Calcutta: Mitra and Ghosh Pvt Ltd, 9th ed. 1998.
120 Banarasidas Chaturvedi, 'Three Letters on Greater India, Indians Abroad', *The Modern Review*, XXXXVII(1–6), 1930.
121 Bibhuti Bhusan Bandopadhyay, Moroner Donka Baje, op. cit.
122 For example, for the study of art, see Monindrabhusan Gupta, Chin ChitrakalarItihash, *Prabashi,* 24(2)(1), 1924, pp. 81–89 and on drama see Kalidas Nag, *Dwip Bharater Natyakala, Prabashi,* 29(1)(6), 1929; Suniti Kr. Chattopadhyay, Javadwiper Pothe, *Prabashi,* 27(1)(5–6), 1927.
123 Jamini Kanta Sen, Chainik Chitrakalar Chhayapoth, *Bharatvarsha*, 26(1)(5), 1938, p. 579.
124 Jagatjit Singh, *My Travels in China, Japan and Java*, London: Hutchinson & Co., 1903, pp. 31–41, p. 174.
125 Rabindranath Tagore, Dhyani Japan, *Prabashi,* 29(1)(5), 1929, pp. 533–535.

3 A woman's perspective

Writings for women, about women and by women

Radha Kumar in *The History of Doing*[1] called the 19th century the Age of Women, and Partha Chatterjee considered that the 'women's question' was the central issue in the age of reform.[2] The *patrikas* were naturally responsive to the 'debate' leading to 'public passion and acrimony' on the position of women in society, and as in real life, men's voices were as loud on issues concerning women and society as that of women. But what is noticeable in the periodicals is greater agency for women than was credited to them in the field of reform. The lines between the 'outer' and 'inner' domains were sometimes drawn deeply and at other times blurred in these essays on Asian women and travelogues. But what is certain is that a bond between women, beyond the nation and self, is being constituted not entirely imaginatively but through knowledge of customs, traditions and real-life experiences, with the unceasing motifs of improvement and empowerment, obviously varying in degree and quality according to the authorship. Defying traditional social binding, women's writings in vernacular journals tried to find a space outside the dual control of patriarchy of the society and state. Rooting for less advantaged women, these essays on information about and travel in Asia try to create awareness against social dominance through intimacy and gender solidarity.

Discussion on Asian women: writing for women by men

One of the earliest magazines started in Bengali was *Bamabodhini Patrika* which aimed at educating women. In a recent anthology of articles on women and family in *Bamabodhini Patrika*, historian Bharati Ray, who edited it, points out that it was the first periodical aimed at casting the 'light of knowledge' for 'improvement of their mental faculties' in a language, 'gentle yet lively' for 'women in seclusion' in Asia.[3] The articles were mostly written by educated Brahmo men and maybe by some women on current topics of health and hygiene, aimed at women's mental and physical well-being. But, strangely enough, most of them have not given their names, so authorship remains a mystery. Most of the articles about other countries, even when they are translations of English articles, contain direct references to women in different countries, aimed at attracting the interest of their women readers. They describe features, attributes, activities and dilemmas of women of Asia as well as similarities or dissimilarities with Indian/Bengali women. One of the first articles on Asia was on Chinese women written anonymously in *Bamabodhini Patrika*.[4] The author starts with the comment:

> the condition of Chinese women is very similar to that of Indian women, who are subjected to male domination. Chinese women cannot sit next to their husbands,

DOI: 10.4324/9781003243786-3

> their opinions even in household matters are never taken into account and they cannot even worship their gods in the temples . . . Their lot is only hard work, thrift in finances and expression, submission to male supervision and will, seclusion and fortitude. Even if the women are dying of starvation or their lifeblood is draining out, they cannot utter a word or complain.[5]

Almost always the description of Chinese women includes the custom of foot binding as the ultimate injustice done to them. It is obvious that the westerners who were encountering local Chinese in the port towns were writing about the custom which was under debate in the wake of the Taiping rebellion (1850–1864). The man at the heart of the rebellion, Hong Xiuquan, was a Hakka and he wanted to remove the alien Qing traditions, including foot binding which was not the norm among the Hakkas. The British and French who encountered the Taipings at Nanjing were impressed by the Taiping discipline and dedication, their idealism and a 'puritanical abstinence unknown among contemporary militia.' The Taipings had assigned an important role to women and were imbued with a 'pervading spirit of fraternity and by the common ownership of resources'.[6] This was reported in contemporary newspapers like *The Times* and the *North American Review*[7] and presumably was read all over the world.

The writer in *Bamabodhini Patrika* claimed men all over the world were opposed to the idea of women going out of the home and it is not surprising that Chinese men would find this custom, which immobilised women, attractive. Along with their feet their minds too were tied down. 'By insisting on total submission to men's will and not allowing women to be educated', except in subjects that kept them confined within the home, 'they have sought to keep male patriarchy alive.'[8]

Description of family structure and family customs were of great interest for these writers since they presumed that their female readers would enjoy them. Again, similarities are explored and differences are analysed in the article. 'Quite similar to the marriage customs of Indians, the Chinese use a match maker to fix marriages and for the bride, pale skin and tiny feet are coveted'.[9] Marriage customs are brought in a discussion on Burmese women in 1870 in another anonymous article in *Bamabodhini Patrika*, but there it is their 'freedom' which obviously intrigues Indians. 'Like French women, the Burmese women are seen to set up shops selling various articles in the markets and they are skilful in this trade'.[10] Freedom of Burmese women is a recurrent theme in articles on women in Asia with opinions for and against.

Refuting 'earlier writing by European adventurers who created a myth about Persian men oppressing women, from only a cursory examination of their society', an article in *Bamabodhini Patrika* in 1867 on Persian women claims to 'hold a more balanced view'. It brings in a discussion of family life negating prevalent views, the men are said to value loyalty and dedication in their marital relations. Though polygamy was prevalent from ancient times, in recent years most men reject the convention. Even though theoretically divorce is possible and appears to be easy, in reality the process is far more complicated and a deterrent. One custom that the author considers an abomination is the custom which allows marriage between first cousins. Even if there is no established caste system, a hierarchy is noticeable in marriage settlements where rich girls cannot marry penniless men.[11] A comparison is brought in between the new bride's position in a Hindu family and a Persian family and says that there are similarities in the fact that the bride is surrounded by a large contingent of female relatives but unlike a Hindu mother-in-law, a Persian mother-in-law does not mentally torture her. Till the bride becomes a mother, she has no freedom to leave the house, but after that she is free to go shopping, as long as she is adequately covered. Another similarity that they have with Hindus is in a custom that when a male child is born, his mother is called in reference to her son's name and her name is no longer taken. But if she has a daughter, her name remains unchanged. When a Persian woman gives birth to a boy, she considers herself very fortunate because she then has the right to a higher position in the household. Finally, he praises the Persian women's contribution to the family and their support to their husbands, socially and in religious ceremonies.[12]

An article in the wake of the ongoing Sino-Japanese war on the contentious Korean issue in 1894–1895 in *Bamabodhini Patrika* was on Korean women which the writer claimed would be interesting to the reader since in general people had not known much about the country till then.[13] Comparisons are drawn with Indian women throughout. According to the article, written anonymously, Korean women are totally dominated by men and polygamy was common there though they considered it dishonourable to live with many wives in the same house. Comparing Indian women with Korean, the writer said that inhibitions about walking in public was present only for women of upper classes who 'cover their face and head by a veil and only their eyes are visible' when they leave the house. Though boys and girls are allowed to play together when they are young and girls are permitted to dress like boys, but thereafter, the girls are strictly disciplined. 'The women wear a dress which is similar to that worn in western India consisting of not a saree but a *pyjama*-like garment. The strange thing is, the Korean women have to wear three pyjamas, one on top of the other, to be conventionally correct.' On top they wear a *piran*-like garment which could be coloured but without pockets and use a cloth pouch tied with laces on their waist[14]

In another article in the same year, a writer discusses certain social rules of Sinhalese women.[15] Observing the Sinhalese women (pilgrims and nuns) who come to Bodh Gaya regularly on pilgrimage, the author initially noticed that 'the women wore plain white sarees in Bombay style, whether widowed or not' (typically married Bengali women would avoid plain white as a sign of widowhood), but on enquiry found out that this was not their normal style of dressing in Sri Lanka. He described the dress he found women wearing there as 'a two-piece draped garment, one covering from hips to toes and the other upwards to the neck'. What was most noticeable in his eyes was that women did not cover their heads and in fact dressed their hair with flowers, beautiful silver or gold hairpins. Unlike Bengali women, the Sinhalese women wear leather sandals on their feet. Sinhalese Buddhist nuns, young and old whom the writer noticed during his visit to Bodh Gaya, do not wear footwear and are dressed in white unstitched cloth. 'Like our widows and other sramanas (monks),' the writer wrote, they eat once a day and are mostly vegetarian …. .Unlike Indian women, they do not have any prayer rituals except that on two particular dates they may keep fast in homage to the Buddha.'[16]

While discussing Sinhalese marriage, the writer writes that the Buddhist marriages are more a civil contract since, unlike a Hindu marriage, there are no priests involved, no rituals or no divine image kept as witness, during the ceremony which is conducted with the consent of the groom who should be between 18 and 20 and the bride who should be at least 16–18. Also, there is only exchange of clothes and ornaments between both parties instead of a dowry. Widow re-marriage is prevalent though there is no compulsion on widows either way.[17]

Even though the writer's aim is to discuss social practices of Sri Lanka, he cannot resist evoking the glory of India's past and starts the essay by reminding the readers of this. He writes:

> Sisters, since you may not be aware of it, I would like you to inform you that Sinhala was really a colony of ancient Bengal. It was established when Buddhism was supremely powerful. That is why many Sinhalese families refer to themselves of having originated from Bengalis families settled there and are, in fact, proud of it. Though all the similarities between the races have been erased by the passage of time, there is still one remaining which will probably remain forever. That is, the shape of the body. It both thrills me and makes me weep to think that there is still a race which considers itself as colonized by Bengalis and that they praise their colonists . . . But I also understand that that is the reason why the Sinhalese have no rituals or social conventions of their own, so ingrained is the foreign influence.[18]

The writer ends the essay by attributing certain peculiarities in Sinhalese customs to 'degradation in Buddhist religion in different Asian countries, like Singhal (Sri Lanka), Tibet, Shyam (Thailand), Brahma (Burma), China, and Japan'. His next statement exposes the biases of a Bengali Hindu against non-Hindus and non-Bengalis, when he writes that the Sinhalese, like Muslims, 'have no inhibitions regarding impurities and they can even sit with their food on their beds.' He adds that it is something 'no Hindu, even if they belong to less inhibited Indian cultures of north western India and Punjab' would do.[19]

An article on Chinese men and women in *Janmabhumi* by Ajit Prasad Sanyal has a section on foot-binding. Following a section called 'men's beauty' where the appearance of Chinese men, their skin colour, moustache, hair dressing styles are discussed, Sanyal then writes how Chinese women are even more beautiful than men but their ideas of female beautification are as far removed from their Indian counterparts as possible.

> All civilized nations, India included, prepare their marriageable daughters to be beautiful in body, as well as be flawless in character and intelligence. But the Chinese look for the size of the bride's feet as the most important criterion. It is only those who possess a three inch feet who are revered as the 'golden lily'. Rich and beauty-conscious Chinese ladies can barely walk a few steps with the support of other women and need to be carried by female bearers when they want to walk in the park. Indian poets refer to a woman's walk as beautiful when they walk like a swan or an elephant while the Chinese consider a walk like a swaying willow tree as beautiful and auspicious. A Chinese woman's gait is a lot like what we will look if we walk on our heels.[20]

Sanyal then repeats a comment made by a friend of his in support of the wisdom of the Chinese regarding foot-binding that the Chinese are cleverer than men or even gods since they have managed to devise a system by which to control 'waywardness of women'.The foot binding custom which makes their mobility difficult 'is the only way women can be controlled and confined.'[21] As a tongue in cheek caveat he adds that 'not all women can be controlled since the painful practice is mainly confined to upper class women who are slaves to beauty.' Women of working classes cannot survive 'celebrating their own beauty alone' and have to earn a livelihood 'using their feet'. Girls of the leisured classes, from the age of five, are shod with iron shoes which are generally cast on by 'foot doctors'and have to bear terrible pain for one year, sometimes succumbing to fever caused by the intense pain. 'Even in winter the young children are afraid to cover themselves with warm clothes in case their pain increases with heat,' the writer adds.[22]

Sanyal ends the essay on a more cheerful note, describing the hairstyling by Chinese women,which differs in different parts of China. 'Generally, women like to use artificial flowers in their hair and like Indian women, who use pins to keep their hair buns tight, Chinese women use long wooden sticks which sometimes become headrests for them.' He also noticed that like Indian women who colour their hand and toenails with saffron and other colouring agents, Chinese women too use red and white colours on their faces to enhance their beauty.[23]

Jnanendranath Chakraborty has a very interesting article on Chinese women, in *Bharati* in 1913,[24] where he writes that one of his Chinese acquaintances commented that what travellers write about Chinese women is only partially true. One can only know about working-class women, or those whom one meets at tea shops or plying boats. But it is next to impossible to know a Chinese woman intimately. Chakraborty on coming across some letters written by a Chinese woman Kui Li to her husband who was an important royal official and was on tour with Prince Chun has translated them for his readers to show the heart of a 'real Chinese woman'. To underline the similarities between married women in China running their husbands' homes and Indian women in the same situation, Chakraborty points out that in China too like in India, men marry and bring their brides to live with their joint families, where they have to live according to the wishes of their mother in law. 'If they so desired, these mothers can make their husband's home, heaven or hell for the daughters in law, he writes derisively.[25] In order to prove the genuineness of the letters, he adds that Kui Li's father Chih Li was an administrator, who was one of the founders of the new education system in China, and who ensured that his son and daughter both got educated. In fact, Kui Li received her lessons from the poet Ling-wing-pu and developed her imagination and ability to express her thoughts so beautifully.[26]

Japan came into the intellectual radar of Bengalis from the turn of the century, especially after her victory over Russia in 1904. The article 'Rise of Japan' by Taraknath Mukherjee, published in 1906 in *Navyabharat*, contained a section on a comparison between Bengali and Japanese women. He draws a picture of the Japanese woman in her husband's home which is bound to raise warmth and admiration for the woman within the Bengali heart. From morning to night, the Japanese bride works hard to keep a beautiful home and look after the welfare of her husband and parents-in-law in a manner similar to a Bengali bride. Quoting from the account of the traveller Chandrasekhar Sen (*A Tour Around the World* – 1890), he highlights the similarities in details of social customs especially around the birth and upbringing of children, marriage rules and customs, despite many western adaptations in dress and hygiene. He also compared between the samurai and Rajput women:

> In ancient times the samurai women were as skilled as the men in warfare just like Chand Bibi, Lakshmibai and many Rajput women for whom warfare was a natural profession . . . In fact local Bengali traditions like *Dharmamangal,* contain instances where loyalty towards their lords and ladies made many women pick up their sword for protection against enemies.

Mukherjee has no doubt that Japanese women when they come into contact with these brave Bengali women, they too will lose their extreme humility towards Japanese men.[27] It is difficult to understand whether the article is in jest or earnest.

Another issue which plays an important role in writings on women is the question of freedom where women of other countries are compared to Bengali women. Taranath Mukherjee in his article 'Rise of Japan' brings in a discussion about the geisha women of Japan who are compared with the dancers of temples, tribal women, actresses and courtesans in different parts of India:

> The geisha women's task was to attract Japanese men not by their beauty but through their sophisticated taste and cultured behaviour and speech . . . the geisha women are always independent and cannot be bought by money. Just like the women of Kamrup are famed to have the ability of enslaving their men like sheep so also the geisha women are considered to be able to control men with a rope through their nose . . . These women are not necessarily from lower classes but are sometimes in later life marry into rich and powerful families.

In that sense, Basanta Sena of *Mrichhakatik* fame may be considered to be an Indian geisha. Holding the British responsible for the end of that tradition in India when 'Bengali families used to send their sons to these sorceresses (courtesans) to learn the art of refinement', he points out that foreign influence could do the same in Japan. He compares the independence of the geisha to the empowered Burmese women. However, Mukherjee succumbs to his own prejudices when he quotes traveller Chandrasekhar Sen who was shocked at both 'women running disreputable tea shops (*Chayas*) in Yokohama' and the performance of 'Jonkino dance in which a woman sits playing a sitar like instrument and three others dance, all totally in the nude'.[28] At pains to point out that 'the geisha women are not representative of the true Japanese womanhood', Mukherjee points out the story of the 'Sati Japanese lady' who on hearing about the martyrdom of her husband in the Russo-Japanese war did not hesitate to plunge a dagger into her heart just like the Rajput women of yore who jumped into the burning pyre. Manmatha Nath Ghosh also quotes stories about the virtues of Japanese women who made huge sacrifices for the war effort. Writing about different aspects of Japanese society in *Manashi* between 1908 and 1913,[29] Ghosh claimed an interest in those aspects which do not 'usually intrigue a casual traveller', which he termed 'the slumbering aspects of Japanese life' (his book is called *Shupta Japan*). Having got a degree in arts and industry from Japan and having lived with a Japanese family, Ghosh vouches for the womanly virtues of Japanese women who are both *teiso* and *misao* (closest to *satitva* considered to be highest virtue for Indian women).[30] Unlike the views of other writers, Ghosh considers Japanese women's freedom as compatible with their womanly qualities of 'grace, temperance, and tolerance' as their qualities of cheerfulness, fidelity, politeness in daily life and strong patriotic values are exemplary. The geisha women of Japan retained interest among other writers as well and Sarojnath Ghosh in *Masik Basumati* in 1923 talks about how the society 'disrespects these women for sticking her foot in the mud yet when she leaves that lifestyle and lifts her foot out of the mud the geisha dancers and marries, the society like her husband erases the memories of her past'.[31]

Women's education claimed the attention of almost all writers from the earliest years of the *Samayik Patrika*. Admiration for Japan's modernisation programme also included analysis of education there. Especially those Bengalis who came into contact with Japan expressed admiration at what was considered to be a unique education system for women. In 1906, Jadunath Sarkar, a student in Tokyo, wrote about the different medical, technical, agricultural, fine arts and music schools for girls in Tokyo, most of which were run by women as well as foreign missionaries. Many societies on education, nursing and sports aided in 'preventing Japanese women from languishing like frogs in a well unlike Indian women', according to Sarkar.[32] There was excitement in India over the establishment of Women's University in Japan in 1901 by Naruse Jinzo whose views have been discussed by Brojosundar Sanyal in *Prabashi* in 1908[33] and Ganapati Roy also wrote an article in *Manashi*, tracing the history of women's education in Japan prior to the establishment of the women's university, Jinzo's quest during his US trip for information about schools and curriculum for women and then a study of the women's university he set up in Japan.[34]

Women's freedom in Burma excited the interest and attention of Bengalis through the entire period of close interaction and almost all the articles on Burma invariably contain at least a mention of the freedom enjoyed by the Burmese women vis-à-vis the Indian – sometimes approvingly and at others disapprovingly. There is a detailed description of the freedom that women enjoy in Burma in an article in *Mahila* in contrast to Bengali women who

> are always secluded within four walls of their home. If a European tourist visited Calcutta, he would think that the city has no women whereasBurma so close to Calcutta has outdone Europe and America in women's freedom.
>
> Be it shops, markets or fairs one can see only women around busy with their wares and at a first glance it appears as if there are no men in this country. Not just that, face to face with a foreign man in the markets or main roads, the Burmese women are never embarrassed or taken aback, they can stare back with aplomb, even smile or laugh out loud at the slightest provocation . . . The Burmese women have great power over their men, who are listless and cowardly and they deal with their men's disobedience with physical violence. The husband is terrified of his wife who often is the main bread-earner.[35]

But in the end mindful of their mission to encourage morality, a warning is sounded discouraging unrestricted freedom like Burmese women, since their freedom apparently was not concomitant with development.

> Many Bengali *babus* believe that if women are brought out of the seclusion of their homes and are allowed to go wherever they wish or converse with whoever they want to, they will have achieved the highest degree of freedom. We do not support them. With the freedom that Burmese women have, it would indicate that they have achieved proportionate development, but that is not the case.

The author then points out their drawbacks citing 'lack of moral discipline and degradation of character' as the reason for the country lagging behind in development. Indian women, he concludes, instead of striving for this false freedom should try to attain 'real freedom which comes only through submission to God's will'.[36]

Even earlier in 1891, Durgadas Bandopadhyay wrote in *Janmabhumi* that women were very independent in Burma and most of the work was done by them. However, he spoke of a system by which Burmese men and women were liable to be bought and sold and in many cases parents sold their daughters for payment. The real empowerment was that wives too could pay off their husbands and return to their parents' home. He ends with a sad commentary on the cruelty of the British commanders of his regiment who bought almost two hundred women for their cavalrymen and some of them even had children by their soldiers. But when the regiment was to return back the women were made to return to their homes, since army rules did not permit these women to accompany the troops back to India. Only one soldier, Resaldar Nizam Khan after a lot of persuasion was provided a reprieve by which he brought back a woman from Burma.[37]

Even before that in 1870, *Bamabodhini Patrika* carried an article on Burmese women in which the writer starts with the sentence, there is no purdah system in Burma. Women are visible on the main streets as well as in all important locations and like French women, they often open shops showing dexterity in selling and buying.' He also describes how Burmese women spend their childhood in playing, flying kites or singing and dancing since they are hardly educated. At the age of thirteen they undergo an ear piercing ceremony which denotes their coming of age. On an auspicious day fixed by the family astrologer, this ceremony, is accompanied with great feasting, singing and dancing. He also points out that unlike Indians, in general, women choose their grooms who are then approved by their parents. But the Burmese have a superstition which somewhat limits the freedom of the women, as the chosen husband's birthday should be the same as the bride's or else it will be considered inauspicious. A distinctive feature of the Burmese wedding ceremony is the lack of presence of a priest since celibate Buddhists monks are prohibited from even attending a marriage ceremony. Thus, for the Burmese, marriage is a very non-religious social affair. The author then describes the Burmese social customs, but one senses that the marriage ceremony, subservience of the husband to the wife's family socially and financially and easy system of annulment of marriages do not really meet his approval and he's simply describing them as curiosities. He goes on to write that Burmese are also allowed to marry outside their community and nation as long as they marry Buddhists. Many Burmese women marry Chinese men and, in these cases the boy born of such marriages are brought up as Chinese and daughters as Burmese. The author also goes on to describe the religiosity of Burmese women who are often seen performing prayers and meditation in the pagodas. Previously, many joined the monasteries and nunneries and though the practice still exists, their number has dwindled over the years. Today they are often seen to work as servers in the pagodas performing various tasks in the service of the Buddha. The author ends by describing the colourful dress of Burmese women –'*Angrakha*, saree and a piece of cloth like *odna* over the *angrakha,* and rich women wear silks and jewellery. They have long hair which they pile up on their head in plaits and buns'. But one custom according to him is repugnant to watch, 'they are always smoking a long cheroot at all hours and in all company and sometime they even do so while minding their small children and in fact even offering it to them from time to time'.[38]

Kalachand Dalal writes in *Bharati* in 1911 an essay about the women of Burma where he starts with the point that Burmese women enjoy a freedom which 'in no way is lesser than men.' They are allowed to go where ever they want, speak to any man who they are not necessarily related to, without any stigma or scandal being attached to their names. According to local customs they need not follow segregation or cover their faces or heads with veils. The writer stresses repeatedly how like men the Burmese women are. 'Even their dress is a lot like that of men.' Their hair is not necessarily tied in plaits but rather piled on top of their heads, 'like a small pyramid.' He finds it amazing that, 'they do not feel self-conscious or shy to speak to men at any time without covering on their face and in fact make fun of Bengali women who hide their faces behind veils.' This freedom from inhibitions that 'plague a middleclass Bengali woman' in the writers eyes makes for the empowerment which he notices in the visibility of Burmese women, 'rich or poor' everywhere- 'shopping in open markets, weaving, making cheroots, stitching clothes, performing agricultural chores, driving carts and boats.' What makes their achievement all round is that, 'they are also experts at cooking, looking after their homes, creating wonderful handicrafts and beautiful embroidery besides being able to write and keep accounts.'

The author is impressed not only by the openness of the society but also by the courage women show in day-to-day life which he also considers a 'manly' virtue in a woman. Once while travelling from Pegu, the author noticed an incident which was an eye-opener for him: A foreigner was sitting too close to an unescorted Burmese woman and apparently insinuated something insulting. Instantly the woman took umbrage and started hitting him with her slippers. The author was astounded at the 'manly courage' shown by the lady. Immediately all the other women of the carriage stood by the enraged woman in a show of solidarity. Dalal concluded that this public show of courage implied that the men in the Burmese society approved of their women enjoying uninhibited freedom[39]

Writing about Turkish women in *Mahila,* Hemendra Nath Dutta compares their condition with that of Indian women, as being much better in the new and changed environment in Turkey:

> The women in this country (Bengal presumably) are always sequestered within the home and are totally unaware of what is occurring in the world but the Turkish women are not. Everyone knows that Turkish women have more legal rights than Hindu women, since all Muslim women can own property separate from that of their husbands. They can also inherit property from their fathers and other relatives. Though polygamy exists among Muslim women, in Turkey it is common practice to have only one wife and though divorce through talaq is legal for all Muslims, very few Turkish men abandon their wives. Within the home of the well-established Turks, there are two sections – the *selamalik* or the outer quarters and *haremalik* or the inner quarters. In most houses the *haremalik* is very spacious and comfortable. Generally only men who are related or well known to the family are allowed into the inner quarters. But under the influence of the enlightened section of Turks, the Young Turks, whose selfless dedication has resulted in a renaissance in Turkey, the system of seclusion is lessening in the Turkish homes.[40]

Dutta describes the life of slave women in a Turkish household who often are bought as children and reared and educated to make them fit to be gifted to the royal family. If they can prove themselves in education and culture, they are often taken as wives by the king, the royal princes or even the royal officials. Sometimes when these slave women bear children they are given freedom and enjoy the same rights as other women of Turkish families. Dutta concludes that though it is true that slaves may not be very unhappy in the society but the very fact of their existence lowers the dignity of the race.[41] Dutta writes in detail about the amusements that Turkish women enjoy and there is reflection of these details in Sita Debi's article many years later. He also talks about the role of the mother-figure in 'fixing' the marriage of the eligible men of the family, the pleasures of bathing at the hamam which could be called a mahila majlis (gathering of women) and a means of making new friends and enjoying the company of old ones,going for picnics at many spots along the Bosphorus Straits,or the shopping expeditions accompanied with 'Negro Khoja pageboys' as special features he noticed in the Turkish society.[42] What remains uncertain is whether Dutta has culled these points from western magazines or books or whether it is a first-hand account. In the discussion on women's education which was *Mahila*'s priority interest, Dutta points out that though the number of girls schools were increasing in Turkey, most Turkish girls are taken out of school early and this lack of education has a detrimental effect on the society. On the contrary, the nomadic tribe Kurd women are more independent. They are experts in riding horses, and can go anywhere with their husbands. They are clever and industrious and have an opinion about everything both personal and public. They do not follow purdah system though at times, they do cover their face partially. Espousing the cause of freedom in movement as the means to women's development, Dutta says that 'these freedoms do not by any means cause any decline in their society, and on the contrary their freedom and hard work contribute immensely to their own self-respect and social ideals.'[43]

Many years later in 1928, Manomohon Ghosh has provided a kind of a survey about the improvement that has occurred in the condition of women under the aegis of the Young Turks.

Writing for women by women

Though a part of the nationalist agenda of improvement, women's writings always create comfort areas for the reader, especially the use of vernacular. They often translate articles from English language newspapers and journals for their Bengali readers, yet always adapt them to make them appealing to their readers. The process of adaptation makes for interesting analysis. It was a great bonus when women travellers write about their travels. They are of course rare occasions since very few women travelled and even when they did it was almost always with a chaperon, barring one unique case discussed later.

Special reference should be made to the journal *Antahpur*, run by women and containing essays written by women on various issues which must have impacted women's emancipation even though as historical research has shown, the fight for women's rights was always subsumed within the nationalist project. This was of course offset by all the other attempts to keep women 'on the right path' so to speak. *Bharat Mahila*, started in 1905, was conservative with womanly ideals being highlighted and education for women through institutional segregation inspired by Japan. In 1909, in its fourth year, *Bharat Mahila* ran an essay outlining the advantages and eulogising the excellence of the women's university in Japan and made a case for the need to open one such institution for women in India.[44] In an article in 1913, Hariprabha Takeda, while describing her trip to Japan, writes about a girls' school in Tokyo that she visited. The headmistress had trained in school education from England and showed her around. 'It became clear to me', Takeda wrote,

> that to be a true human and to teach one's children and other countrymen to be human women's education was absolutely necessary. Apart from lessons in

> chemistry, botany, geography and anatomy, the girls in the school also learn cooking, laundry, gardening, housekeeping, drawing, craft, needlework and also conversational English and elements of ethics.

It was the way these subjects were taught to children that amazed her, instead of books the young children were taught through drawings, origami and models of geographical specialities of Japan and recitation of names of cities and important landmarks.[45] That *Bamabodhini Patrika* played a crucial role in popularising the necessity of educating Bengali women has been well documented in an edited volume in Bengali by historian Bharati Ray.[46] Abala Bose in in her article 'Women's Education in Japan and Our Duty',[47] published in *Bamabodhini Patrika*, draws upon the Japanese experience regarding women's education to say that it is not always beneficial to formulate the syllabus of women's education according to a western model. 'When Japan modernised herself, there was a slavish imitation of western modernity. But to prevent this from becoming widespread, a Japanese style of education for women was proposed'. This according to her meant retaining social distance between men and women, even though Japanese women were free to travel alone in any public transport. While discussing the initiative taken by some Japanese youths, local community leaders and the Japanese government to start schools and institutions of higher education for women, Bose talks about the institution she visited:

> It was like a small village outside Tokyo where education was provided from primary to university level. Along with formal education they also teach home science. It also includes a finishing school where not only training in art is given but also useful crafts like dairy management, maintaining animals and birds and agriculture are taught. The Japanese have developed the course according to their own national requirements. I have been amazed at the simplicity of their living and how they have streamlined their livelihoods and living circumstances according to their own needs. Our Indian living standards on the contrary have become so complex and extravagant. In order to save the country from this extravagance it is important that women are provided higher education . . . It is because of the well-developed educational system for women in Japan that their country is so picture perfect, clean and tidy, . . . why shouldn't we learn from that? Why should our country lag behind in women's education?[48]

Shanta Chattopadhyay visiting Japan in 1938 also visited many schools run by women for young ladies. She describes a whole day she spent in three schools (Jiuaga Kuen) run by Mrs Motoko Hari as well as a school run by Mrs Mochiji and she also includes many pictures which might interest her readers.[49]

Antahpur, on the other hand, keeps at their mission of educating women about other Asian countries either through translation of secondary works in English or through travel writing. Mrinalini Raha,[50] a domiciled Bengali in Burma, writing for *Antahpur* in 1902, speaks of Burma as intimate to India since the fortunes of both countries are tied up with British colonialism.[51] 'It is important for Indians to forget all the preconceived ideas they have had about Burma', she says. She compares the roads and infrastructure of the capital city Rangoon or 'Yanggon as the local people call it' (she inserts the English script when writing the name), with the different Indian cities and points out that 'only Jaipur is comparable in beauty' and 'unlike Calcutta,

Rangoon never suffers from muddy roads'. In Rangoon, the number of expatriate Indians is more than that of the locals and they come mainly for trade, business or professional reasons.[52] She talks about the tourist spots in Rangoon like the museum and the zoological gardens which are enjoyable to visit:

> The Dalhousie park is a beautiful place for a visit. Next to it is the beautiful Royal Lake. In front of the Chief Court, the Fi chi square is also a beautiful place to visit. Here Queen Victoria's white marble statue is worth a visit. The town hall or Jubilee hall is located in the large maidan and the general meetings are held there. Not far from there is the location of the famous Shwe-Dagan Pagoda. The Buddhist Burmese are famous for donating generously for religious favour and that is why there are innumerable pagodas all over Rangoon and other Burmese towns. Dagan means a golden head and there are many small dagons with Shwe Dagan towering over them.

Raha compares the Shwe Dagan with the Vishnu pad temple in Gaya which also has a golden crest but points out that the Rangoon temple has a lot more gold.[53]

Sita Debi, who was a graduate of Calcutta University, daughter of Ramananda Chattopadhyay, doyen of Indian journalism, wrote about Persian women in *Bangalakshmi* in the context of the Asian Conference for Women that was organised in Lahore. 'There is a need now', she wrote, 'to expand the mental horizon of all women through an exchange and sharing of experiences'. It was time she declared that all countries set their women on the path of development and the rise of Persian women from a subordinated condition to their present status may be instructive for Bengali women.[54] Though Sita Debi acknowledges that the article was based on Satindramohon Chattopadhyay's essay in *Modern Review*, the interpretations are all her own. She talks about how women's rights which had been granted by the Akhmani dynasty in the pre-Islamic period was continued by the Sasanians under whom women had equal status as men. But after Islamic occupation the clash between the new and the old civilisations affected women's rights and they were 'bound by the chains of hated rules and for many centuries were interred within the walls of the home. No one cared about their tears'.[55]

Sita Debi's interpretation of the condition of women under Muslim rule was true to the Hindu nationalist discourse as she wrote that

> Muslims did not believe that there could be social equality between men and women and they only considered women as objects of desire with no faith at all in the integrity of their character . . . There was no expectation of help, knowledge or friendship from women so there was no effort to educate women. To maintain their dominance, they were not only satisfied with keeping women illiterate, they also popularised the right of four simultaneous marriages. Not just on paper, most men actively exercised the right . . . Women lived in the inner quarters like men's playthings, their age increased but knowledge did not. They were denied of even the basic literacy and had no knowledge or awareness about the world.[56]

She is quite scathing in her description of the *burqah* describing it as a 'shapeless dark coloured garment with two slits where eyes should be' so that though the wearer can see everything the person she is facing does not 'know if they are ghosts or human'. She roundly blames the men saying that by implementation of the purdah system, they 'attempt to cover up the flaws in their own characters.'[57]

Sita Devi is equally scathing when she talks about the lack of education of Persian women in the past and they could not read classical Persian and spoke a mixed language called *Dhari*. It was obviously shocking for the educated Sita Debi that the only relief from the monotony of existence for these women was their supervised visit to the *hamams*, though according to her this freedom was like that accorded to 'state prisoners'. The writer is glad that in recent years protests have been made against these oppressive customs by Persian women supported by the Sufis and the Bahais, though 'it was the political change that opened the floodgates and broke down the stone walls'. With Reza Shah Palhavi inaugurating the new age in Persia a *Persian desh sevika sangha* (presumably Society of Patriotic Women or Jam'iyat-e Nesvân-e Vatankhâh) emerged which concentrated their activities mainly on women's emancipation through grant of important civil rights. Sita Debi introduced her readers to those courageous women who initiated reforms in the face of opposition by religious conservatives, namely Khanum Shahnaz Azad and Khanum Eskandari. Sita Devi concludes that when women take the lead in women's movement, their success is inevitable as was the case with the Society.[58] She wrote:

> this association has received sympathetic support from various parts of Europe and looks forward to working with the women's organisations in India. When they received invitation to the All Asian Women's Conference (1931) they were the first to acknowledge it and sent their representative at the meet. They are an example of how women can rise above degradation and create a new future.[59]

Women's travels in Asia: written testaments

It is true that compared to the travel narratives by men, the number of women travelling was much less but the very fact that women were able to ignore or circumvent the normative practices of the time and become trendsetters not only in practice but also in writing was a unique factor. Women's travel narratives which came in the different issues of the periodicals have not found much place in the academic discussions on Bengali travel writing till recently, though they form an important element in the understanding of women's self and their position and role in society. It must be remembered that these travels by women were not only within the country but also outside to other Asian countries and Europe. The conventional studies on women's travels narrative have in general been monotonously and invariably directed towards the colonial gaze. It is only rarely that the reverse is studied. Even in those rare cases, the concentration is on migration studies and the women's experience in settling in a new place. The exploration of the western countries – Europe, England and the United States – by women belonging to a colonised nation and then sharing of their experience through travel narratives in the form of a diary entry or letters has not been documented at all. The connection between travel narratives and the use of the letter form has been discussed by scholars like Amy E. Smith who argues that travel narratives were better received when they were written in the same style as a letter.[60] She says that this form of writing is more likely to produce a stylistically enjoyable narrative that has 'an inherent sense of audience'.[61] The addressing of the recipient of the letter by name or a family relation gave the reader a sense of closeness with the writer and a sense of sharing like a family member. The use of the form of diary entry or letter writing creates an aura of authenticity since it is assumed that the traveller is writing down their entire experience immediately leaving no room for imaginative or subjective manipulation. However, Clare B. Saunders points out that 'the assumed authenticity and greater honesty of a personal diary or correspondence which records personal experience, . . . can easily be manipulated with omissions and elisions to meet the agenda of the writer'.[62] The travel narratives[63] I discuss here are written by women belonging to Hindu/Brahmo *bhadralok* class, affluent and well connected and well educated in Bengali and some English who are travelling to the east, mostly they are travelling with male family members with the important exception of Sarala Debi.

Rajkumari Bandopadhyay was the first woman to travel to the west in 1871,[64] though she did not leave an account of her travel. Krishnabhabini Das's account of her travel to England, *A Bengali Woman in England* (first published anonymously in 1885)[65] was not published in the journals but came out as a separate volume. Her later essays about her experience in England, however, were published from time to time in the periodicals. Pramila Debi's travels to England came out in *Mahila* in 1903 and one can decipher from her writing that she was socially an important woman, belonging to famous families on either side – her husband appears to have been well connected to the British administration while Pramila herself was a prominent member of the Bengali society as the niece of the Brahmo leader Keshav Chandra Sen. However, in this book, I do not discuss travel writings to the west but only mention them because of their importance as colonised women looking at the west with admiring but uncolonised eyes. Himanghubala Debi, Sukumari Debi and Bimala Dasgupta also travelled to the west and left interesting travel accounts which I have discussed elsewhere.[66] Sukumari Debi was probably the wife of K.C. Roychowdhury and accompanied her husband who was Member of the Bengal Legislative Council and President of the Kakinara Labour Union to attend International Labour Conferences abroad. One such trip was covered in her travelogue in *Bangalakshmi* in 1930.[67] Sukumari Debi's writing is remarkable because one finds a woman very much involved with her husband's work and very aware of the world that she finds herself in, in Europe. Bimala Das Gupta travelled to Norway and Sweden with her husband and published her narrative in *Bharatvarsha* in 1914[68] and Himangshubala Debi travelled from her home in Edinburgh, where her husband Dr Dwijendranath Bhaduri was posted under the Indian Medical Service, to Glasgow, Lake District, Cambridge, and many parts of the continent.[69] Two other interesting articles are by the 11-year-old Tapati Sarkar who travelled to London with her parents and shared her experiences in the children's magazine *Ramdhanu*[70] and Sudha Sen's article on the Niagara Waterfall, which is the only travelogue written by a woman on travels in America to my knowledge at least and is written in 1934.[71]

We have some details about two women travellers. Firstly, Sarala Debi Chowdhurani,[72] who travelled to Burma for a conference, is well known for posterity through her multifaceted activities – inspiring the youth to physical activity and associations with journalistic ventures in both Lahore and Bengal. Her writing and role in freedom movement is well known and documented.[73] Secondly, Hariprabha Takeda, a Bengali social worker married to a Japanese businessman Uemon Takeda, who sent her travel account to the editor Saraju Bala Dutta of *Bharat Mahila* for publication in 1912.[74] Luckily, the editor wrote a few lines explaining who the diary writer was. For understanding who the others were, I had to pick up clues from the narrative to trace their background and realised that though they are unknown today, they were probably socially famous and relevant then which is why no introductory remarks precede their accounts. These women hardly provide any biographical details and rarely mention their husbands' names. Even Sarala's accounts in 1931–1932, which make wonderful reading in her description of sights and her own insights, is threadbare in details of the work she has gone for. It is also intriguing why the series instead of being published in the family-run *Bharati* came out in *Bharatvarsha*. Another traveller, Saratrenu Debi[75] has turned to be an enigma in more ways than one. My guess is that she might have been comparatively unknown in the Calcutta society since she could have been based in Bombay. She starts her travelogue from Bombay but since it was customary to go to Persia from Bombay and many Calcuttans do that as well, it's not conclusive that she lived in Bombay based on that fact alone but the fact that her comparisons of foreign lands are with the Bombay city and society makes it plausible that she may have originated there. The publication of her unique article was unfortunately incomplete and Persia was not even reached. Abala Bose,[76] brought up in a Brahmo environment, along with her sister Sarala, learnt from their father Durgamohon Das, the importance of education and open mindedness in life. Later after her marriage to the scientist Jagadish Chandra Bose, Abala gave up her medical training and travelled extensively to Europe, America, China and Japan. From her extensive experience, she writes,

> we need to travel to get out of the monotony of our daily existence in order to find our strengths and lift our minds above our problems . . . When we are in another country we forget our daily inconsequential irritations and only recall the pleasures that lie in our subconscious. We understand and love our country better and through visiting a new place we are imbued with a self-confidence and self-reliance.[77]

Some travellers are famous for their fictional writing and essays even if they do not write travelogues. Sita Debi, who was socially well known as a famous daughter of a media baron Ramananda Chattopadhyay, lived for a long time in Burma after marriage (1923–1930) and only wrote one article on Burmese women[78] with hardly any description of her life there, though much of her creative work is published in the periodicals, and her reminiscences of Rabindranath Tagore are well known.[79] Shanta Chattopadhyay Nag, her sister, on the other hand, accompanied her husband Kalidas Nag abroad and her long serialised travelogue on her visit to Japan with her husband and daughter is one of the best by a Bengali woman.[80] Her fictional writing and compilation of folk tales along with her reminiscences of her father, Ramananda Chattopadhyay and Rabindranath Tagore are also very well known.[81] One article by her came out in *Prabashi* in 1914, but though she writes about Boro Budur temple in Java, its discovery and preservation by Dutch archaeologists and scholars, she does not appear to be visiting. The tone indicates that she is aware of the Greater India ideas prevalent in Calcutta a decade before the Society is established.[82] Two writers based in Rangoon wrote interesting travelogues – Mrinalini Raha, a resident of Burma and writes about the various places of interest,[83] though it is as if she is in an Indian bubble, so to speak, and one does not get a glimpse of Burmese people or life in her writing. Another travelogue is by Pushpalata Debi writing in *Mahila* in 1903, about her travel to Malacca with Singapore as a base.[84] Aparna Debi's 1933 article on Japan is both informative and analytical.[85] Chittaranjan Das's daughter, who in her reminiscences of her father, mentions that out of deference to her father's wishes, she never travelled outside Bengal as long as her mother was alive, and went to Japan much later.

These women who are travelling were educated – not only in their mother tongue but in English literature as well. What they see, especially in the west, reminds them of English stories, poems and dramas during their travels and they do not hesitate to use the references when writing the articles inferring that the readers will also automatically associate with their thoughts, while in the east the visuals bring out poetry not only in their descriptions but as praise of the country as by Sukumari or Lord Buddha, as by Sarala. Coming from well-to-do and well-connected families, they stay in the best hotels, speak of going to lunches and teas with all the rich and famous personalities and seem to be very comfortably placed in the best rooms in the ships, though Saratrenu Debi and Hariprabha Takeda complain about their journey as uncomfortable. Saratrenu was booked on the second class with her husband and even that accommodation came a day later, while Hariprabha and her husband had to share a tiny cabin in mixed company. The mention of famous men and women whom they meet may be for the entertainment of their readers. Pramila Debi mentions being invited to lunch by the former Governor General of India, Lord Ripon and his Lady, visiting Sir John Phear's home at Marpool hall, lunching at Oxford with Prof and Mrs Max Mueller.[86] Sukumari Debi too talks about her meeting with the most highly connected people in Europe and England, but she also expresses her great pleasure in making friends with young and talented Bengali students and professionals abroad. Sarala Debi, invited to an international meeting, also mentions the Burmese elites whom she meets during her trip, and Shanta Debi during her travels in Japan refers to many individuals from different countries living there.

Though these women are not going for higher education nor are they professionals and are probably housewives in today's sense, but they are socially prominent, hence they are being invited to write in the magazines. Not only are they exemplar women, travelling with elan in foreign countries and interacting with all sorts of people, they were probably also associated with social work at home since both *Mahila* and *Bangalakshmi* magazines were associated with women's organisations. But they are almost always chaperoned by their husbands and family members, and only Sarala Debi is invited on her own merit and is travelling alone to give a keynote address at a conference. Sarala Debi is, of course, a class apart in her confidence in herself and her lineage and in her ability to deal with the unexpected and untoward in her travels. The artistry of the language of her narrative raises it far above the other writings and her insightful descriptions of the people and religious sites in Rangoon together with the comparisons with Calcutta and India make it one of the most interesting travel narratives.

There is no real way to assess how many women travel out of Bengal since there is no record of it. Pilgrimage was always popular among the older women, so presumably middle-aged women have travelled continuously. The bar on crossing the seas became applicable only when women started travelling outside the country, to the west – to study or accompany their husbands. The literary journals of the time abound in descriptions of train rides to pilgrim spots or even travel to distant mountains or hill stations for improvement of health. There is an interesting letter to the editor of *Mahila* in which the writer describes herself as *kupamanduka* or a frog in a well who has had the good fortune to view the Himalayas in Kurseong. She says that the travel opened her eyes in a way no book had ever been able to do.[87] Mentioned only as R.S

Hossain, it may be Begum Rokeya Sakhawat Hossain, which of course meant that this 'travel' was much more worthwhile for 'picking up attractive stones . . . and seashells' symbolising freedom instead of earning merit as a good woman in the household or as in her case the 'curses of the die-hard Mullas' for her service to the society.[88] Travelling overseas was rare. Perhaps that was why these rare women who did travel were encouraged to write in the periodical journals to make them an exciting read for the literate public. Unlike today, many of these women who travelled did so for extended periods. Some of them also may have been domiciled abroad for some years. The idea that had become popular in the 20th century was that of companion wives as the real identity of the new Indian women. With the spread of women's education, women travelling to different parts of India with their husbands as well as outside the territorial boundaries of the country was socially condoned.

Description of the route of travel and the sights

All travelling women start their journey from the preparations at home and then describe their travel through the ocean and the road or rail in detail. Presumably, they are the first women in their families to be making this arduous journey which is why they go into details describing not only the view but their rooms, the ship as well as the places they touch on the way. What is generally considered stereotypically a 'woman's touch' in travel narratives is actually very helpful in the reconstruction of a journey by sea. For all the women describing the sea, seasickness, fellow companions, food, entertainment seem to be of first importance while there is less detail in the travel narratives by men. Sarala Debi's description of seasickness is artistic to say the least. She writes:

> while talking to them (two young Burmese students) I realized a known enemy in our midst was making me disbalanced . . . I sat in my deck chair in a stupor, realizing that speaking might have serious repercussions . . . The moment I reached my cabin whatever was inside emerged out. It was as if a giant had put a pump in my innards and was determined to rid it of all it possessed. That giant's torture doesn't work on land, or in sweet waters. Only in salt water does he emerge to dominate and annihilate his victims.[89]

Others are more prosaic. Saratrenu Debi describes her trauma on board the S.S. Chakla when on embarking the ship, she was informed that their second-class cabin, uncomfortable as it was, had been allotted to someone else and they would have to sleep on the deck. She suffered from seasickness for two days and even when their allotted second-class cabin became available, she found it 'too uncomfortable because it had no fan and only one porthole'.[90] Hariprabha writes that her cabin 'which was barely 7 ft by 4 ft and 5 ft in height was hot and stuffy', so she could barely sleep. The bunk beds were tiny and the room was stuffed with boxes. She and Uemon had to share with three other Japanese people and a stink from the boxes, which she thought may have been from preserved fish, made it impossible for her to stay there, despite the perfumes she sprayed in it. But the situation improved gradually when the cabin was emptied of the other passengers and luggage, and she speaks about sleeping well and even singing songs while playing the esraj.[91] Though she had a comfortable stay, that she was not as well-off as the other travellers is evident because she had a third-class cabin and needed financial assistance for the expenses of her travel.

The women describe in detail the route they follow. Since the narrative follows the form of diary entries or letters with dates (with some exceptions), the reader journeys with the writers. Saratrenu Debi travelled via Karachi, Muscat, Bushahr and Mehamera to Persia. Since she compares the streets of Mehamera with Bombay, it is possible that she was based there. Saratrenu Debi describes her stay in Mehamera in detail mentioning that there were an equal number of Persians and Arabs. She describes the presence of the British consul to look into the affairs of the domiciled Indians who worked for the Anglo Persian Oil company and the Strick Scott and company. Besides the consul, Persian sultan had his representation there in the person of an official and a minister. Saratrenu Debi's Persian sojourn was not completed by the journal and ends with her stay at Mehamara.[92] Hariprabha mentions Singapore which was 'clean and oily' and Hong Kong which was 'decorative and beautiful' and describes the 'charming journey via the peak tram to the peak hotel' and the lovely view of Hong Kong at night.[93] Takeda then visited Shimonoseki where she visited Tenjim Sama temple before reaching Kobe. On the other hand, Shanta Chattopadhyay's travelogue describes Hong Kong and Singapore on the way back.[94]

Mahila in 1903 brought out a travelogue of Pushpamala Debi described as a resident of Rangoon who makes Singapore her base and journeys through some towns of Malaya – Johor, Malacca, Deli and Perak. She embarks on her journey from Singapore by road to Kranji by horse carriage and then crosses the Tebrau Straits to reach Johor. She gives an interesting description of crossing the waters.

> The sky was overcast from the morning and intermittent rain started when we got off the carriage. The strong winds discouraged us from embarking on our journey by *sampan* (a flat bottomed boat) through the deep straits. But there was an old Malayan passenger with us who was travelling with his two daughters. He said, the straits were only one and half mile long and it will take us only half an hour to cross it. We will reach out our destination before the storm breaks. We were convinced by his brave words but very soon realised that it had been foolhardy to start in the storm. The strong winds buffeted our *sampan* from one side to the other and heavy rains pelted on us. We all gave up hope of surviving the ordeal and began to call upon all our gods for deliverance . . . Finally it was the dexterity of the Chinese sailors which saved us, though we covered the half hour journey in three hours.[95]

Pushpamala Debi was shocked to discover the flourishing gambling going on in Johor, though 'the King of Johor who was a frequent traveller to Europe, had improved the roads and infrastructure of the city on European lines'. It was a pity according to the writer that 'though he had imitated much from England for the development of his country, he could not adopt the civilized English law against gambling'. She visited the museum at the palace of the Sultan and the garden adjacent to it. After that she went to the Chinese quarters which appeared to her like a 'small Chinese kingdom' with many Chinese families living there for generations and most have not even been to China. Her description of the Chinese women is similar to others on the Chinese and she too succumbs to all the stereotypes of her compatriots.

> The tall Chinese women had such tiny feet that they walked with difficulty leaning on their sticks. I know that women are willing to bear a lot of discomfort for

> enhancing their beauty but what beauty was enhanced by this (foot binding) I couldn't fathom.[96]

Similarities with home country and gender perspective

All the travel writers remember their own country from the moment they leave it, whether they are off on a short tour or on a prolonged stay. They compare every aspect of the places they visit with comparable situations in India and create a sympathetic bond between the traveller and the reader. Sarala Debi compares Rangoon with Calcutta saying that both were cosmopolitan cities and just like in certain localities of Calcutta one cannot see Bengali faces, so also in Rangoon, some streets are devoid of Burmese. There are large numbers of Indians in Rangoon whom she describes as

> Madrasi of low class, Gujarati genteel folk, Muslims of all classes. Those who marry and settle there are referred to locally as *Jerwadi.* There aren't too many Bengalis visible on the streets nor Punjabis. Later however, I came into contact with Bengali and Punjabi associations in the different ports of Burma.[97]

Mrinalini Raha writing for *Antahpur* in 1902, held similar views:

> in Rangoon, the number of expatriate Indians is more than that of the locals and they come mainly for trade, business or professional reasons . . . India and Burma's destinies are tied by the same thread – the same British monarch rules over both countries.[98]

She compares the roads and infrastructure of the capital city Rangoon or Yanggon as the local people call it, with the different Indian cities and point out that 'only Jaipur is comparable in beauty' and 'unlike Calcutta, Rangoon never suffers from muddy roads'.[99] Similarity for Hariprabha Takeda had a different meaning altogether as she embraced her new family. When she landed in Japan, a Japanese newspaper wanted her reaction regarding her decision to join her new family. Knowing that her father-in-law was a well-known man in Japan, Hariprabha in her interview said that she had already been prepared by a Japanese friend Kawaguchi based in Banaras, who had soon after her marriage warned her not to destroy the meaningful bond between the two homelands.[100] Hariprabha's descriptions of the city of Kobe, cleanliness of the roads and parks, the efficient railway system which makes it very convenient even inside the city where 'a sense of national unity visible everywhere' in the 'lack of pushing and shoving' with people looking after the comfort and well-being make interesting reading. The welcome that she was given by her Japanese family was unexpected, yet very familiar because of the similarity with the Bengali way of greeting a new bride. A large number of family and friends greeted her with food and gifts, 'grateful that the son whom they thought they had lost in an alien place was not only alive but had come visiting with his bride'. Hariprabha describes her home and its admirable cleanliness, the food they ate and the clothes they wore, stating the differences yet in a sympathetic manner looking beyond differences to the warmth and caring that she felt and the interest towards Indian customs and religion that they showed. Like most of the women writers of her time, Hariprabha showed a keen interest in the work of the village women and the duties expected of them.[101]

If gender is bound in hegemonic ideologies and women were made an instrument of and/or were complicit in politics of imperialism, the corollary was also true of the nationalist project. Partha Chatterjee's idea that educated colonised women within the nationalist discourse internalised 'material/spiritual distinction' condensed into 'outer' and 'inner' dichotomy[102] may be extended here to see how they articulated this in their travel encounter in the east, differently from their experience in the west. From engaging with differences with the west they encounter while travelling to Europe, in Asia, they articulate similarities, even when they find themselves face to face with dissimilarities. In their writing, these women travellers stress similarities of gender and culture as being more important than political or economic differences to underline solidarity of inner self and spiritual values. It is not that these women did not consider their readers as competent to imbibe information on politics, because one can see admiring references to both in western travels. Even if in the case of Japan, they may refer to modernisation or development, in the case of South-East Asia at least, they highlight cultural ties. Except in Sarala Debi's oblique reference to 'Rangoon as part of Greater India and expressing pride in the Indic connections in the past' yet showing awareness of the innate Burmese distaste for it and the accompanying anti-Indian feeling present there[103] and a stereotyping of Chinese as involved with spurious gambling and opium dens,[104] there was much more discussion of Buddhist architecture, women's education and new meanings of gender freedom in their writing. What the women did was to create a new site outside the bindings of patriarchal domination where they articulated their own ideas and visions of looking at the 'new and foreign', in a sense exoticisation reversed in the west and un-exoticisation in the east.

A slightly later article in 1933 by Aparna Debi in *Masik Basumati* is refreshing in its political tone, though what she writes, as is apparent today in retrospect, was imbibed over the past few decades. At first glance, the reader is unsure whether this is a travelogue (despite the title 'What I Saw in Japan') or it is a knowledgeable essay. But as the narrative progresses, one realises how she weaves in her argument with what she sees during her visit. She describes:

> how the east and west has met in Japan despite Kipling's famous assertion, and how Japan has emerged not only as the veritable leader of the East, the master of the Pacific and a part of the Big five of Finance and Commerce. Japan, who has not only proved Kipling wrong, is neither of the East nor of the West but is the beautiful combination of both separate components. Japan has respectfully absorbed elements from many cultures – China, India, Europe and America. But its own characteristics were so strong that they have assimilated the received elements within their own self. What they have preserved intact is the core element of their civilization – they are Japanese patriotism, Japanese religiosity and Japanese bravery and enhanced them with elements received from other cultures . . . not blindly but with great sagacity.[105]

Aparna Debi then describes 'qualities of Modern Japan', where 'following the Bushido code (samurai codes of honour and ideals) which brought success'. The qualities she stresses are 'devotion to the Emperor, constant alertness, faith, belief in religion, maintaining one's reputation, martial spirit, and helping others in distress.'[106] She then provides a pictorial survey of the great developments of the past 60 years ever since Commodore Perry made his landing on the shores of Japan – in politics, economy, administration, lifestyle and civic rules. Culturally too, Japan leads in literature and theatre. She concludes the high position that Japan holds in the world is something that Indians cannot even comprehend. 'Until I saw it with my own eyes, I did not realise how advanced Japan was. I never thought till I visited Tokyo that I would find it comparable to those developed cities like Paris and London.' And yet for Aparna Devi, 'Japan's modesty, her respect for women, natural beauty, colours of cosmopolitan life, and above all the ideal of motherhood' was most impressive. From her own experience she does not think she can convince her readers by her words alone and says that they should visit Japan and discover the spirit of the country for themselves.[107]

Shanta Chattopadhyay's eye too notices and reproduces certain political elements in Japan, though the interpretation she gives is her own. She provides a picture of an Anti-British Public Meeting that was held in Tokyo saying that 'due to an imaginary accusation, that the British was helping China, an anti-British feeling was building up in the minds of many of the Japanese people'. But beyond that she doesn't mention anything more.[108] She is obviously proud of their association with many well-known scholars and poets of Japan whom she meets through the P.E.N association of which her husband Kalidas Nag is an important member or through her connection with Shantiniketan. She mentions names of Mr Simayaki, President of P.E.N, poet Noguchi, the painter Kampo Arai who stayed in Shantiniketan with his wife and whose quick sketch of her daughter became Shanta's pride possession, Mr Sakai who was secretary of Indo Japanese cultural association, her dear friends Mrs Kora, Mrs Shimiji, Mrs Sakurai, Professor Kamra who studied at Sanskrit College, Mr Kimura who spoke Bengali and sent articles to Bengali periodicals and Mrs Tomiko Wadakora who helped Tagore during his visit to Japan among others.[109]

An important part of the gendered vision is that women are much more visible in women's eyes. Sarala Debi referred to the attractiveness of the Burmese women and the culinary ability of her hostess Mrs Vardun who made several vegetarian dishes. She refused to sit down for dinner with her guests and preferred to serve the meal herself. 'Just like a doting mother she made sure that I ate the meal like a proper Burmese and not like an ignoramus'.[110] She also discusses the changing fashion in Burmese women's clothing.[111] That Sarala was different in her writing compared to the other women travellers is evident when she describes the young women Mrs Vardun invited to meet her. One of them specially caught her attention. She was a Christian, brought up by the missionaries since childhood, had college education and was, very vivacious. A young man Moung a serious theosophist, vegetarian, and unable to converse, volubly on the dinner table appeared to Sarala Devi as this Burmese debutant's special subject of ridicule. She struck out at him verbally at every chance she got making the other guests uncomfortable till the embarrassed Moung told her unobstrusively at one point, that 'considering this girl to be an example of the educated Burmese women would be a mistaken idea to take back home, . . . our girls are . . . well mannered and disciplined, this girl is a result of the missionary education'".[112] Struck by this Sarala writes that that girl though outspoken had many talents and was soon going abroad for higher education. 'This girl', Sarala wrote,

> is an example of the mixture of the Orient and the Occident, both in her virtues and her faults . . . she will get a passport to any social gathering . . . such a smiling, lively, vivacious girl brings everyone present alive. May be that is not an ideal of an oriental society, but it is appreciated in the rest of the world.[113]

Shanta Chattopadhyay's travelogue is replete with mention of Japanese women and in one place she says:

> Most of the women do the general work here, so the selling of the tickets in the museum, storing the sticks, selling catalogues outside, all were done by them. Innumerable foreigners visit these places, Americans in particular. These girls, manage the work, without speaking a word of English. They said that they were very happy when they heard that we were Indians. They showed us many pictures with a lot of care and all of them came forward to meet us. Perhaps, there is still, some attraction to the birthplace of the Buddha in some parts of Japan.[114]

Throughout her travelogue women are visible and unlike many others, she continuously analyses what she sees. There is a charming description of her daughter and the little Japanese girls they met while travelling, and she writes:

> My daughter would make friends with all the little girls she met on the trains. There was a deficiency of language skills in both parties, so the friendship blossomed through the exchange of oranges and toffees. At the time of bidding farewell, these little girls would keep turning around, bowing and saluting in the Japanese style, as long as we could be seen.[115]

Chattopadhyay also describes her visit to a Japanese ladies Monday Club meeting. In her words,

> the club meets in a large building, in a room on the fifth floor which we went up by lift. The ladies were sitting on both sides of a long, dining or library table. There was only one man, an invited guest. He had probably been called to give a talk on their country that day. . . After that, everyone was served with strawberries and cream, cakes and tea. After the gentleman left, we were introduced to the ladies. Of them, some were novelists, some journalists, some were social workers, some teachers and some others were suffragettes. One lady said, 'I would like to go to India to study Indian Philosophy'. We met a lady who was the editor of a monthly magazine. Her magazine was the one which had a sale of 60,000 per month. Of these ladies, about seven or eight were in European clothes. Except for school girls, we had not seen so many people in European clothes in the same place before. It clearly showed that the European attire was gaining popularity very quickly among educated women . . . whatever the style of clothing the members of the Monday club wore, frocks or kimonos, they were in plain colours and without any frivolity. Most women wore black, though, a couple of them were in other colours, but always dark colours, close to black. I have noticed that most of the older ladies in Japan, wear black. But here, even younger women had come in black. Japan is such a country of colours, I wondered what these ladies wear during festive times. In our Bengal these days, the educated westernised women, young and old, wear clothes in various colours and designs. The variety of colours seen in the sarees at places like the assemblies of the All India Women's Association, are not seen anywhere else. Many of the members of the Monday club were married, though there were some were unmarried middle-aged women. Not everyone spoke English but the lady who taught English spoke to me in that

> tongue . . . Looking at them, it seemed to me that the educated Japanese ladies of noble birth are quite different from the ordinary Japanese women.[116]

Talking about gender, empire and cultures of travel, a recent writer Inderpal Grewal examines how Indian women travellers within the discourse of European travel and its politics utilised these practices and altered colonial modernity to lead the way towards 'modernist feminism' often in opposition to nationalist and colonial patriarchy.[117] These women often used the trope of 'freedom' outside versus un-freedom within the country. There is also an awareness of doing something which needs legitimisation and support from others, since they are doing something not usually condoned for women, even by other women. This is applicable to travel even within the country. Swarnakumari Debi's travelogue to Prayag while showing her professed dependence on her travel companion, her elder brother Dwijendranath Tagore, writes about her experiences in 1886, as an exemplar for a conservative society despite the fact that she is already an empowered woman, educated and professional as editor of successful magazines.[118] These hesitations are not visible in her daughter Sarala Debi, travelling in 1930, who also has a preliminary statement, not about fear of social ostracism, or travelling alone but revealing her surprise that it took so long for an opportunity to present itself. Sarala Debi, writes that 'one must draw a connection between divine will and human endeavour for a journey to be successful, since both inner compulsion and external inspiration are necessary'.[119] Instead of expressing eagerness at the opportunity she got to lecture at the Rangoon conference, Sarala is obviously annoyed that instead of a longer visit to the west that she had craved, she only got the chance to travel a short distance. That irritation probably stayed with her since she looks down on the excited women on board the ship referring to them as 'birds freed from their cages roaming restlessly from one deck to the other' in a purposeless manner. It was freedom from their monotonous existence where there was no fear of reprimand.[120] Obviously, Sarala feels isolated from these women who she knows have led much more restrictive lives compared to her but she recognises the value of travel in consciousness of freedom. Hariprabha Takeda is different from Sarala (though her travelogue is equally detailed and recently has been getting a great deal of attention) since she is doing the highest duty of a married woman, travelling with her husband to her in laws and enjoying a good relationship with them. In fact, at the end of her travelogue, she expresses her guilt that she could not reciprocate the affection of her Japanese family by staying with them and taking care of them.[121]

Freedom from social patriarchy and colonial hegemony remains partial for these travellers. Most of them travel with their family heads to places where western influence is predominant. In that sense, the writings do not really signal freedom, but what is evident is that there is less articulation in their writing compared to those of men, of western or British imperial appreciation and more horizontal appreciation of people and places they are visiting. Even more than the travelogues to western countries, these women who are travelling eastwards within Asia concentrate on Asian women and establish a homogeneity of their gender appreciating good qualities in public life but more importantly bringing to the fore special eastern/Asian features. Finally, what one realises is that these writings for women, travel or knowledgeable essays, are not only for entertainment, they want to set an example for other women. Besides stressing commonalities and universal values, a sense of self-worth and self-confidence is also conveyed in the writing.

Notes

1 Radha Kumar, *The History of Doing: An Illustrated Account of Movements for Women's Rights and Feminism in India*, 1800–1990, Delhi: Zubaan, 1993.
2 Partha Chatterjee, *The Nation and Its Fragments: Colonial and Postcolonial Histories*, Delhi: Oxford University Press, 1994, p. 116.
3 Bharati Ray, ed., *Nari o Paribar: Bamabodhini Patrika*, Calcutta: Ananda Publishers, 2002, p. 8.
4 Anon., Chindeshiyo Strijati, *Bamabodhini Patrika*, 3(54), 1867, pp. 678–680.
5 Ibid., p. 678
6 John Keay, *China: A History*, London: Harper Press, 2009, p. 474.
7 Ibid., p. 467.
8 Anon., Chindeshiyo Strijati, *Bamabodhini Patrika*, op. cit., p. 679.
9 Ibid., p. 680.
10 Anon., Brahma Mahila, *Bamabodhini Patrika*, 6(2)(393), 1870, pp. 14–17.
11 Anon., Parashya Ramani, *Bamabodhini Patrika*, 3(3) 264, 1867, pp. 259–262.
12 Ibid.
13 No author, Korea Pradesher Mahila, *Bamabodhini Patrika*, 5(3)(361), 1895, pp. 313–314.
14 Ibid., pp. 313–314.
15 Anon, Sinhaler kotokguli Achar Byabohar, *Bamabodhini Patrika*, 5(3) (362), 1895, pp. 335–336.
16 Ibid.
17 Ibid., p. 336.
18 Ibid., pp. 334–335.
19 Ibid., pp. 336–337.
20 Ajit Prasad Sanyal, Chin chitra, *Janmabhumi*, 11(9), 1902, p. 340.
21 Ibid., pp. 340–341.
22 Ibid., p. 341.
23 Ibid.
24 Jnanendranath Chakraborty, Chin Ramanir Prempatra, *Bharati*, 37(11), 37(12), 1913, pp. 1194–1198; 1291–1297.
25 Ibid., p. 1194.
26 Ibid.
27 Taraknath Mukhopadhyay, Japaner Abhyudoy(2), *Navyabharat*, 24(2), 1906, pp. 110–112.
28 Ibid., pp. 112–113.
29 Manmatha Nath Ghosh, Japane Stri Charitra, *Manashi*, 1(2), 1908, pp. 93–96; 1(6), pp. 252–255; Japane Bibaha, *Manashi*, 1911, 3(9), pp. 599–603; 4(2), pp. 112–115.
30 Manmatha Nath Ghosh, *Sachitra Shupta Japan*, Calcutta: Devakinanadan Pub., 1915.
31 Sarojnath Ghosh, Japani Nartaki, *Mashik Basumati*, 2(2)(1), 1923, pp. 82–87.
32 Jadunath Sarkar, Japaner Obhyudoy, *Bharati*, 30(11), 1906, pp. 1064–1069.
33 Brojosundar Sanyal, Japaner Nari Samaj, *Prabashi*, 8(6), 1908, pp. 315–320.
34 Ganapati Roy, Japane Stri Jatir Itihas o tahader shonge Hindu lalanagoner Shikshar tartomyo, *Manashi*, 2(12), 1910, pp. 732–739.
35 Anon, Brahmadeshe Srtiswadhinata, *Mahila*, 12(9), 1907, pp. 196–198.
36 Ibid., p. 198.
37 Ibid., p. 470.
38 Anon., Brahma Mahila, *Bamabodhini Patrika*, 6(2)(393), 1870, pp. 213–216.
39 Kalachand Dalal, Brahmadesher Ramani, *Bharati*, 35(8), 1911, pp. 801–804.
40 Hemendra Nath Dutta, Turashka Ramani, *Bharat Mahila*, 4(8), 1908, pp. 171–174.
41 Ibid., p. 172.
42 Ibid., pp. 172–173.
43 Ibid., p. 173.
44 Women's University in Japan, *Bharat Mahila*, 4(5), 1909, pp. 97–101.
45 Hariprabha Takeda, Bangamahilar Japan Jatra, *Bharat Mahila*, 9(4), 1913, pp. 110.
46 Bharati Ray, *Shekaler Nari Shiksha: Bamabodhini Patrika (1270–1399 Bengali Year)*, Calcutta: Women's Studies Research Centre, University of Calcutta, 1998.

47 Abala Bose, Japane Stri Sikhsha o amader Kartabya, *Bamabodhini Patrika*, 10(4)(53), 1915, pp. 174–180.
48 Ibid., pp. 177–178.
49 Shanta Chattopadhyay, Japan Bhraman, *Prabashi*, 9 issues 38(1)(1–6), 38(2) (1–3) 1938 and Hongkong and Singapore, *Prabashi*, 39(1), 1939, pp. 149–152.
50 Mrinalini Raha, Barmadesher Kotha, *Antahpur*, 5(8), 1902.
51 Mrinalini Raha, Mrinalini Raha, Barmadesher Kotha, *Antahpur*, 5(8), 1902. Barmadesher Kotha, op. cit., pp. 161–164.
52 Ibid., p. 163.
53 Mrinalini Raha, op. cit., pp. 161–164.
54 Sita Debi, Parasyer Nari, *BangaLakshmi*, 6(5), 1930, pp. 387–391.
55 Sita Debi, Parasyer Nari, op. cit., p. 388.
56 Sita Debi, Parasyer Nari, op. cit., p. 388.
57 Ibid.
58 Sita Debi, Parasyer Nari, *BangaLakshmi*, 6(5), 1930, pp. 390–91.
59 Sita Debi, Parasyer Nari, op. cit., p. 391.
60 Amy Elizabeth Smith, Travel Narratives and the Familiar Letter Form in the Mid-18th Century, *Studies in Philology*, 95, 1988, p. 81.
61 Ibid., p. 83.
62 Clare Broome Saunders, ed., *Women, Travel Writing and Truth*, New York: Routledge, 2014, Introduction, pp. 1–2.
63 A volume with translation of 16 travelogues to east and west is forthcoming. Sarvani Gooptu, ed., *Wandering Women: Travel Writings in Bengali Periodicals 1900–1940*, translated by Indrani Bose and Sarvani Gooptu.
64 Kashi Chandra Ghoshal, Sarbaprothom Bilat Jatri Banganari, *Prabashi*, 11(1)(5), 1911, pp. 489–492.
65 Simonti Sen, ed., *Krishnabhabini Daser Englande Banga Mahila*, Calcutta: Stree Publishers, 1996.
66 Sarvani Gooptu, Crossing the Threshold into the World: Travel Narratives by Bengali Women in the 20th Century, *Asian Studies*, 35(1–2), 2017, pp. 1–15 and Sarvani Gooptu, Introduction: 'The Travelling Women', in Sarvani Gooptu, ed., *Wandering Women*, op. cit.
67 Sukumari Roychowdhury, Genevajatri Banga narir patra, *Bangalakshmi*, 5(9) 1930, pp. 695–700; 5(11) 1930 pp. 820–825; 6(3) 1931, pp. 184–188; 6(7) 1931, pp. 549–554.
68 Bimala Dasgupta, Sweden Bhraman, *Bharatvarsha*, 2(2)(2), 2(2) (4), 1914, pp. 237–243, pp. 618–623.
69 Sarala Debi Chowdhurani, Burma Jatra, *Bharatvarsha*, 19(1)(5), 1931, pp. 779–780; Rangoon, *Bharatbarsha*, 19(2)(4), 1931, pp. 605–611; Shwe Dagon, *Bharatbarsha*, 20(1)(2), pp. 262–268.
70 Tapati Sarkar, Londoner Kotha, *Ramdhanu*, 2(11), 1929, pp. 568–572.
71 Sudha Sen, Niagara Prapat, *Bharatbarsha*, 22(1)(6), 1934, pp. 908–914.
72 For her travel to Burma see Sarala Debi Chowdhurani, Burma Jatra, *Bharatbarsha*, 19(1)(5), 1931, pp. 772–782; Rangoon, 19(2)(4), 1931, pp. 604–613; Shwe Dagon, 20(1)(2), 1932, pp. 260–268.
73 See Bharati Ray, *Early Feminists in Colonial India: Sarala Devi Chowdhurani and Rokeya Sakhawat Hossain*, Delhi: Oxford University Press, 2002; Geraldine Forbes, *Women in Modern India*, Delhi: Cambridge University Press, 1998; Srubabati Chakraborty, *Changing Face of the Women in Colonial Bengal: Krishnabhabini Das and Sarala Debi Chaudhurani, Foremothers of Indian Feminism*, PhD thesis, Vidyasagar University, 2015.
74 Hariprabha Takeda, Bangamahilar Japan Jatra, *Bharat Mahila*, 8(8), 1912, pp. 252–256; 9(3), 1913, pp. 82–88; 9(4), 1913, pp. 109–114.
75 Saratrenu Debi, Parashye Banga-Ramani, *Bharatvarsha*, 4(1)(1), 1916, pp. 30–33.
76 Abala Bose, Japane Strisiksha o Amader Kartavya, *Bamabodhini Patrika*, 10(4)(53), 1915, pp. 174–180.
77 Ibid., p. 175.
78 Sita Debi, Brahma Naari, *Bangalakshmi*, 4(8) 1928, pp. 551–553.
79 Besides her articles in *Prabashi*, also see Sati Debi, *Punyasmriti*, Calcutta: Maitri, 1942 (1963).

80 Shanta Chattopadhyay, Japan Bhraman, *Prabashi* (1938–39).
81 Shanti Nag, *Bharat Muktisadhak Ramananda Chattopadhyay o Ardhashatabdir Bangla*, Calcutta: Firma KLM, 2000 and Purba Smriti, Calcutta: Papyrus, 1956.
82 Shanta Chattopadhyay, Boro Budur, *Prabashi*, 14(2)(4), 1914, pp. 397–402.
83 Mrinalini Raha, Brahmadesher Kotha, *Antahpur*, 5(8), 1902, pp. 160–164.
84 Pushpalata Debi, Malay Rajya, *Mahila*, 9(3), 1903, pp. 71–2.
85 Aparna Debi, Japane Ki Dekhilam, *Mashik Basumati*, 12(2)(5), 1933, pp. 703–710.
86 Pramila Debi, op. cit., pp. 218–219.
87 Letter to the editor of Mahila by Mrs R.S. Hussein, *Mahila*, 10(4), 1905, pp. 108–112.
88 Quoted in Bharati Ray, *Early Feminists of Colonial India: Sarala Devi Chaudhurani & Rokeya Sakhawat Hossain*, op. cit., p. 62.
89 Sarala Debi Chowdhurani, Burma Jatra, *Bharatvarsha*, (19)(1)(5), 1931, pp. 779–780.
90 Saratrenu Debi, Parashye Banga-Ramani, *Bharatvarsha*, 4(1)(1), 1916, pp. 30–33.
91 Hariprabha Takeda, op. cit., pp. 254–255.
92 Saratrenu Debi, Parashya Bangamahila, op. cit., p. 675.
93 Hariprabha Takeda, Bangamahilar Japan Jatra, *Bharat Mahila*, 9(3), 1913, pp. 82–88.
94 Shanta Chattopadhyay, Japan Bhraman, *Prabashi*, 39(1), 1939, 249–255.
95 Pushpabala Debi, Malay Rajya, *Mahila*, 9(3), 1903, pp. 71–72.
96 Ibid., p. 73.
97 Sarala Debi, Rangoon, *Bharatvarsha*, 19(2)(4), 1931, p. 606.
98 Mrinalini Raha, Bharmadesher Kotha, *Antahpur*, 5(8), 1902, pp. 161–164.
99 Ibid., p. 163.
100 Hariprabha Takeda, Bangamahilar Japan Jatra, *Bharat Mahila*, 9(3), 1913, pp. 85–86.
101 Hariprabha Takeda, Bangamahilar Japan Jatra, op. cit., 1913, pp. 87–88.
102 Partha Chatterjee, Colonialism, Nationalism and Colonised Women: The Contest in India, *American Ethnologist*, 16(4), 1989, pp. 622–633.
103 Sarala Debi Chaudhurani, Rangoon, *Bharatvarsha*, 19(2)(4), 1931, pp. 604–613.
104 Pushpabala Debi, Malay Rajya, *Mahila*, 9(3), 1903, pp. 71–72.
105 Aparna Debi, Japane Ki Dekhilam, *Mashik Basumati*, 12(2)(5), 1933, p. 703.
106 Ibid., p. 704.
107 Ibid., p. 710.
108 Shanta Debi (Chattopadhyay/Nag), Japan Bhraman, *Prabashi*, 38(1)(2), 1938, p. 268.
109 Shanta Debi, Japan Bhraman, op. cit., 38(2)(2), 1938, pp. 292–293.
110 Sarala Debi, Rangoon, *Bharatvarsha*, 19(2)(4), 1931, pp. 610–611.
111 Ibid., p. 612.
112 Sarala Debi, Rangoon, op. cit., pp. 609–610 (translated by Indrani Bose).
113 Ibid.
114 Shanta Chattopadhyay, Japan Bhraman, *Prabashi*, 38(1)(1), pp. 101–110 (translation of Shanta Chattopadhyay's travelogue by Indrani Bose).
115 Shanta Chattopadhyay, op. cit., 38(1)(2), p. 269.
116 Shanta Chattopadhyay, op. cit., 38(2)(2), 1938, pp. 292–293.
117 Inderpal Grewal, *Home and Harem: Nation, Gender, Empire and Cultures of Travel*, Durham: Duk University Press, 1996.
118 Swarnakumari Debi, Prayag Jatra (Travelling to Prayag), *Bharati o Balak*, 1886, reprinted in Abhijit Sen and Ujjal Ray, eds., *Pother Kotha: Shatabdir Shondhikkhone Bangamohilar Bhraman*, Calcutta: Stree, 1999, pp. 1–36.
119 Sarala Debi Chowdhurani, Burma Jatra (Travel to Burma), *Bharatvarsha*, 19(1)(5), 1931, pp. 771–773.
120 Sarala Debi Chowdhurani, Burma Jatra, *Bharatvarsha*, 19(1)(5), 1931, p. 777.
121 Hariprabha Takeda, Bangamahilar Japan Jatra, *Bharat Mahila*, 9(4) 1913, p. 114.

4 Beyond the classroom

Teaching about Asia in children's magazines

Even when the concept of the nation was still 'fuzzy' and European thought 'was both indispensible and inadequate',[1] vernacular literary magazines interpreted in their own way modernity which impacted families, specifically children. As Partha Chatterjee points out, this was the 'own domain of sovereignty within the colonial society' created well before 'it begins its political battle with imperial power', which he called the 'inner' domain which was yet unconquered, distinguished from the 'outer' public domain where the colonised were defeated.[2] But this journalistic domain was sovereign because its language was its own, incomprehensible by the colonial state, except in translation, yet it went beyond its own limits to absorb and adapt the tools of the 'outside' domain of western knowledge to educate the family, informally yet with serious intent. In this education, not only the west but also great Asian nations played an important role in the pride it evoked at both the 'public domain's' development and the 'inner domain's' cultural and spiritual treasures. Besides Asian solidarity, the other aspect of this awareness campaign was to create a sense of peoples' bonding at all levels. As Sumit Sarkar shows, there was a difference between 'formal pedagogical methods' and 'literature for children', and the latter went beyond the 'purely didactic' and explored 'ways for stimulating the imagination of the young and providing entertainment'.[3] As the children's magazines that I will discuss in this chapter showed, this occurred simultaneously with the nationalist project but was not engulfed by it. It was to create not only ideal citizens for the imagined nation but also an intelligent childhood and well-aware youth able, if necessary, to interact with their peers in the world through this information with entertainment strategy.

Sakha has been considered to be the first monthly periodical for children, and its high standard was attested to by Bengal's famed novelist Bankim Chandra Chattopadhyay, who praised its language style and content in a letter to the editor saying that all young Bengalis should make friends with *Sakha* (a pun on the word, which means friend). Edited by Pramadacharan Sen during 1883–1884, the later editorship was taken up by Shibnath Shastri during 1885–1886 and then by Annadacharan Sen during 1887–1892. It was a periodical for children, dealing mainly with the history of India and science. The spectacular success of *Sakha* led Gyanadanandini Debi, wife of Satyendranath Tagore, to draw in the Tagore house children to a new magazine for the young called *Balak*. The pictures including maps that were published in *Balak*, at least in the initial phase, were important attractions for the readers. Soon Rabindranath Tagore took over as executive editor, but after a year it was amalgamated with *Bharati* published thereafter as *Bharati O Balak*. Another children's magazine in 1898, *Anjali*, was edited by Rajeswar Gupta, and

DOI: 10.4324/9781003243786-4

from the very first issue learning about the geophysical features of Asia and understanding its politics was stressed.[4]

Shishu, a monthly literary periodical for children from Calcutta with Baradakanta Majumdar as editor, started in 1912 and combined fairy tales, mythological stories and poems, as well as current events and important landmarks in Asia, as its content. But by far the most popular magazine for children was *Sandesh*,[5] which was first published by Upendrakishore Raychowdhury in 1913 through his publishing company, M/s U. Ray and Sons. Upendrakishore's eldest son Sukumar Ray went to Great Britain for advanced training in printing technology, and he joined as an active partner after his return. After the death of Upendrakishore Raychowdhury in 1915, Sukumar succeeded as the editor of the magazine. Under Sukumar Ray, *Sandesh* was established as a unique magazine that combined literary values with humour and fun and a lot of information from different parts of the world. In 1923, Sukumar's younger brother Subinoy took charge after his untimely death. However, the publication of the magazine was stopped in 1925 and then revived later by the famous family scion Satyajit Ray. *Ramdhanu* was also a monthly literary periodical from Calcutta with editor Bisweswar Bhattacharya at the helm during 1927–1929; Manoranjan Bhattacharya during 1929–1938; and Kshitindranarayan Bhattacharya during 1938–1988. Another magazine, edited by the famous children's novelist Hemendra Kumar Roy, was *Rangmashal* which was published from 1937 to 1946, with Kamakshiprasad Chattopadhyay and Debiprasad Chattopadhyay taking over after Roy. It was an important periodical for children dealing with essays in literature and popular science in the 20th century.

An important point of interest was that far more than the countries of South or South-East Asia, the main focus of interest of the writers of the period in the children's magazines was on China and Japan. This could partly be because Chinese and Japanese news and literature were more accessible to the literate public of Calcutta as translated works, but also because the so-called Far East was closer in the minds of ordinary people than the countries of South-East Asia. Ultimately, these magazines had to sell, and so writing interesting facts about lands the children have heard of would be far more worthwhile than the informative essays about lands they knew precious little about. It must be pointed out that West Asia is not neglected in the periodicals, and stories based on Arabia and Bagdad are frequent.[6]

Information through entertainment

The first step in this process was to know about the life and culture of the people of Asia, and since these writings are meant for children, they aim at an educative value or moral and generally contain an idea or value which is familiar to the Bengali reader. There are translations of travel writing by famous western travellers like the Swedish traveller Sven Hedin on his visits to Kirghisthan and Chinese Turkistan, Dr Aurel Stein's and Raffles' works, in the children's magazine *Sandesh*, appealing to the spirit of adventure as well as the spreading of knowledge by throwing light 'on parts of the world which no one knew anything about'.[7] Subimal Ray describes these discoveries of how despite the Gobi desert being more terrible and lonely than other places in the world, the local people still remember the pre-existing cities and there are many tales and proverbs that circulate among the people in the neighbouring forests and mountains about the lost city. Almost a thousand years ago a Chinese pilgrim had discovered the ruins in the desert and wrote about them in a book. Many years later the famous Swedish traveller Sven Hedin visited Chinese Turkistan and heard about the ruins from the local people. He then decided to enter the desert and discover the truth for himself. Organising a party of explorers, camels and dogs he entered the desert but was deserted by many of his companions while some died or became mad. After a lot of trouble he discovered the ruins and entering a temple he found beautiful paintings on the walls – not only of people, animals, boats but also found spinning wheel, pots, wooden screws and books whose script he could not read. After Hedin, Dr Aurel Stein too made more discoveries in the desert. In a ruined temple he found pictures of Greeks and Romans, as well as Greek coins. He also found books written in ancient Turkish and Chinese. Not only did he discover connections between China, India and Persia, he found the influence of Buddhism and Buddhist relics. Sven Hedin discovered images of people who were a lot like the ancient Aryans and many experts say that almost 4000 years ago the people of the Gobi desert were a branch of the ancient Aryans of central Asia.[8]

The spread of knowledge of the archaeological discoveries is combined with the appreciation of the spirit of adventure of these intrepid explorers. In 1885, Sris Chandra Majumdar's article on the Parliament of the Tahiti Islands, in the magazine *Balak*, shows how all the island's chieftains came together to sacrifice their own royal rights and establish a representative body to establish their own rules and end capital punishment, with some help from the Christian missionaries.[9]

A similar method of dissemination of knowledge about distinctive flowers, trees and animals found in different parts of Asia is identified for the young readers through an appreciation of their scientific knowledge and background. Upendrakishore Raychowdhury's article on *Rafflesia*, found in the forests of Sumatra by the English explorer Raffles, describes the flower with its large petals which are the size of a full arm and one finger thick and its leaves containing an urn like structure which can hold large quantities of water. It is a parasite, emitting a smell like that of rotting dead bodies, attracting large drones of flies.[10] For full effect on the readers a picture has been provided for Rafflesia.

'Banraj Pukan Sen' (King of the Forest) is a story of a pet elephant who saved his master James Anderson from wild elephants in forests of North Siam (Thailand), which came out in the *Pearson Magazine* and has been adapted for readers of *Sandesh*.[11] All the children's magazines contain such informative articles.

Places and people of interest are showcased in different magazines. Rabindranath Tagore's visit to Japan created a furore not only because of the publication of his book *Nationalism* criticising Japanese aggression that had led to mixed reactions but also people's interest in the country had been piqued by Japan's success as well as his criticism of it. In the years 1917–1918, a number of articles on Tagore's visit to Japan were discussed by Mukul Chandra De, who accompanied the poet and Andrews and Pearson in 1916 in the form of a travelogue of interesting places[12] or wonderful sights like Mt Fujiyama.[13] De describes Yokohama and the house of their host Hara San, on top of a cliff overlooking the sea, where they stayed during the visit. He describes the view of Mt Fujiyama and their rooms with flowers, paintings and mat carpets.[14] 'It is wonderful', he wrote,

> how much the Japanese love Mount Fuji. Either they sit quietly and watch the mountain, or their artists paint in portraits, and handkerchiefs, even pots and pans

> or fans. There are many stories, songs and expressions of love about Fujiyama that I have never seen about any other mountain. I have never in my life seen a more beautiful mountain – if you ever go to Japan then you will realise the truth of my words.[15]

Like Mt Fujiyama, another landmark which has excited the wonder of observers and travellers for ages is the Great Wall of China. In 1913, an article in *Shishu*, titled 'The Frontier Wall of China', discusses the Great Wall considered to be one of the world's seven wonders and how its maintenance has been neglected in recent years.[16] *Sandesh* published in 1920 an article on the Great Wall of China with pictures and the story of Qin Shi Huang who, despite being a despot destroyed and burnt all previous history records, retained one achievement – that of building the Great Wall, which has immortalised him. Sukumar Ray, in this essay, imagines the Great Wall as a 2000-year-old man who has seen thousands and thousands of travellers cross over its broad road and has also seen hordes of enemies among the Turks, Tartars, Manchus and Chins test the might of their weapons over it. The Wall has seen successive dynasties rule China and 'bury the bodies of their dead kings near it . . . It is now on its death bed and a few centuries later one will have to hunt for its history from the remaining rocks'.[17] In 1931, Biraj Kumar Bandopadhyay, in *Ramdhanu*, started by writing that one builds high walls around a house to keep the thieves out, and in the same way, earlier even cities built walls around themselves to protect the people from raids.

> It was many years back, two thousand to be precise, when a Chinese king called Shi Howangti ruled who was rather whimsical. Do you want to know how whimsical he was? Once he asked the people of his kingdom to consider him as the oldest king of China. But in order to achieve that one has to remove the visible proof of achievements of the previous kings. The king ordered that all the books which contained past history should be burnt. But even that would not solve the problem. What about the old learned men who could pass on their memories to the next generations? He ordered that the heads of all the old scholars be cut off. But despite all his efforts, he could not erase the past history. But this whimsical king had an achievement which has remained one of the greatest achievements of China. Just like the Bargi raids evoked fear in Bengal, the Tartars and the Manchus also invaded China wreaking destruction in the countryside and killing millions. When all efforts to combat the raids were unsuccessful the king decided to prevent them totally by building a huge wall at the border. Ten thousand people were employed to build the wall and after some years of perseverance, a 15,000 miles long wall came up which has no parallel in the world . . . However today after 2200 years it has been almost destroyed by time.[18]

China has attracted the interest of Bengalis from the very beginning of writing in the journals. Keeping in mind that *Sandesh* was written for children, descriptions of unfamiliar practices and dressing habits are often discussed humorously, rather lightly, acquainting young minds through stories and jokes. In 1915, Upendrakishore Raychowdhury started his 'Stories about the Chinese' with a funny tale of how a Chinese envoy was sent to India by the Chinese Emperor to taste and bring back the famous mango. Though he enjoyed the mangoes, the envoy was unable to carry a sample back. Fearing the wrath of the king, he devised the plan of rubbing some tamarind in his own beard and asked the king to suck it, saying that was the taste of mango. The king was furious at the taste and blamed those who praised India as the country of such a magnificent fruit for misleading him.[19] 'It was fortunate', the author continues,

> that the envoy had a beard otherwise how would he have hoodwinked the king. In fact, very few people in China have beards or moustaches. It is the symbol of age there so until they become grandparents, Chinese do not keep beards. When they finally do keep a beard, they take good care of it by oiling it and tucking it away in a tiny bag when they go to bed. It is always well combed and oiled.

Again, Raychowdhury tells a story that once a king admiringly asked his minister how he managed to keep his beard beautiful. When the minister replied, he did it by tending to it very tenderly, the king got very annoyed at the time he was wasting on the beard and reduced his salary.[20] The author then talks about the ponytail that the Chinese keep behind their head, similar to the familiar 'tikis' sported by the Indian Hindu Brahmins.

> The Chinese 'tiki' proved to be very helpful. If one wanted to fight, the tiki proved to be a good place to hold while it could also be a cane to smack naughty children on their backs. It was considered a matter of great humiliation to deprive a Chinese of his hairpiece. When a thief was sent to jail his hair was cut off so when he was released his first job was to attach a fake one. It also helped when he was caught stealing again because when the police caught him by his hair, he simply evaded being caught by leaving the false hair in their hands.[21]

Two other things that the author describes as essential for the Chinese are their fans and chopsticks. Raychowdhury wrote that the Chinese are very intelligent people which Indians have known for a long time. They have invented many things like, telescope, printing, and gun powder. The largest wall in the world, largest canal, the oldest newspaper all came from China. Even astronomy was practiced in China for a long time. He adds a humourous touch for his young readers when he writes that 'the Chinese astronomers said many peculiar things – the world is a square, and eclipses take place because a large dog swallows the sun and the moon.' But he admits that it is very similar to the ancient beliefs in our country as well. Another similarity that Chinese have with Indians is the zodiac, though they are named differently. 'We talk about *mesh, brisha, mithun, karkat, singha, kanya, tula, brishchik, dhonu, makara, kumbha* and *meen* and the Chinese have their rat, cow, tiger, rabbit, dragon, snake, horse, sheep, monkey, hen, dog and pig'.[22] A number of pictures have been added of Indian and Chinese zodiacs.

Another article also unnamed but possibly one of Upendrakishore's last was 'Chindesher Kotha' (Tales of China). It was very similar to his 1886 article in *Sakha*, titled 'Chiner golpo' (Story of China), where he describes a Chinaman in the following way.

> Many of you may know where China is and many of you have seen a Chinese man. Those white men, with flat faces, snub noses, twinkling eyes, long hairpiece at the back, who make shoes, do carpentry, speak using words like wah kwah, wang chung, those people who have opium.[23]

After this rather objectionable beginning (which he claims comes out of a book he had read), however, the author reminds his youthful readers that the Chinese had become civilized long before others. They were the first to begin printing and they were the first to invent gunpowder. Because they used to suffer from foreign attacks the Chinese built a wall such as the world had never seen before and after all there is no other country in the world which can make and fly kites better.[24] He then describes the birth of a daughter in a Chinese household where 'she is treated poorly, neglected and not even named,' while a boy is bathed in water containing many perfumes and oils to wish him good fortune. Gold and silver coins are added to the bath water for future wealth and egg-whites are rubbed on his body so that he becomes fair-skinned. Finally, the boy's buttocks are slapped with onions so that he becomes intelligent. Sometimes the boy's hands are loosely tied with a red string for days so that he doesn't grow up to be naughty and to ward off evil spirits coins are tied to their wrists. Within a few days the boy's hair is shaved off so that he has thick hair growth and when the hair grows a tiny ponytail is made which is hung from a hole in the cap that the boy wears. When a girl is born in a Chinese household, they are not looked after at all. In many cases they are killed off most of the time their father performs this heinous act. They are thrown into the water with a stone tied around their necks or some cruel people burn their new born daughters[25]

After giving instances of how they kill their unwanted daughters, Ray writes that

> when children die in a Chinese household it is believed that father or grandfather owed money to someone who is then born in their house so that they can waste their money before dying. So, though the Chinese care for children when they are sick, as soon as they die, they are considered to be ghosts who must be removed from the house and dust the house thoroughly and burst crackers to ward off evil.[26]

Raychowdhury also discusses the importance given to education from a young age by the Chinese. Along with a picture of a classroom, the author says that the student's time to play ends when he joins school because he studies from morning till evening. Interestingly, even in a children's magazine, or may be because of it, Raychowdhury reminds his readers of the universal Chinese vice of opium smoking which become counterproductive in all spheres and must be avoided at all costs by Indian youth. Many years later, while writing 'Tales of China' for his own magazine *Sandesh*, the author is much less scathing, though he still hovers over the dissimilarities between Chinese and Indian customs – like using their surname before their first names, giving the year before the month followed by the date, shaking their own hands in greeting, repeating lessons to the teacher while backing them instead of facing them, paying money to the doctors when they are well instead of when they are being treated for illnesses, using a hard board under their heads for comfortable sleep and last but not the least, punishing a thief by committing suicide in front of their house.[27] He then provides many instances where laughter is evoked in those who are unfamiliar with the Chinese language and refers to a group of people whose profession is making up stories. But in the end he describes the industrious nature of the Chinese and their proficiency in paper production, printing of books, discovering telescope and gunpowder and, of course, the longest wall in the world 'which will take a horse rider almost a month to travel the entire length'.[28] A year after Upendrakishore's article on China came out in *Sakha*, Bihari Lal Gupta, who was an ICS and first Indian Chief Presidency Magistrate and Coroner of Calcutta, wrote a sequel to Ray's article on China. He told his readers that he hoped his article would satiate to some extent the thirst for knowledge that had arisen from Ray's earlier article about Chinese people. Addressing what for Indians is the most curious thing about the Chinese, he writes that

> unlike India where four brothers of a family may look completely different in colouring or features, in China most people have same skin tone and similar features. Also the Chinese are much fairer which is why when an Indian sees a Chinese man on the streets of Calcutta people address them as '*Chine Sahe*b'[29]

putting them at par with Europeans. Gupta however is rather scathing about their looks when he says that 'it is not that just because they are fair the Chinese are very beautiful. While they are young, they look quite attractive but as they grow older their face becomes more and more flat and unremarkable'.[30] Gupta then points out two customs which the Chinese follow to supposedly enhance their looks, but which in his eyes prove to have quite the opposite effect. 'One is the habit of growing the finger nails of their left hand to show off their high social and financial status, since only the idle rich who can afford to grow them'. He then describes in graphic detail the pain of Chinese women who beautify themselves through foot binding and ends with the comment that 'though the Christian missionaries have tried very hard to eradicate this custom, they have failed'.[31] He also ponders on the difference in the ideas of beauty that prevails among men and women in different countries and how he as an Indian finds it difficult to comprehend the Chinese concept of beauty where 'the girls make their face very white and add a lot of red colour'. He considers it unnatural and therefore ugly and ends his article with the comment, 'If the Chinese had not tried to change their natural God-given looks they would indeed look beautiful. Isn't there a lesson for us to learn from this?'[32]

A grandmother writing to her granddaughter in 1917 writes about her visit to Sri Lanka (which she refers to as the land of King Ravana) in her childhood with her mother after travelling to many places. She describes her journey from a coral island where she travels by train until she boards the ship Curzon to take her to Sri Lanka. She describes her journey by train when she notices the most beautiful coral scattered on the beaches of the island, just like 'flower bouquets'. The froth of the sea too appeared to be like the *kunda* flower, though when the froth dried they became deposited into salt-like formations. Sometimes people mistake the cuttlefish bones for seafoam too.

> When we got off the train and crossed the wooden pool to the ship, a sea wave came in through the gap in the bridge and wet my socks and shoes.[33]

In the next issue, she described the places she visited

She travelled 56 miles from Colombo to a rubber factory and enjoyed watching the coolies cut out a part of the bark of the rubber tree and picked out the sap in coconut pots. Each person cuts about 200 trees and then collects the sap in a bucket which he takes to the factory. All the sap is collected and solidified and cut up into pieces. She compares the thin cloth like strips that emerge when the sap pieces and thrown into a machine, to an Indian folded dhoti. Later they are then dried by fire and then coloured red with smoke. Then they are ready to be packed. She was charmed to see the leaves of the rubber plants becoming red and falling off and soon the new leaves and flowers with three seeds would bloom. She also described her journey to Kalayani (or Kalyani) where there was a Buddhist temple. There below a very large stone Buddha's tooth is preserved. It is said that Hemmali, an Oriya princess hid the tooth in her hair and brought it here. There is a marble image of Buddha in this temple where he is lying resting on one hand. The costume and ornaments of the image are made of gold. The author whose name is not mentioned anywhere noticed that someone had donated a gold pineapple there. There are many images of gods and goddesses on the walls but they were not familiar to the Indian eye. The temple too is not very beautiful. There are generally three parts in a temple – the stupa below which the relic of Buddha is generally hidden, a room where his image is kept and a Bodhidruma that is an oval tree.

> I noticed some young girls go to that temple in a bullock cart . . . They are similar to ones that are used in our country as well. The driver here says the words 'jack' and 'mack' for right and left when they drive.[34]

Burma's occupation by the British in 1885 not only heralded political articles in *Bharati*, an anonymous writer also tried in *Balak* to make the present king Thibaw's predicament understood even by young India.[35] The article is based on British newspaper reports, but the presentation of the sad but dignified figure of Thibaw at the transfer of power ceremony is the author's own. He, or it could have been the editor herself, also adds at the end, the latest available news was that Burma has now been 'incorporated into the British empire, that the British should beware of the amount of straw they were saddling on a camel since it was the last one which proverbially broke the camel's back.'[36] Nripendra Chandra Bandopadhyay serially in *Ramdhanu* describes the places of interest and the people's lives in Burma in 1927. However, even in his innocuous way of describing the city and the people, Bandopadhyay is true to a stereotype when he glibly mouths the Indianisation ideas by attributing Burma's artistic excellence to Indian talents and is also true to an Indian patriarchal stereotype in judging Burmese women. He had been full of praises when he spoke about the neatness in the dress and manner of the Burmese, but then he writes that despite

> the silks and jewels that the Burmese men and women wear, their home are rather unclean. This is bound to happen when the women roam around freely in the streets – even when they are doing most of the work compared to their men, they obviously do not have the time to look after their homes or do housework. In our homes, the women keep busy with cleaning the house and doing the cooking and do not have any connection with the outside world, the Burmese women on the other hand work both at home as well as outside. When they spread pearls outside, the oysters form inside, when the outside is beautiful, the inside of the home may often accumulate dirt.[37]

Bandopadhyay, who finds Burma to be 'a land of magic and dreams', hopes that 'one day when the readers of *Ramdhanu* grow up and visit Burma, they will present to their readers, accounts of India's connections with that country not only in the past but discuss their intellectual legacy in contemporary times'.[38]

An article by Manoranjan Bhattacharya introducing the young readers to Shyamdesh or Thailand came out in *Ramdhanu* in 1932. A multifaceted writer, combining his work as editor of *Ramdhanu*, Professorship at Ripon College and a writer of children's stories and teen detective fiction (starring the Japanese sleuth Hukakasi), Bhattacharya starts with the name Siam (spelt in Bengali as Shyam), which is how 'the English atlas refers to Shyamdesh'. He writes that the reason why it was so called was because though the locals called their country Sayam, the neighbouring Malay people called it Siyom. Today the local people of Siam do not get into this controversy and call their country *Muang thoi* which means independent country.[39] The article describes the appearance of the people of Thailand, the main industries like tin (controlled mainly by the Chinese), gold and silver ('which the Siam government takes keen interest in and sends the intelligent students abroad to learn the best production techniques'), agrarian crops and forest products and which country controlled which industry (Chinese and British). It also describes the rich natural resources in wild and domesticated animals who are used as beasts of burden. To pique the interest of the readers he mentions the presence of 'atleast fifty-six species of snakes.' The rivers not only consist of crocodiles, but also many types of fishes. The main food items of the people are rice and fish. The incidental comments he makes are obviously jocular in a journalistic fashion. 'They also like mutton but being Buddhists, they don't like to kill animals themselves. Luckily the Chinese who have no such qualms do the needful.' In a more serious note Bhattacharya describes how in recent times, Siam has been modernised through European contact and are now enjoying modern education, modernised army with heavy artilleries, and warships. The fact that the monarchical system was ended in 1932 and the people were granted a constitution has been expressed to suit his youthful readers. 'Recently the people of Siam have extracted a promise from the King that he will no longer administer the country but only remain as a figure head.' For those interested in travel to Siam, the author writes that Siam has not really developed large cities and only Bangkok has a large population of six and a half out of which almost half are Chinese. Railways have been established but majority of the population still use the water ways for movement. The reason for this is that large areas of Siam contain low and soft land and rocks are very difficult to obtain which makes building roads and maintaining them very difficult and cost intensive. On the other hand, there are many large and small rivers and streams. That is why the government has concentrated more on building canals rather than roads and travelling by boats is most common there[40]Like most other writers, Bhattacharya ends his description by recalling 'Bharat-Siam links in ancient times'. He writes:

> even today one can notice similarities between the customs of the two countries. Ancient Puranic sources state that during the age of Buddha, two Indian Brahmins went travelling and established the kingdom of Siam. But this is not a historical fact but a legendary myth. But one must remember that before Bangkok, the capital of Siam was Ayuthia which still exists today. According to experts, Ayuthia was named after the capital of the legendary king Ram's capital at Ayodhya. Initially its name was Ayodhya but over time, the name changed to Ayuthia.[41]

Translation of stories and folk tales

Most of the translated stories and folk tales have a moral which appeals to the Indians and make them suitable for the young mind. But it is striking that there is no attempt to Indianise the stories through changing names of the characters or context, and in fact the place or language of origin is always mentioned. A majority of the translations of fairy tales or folk tales are seen in *Sandesh*. In 1913, a Japanese story was translated by Upendrakishore (though the name is not mentioned) called the Japanese God, where the youngest grandson of the light of the sky, Triptanol, wanted to switch practices with his eldest brother Diptanol and borrowed his fishing rod. But due to his inexperience in fishing, he lost the fishing rod when a fish dived into the sea with it stuck in his throat. Triptanol tried to replace his angry brother's hook with others, but Diptanol was extremely unforgiving and insisted that he find his lost rod. Spying Triptanol sitting with a dismal face on the seashore, the sea god sent him to court the Sea King Sindhupati's daughter. In due course, Triptanol was welcomed into the court of Sindhupati, who gave his daughter in marriage to Triptanol and located the fish who carried the pierced rod. Then Triptanol returned home riding a giant crocodile and armed with two jewels to control the tides and was able to pacify Diptanol and win his father's throne.

This was the first of many Japanese stories that were translated for the Bengali children over the next decade. Another story by Upendrakishore which also 'The Frog and the Sea, though it does not mention the author's name'[42] was also a translation of a Japanese story. It spoke of the lack of farsightedness in the frog who on his way to discover the sea lost his way and standing on a hill found another village before him. So he returned and informed his fellowmen that there was nothing known as the sea and it was a false story. This corresponds to the popular Bengali phrase of *kuyor bang* or *kupamanduka* where a frog thinks that the well he is in comprises the world. The whole idea is to exhort the Bengalis to give up their lazy and easy life and discover a world beyond. 'Ashchoyjyo Chhobi' by Subinoy Ray in 1918 is a story which had as characters a simple rustic Japanese family and a village chief, discovering the wonders of a mirror, but the underlying philosophy is universal that truth is one, but it takes different meanings when viewed differently.[43]

In 1919, *Sandesh* brought out two Tibetan story translations by Shobhanlal Mukhopadhyay ('Kak O Bang') and Mohonlal Gangopadhyay ('Shonar Jharna'). The first story (The crow and the frog)[44] narrates how a little baby frog managed to use his ready wits to hoodwink a crow who had caught him to eat. This style of using animal stories with morals and values is universal and timeless in educating children and the uneducated. The second story, 'Golden Waterfall', is about two brothers – the elder clever and selfish, while the younger simple and kind. The elder brother threw the younger one and his mother out of the house, and they started living in the forest where the boy cut and sold wood for food. One day he discovered a huge stone lion on top of a hill and started to worship him. The lion suddenly roared and offered to give him a boon of molten gold. His elder brother, hearing of his brothers' change of fortune, tried to replicate the boon, but because he was greedy he was punished.[45] This story too can find resonance in every culture but that it is a Tibetan story is mentioned.

Jotirmoyee Debi's 'Dushtu Gemunu', or 'Naughty Gemunu', is a story based in Sri Lanka, where the young boy Gemunu decides that he has grown up and must fight the Tamils to protect his maternal grandfather's kingdom against his father Kabbantishya's wishes. He was able to defeat the Tamil king Ellara, but instead of disgracing his enemy, he made a monument over his dead body and ordered that all should show respect to the fallen king. Thus, the naughty boy Gemunu was transformed into a legendary hero.[46] This story is interesting not only as a simple story but for its context which is stated plainly and not disguised. By publishing a story for children where the protagonist is a Sinhalese and the enemy are the Tamils from South India who are mentioned are raiders and marauders[47] in 1920, it shows the commitment to and highlights the new universalist ideas which were criticising and cautioning against excessive nationalism that had already brought about a World War.

Punyalata Chakraborty, Upendrakishore's daughter, writes a story, 'A Man from Afterlife', about a simple Turkish couple who were hoodwinked by a clever thief who took advantage of the woman's simplicity saying that he was from the world of dead and promising to give the money she offered to her dead son.[48] Some of the stories, whether as translated works (where the origin is mentioned) or simply stories told, have an appeal to universal values and ideas even though the backdrop is from different lands. To my mind, the very site of the story in different countries stresses the universality of a value which then claims greater legitimacy for it.

In 1918, Subinoy Roy translated a Chinese fairy tale where Wang, who got a boon to climb above the clouds when he helped an old man, climbed to the cloud to see that lightning was caused by the brushing of an ogre's tail. He picked up a diamond-like star and realised that rains were caused by the pouring of water from a jug by three ghosts sitting on top of the ogre. They invited him to make rain, so Wang poured water over his village which helped his family to improve the farming and then he sold the star to the Chinese king for a huge sum, which ended all his family's problems.[49] Punyalata Chakraborty translated 'Pratigyar Daye' ('For the Sake of a Promise') which is about an Arab Bedouin who bought the most fabulous camel at a huge price. Having brought it home, the Bedouin took such good care of it that the neighbours were amazed. But one day the camel vanished. The Bedouin was devastated and hunted for him high and low. Then after a few days angry at what he considered a betrayal by an animal he loved and cared for so much, he promised in a mosque that if the camel returned, he would sell it for one paisa. When he reached home, to his surprise the camel was there. Though he was happy at his favourite camel's return, he knew that he would have to honour his promise and the next day hundreds of people including the local Qazi came to his house to buy his camel. Soon the Bedouin came out followed by his camel, and, lo and behold, there was a dirty black cat on the back of the majestic camel. The Bedouin then said that just as he had promised to sell his camel for one paisa, he had also promised to sell his cat for one lakh and both would have to be bought together. The people and the Qazi burst out laughing at the clever wit of the Bedouin and the way he had saved his precious camel.[50]

Kuladaranjan Ray's 'Blind Lo San' ('Andha Lo San'), a translation of a Chinese folk tale about how good deeds and the loyalty of his dog Fan bring back sight to a homeless blind beggar,[51] or the story about love and friendship between a little beggar girl and a horse – 'God in God Knows' ('Devata Janen'),[52] a Chinese tale, has remained as one of children's favourite stories. Kuladaranjan Ray, younger brother of Upendrakishore, was a prolific writer of children's stories based on not only Indian Epics and Puranas but also Asian folktales. Almost every issues of *Sandesh* carried some translation or other which became a favourite for years to come. 'Rustom and Sorab', a Persian tale of a father and son warrior duo, was one such story which came out in two parts in 1915. Rustom was a great warrior who often came to the aid of the Persian king when he was attacked by the Tatar king Afrasiyab, who never managed to evade the might of Rustom's arms. After every victory, Rustom went away on his travels, always refusing to join the Persian army. Once when he was resting on the roadside, he was approached by the Kurdish king to accept his hospitality. There he met the king's beautiful daughter and proposed marriage to her. They had a child called Sorab, but Rustom who had left for his voyages never saw the baby. Fearing that Sorab too would follow in his father's footsteps and live dangerously, the princess lied to her husband that they had a daughter and not a son. Soon however what she feared came to pass, and inspired by stories of his father's valour, Sorab too joined the Afrasiyab's army. The Tatar king decided that now was the chance to avenge all his defeats and attacked Persia. The Persian king after a lot of persuasion managed to make Rustom agree to lead his army. Soon the father and son face each other on the battlefield on the banks of the Oxus river, though neither recognised each other. That night Sorab who had heard his father was his opponent in the war could not sleep in excitement at the chance of finally meeting his father even if it meant fighting with all the Persian generals.[53] During the battle that ensued between father and son, Sorab could not inexplicably raise his weapon against his opponent, whereas the similarly unaware Rustom was determined to defeat his foe. Finally, when he was fatally wounded, Sorab heard someone call out to his opponent by his name and realised it was his father. He then told Rustom that he was his son and showed his signet ring as proof. Rustom was mortified and wanted to commit suicide but the mortally wounded Sorab requested his father to bury him with the epitaph that 'here lies the warrior Sorab, son of Rustom, killed by the hands of his father who had not recognised him'.[54] Three other stories translated from Turkish folk tales by Kụladaranjan Ray came out in 1922 – 'Kuyor Bhoot' ('The Ghost in the Well'), 'Saptanon Daitya' (the seven-faced ogre) and Ganatkat ('The Fortune-teller'). In the first story, a carpenter's truculent wife fell into a well when she disregarded her husband's warning. Initially relieved by her absence, the man tried to pull her out but got an ogre out instead. The ogre had been so terrified by the carpenter's wife's anger that he decided to give his rescuer a boon of three leaves which would cure anyone whom the ogre possessed. In due course, he was able to save a princess whom he married and when another princess was captivated by the ogre, the clever carpenter pretended that he had got his wife out of the well and the ogre overcome with fear vanished forever.[55] The second story was that of 40 sons of a *badshah* who decided that they would only marry 40 sisters of the same parents. One family had 39 daughters, but the 40 sons did not want to separate their youngest brother from them and decided to look for their own brides. Their father agreed but warned them that on their way, they should not rest near a large waterfall, an inn and a large field which they would come across on their journey. After travelling the whole day, the tired brothers fell asleep in front of the waterfall while the youngest brother stood guard. At night, an ogre with seven heads came near and a battle ensued. The youngest brother managed to cut off six heads with his sword and the seventh head rolled away. The boy ran in pursuit till the head came near a well and said that the person who has killed me will get all the jewels and jumped into the well. The youngest son then climbed into the well and found an iron gate through which he came before a palace with 40 doors behind which sat 40 beautiful princesses with a mound of jewels before them. The princesses were very happy to hear that he had killed the ogre who had imprisoned them, and promising to come back with his 40 brothers, the youngest brother returned back. The next morning, the story forgotten, the brothers came in front of an inn at dusk and decided to fall asleep without heeding the youngest brother's advice. Once again, the seven-headed ogre appeared, and once again the same thing happened with a larger palace than the first. Here there was more wealth, but there were no princesses. The third day the brothers reached a field where they again fell asleep. This time a third ogre came furiously spouting fire in anger against the person who had killed his two brothers. The noise woke the other brothers who became terrified at the fierce ogre. The youngest brother bade them to leave with the princesses and jewels in the wells and decided to deal with the ogre himself. After a fierce battle, the boy became very tired, so the ogre promised to let him go if he got him the princess of Chinimachin country where a horse named Agjir would take him. The story goes on how the boy managed to meet the princess who fell in love with him and how the two made a plan to trick the ogre Champalak whose life was safely kept in a palace. Finally, free of the ogre, the happy couple was reunited with the 39 brothers and their wives and the 40th princess was married to the Chinimachin princess' brother.[56] The third story was about three intelligent girls who made use of their circumstances to find themselves good grooms. A soothsayer had predicted that their lives would change in three different ways, but unlike other stories where it was supernatural events which got them good fortune, here all the three sisters used their natural wits and found their husbands. The elder one putting her shawl on a couple sleeping in a well so that the fairy who had bewitched the man was frightened away, the second one eavesdropped in a graveyard a conversation between a king's son who was presumed dead and his evil doctor and informed his mother and the youngest one married a bewitched man who was saved when he was forced to look at his wife.[57] The next year Kuladaranjan Ray translated another story from Turkish folk tales, 'Price of Being Too Clever', in which a good man of Damascus, Hasan, was able to please a Brahmin Padmanabha by his good nature and musical abilities who wanted to reward him by showing him a well where by reciting magical mantras Hasan was able to carry a large wealth home. But his wicked stepmother's greed forced him to take her and his father to the well. But without the Brahmin's magic, they were killed by the fearful giant who was guarding the treasure when a divine voice said that Hasan had not respected the fatherly love that the Brahmin had given him out of greed and all three of them deserved to die.[58]

In the next issue, Kuladaranjan Ray's 'Sing li's Fate' is a beautiful story adapted from a Chinese folk tale of how a young boy was told by a fortune-teller that he would die at the age of 18 and how he wins over the God of Death by his pleasing manner and respect for the old, to win a boon of long life.[59] In 1924, a Korean story was translated by Subimal Ray, which is about a very clever man Ken Chung who managed to survive the enmity of the king's minister by his wits. When he was jailed for owing money to the king, he spun a tale to a foolish cousin of the minister that he needed a very special nose for the king's uncle who was suffering from a boil on the nose. The foolish Lang Ting was terrified when Ken Chung said that his nose had been chosen as the most suitable and said that he would rather pay the ransom that the prisoner had to pay to be free from the king's demand. Thus, Ken Chung was saved when he took the thousand gold bars and paid off his loan.[60]

'Kajir Bichar' by the famous Bengali short story writer Prabhat Kumar Mukhopadhyay in *Ramdhanu* in 1927 is about a rich village landlord Kudratullah Khan in ancient Persia, who was rich, obese and indolent, and a poor peasant Abdullah, who lived at the edge of the village and made baskets out of cane. The rich nobleman omrah envied Abdullah's ability to eat whatever he could lay hands on and sleep soundly at the end of a hard day while Khan suffered from dyspepsia and insomnia. In anger Khan burnt the cane forest and the poor man's cottage. Abdullah in despair went to the capital and complained to the Qazi. The wise Qazi after deliberations came up with the punishment that the two men would be sent to an island where they would have to survive on their own. The story goes on to show that the poor man had no trouble in settling in the new place and was deeply appreciated by the local people. Initially, the omrah had trouble because he had got used to an easy living, but with hard work he too realised that he could eat more and sleep better in this new life.[61]

Ideal children for ideal Asia

Besides entertainment, there was also the consciousness that an ideal nation would include an ideal child. As expected, moral lessons in values and ethics even with an eastern stress were present in these periodicals. *Sishu* contained a statutory warning on its front page that it was a magazine permitted by the Director of Bengal School Society. Besides containing informative articles on the Chinese wall,[62] or mythological stories and fairy tales, it included stories of moral lives – stories of Christ's sacrifice,[63] Ramakrishna Paramhamsa's religiosity,[64] the motherly love of Hazrat Abdul Qadir Jalani[65] and the spiritual life of the Chishti ancestor Sufi Ibrahim Ibn Adham of Balkh.[66]

There is an implicit idea in all the writing of the time that the Asian nations should be aware of each other's strength and tie themselves in an unshakeable bond of friendship which would be mutually beneficial. The admiration of Japan and China who had risen to become powerful nations without western help is stressed, but always the emphasis is on the perpetuation of their past glory and spiritual and ethical strength. There was never in this admiration any sense of envy; rather, the articles are inspirational, exhorting the Indians to emulate the discipline and values which have made them great nations. It would be interesting to place the pedagogy and children's literature of the late 19th- and 20th-century Bengal in the context of developments in the critical analysis of world literature for children. Romantic writers like Charles Lamb and William Wordsworth in the 19th century condemned that pedagogy which 'crammed' children's mind with 'geography and natural history' was 'oppressive of childhood's natural energies, imagination and sense of wonder' was a nostalgic conservatism indicating a longing to return to simpler and more innocent times.[67] The early 19th century also saw the re-emergence of fantasy within middle-class ideology and pedagogy without a radical break from the moral and rational mode. The productive and pedagogical ends 'were more concealed in a delightful packaging'.[68] Philippe Aries, in re-creating the world of childhood in Europe, claimed that 'to every period of history, there co-responded a privileged age and a particular division of human life: youth is the privileged age of the seventeenth century and eighteenth, childhood of the nineteenth and adolescence of the twentieth'.[69] Even without distinguishing age group since magazines had to target a reading group (probably tweens and teenagers), it was this impressionable age group which was targeted for creating awareness regarding Asia and the world, keeping in mind the vital role they would play in future as modern world citizens as well as model sons of the nation fighting colonialism. It was the diet of the best values of the east and west through fun and riddles that would go into the making of the new Indian youngster.

Much before national virtues were highlighted as needed for the ideal son of the ideal nation, Biharilal Gupta in *Sakha* in 1887 upholds those values that Indian children could learn from Chinese children, like industriousness, politeness, respect for women and reject 'harmful' ones.[70] Mahendranath Maitreya, in the journal *Grihastha*, speaks about age-old practices in China which need to be adopted in other countries as well. He translates normative practices prescribed by *Li ki* written in 500 BC as well as a book by the Sung period writer Ching Tsi Jhi to highlight the importance of children's education and social behaviour. Children's education cannot be neglected since, as Tsi Jhi points out, 'children do not have a discerning mind when they are little so they must be given moral and ethical instruction so that their senses may be prepared for their future development'.[71] Maitreya quotes from the texts by leading Chinese thinkers to point out the features of an ideal child in school and at home.

> All children must come to school very early and as soon as they enter school, they should say a prayer to Confucius and then pay respects to their teacher. In the evening before leaving they have to recite a poem which should be simple yet touch the hearts of the listeners. Once they reach home they should pay respects to their forefathers, then their grandparents, parents and other elders at home . . . While learning by rote, a student must remember to concentrate three things, eyes, face and mind. If the mind is distracted then repeated uttering of lessons becomes useless and should be discarded. . . . The student should remember the explanations and implications of all lessons that the teacher teaches and keep them in mind so that they can use them in their real life as well as for examinations.[72]

But as Maitreya adds, it is important to remember that the teaching of the schoolteacher must be appropriate and relevant to his time and for the students; otherwise such model education has no value and would not last outside the classroom.

It is the future children who will have to find commonalities between the different peoples and who will have to make peace with each other's differences. This logic lurks behind the story by Dhirendralal Dhar (*Ramdhanu* 1938), when the Japanese army is about to capture the city of Nanking in December 1937 after the battle of Nanking, which speaks of the tragedy of war and how little imperialistic ambitions of nations appeal to ordinary people who long for ordinary lives and peace. *On the Nanking Front* speaks through the voice of a Chinese soldier, Neng Chu, who is happy because in the midst of Japanese shelling the post had brought a letter from his mother. But he is sad because he cannot read the letter in the trench since they are not allowed to switch on any light since it will attract an attack by the Japanese hidden in opposing trenches. So Neng Chu is waiting for dawn and falls asleep with his head on the walls of the trench. He is awoken before dawn with the call to march towards the Japanese lines in front. He crawls on all fours to avoid visibility towards a Japanese trench where he finds a Japanese soldier, stunned by a shell attack and when the Jap soldier tries to escape on seeing Neng Chu approach, Neng Chu sticks his bayonet into him and kills him. When the sun rises, he realises that the fallen soldier is a young boy whom 'he would have liked to befriend rather than kill in normal circumstances'. Out of curiosity he looked for an identity and found an envelope in his pocket, which he opened to find a picture of a smiling lady with eyes just like his own mother and a letter addressed to Sinyo by his mother in which she writes how she dreads to open the newspaper every morning in fear that she might find his name in the list of fallen soldiers and how she longs to see his dear face again. In another letter in the same envelope, Neng Chu finds a reply by Sinyo to her where he writes:

> I don't feel like fighting any more, mother. We have won Nanking. We destroyed the city with cannon fire but I don't exult in this victory. I saw the other day in

> front of our trench the body of a young girl clutching her baby in her arms in death, victim of our bombing. The smile was lingering still in the baby's face. As I gazed at the innocent face, I wondered why we were killing all these people. What would we gain from it? Even if we occupied the whole of China, what would we achieve? The powerful will rule, men with arms will become generals, the rich will increase their business and the rest of us will be clerks at the most. Those who are today sitting in comfortable armchairs, sipping tea and reading in the newspapers about the wars, will become all powerful and while we will possibly lose our lives for our countries . . . We have no real conflict with any Chinese – then why are we murdering them every day? For the past few days every time I hold up a gun, the image of that dead woman and her child creeps into my mind. The smile that the child has even in death reminds me of Lord Tathagata. I'm no longer enjoying my assignment as a soldier and have applied for leave to visit you at home.

Neng Chu sighs in sadness and to take his mind off his own guilt takes out his own letter from home, which he had not yet read. His mother writes in the letter,

> It is my only prayer that you return home hale and hearty. Every evening I pray at the temple of Buddha that His blessings always be with you. I can barely sleep at night thinking of the danger that you are facing in the midst of all the bombing and shelling.

Neng Chu's eyes fill with tears at the thought of both mothers of young boys of different countries praying to the same God for the war to end and keep their sons safe. He realised that if a Japanese aircraft dropped a bomb, then like Sinyo's mother, his mother too will not get the news of his death. Holding the picture of Sinyo's mother before him, he realises that there was even a similarity in her expression with that of his own mother. At that moment, Neng Chu feels that the only thing he wants is to ensure that Sinyo's letter reaches his mother. Without wasting a moment, he inscribes on top of Sinyo's letter, the following words in large letters: Killed in a trench on Nanking Front. He then wraps the letter along with a small stone in a handkerchief and throws the letter with all his might towards the next Japanese trench. Neng Chu did not even get the time to see if his letter missile reached its destination, because the Japanese soldiers in the trench, thinking that it was a Chinese attack retaliated with a series of bombs towards the hand that was lifted out of the trench to throw the letter. One bomb landed right next to Neng Chu, and instantly his body was torn into bits. The very next day, Neng Chu's mother gets a message saying that her son was 'killed in a trench on Nanking Front'. When he wrote that line in Sinyo's letter little did Neng Chu think that his mother would be the one to get that message first. The sons of two mothers, Japanese and Chinese, were laid down and buried side by side by the Chinese soldiers, since the stench of the decomposing bodies became overpowering.[73]

Notes

1 Dipesh Chakraborty, *Provincializing Europe: Post-Colonial Thought and Historical Difference*, Princeton: Princeton University Press, 2000, p. 16.

2 Partha Chatterjee, *The Nation and Its Fragments: Colonial and Postcolonial Histories*, Delhi: Oxford University Press, 1994, p. 6.

3 Sumit Sarkar, *Modern Times: India 1880s–1950s, Environment, Economy, Culture*, Ranikhet: Permanent Black, 2014, p. 372.
4 Anon, Atlas Shiksha, *Anjali*, 1(1), 1898, pp. 37–40; Anon, Chin Porachinporotar Parinam, *Anjali*, 1(1), 1898, pp. 40–42 (discussed later).
5 Certain sections of this chapter was published in 2016 as Mapping Asia for Children: Pedagogy and Nationalism in Sandesh (1913–1926), *Asian Studies*, xxxiv(1&2), Jan–Dec 2016, pp. 21–35.
6 Upendra Kishore Ray-Napit Pandit (Puraton Lekha-Older Writings), *Sandesh*, 5(6), 1917, pp. 176–181 or Kuladaranjan Ray's Sindhu Pori: A Folk Tale from Turkey, *Sandesh*, 7(2), 1919, pp. 34–37.
7 Subimal Roy, Sven Hediner Bhraman Brittanto, *Sandesh*, 10(11), 1922, pp. 383–385.
8 Subimal Ray, Morubhoomite Prachin Shahor, *Sandesh*, 11(2), 1923, pp. 35–40.
9 Sris Chandra Majumdar, Tahiti Dviper Parliament, *Balak*, 1(4–5) 1885, reprinted in *Balak*, Calcutta: Dey's Publishing, 2010, pp. 313–317.
10 Upendra Kishore Ray, Ashchoyjjyo Phul, *Sandesh*, 3(9), 1915, pp. 274–275.
11 Banraj Pukam Sen from the Pearson Magazine, *Sandesh*, 13(10), 1925, pp. 348–358.
12 Mukul Chandra De, Japaner Kotha, *Sandesh*, 5(9), 1917, pp. 264–268.
13 Mukul Chandra De, Fujiyama, *Sandesh*, 5(10), 1917, pp. 302–304.
14 Mukul Chandra De, Japaner Kotha, op. cit., pp. 265–268.
15 Mukul Chandra De, Fujiyama, op. cit., pp. 302–304.
16 Sri Harsha, Cheener Sheema Prachir, *Shishu*, 2(1), 1913, pp. 41–43.
17 Sukumar Ray, Cheener Panchil, *Sandesh*, 8(2), 1920, pp. 82–86.
18 Biraj Kumar Bandopadhyay, Ashchorjjyo Prachir, *Ramdhanu*, 5(1), 1931, pp. 28–30.
19 Upendrakishore Ray (possibly), Chineder Kotha, *Sandesh*, 3(2), 1915, p. 54.
20 Ibid., p. 55.
21 Ibid.
22 Ibid., pp. 55–56.
23 Upendrakishore Ray, Chiner Golpo, *Sakha*, 4(1), 1886, p. 10.
24 Ibid.
25 Ibid., p. 11.
26 Ibid., p. 12.
27 Anon. (Sukumar Ray), Chindesher Kotha, *Sandesh*, 3(10), 1915, pp. 314–318.
28 Ibid., p. 318.
29 Bihari Lal Gupta, Chine Saheb, *Sakha*, 5(4), 1887, p. 60.
30 Ibid.
31 Ibid., pp. 60–61.
32 Ibid., pp. 62–63.
33 An unnamed grandmother, Rabon Rajar Deshe, *Sandesh*, 5(11), 1917, pp. 333–334.
34 Ibid., pp. 367–368.
35 Anon., Brahmaraj Thibaw, *Balak*, 1(10), 1885, reprinted in *Balak*, Calcutta: Dey's Publishing, 2010, pp. 429–432.
36 Ibid.
37 Nripendra nath Bandopadhaya, Burmar Kotha, *Ramdhanu*, 1(3), 1927, pp. 115–116.
38 Ibid., p. 118.
39 Manoranjan Bhattacharya, Shyam Desh, *Ramdhanu*, 6(1), 1932, pp. 48–52.
40 Ibid., pp. 50–51.
41 Ibid., pp. 51–52.
42 Upendra Kishore Ray, Byanger Somudro Dekha, a Japanese Story, *Sandesh*, 3(3), 1915, pp. 93–94.
43 Subinoy Ray, Ashchorjjyo Chhobi, *Sandesh*, 6(4), 1918, pp. 113–116.
44 Sobhanlal Mukhopadhyay, Kak o Bang – Tibbotigolpo, *Sandesh*, 7(2), 1919, pp. 50–51.
45 Mohonlal Gangopadhyay, Shonar Jhorna, *Sandesh*, 7(5–6), 1919, pp. 194–199.
46 Jyotirmoyee Debi, Dushtu Gemunu, *Sandesh*, 8(2), 1920, pp. 40–44.
47 Ibid.
48 Punyalata Chakraborty, Poroloker Manush, *Sandesh*, 11(2), 1923, pp. 34–35.
49 Subinoy Ray, Wang, Cheena Golpo, *Sandesh*, 6(4), 1918, pp. 162–164.
50 Punyalata Chakraborty, Protigyar Daye, *Sandesh*, 7(12), 1919, pp. 333–335.
51 Kulada Ranjan Ray, Andha Lo San, *Sandesh*, 8(9), 1920, pp. 264–270.

52 Kulada Ranjan Ray, Devata Janen, *Sandesh*, 8(7–8), 1920, pp. 247–254.
53 Kulada Ranjan Ray, Rustom o Sorab (i), *Sandesh*, 3(9), 1915, pp. 258–260.
54 Kulada Ranjan Ray, Rustom o Sorab (ii), *Sandesh*, 3(9), 1915, pp. 297–301.
55 Kulada Ranjan Ray, Kuyor Bhoot (Turkish folk tale), *Sandesh*, 10(2), 1922, pp. 50–54.
56 Kulada Ranjan Ray, Saptanan Daitya (Turkish folk tale), *Sandesh*, 10(8), 1922, pp. 245–251.
57 Kulada Ranjan Ray, Ganatkar (Turkish folk tale), *Sandesh*, 10(10), 1922, pp. 320–326.
58 Kuladaranjan Ray, Oti Lobher Shaja, *Sandesh*, 11(5), 1923, pp. 144–150.
59 Kuladaranjan Ray, Sing Lir Bhagya, *Sandesh*, 11(4), 1923, pp. 99–104.
60 Subimal Ray, Naker Jonyo, *Sandesh*, 12(7), 1924, pp. 252–255.
61 Prabhat Kumar Mukhopadhyay, Kajir Bichar, *Ramdhanu*, 1(1), 1927, pp. 33–42.
62 Sri Harsha, Chiner Shima Prachir, *Shishu*, 2(1), 1913, pp. 41–43.
63 Satyacharan Chakraborty, Mahapurush Jesus Christ, *Shishu*, 2(9), 1913, pp. 391–411.
64 Satyacharan Chakraborty, Paramhamsa Sri Sri Ramkrishna, *Shishu*, 2(11), pp. 497–510.
65 Md. Ahbab Chowdhury, Matri Bhakti, *Shishu*, 2(10), 443–446.
66 Anon, Tapash Ibrahim Adham, *Shishu*, 2(3), 1913, pp. 121–125.
67 Andrew O' Malley, *The Making of the Modern Child: Children's Literature and Childhood in the Late 18th Century*, New York: Routledge, 2003, pp. 129–130.
68 Ibid., p. 137.
69 Philippe Aries, *Centuries of Childhood: A Social History of Family Life*, Translation from French by Robert Baldick, New York: Alfred A. Knopf, 1962, p. 32.
70 Biharilal Gupta, Chiner Kotha, *Sakha*, 5(4), 1887, pp. 59–63.
71 Upendranath Maitreya, Chine Shishu Shiksha, *Grihastha*, 8(8)(2), 1916, pp. 122–123.
72 Ibid., pp. 124–125.
73 Dhirendralal Dhar, Nanking Fronte, *Ramdhanu*, 11(5), 1938, pp. 292–296.

5 Cultural intimacies

The quest for an Asian art and culture

Discussions about art and culture were important features of these periodicals, and it was both the world and the local and national context where it was played out. Besides connecting the reader to important debates and discussions going on in the art world, these articles discussed through a comparative manner, differences in art and culture styles of the Asian nations in the past and present. In the case of performing arts, the theory of Indian influence was much more widespread as far as the South and South-East Asian nations were concerned compared to China and Japan. I would like to highlight in this regard the distinctive case of Rabindranath Tagore who went the whole way in the opposite direction to the Greater India enthusiasts and tried to bring in the art and culture of the rest of Asia into India in a reverse assimilation to highlight universalism which he wanted to develop as the motto of Visva Bharati, his world university. It marked a full circle for him in cultural connectivity.

Art

A new trend started at the beginning of the 20th century in the journals, and *Prabashi* led the way in it, which was inclusion of print copies of great works of art from all over the world in the magazines, specifically Asian art. Appreciation of western art was popular in 19th-century Bengal among western educated men, while women brought this 'new mentality' into their 'inner quarters' by 'adorning their walls' with 'prints of famous world art', according to Nirad C. Chaudhuri.[1] Art appreciation in the press was rarer and appreciation of Asian Art probably started in the first decade of the 20th century. In the meantime, the colonial government's efforts to set up art schools for Indian artisans were hijacked by the young Indians from respectable families and cultural nationalists with Rabindranath Tagore in the lead, who 'discovered the Theosophists and other European enemies of Victorian materialism to be soul mates' and debates on Indian identity, 'mirroring developments in nationalist politics', started.[2] E.B. Havell, who had been given the charge of heading the Calcutta art school, with the support of Abanindranath Tagore, who was not only Vice Principal of the school but also the pioneer of the Bengal School and Indian Society of Oriental Art, proclaimed that India's spirituality, which he called 'Indian idealism', was reflected not only in the art of the ancient period but also in 'Mogul art ... and in the great schools of China and Japan'.[3] Abanindranath Tagore had a huge impact on the artists and art critics of the period and a debate raged between the Bengal school that wanted to create an 'oriental art' by assimilating the different Asian cultures and Academic art which was branded as a colonial hybrid lacking authenticity with the painter Ravi Varma as the main target.

DOI: 10.4324/9781003243786-5

Kakuzo Okakura, the Japanese art critic who arrived in Calcutta in 1900 to find support for his cultural movement that challenged western values and art which had flooded Japan, found that his movement had a resonance in the Tagores' desire to search into the indigenous traditions for an Asian spirituality to fight against western materialism. Okakura was followed in his traditional art movement *nibong* by Yokoyama Taikan and Hishida Shunso who came to work in Calcutta with Abanindranath, bringing about distinct influences in Indian art of the Bengal school. As an art historian, S.K. Bhattacharya wrote for a textbook in 1966 about this art movement, the 'accent was on Eastern tradition borrowing in profusion from Chinese calligraphy, Japanese colouring and Persian finish'.[4] As Kalidas Nag pointed out:

> the study of Indian art and archaeology is undergoing a rapid and remarkable orientation ... while it is possible for Mr Havell and Mr VA Smith to write elaborate histories of Indian art with only desultory allusions to Java or Cambodia, Coomaraswamy and his co-workers on the same field find it difficult not to devote a considerable part of their works to the detailed and intensive study of Far Eastern families of art and their Indian origins or affinities. It is no longer possible to discuss adequately the problems of Indian architecture, sculpture or iconography without reference to their Asiatic context.[5]

Ananda K. Coomaraswamy's books *Introduction to Indian Art* (1922) and *History of Indian and Indonesian Art* (1927) were probably the first books in English by a South Asian on art and in his quest of interpreting Asian art to the world, Coomaraswamy used the comparative method and was intellectually close to the Tagores and the Greater India Society established in Calcutta in the 1920s.

Art journalism undoubtedly played an important role in introducing Asian art to the general public and also popularising appreciation of Indian and Asian art in a nationalistic spirit, delineating clear differences between Asian and European art and challenging the cultural criticism of Asian culture. As Aurobindo Ghosh in his reply to the criticism of William Archer referred to a mental block of the western critic who demands 'something other than what its characteristic spirit and motive intend to give'.[6] Manindra Bhushan Gupta in an article in *Prabashi* actually refers to these art debates when he talks about the similarity of Asian art and how different it is from western art. He writes:

> The whole of Asia is united by a similarity of strokes which is distinct from the portraiture of European art. That is why European art leans towards realism while Asian art towards idealism though there are exceptions in the ancient Christian art which was close to Asian art.[7]

Gupta also makes a distinction between intellect/scientific art which European art evolved and imaginative/creative aspect which Asian art believed in. He thought that it was regrettable that the educated people in India did not appreciate traditional ancient art enough because their heads were filled with bookish knowledge and they perceive everything analytically. .... They were not imaginative enough and they only appreciated those painters who reproduce reality in their art because then it is easily comprehensible. He believed that though China has been able to break the shackles of colonisation and evolve her own nationalism, she needed to find her own art as well. Only then will her culture evolve.Gupta writes that 'it is mainly through paintings that the Chinese genius has manifested itself. If one has to understand China, one must acquaint themselves with Chinese painting'. Using three books – *La Peinture Chinoise* by Tenhang Yi-Tehon and J. Hackin, *Encyclopaedia de la Peinture Chinoise* by Raphael Petrucet and *Painting in the Far East* by Laurence Binyon – as his sources, Gupta says Chinese alphabets and painting emerged from the same source in ancient China when a letter denoted portrayal of an article. This attempt at creating a likeness was called *Wen*. This writing depicted through painting a particular event and not the feelings or ideas of the painter. Gradually this stroke was developed into a character or letter as a medium of expression of a personal feeling. This stroke letter is called ideograph in English which only expresses emotion but not a word. Much later this letter became phonetical and from then the written language was separated from painting. Chinese painting began from this time to be considered as an art form.... It would be more accurate to say that the Chinese painters do not to paint pictures but rather write them. This is called calligraphy art in English to which the Japanese and the Persian painting too belong.

His conclusion in this regard was that Japanese painting was close to the Chinese since China was Japan's mentor but Persian painting's history was different. Their painting started as illustrations for their books. The strokes denoted the limit of the object they portrayed, while in the tone and stroke of Chinese paintings there was a rhythm and logic which expressed the character of the object they aim to depict. Having delineated the differences, Gupta says that it was 'in the stroke of the brush that the Chinese painters excelled. There was both strength and softness in the stroke work. They create pictures with such spontaneity that it verges on playfulness'. Gupta refers to Chinese painting as a 'lyrical poem or as the ancient Chinese proverb says a picture is like poetry without words'. He says that 'Chinese art was influenced by the teachings of both Lao Tse, the mystic and Confucius, the contemporary of Buddha bringing dual qualities of harmony and discipline as well as strength and independence'. From the *Encyclopedie de la Pointure Chinoise*, the author translates the six principles of Chinese art,

> a) In order to introduce through art a life spirit or rhythm in all articles a painter must internalise spiritualism. b) One must use brush strokes to recreate bone-structure. c) Ability to equate one's nature with the object painted. d) To create similarity between the object and writing. e) To organise the strokes through a need-based and importance-based priority. f) To create beauty in compliance with imagination. What is harmonic unity (samanjasyaer aikya) for Rabindranath Tagore is rhythmic vitality (chande pranshakti) for the Chinese.[8]

At the end of his 'History of Chinese Painting', Gupta pleads that 'today the great Chinese nation has woken up from slumber due to the clash of foreign civilizations on her soil in the political sphere. When will there be an awakening in her culture and art?'[9] At the time of writing the article, he was already a teacher of English, Mathematics, Bengali and Art in Santiniketan while taking training from Nandalal Bose. Gupta was also trained in French and had translated the section on Raphael Petruce from the original. He was then sent to Sri Lanka to teach art at the Ananda College in 1925, where he met the Inspector of Art of Colombo, artist C.F. Windsor. They admired each other's art and Windsor wrote about Gupta's new style of painting: 'His interest in acquiring knowledge and culture places him in the foremost rank of Indian artists and gives him a very definite personality'.[10] He travelled widely in Sri Lanka and visited historical ruins at Anuradhapur, Polanarua, Sigiria, Kandy, etc. He even stayed at the Buddhist viharas and his paintings were greatly influenced by the ancient art. He also contributed knowledgeable articles on Sri Lankan art to *Prabashi* and *Modern Review.*[11]

Nandalal Bose in *Chin Japaner Chithi* discussed the different categories of painters of China –

> artist craftsmen who were traditional; the mad artists who were cultured and aristocratic and did not need to worry about earning; the sane artists who were professionals who were skilful and sometimes are patronised by aristocracy and royalty; the thief artists who copy the work of others; and the pottery painter. The first group are impossible to imitate and they are the path breaking artists. The second and third groups may be copied and the fourth group specialized in doing that from the second and third group.

Bose was even trying to translate a paper by one Chinese artist. However, he felt that Rabindranath Tagore's vision of a unity between India and China would not be possible because the people there were interested only in meetings and lectures. He regretted that ornamentation in architecture was coming to an end in China. He believed that the people have lost their originality and are copying the west because they are embarrassed by their past traditions and are being trained by the 'civilized' artistes from England.[12]

Bimalendu Koyal, writing in *Bangasri* in 1935, said that the Chinese painters had never traditionally visualised painting as a profession.

> The genteel folk took up the brush for passing their leisure hours in pleasure and occasionally some of them were appointed as painters in the royal court. It was only when the western trained painters returned home that a class of professional artists developed who are not only enjoying their earnings from art but are also experimenting with western influences on their art.[13]

He is effusive in his praise of the painting of Chinese painters like Tai Chin and Jang In who during the Ming era had 'broken the barrier of the orthodox Chinese painting style which was thousands of years old' and who had been trying to establish a new art form. The paintings of Tai Chin displayed in Freer Art Gallery of Washington are testimony to the greatness of Chinese art. If the modern painters of China have to achieve the same brilliance, they will have to combine traditional styles with modern western styles.[14] Koyal categorises the modern Chinese painters into four divisions: The first category comprises the majority of the Chinese painters who belonged to the old school. They mostly re-created the old masters with their own imagination and ability. These paintings were sometimes sale worthy, but mainly were labours of love. The leading painter of this school was Chi Pai Shih, who at the time was residing in Peeping. Aged sixty one he had not let western influence touch him in the slightest. The contemporary painters referred to him as a rough diamond who may not shine as brightly as a polished one but which emits a brilliant light of its own.... The celebrated painter Ju Pian was his student. The second category of painters were led by Kung Pa King. When the traditional Chinese art was in a state of decline it was Kung Pa King who had breathed life into it. His immortal contribution would never be denied by all those who have love for Chinese art. He belonged to a rich and elite family and used his own resources to establish an academy where the students were trained to imitate the works of the old masters and thereby create an archive of ancient and modern art. His brother Wang too was an accomplished and established artist. Despite their training in western art, this school managed to keep the ancient art forms alive in modern China. The third category of painters stayed true to their western training. According to Koyal, this group of painters took this way out since ancient Chinese painting style required a particular type of colouring which was very expensive to maintain in the present times. This group led by Liu Su was trained in western art and portrayed realism and positivism. 'In 1932, Liu painted the Sino-Japanese war, a realism which had hitherto never been seen in Chinese art'. Koyal referred to some others belonging to this group of western trained modern artists like Ju Piyan, whom he called the best of this group who was trained in Paris but was trying to combine western techniques with traditional Chinese art, and Ko Ki Feng who was an artist of the material world. The fourth group was inspired by Russian art and majority of their paintings were motivated by some political message. Most of their paintings were cartoons or satires which is a new development in Chinese art. Koyal ends with a quotation from Dagny Carter on whose book (*China Magnificent: Five Thousand Years of Chinese Art*) he probably relied on for his information: that 'Chinese painting today, far from resembling a corpse is more like a new born babe.' The future was still uncertain but 'Chinese painting in the new era holds great promise in the future.[15]

There is a descriptive essay on the Chinese art in *Bharatvarsha* where the writer, Jamini Kanta Sen, says with pride that the paintings may be incomprehensible to the Europeans but to the Indians they are familiar.[16] Three years earlier, this art teacher of Tagore's school at Bolpur wrote a detailed history of Chinese art over the ages while looking for signs of 'Indian glory in Chinese art'.[17] This article appears to have been based mostly on secondary writing of art historians like Waley, Coomaraswamy, Okakura, Larence Binyon and Andrew Lang and traces the influences on the Chinese artists and their works right down to the modern times. He rues at the end that

> in the modern period the transience of art production is a universal phenomenon all over the world when people's attentions span is limited and being 'new' is the watchword. This western outlook has recently affected Japan, Turkey and Persia and China could not protect herself from this any longer. Modern China is now following the expressionism in the European fashion in art – not all over China it is true but the beginnings are quite visible. In recent times, art has been revolutionised when Liu Hi Su was imprisoned in 1920 for using a naked model in Shanghai. It is true that that time has passed but in the 1930s a new art form is being created. Deep depression due to bloody revolutions and the pain of famines and poverty is being reflected in the art forms which has replaced the beautiful dreamy impressionism of the past. In the new China oil paintings and woodcuts are popular. In their desire to chalk out a new path in art, modern China seems to be eager to abandon its past art tradition.[18]

Jadunath Sarkar in analysing the Indian influence on the art of Indo-China reviews the research of Groslier and points out that the artists were in the service of an aristocracy which was half Indian and half native whose sole preoccupation was to build temples and embankments to live in luxury, to use elegant and decorated utensils, to accumulate riches and religious merit. The influence of South India on Cambodia was local and accidental. There was both Chinese and Buddhist influence on art in Cambodia.[19] In 1924, in a series of articles on Thailand (Shyamdesh), Narendra Dev describes the art and craft of Thailand as having developed under the shadow of religiosity since they were concentrated in the Buddhist viharas, but he is hopeful that with the spread of education, 'more secular trends are visible in the work outside the monastic establishments. The popular works of Thai art are wood work, silver work, articles made of lac and bronze as well as cloth with chikon embroidery and paintings'.[20]

Cultural nationalism to be successful needed to be brought to the level of the ordinary people. Together with the idea of improvement, nationalism meant the use of all methods possible to arouse a spirit of unity by appreciation of the past achievements in all fields. Culture and art, being part of the spiritual domain, were inviolable since they could not be appropriated by an alien political power. The links with Asia in the past in the field of art and culture thus formed another source of power, which was outlined to the common reader through the journals. The final question that arose was how this appreciation could be filtered to all levels of the population. 'The poverty of the Indians at the present time has made art a luxury', whereas 'in olden days it was considered a necessity . . . Economic distress cannot make ordinary run of people sensitive to art', says Sris Chandra Chatterjee in an article in *The Modern Review* in 1930,[21] the only solution for this problem is if art could be made a part of the daily life of the people like it was in the past. This can be possible only if art education was made a part of general education, as V.V. Vadnerker points out in another article. Only then could a revival of the art and architecture of the country be envisaged. However, in this process, one must make a distinction between reproduction of natural forms which is mainly an education of hand and eye and should be regarded as part of education in empirical science'. What was distinct from this was the 'teaching of drawing as an education of the imagination and of the emotional side of the self' and as a means to a 'fuller grasp of the national culture.'[22]

Sris Chandra Chatterjee speaks of a strong movement in certain quarters in the country for inclusion of at least an elementary training in art in the curriculum of the universities. But this education must also be one which becomes an effective force in life. As he says, art should be brought to everyone's door since it is not merely an 'embellishment of life but necessary in order to redeem life from brutality.' Only then could art education become fruitful. Chatterjee believes that Indians 'must come to a better understanding of their artistic heritage and bring about a true renaissance of Indian architecture', if she ever hopes to find an honourable position for herself in the community of nations in the world.[23]

That Asian art had caused a revolution in the western artistic world is attested to in an essay on Indian art by Nalinikanta Gupta in *The Modern Review* where he tries to answer some allegations.

> Indian art is not in truth unreal and unnatural, though it may appear so to the eye of the ordinary man or to an eye habituated to the classical tradition of European art.... Indian art too possesses a perspective and an anatomy, it too has a focus of observation which governs and guides the composition in the ensemble and the detail. Only it is not the physical eye but an inner vision ... the angle of a deeper perspective or consciousness.

He points out that schools of the East – Chinese, Japanese or Persian masterpieces – 'have also moved very far away from the naturalistic view, yet they have kept if not the form, at least, the feeling of actuality in their composition'. Gupta has compared Indian, Asian and western art in the form of a scale: European (the far western art) gives a front view of reality; the Japanese art (the far eastern) gives a side view; the Indian art gives the view from above. Or as we may say, in psychological terms, that European art embodies experiences of the conscious and external senses, Japanese art gives expression to experiences that one has through the subtler touches of the nerves and the sensibility and Indian art proceeds through a spiritual consciousness and records experiences of the soul.[24]

A search for past Indian glories in South-East Asia is seen in Swami Sadananda's article in *Masik Basumati* where he tries to locate the sources of the 'Icons of Greater India'.[25] His article compared to most is far more aggressively nationalistic in tone, not only in the title but in the text as well. He writes:

> Indian Hindus first established colonies in Cambodia and Siam, and then in Javadvip, Balidvip and other surrounding islands. Besides the historically famous Ankor Vat where Vishnu's image was established there are many other temples where Shiva icons are established. Cambodia also has other temples dedicated to Brahma and other gods. Not only is the architectural splendour of Ankor praiseworthy, everyone is impressed with the beauty of Vishnu's figure.... One notices in the National Museum of Bangkok, the capital of Siam, beautiful sculptures of Vishnu, copper images of Dharitri Devi and ... images of Ganesha ... and Shiva at Batavia museum is proof that Indian gods had an important impact on the hearts of the colonized people.[26]

He concludes that 'just like in the temples of greater India there are Hindu gods and goddesses, the carvings on the temple bodies contain stories of the epics Ramayana and Mahabharata'.

In comparisons of art among Asian nations, Indian influence was not so readily considered a one-way traffic. Jogindranath Samaddar in *Bharatvarsha*, in 1923, translated the speech by F.C. Manuk, Bar-at-law at the Annual Conference of the Bihar and Orissa Archaeological Research Society, who had said that 'though Mughal painting style was born in Persia it was consolidated in India and undoubtedly the Persians learnt this art from the Chinese.' He admitted that this view was not accepted by many who believe that only the art of Eastern Persia developed from Chinese art and there was no connection between the art of western Persia and China. On the other hand, much of the art of mid and later Mughal period can be called Indian. Samaddar adds that many critics use this theory to draw the conclusion that all Mughal art is totally Indian but this statement has no historical basis. 'In reality the Persian painters worked with the Indian painters and imbibed their art forms partially.'[27]

Suniti Chatterjee's lecture at the Patna session of the Oriental conference, published in the *Vishwa Bharati Quarterly*, summed up the history of Indian art as one of assimilation and connectivity. The pre-Aryan art, he believed was connected to Sumerian Art and it seemed likely that 'some elements of architecture and decorative art in India, South-Eastern Asia and Indonesia originated with the Austrics'. He then described how Indian art was formed through assimilation of imported styles with

Indian spirit and then how it was passed into Indo-China and Java where modified by the local native character and contribution, it was transformed to what he calls 'Hindu Colonial Art of South Eastern Asia.' He distinguished the different degrees of influence on the art of different countries and said that 'the Buddhist art of Serindia, China, Korea and Japan in which … (Greek and Gandhara) met with fresh influences from Persia (Sasanian Art) and later on was further modified by … (Gandhara) and varieties of … (north and south Indian art). There is also profound modification by the native art and the spirit of China.'[28]

It is not just that art of the different nations was seen as influencing each other, for the colonised east there was a sense of pride in establishing difference with the west. Jamini Kanta Sen referred to the similarities of eastern art as the 'triumph of oriental spirit' when he says proudly: 'Oriental idealism is burning bright all over Asia'.[29]

It must of course be remembered that these discussions of art in the 1920s and 1930s came in within a broader discussion and debate about Indian and Asian art in the world as people travelled and came into contact with world art. Benoy Kumar Sarkar, referring to articles in *The Modern Review*, referred to this art appreciation debate as based on two broad categories – one was seeking sources of inspiration, which was connected to the 'alleged anti-thesis' between 'ideals of the East and those of the West'. The other was about the 'very nature and functions of art' which he called '*swaraj* in *shilpa*' or 'art in itself'.[30]

Cultural performances

Not only in the case of art, other forms of culture like drama, music and dance are also discussed in detail and a consistent comparison is made with India. Much before Tagore ventured to popularise Asian theatre and dance in India, there are references to them in the journals. Interestingly, the distinctions made today in performances with regard to drama, music and dance were not so strictly visible in the discussions throughout the period I am writing about. This was probably because all three were vital elements of all performances in most of Asia. In *Bharati*, in one of its first issues, there was a discussion on Burmese drama as well as translation of a Burmese play. The essay starts with the following words:

> we consider the Burmese (or Mogs as they are colloquially referred to) as uncivilized but how can a people who have a culture of drama and a love for dramatic art be considered to be uncivilized? This is worth pondering over. Dramatic performances for the Burmese are national festivals. It casts a tremendous influence over all classes of Burmese who wait eagerly for an occasion to witness a *poye* performance. There is generally a very large crowd who come to such a performance but there is great discipline among the audience who watches the play in rapt silence. They get so involved with the play that at times they suffer with the pain of the characters while at other times they burst out laughing at the comic characters.[31]

The writer whose name is not mentioned also describes the performance and stage:

> The dress of the performers is very bright and gorgeous but the stage and backdrop is simple. The theatre hall is constructed with bamboo sticks and the roof is thatched with grass but the whole stage is covered with colourful cotton and silk

> cloth. The stage is in the middle of the hall and a tree branch is planted to indicate a forest scene. It is amazing how a single branch can represent the whole forest in the imagination of the viewers. The tree branch is surrounded with lamps created from the boat-like stems of banana tree in which petroleum oil is poured in and lit. For the well to do audience, seats on higher ground were prepared while the ordinary folk, were seated huddled together on the ground. The musical instruments which accompanied the performance were seated behind the stage and behind them was the so called green room where the actors changed their costumes as well as entered and exited.[32]

The writer highlighted the similarities in the plots of the difference Burmese plays which invariably include a princess for whom the prince pledged undying love, the King who the prince's guardian, strict and wise ministers, the obedient courtiers and the princess' companions. There was bound to be a royal court with music performance, and the prince would always have a companion whose role was like that of a *vidushak* (a jester) like the Indian plays. His performance inevitably kept the Burmese audience in splits[33] Having provided a similarity with Indian plays, the writer underlines the difference as well:

> In Burmese language the same word takes on a different meaning with a change of the intonation. That is why the language is very favourable for satires and farces because of the use of double meaning. The dialogues were mostly conversational though at times there were soliloquy and music and dance sequences to break up the monotony of continuous dialogues.[34]

As proof of the high lyrical quality of the plays, an example has been provided for the enjoyment of the readers of *Bharati* – a play called *Rajatgiri*. Though the writer's name is not mentioned, one can guess it was Jyotirindranath Tagore since he wrote a play of the same name 'based on a Burmese drama' in 1907.[35]

There was apparently less discussion about East Asian theatre in the west, barring references to scholars like H.H. Wilson while discussing Hindu drama,[36] till relying on travellers' tales and translation of a few play texts by scholars like Arthur Waley, directors and designers saw in the elaborate symbolism and apparent simplicity in the Far Eastern stage a way out of the dead end for the western theatre. Some of the innovations were due to their inspiration – revolving stage introduced in 1896, the 'flowery way' through the audience, the use of masks and the relevance of incidental music.[37] As far as Chinese theatre was concerned, only the name of May Lang Fong of China became famous in the west, more of a curiosity since despite the name May, he was a man. *The Modern Review* in the sections Gleanings wrote in 1920 about May, 'when he acts he transforms his spirit into that of the one whom he imitates'. The article explains the reason why Chinese theatre is not understood in other nations where theatre was meant to entertain. In China, a play is created not only to amuse and entertain the public but had a deeper purpose of promoting 'education and morality of the society'. According to the author, the Chinese people are so accustomed to such plays that they cannot bear those which show the weakness of human minds and the defects of human action and the good Chinese actors and actresses 'would never dare or care to take part in a play which is generally considered to be not high class.' More than loss of fame they are mindful that enacting the role of a bad character might cast a shadow on their personal integrity which they considered a worse prospect.[38] This clinging to a traditionally high quality style and content became a heated issue in the 20th-century Bengali public theatres,[39] this high praise of tradition in Chinese and Japanese plays should be seen in that light.

Travellers to different parts of Asia often write about the dramas and other cultural performances they attend. Ramlal Sarkar who stayed for extended periods in China and was a regular contributor on China to the periodicals wrote on the various theatrical performances he attended. It is true he is critical of certain elements which are discordant to his Indian ear, but in general he is quite balanced. He describes theatre performances in temples, at weddings and feasts, where young boys perform female roles and after the performance mingle with the guests as if they were real women. Sarkar also gives details of a Chinese play *Chanchiyentao*.[40] Benoy Kumar Sarkar, travelling in Japan in 1915, describes his visit to the famous Imperial theatre:

> One can see the latest English and American interiors and costumes in these theatres. The stage, gallery, chairs, guards, ushers, ticket rooms, etc were all styled as in Europe and America. But the tickets are a little cheaper – first class was priced at 4/- only. One major difference is that the performance here lasts for five hours, from five in the evening to ten at night. There are breaks in between during which one can grab food and drinks from the Japanese restaurants within the theatre.

From an English pamphlet which the guide bought for him, Sarkar was able to decipher the substance of the plays he was about to watch. The first play was a 3 act one and that was followed by a one act play. In the performance of the play there were some songs and dances. Though Sarkar had become familiar with Japanese songs, the performance seemed rather monotonous 'as if it was an unending *jinjhint* raag performance' as he described it. To his ear it appeared as if the actor used an opium-induced rough voice in his dialogue delivery. He could not gauge whether this was natural or intentionally done to entertain the audience. Sarkar had noticed this tone of voice even on the performance on the ship and had wondered if it is not a style like the use of nasal tones of Indian Jatra performers. The first play was called the 'Prostitute and the Samurai'. The medieval Japanese society has been portrayed in this lyrical play. The setting of the play was pre-modern Japan and Sarkar found the three acts to contain separate unlinked stories without complexities of plot or character. But one got a very vivid picture of Japan's feudal age in the play. The large number of performers created variety for the audience. Just as the English try to understand the Muslim society by watching the play *Kismet*, Sarkar tried to understand the Japanese Shogunate period through this play. The English programme of the play said that it was a historical drama in three acts, plotted by Takenoya and adopted by Torahiko Migita and was set in 1673 in Yedo and Shimotsake province".

Sarkar discusses the play in detail. In the first act there was a conflict between a *Daimo* and a *samurai* regarding Takao, a prostitute who fell in love with the samurai, though the Daimo coveted her and finally kills her in desperation. In the second act, the play gave a vivid description of Shogun administration, roads, protection of property, inns, etc. under the Daimo's rule, when the samurai attacks the Daimo for revenge for the murder of his beloved Takao. This act was entertaining for the audience because of the display of Japanese style fighting with sticks and swords and jiujitsu. In the third act, there was influence of Buddhism, belief in spirits and supernatural elements, etc. during the funeral rites of his wife performed by Takao's father who didnt yet know that his daughter was dead. He became remorse because he was unable to look after her he had handed her over to a businessman who had sold her to a brothel. Takao appears as an illusion before the father who decided to embrace Buddhism, but later hears from the samurai that his daughter was dead. The Daimo reappears to avenge the attack by the samurai and finally captures him and Takao's father. In despair, the samurai commits hara-kiri in the end.[41] The second play was '*Koharu and Jihei*' which Sarkar describes was also based on the shogunate period. In his words, 'It was a love story, the Romeo Juliet of Japanese literature'. From the English programme, it appeared to be written by Chikamatsu Monzosmon in 1720. The story was rather a simple romance between Jihei, a married man, and Koharu, a prostitute of Osaka. Their love was mutual but realising that there could be no solution to their love story, they decided to commit suicide while Jihei's brother and wife tried to convince Koharu to simply forget him. Despite many twists and turns, the couple could not give each other up and committed suicide.[42] Sarkar ends with the comment that suicide was common in Japan.

Writing about Burmese culture on the celebration of the Burmese New Year, Kumudnath Lahiri in *Prabashi* (1910) refers to the word *poye*, meaning in general Burmese theatre, also used as picnic or even an examination. He writes:

> a person goes through many poye ceremonies from his birth to death. In the new year *tinjan(Thingyan) poye* is celebrated. The first month Tagu is of 29 days generally in April, followed by 30 day months. The imaginative Burmese have a story about Tinjan. In the ancient times, an argument started between the gods Indra and Brahma regarding the system of foretelling the future and then went to the King for settlement. They tested the capability of the King to judge their case by asking him questions and then requested him to suggest a solution to their argument. The king pronounced Indra the winner and the defeated Brahma, decided to surrender his head as price of defeat. But Indra was reluctant to take responsibility of his head which might fall on any part of the world and cause famines, floods or fire. Finally Indra called upon the *nat* fairies who were asked to hold the head for a month each till the whole year passed and a new ceremony again restarted the process of chare, chatte and tete which takes place on three days.[43]

Lahiri also describes the water festival taking place on the New Year, though he refers to a debate among those who believe that there is no connection between the water festival and Thingyan. Some refer to the sprinkling of water as a means to purifying the soul at the start of a year though Lahiri believed that water was a means of providing relief from the heat of April and source of happiness. He found it very similar to the Indian Holi festival. Men and women wait with pitchers or tubes of water so that they can sprinkle them on unwary folks. For the tourists it was a happy occasion watching children rush around holding *pichkaris* containing water. Lahiri also points out that the water festival also meant showing respect to animals by freeing cows from the butchers, setting them free, or release fish into ponds symbolically. The festivities are always accompanied by performances of plays, puppet shows, songs and dances. He writes, 'they dress up as clowns and walk down the streets singing and dancing.

In fact, the Burmese become so engrossed in these performances and ceremonies it appears as if they do not have any trouble in the world'.[44] 'Nat Puja in Burma' and its cultural aspects were discussed a decade earlier in *Bharati* in 1900 by presumably the editor Rabindranath Tagore, since no author is mentioned. The author starts the essay by the statement that

> in large parts of Eastern Asia there was so much worship of spirits and ghosts among the uncivilized and half civilized people that it impacted those civilizations where Buddhism was the main religion. In Burma this worship of spirits was called Nat puja specially by the Nath worshippers. It was quite widespread and only a small section of the educated do not believe in worship of spirits. The word Nat was used to denote the gods as well as demi gods who are worshipped by the Mogs (referring to the Arakanese presumably).... The mogs believe that Brahma descends from the heaven to earth on new year's day and stays for three days but very few people worship this Brahma and prefer to worship the murderous demigods.

The author writes that the Mogs believe that nat spirit exists in all things, living and non-living while many spirits wander around homeless. They believe that these spirits in a previous life had a human existence and due to a fearful death or accident they were converted into spirits. There seems to be a similarity between these beliefs and that of the Hindus regarding restless ghosts from unnatural deaths. In a perpetual state of fear of these demon spirits, the Mogs try to keep them as far away as possible and pacify them by food and offerings. At the end of the rainy season in Burma, for relief from fevers and diseases elaborate offerings of eggs, fruits and coins are made. During that festival a woman dances for the Nat god as his wife (Nat patni).[45]

In an article 'Islands of Eastern India', Narendra Dev stresses that the performance style of Java differs from that of India: 'Here the poet narrates/recites his drama and the actors wearing masks and costumes, act it out without speaking'. He provides a picture of performers wearing masks as illustration.[46] Kalidas Nag discussed the drama forms of Java in an article curiously called *Dwip Bharater Natyakala* (the Dramatic Art of Island India). This article tries to trace similarities between the dramas of India and Java in different ways. He finds similarities between the Wayang Orang portrayal of the epics Ramayana and Mahabharata and the Yatra performances. He says that there are similarities between the masked dance drama of Wayang Topeng of Bali and the Ramleela of North India and the Kathakali of South India. He also compares a Puppet drama performance he saw at a funeral service in Bali to the creation of kush (grass) puppets at a Hindu *Shraddha* (funeral) ceremony. Nag also finds similarities between the Wayang golek puppets of mid-western Java and Indian puppets. The shadow play 'Wayang Purva' is based on Indian epics while the 'Wayang Gedok' is based on local traditions and myths called Panji literature. He expressed hope at the end that there would be joint research on drama by Indian and Indonesian scholars.[47] Suniti Chattopadhyay provides detailed descriptions of Chinese theatre in Singapore in *Prabashi* when he stopped at Singapore on his way to South-East Asia – the costume and make-up of the artists and the very loud orchestra which sound strange to Indian ears.[48]

One of the first articles on music in the journal *Aryadarshan*[49] traces connections with Chinese music and translates Chinese songs into Bengali notations. I have referred to his travelogue before as a 'different' journey and here only refer to the comparisons made between Chinese and Indian music. The music traveller (*Sangeet Pothik*) writes that despite dissimilarities, music in China and India is the same.

> Such a long time has elapsed since the inception of the two nations that it is difficult to say with any degree of certainty which country influenced which. But if one listens to Chinese music, one feels that it is a replica of Indian music – what difference there is, is due to passage of time and social differences. Since maintenance of traditional practices untainted by foreign influences is of utmost importance in that country, the old Chinese music is continued even today.[50]

The author's intention in discussing about the Chinese music is to trace similarities with Indian and to establish an Asian solidarity and also subtly praise the tradition living on in Chinese music. He writes:

> it is difficult for the Western musicologists to comprehend the nuances of Chinese music[51] which is why they are not enamoured by it. The understanding of the grace-notes or srutis requires an oriental musical ear. However, to us Chinese music seems melodious and familiar, very similar to the ragas *Bhupali* and *Bibhas*.

In the end, he demonstrates this through applying Chinese music to Indian notations to show the similarity between *Mu-li-hoya* and *Bhupali* ragas.[52]

Narendra Dev in his essay on Thailand says that music permeated their lives much more than any other country. Almost everyone trains in singing and it was considered a matter of shame if one couldn't sing. They also have many musical instruments which are performed solo as well as in an orchestra. Even the soldiers march during a military campaign while singing marching songs.[53] Describing the lifestyle of the aboriginal negro tribes of the Philippines, Narendra Dev also described their music practices. The inhabitants of Philippines love music and dance and their instruments reflect those of the ancient period. Bamboo flutes, brass gongs, handloom sarong, copper bells, leather drums etc. And a favourite instrument of theirs which Dev called *banshtaranga,* though it does not necessarily have to be made of bamboo. It could also be a long piece of sal or goran wood which is scraped and cut to make sounds. It is then strung up with rope like a cradle. Groups of girls stand on two sides and beat on it with wooden sticks and dance and sing in tune with the different notes that emerge from it. Sometimes men join them with drums and bells. Dev ends by saying that 'one can see a high culture and imagination in the dance of these unsophisticated barbaric tribal people.' Visions of bees hovering on the flowers, peasant women gathering corn from the fields, youths enacting rituals of romance, and brave warriors taking leave from their tearful lovers before going to their battles are portrayed by poets in the dances, Dev writes.[54] He contrasts this with the Muslim Moro tribes in the same region who do not really care for dancing, though the men perform a dance-like sword fight. The Moro women dance in festivals but their dance has no foot movements. 'They sit and sway their upper bodies and use hand movements and dramatic facial movements, similar to the baijis in our country.'[55]

Javanese dances were discussed by JVH Labberton when a Javanese troupe arrived in Madras and a performance was organised at the Jubilee Convention of Theosophical Society. He wrote 'Wayang Wong is from the standpoint of art a most beautiful expression of human soul dancing. These aristocratic dancers have an unimaginable grace.' This romantic dance drama is an episode of the Indian epic Mahabharata which is called the *Bharata Yudha* in Java. Labberton described the Pandava dances as 'delicate and refined' while the 'Kaurava dance is more wild and aggressive and the Danava dance is a savage dance.' Arjuna was accompanied by three clowns who 'represent the powers of good'[56]

B.R. Chatterjee looking for Indic connections as a Greater India scholar finds it interesting that 'in the Javanese puppet show known as Wayang, old Hindu tradition has been preserved even now though Java has been a Mohammedan country for more than five centuries'.[57] There are a number of essays which give details of adaptations of Ramayana and Mahabharata in the lands of South-East Asia and point out the differences with the Indian epics. Amulyacharan Bandopadhyay tells the story of Brata Yudha or Mahabharata as told in the ancient language of Java called Kavi completed in 791 slokas.[58] I have discussed cultural intimacies among Asian nations in more detail elsewhere.[59]

Santidev Ghosh after graduating in music and dance from Visva Bharati visited many Asian countries with the blessings of his Guru Rabindranath Tagore, in the search of best cultural techniques in the east, in true universalist belief that Tagore had. In his book *Java and Bali's Dance and Music*, there is a chapter on the shadow play of the two countries which he says was popular in every village there. The royal family took a keen interest in all the cultural performances. The main performer is the Dalang who sings the songs and the puppets are manipulated against a white screen with red border (called kleen). Behind the Dalang sits the Gamelan musicians who provide musical support. The Dalang changes his voice according to the characters his puppets portray. According to the Java dance drama tradition the series of puppets on the right of the Dalang are good and the ones on the left are bad. When the play is Mahabharata, the right puppets are Pandavas and the others are Kauravas.[60]

The play that Santidev described was on Arjuna's stealing away of the beautiful daughter of Shakuni. He writes that according to scholars of Java, the companions of Arjuna (a short old man, and his three sons) were probably a part of the Javanese tradition which had been adapted here. These puppets look different from the other puppets and always act like a clown. 'They have an instinctive native intelligence like Gopal Bhand of Bengal.' he added. The Javanese puppets do not have any ornaments but wear a flower chain around their waist and though they can move their limbs their mouths do not move. There is a strict tradition of how the audience should sit. The men sit on the lit side where the Dalang sits, while women sit on the shadow side.[61]

Santidev also describes the shadow play in Bali. It is similar to that of Java except that their puppets are more masculine. Before the play commences, the Dalang performs a prayer. In Bali, the names for the puppet box are different and the Dalang has two assistants. The shadow plays of both the countries have one commonality. That is the sculpted leather fork. It has multifarious meanings in the play. When placed against the screen, it indicates beginning or end and it is visible when the scene has to be changed. It also indicates wind, fire or water. The rule is to take the Kayonan, as the fork is called, out of the box (Kropak) before taking the puppets out. The puppets of Bali unlike the Javanese puppets can move their mouths. The shadow plays were often used in Java and Bali as instruments of education. Santidev Ghosh ends with an interesting observation:

> It is often a matter of pride to the people of these countries that the shadow play belong to their own tradition and did not come from India since there is no

> shadow play present in India today. But they do not know that in some areas of South India shadow play is present till today and the dolls are in fact very similar and made of the same buffalo skin. In Java they are called Owangwang in South India they are called Bammalat.[62]

Shadow play at the palace of Raja of Soerkarta was described in detail by Tagore himself in a letter to Pratima Debi[63] which was also printed in *Visva Bharati Patrika*[64] in which he ends the description by saying that 'If only we could have given our history lessons like that – the schoolmaster narrating the story, a marionette show giving a visual representation of its main incidents and a musical accompaniment voicing the emotions with various tune and time!'

The stress on a common past and common tradition is seen in discussions on economy, culture, health, military policies or when discipline and ethical values present in the Asian nations are upheld. Even in discussion of art and theatre, commonalities are underlined and stress laid on the distinctiveness of Asian art in contrast to western culture. In one discussion in 1904, by Ramlal Sarkar on Chinese life, a comparison is made between Sri Panchami or Saraswati puja celebrated in Bengal with the spring festival in China. Unlike our country where the pujas are celebrated in every household, in China this festival is organised by the state and royal officials. Much like the *panjika* or the almanac prepared by the Sanskrit pundits of Navadvip fix the date of Sri Panchami, the almanac prepared by the astrologers of Peking fixes the date of the spring festival. In due course the idol of a buffalo is prepared from bamboos, straws and clay. The colour of the buffalo changes according to the year's prediction – fear of fire will make the colour of the buffalo red, colour yellow will indicate a year of high winds and black indicates heavy rains and white epidemics. A particular family prepares the idol every year partly with the help from the government and partly from funds raised from the market.[65] Sarkar then describes the procession that is organised by the government, marking the worship of the Buffalo god. Many floats called thaig accompany the procession with young boys dressed as women which Sarkar compared to the Janmashtami procession floats in Dhaka.

> Behind the Idol and the floats young boys follow carrying triangular red flag and then men bearing spears and swords are followed by the soldiers on horses. They are followed by decorated palanquins bearing royal officials in full regalia ... once the procession after traversing the main streets reach their starting point, the idol is then ceremoniously placed on display. The next day at a propitious time fixed by the astrologers, the officials beat the idol with sticks till it disintegrates. Amazingly from the inside of the idol emerge twelve small images of buffalo calves which the image maker had skilfully hidden inside the image. Everyone wants to own one of these tiny images and often riots occur on these occasions.[66]

This Chuyen nyu worship is more a local tradition and Sarkar claimed that he could not discover any reference to this in any book.

Rabindranath Tagore was so determined to undo pride evoked in the memories of past colonisation of parts of Asia by India that he decided that the only way to mitigate it was through an inverse colonisation. Not content with simply creating awareness, he devised a unique plan of cultural assimilation in his university curriculum. He invited scholars to lecture and teach various subjects and Asian languages at Vishwabharati,

Santiniketan. His large repertoire of songs he set to tunes which were influenced by world music and in the dance dramas he decided to experiment with dance forms of Asia. An excellent description of this has been given by Santidev Ghosh, a student who later adopted his guru's principles in the curriculum of Kala Bhavan. Ghosh travelled in different parts of India and Asia to absorb basic techniques of dances and theatrical styles of Asia. After Manipuri and Kathakali, Tagore sent him to Sri Lanka four times between 1936 and 1938. There he trained in the men's Kandi dance. In 1937, Santidev went to Burma and learnt the hand movements of the Rampoye dance drama style from a veteran dancer and two years later he went to Java and learnt the Nari, Legong and Kobiyar dance at the invitation of the king and later spent a month in Bali learning the popular dances there. He was particularly impressed with the Gamelon music there. Rabindranath's efforts were supported and popularised not only by his associates like Suniti Chatterjee, Kalidas Nag and Nandalal Bose who serially wrote about their visits to the Asian countries in the periodicals of the day but also by others. Sylvain Levy in a lecture in Madras under the auspices of the Sanskrit Academy contained a suggestion and an exhortation to Indian students to go to Japan, Java, Bali, etc. to study the cultural achievements of their ancestors. *The Modern Review* while reporting this and the efforts of Rabindranath Tagore in this direction also added that 'if funds had been placed at his (Tagore's) disposal by munificent lovers of Indian history and culture, he could have sent competent young scholars to study and work there for a year'.[67] These dreams of Asian interconnections that Tagore and other intellectuals saw left many legacies in Santiniketan[68] as well as in the associations and writings of those who interacted and visited Bengal then and in the later period.

Notes

1 Nirad Chandra Chaudhuri, *Atmaghati Bangali*, Calcutta: Mitra and Ghosh, 1988, pp. 38–39.
2 Partha Mitter, *Indian Art*, Oxford: Oxford University Press, 2001, p. 177.
3 E.B. Havell, *Ideals of Indian Art*, London: John Murray, 1920 (1911), p. Intro., pp. xiii–xv.
4 S.K. Bhattacharya, *Story of Indian Art*, Delhi: Atma Ram & Sons, 1966, p. 99.
5 Kalidas Nag, Art and Archaeology in the Far East-French Contribution, *The Modern Review*, XLVII (1), January 1930, p. 63.
6 Sri Aurobindo, *The Significance of Indian Art*, Bombay: Sri Aurobindo Circle, 1947, p. 29.
7 Manindrabhusan Gupta, Chin Chitrakalar Itihash, *Prabashi*, 24(2)(1), 1924, pp. 81–89.
8 Ibid., p. 85.
9 Ibid., p. 89.
10 Manilal Sensharma, Shilpi Manindrabhushan Gupta o tar chitrakala, *Bichitra*, 7(1)(4), 1933, p. 486.
11 Ibid.
12 Nandalal Bose, Chin Japaner Chithi, *Prabashi*, 28(1)(1), 1932, pp. 784–787.
13 Bimalendu Koyal, Adhunik Chiner Chitrakala, *Bangasri*, 3(2)(3), 1935, p. 427.
14 Ibid.
15 Ibid., p. 431.
16 Jamini Kanta Sen, Chainik Chitrakalar Chhayapoth, *Bharatvarsha*, 26(1)(5), 1938, p. 579.
17 Jamini Kanta Sen, Chainik Shilpakalay Bharatiya Aishayjjya, *Mashik Basumati*, 14(2)(3), 1935, pp. 480–488.
18 Ibid., p. 488.
19 Jadunath Sarkar, Indian Influence on the Art of Indo China, *The Modern Review*, 39(1), 1926, p. 43.
20 Narendra Dev, Shyambhumi, *Bharatvarsha*, 12(1)(6), 1924, p. 905.
21 Sris Chandra Chatterjee, Indian Fine Arts, *The Modern Review*, 47(5), 1930, pp. 591–596.

22 V.V. Vadnerker, Revival of Indian Art and Architecture, *Welfare*, 3(7), 1925, pp. 30–31.
23 Sris Chandra Chatterjee, op. cit., pp. 591–596.
24 Nalinikanta Gupta, The Standpoint of Indian Art, *The Modern Review*, 49(5), 1932, pp. 493–496.
25 Swami Sadananda, Brihattara Bharater Dev-Devi, *Mashik Basumati*, 14(2)(4), 1935 pp. 552–558.
26 Ibid., pp. 502–507.
27 Jogindranath Samaddar, Bharatiya Chitrabidya, *Bharatvarsha*, 2(2), 1923 pp. 161–167.
28 Quoted in Origin of Art and Culture in India, Indian Periodicals, *The Modern Review*, August 1931, p. 212.
29 Jamini Kanta Sen, Chainik Chitrakalar Chhayapoth, *Bharatvarsha*, 26(1)(5), 1938, p. 579.
30 Benoy Kumar Sarkar, *The Futurism of Young Asia and Other Essays on the Relations between East and the West*, Berlin: Julius Springer, 1922, pp. 116–143.
31 Brahmadeshiya Natok o Natokabhnoy, *Bharati*, 2(7), 1877, p. 306 (pp. 306–314).
32 Ibid., p. 307.
33 Ibid.
34 Ibid.
35 Jyotirindranath Tagore, *Rajatgiri (Brahmadeshiyo Natok)*, Calcutta: Sanyal and Co., 1903.
36 H.H. Wilson, *Select Specimens of the Theatre of the Hindus*, 3 vols, Delhi: Asian Educational Services, 1984 (3rd ed.).
37 Phyllis Hartnoll, *The Theatre: A Concise History*, London: James and Hudson World of Art, 1985 (3rd ed.) pp. 229–230.
38 Gleanings, *The Modern Review*, XXVII, January–July 1920, p. 286.
39 For one aspect of the debate, namely between good 'traditional' and 'bad' modern practices in public theatre, see Sarvani Gooptu, Caught between Tradition and Modernity, in *The Actress in the Public Theatres of Calcutta*, Primus Books, 2015, pp. 50–67.
40 Ramlal Sarkar, Chindehe Natyabhinoy, *Prabashi*, 5(3), 1905, pp. 143–147.
41 Benoy Kumar Sarkar, Swadhin Ashiar Rajdhani, *Grihastha*, 7(7) (4), 1915, pp. 343–345.
42 Ibid., pp. 340–342.
43 Kumudnath Lahiri, Brahmer Nat Utsav, *Prabashi*, 10(6), 1910, pp. 536–538.
44 Ibid., pp. 537–538.
45 Anon. Presumably editor Rabindranath Tagore, Brahme Natpuja, *Bharati*, 24(10), 1900, pp. 922–924.
46 Narendra Dev, Purba Bharater Dvipabali (the Islands of Eastern India), *Bharatvarsha*, 12(1)(1), 1924, p. 125.
47 Kalidas Nag, *Dwip Bharater Natyakala*, *Prabashi*, 29(1)(6), 1929.
48 Suniti Kr Chattopadhyay, *Javadwiper Pothe*, *Prabashi*, 28(1), 1928.
49 Sri Shou/Sri Sourindro.. (name withheld, possibly Sourindra Mohon Tagore), Sangeet Pathik, *Aryadarshan*, 1(1)(3)(4)(6)(7)(9), 1874, pp. 51–54; pp. 134–142; pp. 192–199; pp. 295–346; pp. 434–439.
50 Sri Sourindro, Sangeet Pathik, op. cit., 1(6), pp. 295–296.
51 He analyses the works of western scholars on Chinese music to prove his point. Sri Sourindro, Sangeet Pathik, op. cit., 1(7), pp. 344–346.
52 Ibid., pp. 299–300.
53 Narendra Dev, Shyambhumi, *Bharatvarsha*, 12(6)(1), 1924, pp. 905–907.
54 Narendra Dev, Philippine (Philippines), *Bharatvarsha*, 12(1)(3), 1924, pp. 456–457.
55 Narendra Dev, Philippine (Philippines), *Bharatvarsha*, 12(1)(4), 1924, pp. 595–596.
56 J.V.H. Labbeton, Javanese Dances, Gleanings, *The Modern Review*, XXXIX, January, 1926.
57 B.R. Chatterjee, Mahabharata and the Wayang in Java, *The Modern Review*, XXXXVI, July–December 1929, p. 658.
58 Amulya Chandra Bandopadhyay, Javadwiper Mahabharata (Story), *Bharatvarsha*, 18(2), 1930–31, p. 601.
59 Sarvani Gooptu, The Politics of Cultural Intimacies in Asia: Writings on Drama and Musical Performances in East and South East Asia in Bengali Literature and Journals, in

Sarvani Gooptu and Mimasha Pandit, eds., *Identity at Crossroads: Performance and the Culture of Nationalism in Asia*, Delhi: Routledge (forthcoming).

60 Santidev Ghosh, *Java o Balir Nrityageet*, Calcutta: Visva Bharati Patrika, 1952 (new ed. 1994), pp. 26–27.

61 Ibid., p. 28.

62 Ibid., p. 30.

63 Rabindranath Tagore, *Letters from Java: Rabindranath Tagore's Tour of South East Asia 1927*, Translated by Indira Devi Chaudhurani and Supriya Roy, ed. by Supriya Roy, Calcutta: Visva Bharati Publishing, 2010, p. 114.

64 Quoted in Indian Periodicals section of *The Modern Review*, XLIV(1–6), 1928.

65 Ramlal Sarkar, Chindeshe Basantotsav, *Prabashi*, 4(2), 1904, pp. 81–82.

66 Ibid., p. 83.

67 *The Modern Review*, XLIV(1–6), 1928, p. 492.

68 A discussion on Santiniketan's lasting connection with China can be seen in the chapter Pan Asianism and Renewed connections in Tansen Sen's *India, China and the World: A Connected History*, Delhi: Oxford University Press, 2018, pp. 293–377.

6 Buddhist ideas and pilgrimage as a means of connectivity

Connection with Outer Asia was most evident in the rediscovery of Buddhism. Buddhism was identified as originating from India, through its living presence in the other Asian countries. Buddhism thus acquired for Indian intellectuals a new area of pride, intangible yet strong. Intangible because Buddhism was not a reality in the lives of the Indians and so could not become a source of weakness, being out of reach of all hegemonic control. This idea of Buddhism, unsullied, untainted by colonial disdain could become a source of pride in place of Hinduism which was prone to attack and vilification since the beginning of colonisation. Taking pride in the ownership of Buddhism, especially since archaeological discoveries uncovered its splendours outside the territorial limits of India where the religion seemed to have survived so strongly as well as within where only the memory survived, was now linked to an academic enterprise of 'pilgrimage'.

The recovery of lost memories of Buddha and Buddhism was a unique history and Indians eagerly and strategically joined with the British in this journey of rediscovery as a means to discover their own history and philosophy. A large amount of writing exists in Bengali on Buddha and Buddhism like Sadhu Aghorenath's *Sakyamuni Charita* (1882), Krishna Kumar Mitra's *Buddhadev Charita* (1887), Ramdas Sen's *Buddhadeva* (1891), Upendra Kumar Ghosh's *Buddhacharita* (1894), Satyendranath Tagore's *Bouddhyadharma* (1901), Acharya Satishchandra's *Buddhadev* (1904), Narendranath Bhattacharya's *Buddha* (1910), Baradakanta Bandopadhyay's *Buddha* (1910), Atulchandra Mukhopadhyay's *Sakyasingha* (1911), Sarat Kumar Ray's, *Buddher Jibon o Bani* (1914), Adyanath Ray's, *Chhleder Buddhadev* (1923), Pramathanath Dasgupta's *Gautam Buddha* (1927), Hirendranath Dutta, *Buddhadever Nastikata* (1936), Haraprasad Sastri's *Bauddhyadharma* (1948), U Nu's *The Buddha* (1961) and many more published in the 1950s and 1960s. Rabindranath Tagore along with many others wrote articles on Buddha's life and philosophy in the various journals in Bengali which were later collated into books. Some of them at least discussed the spread of Buddhism in South, South-East and East Asia underlining the commonality of values that Buddhism brought in these countries despite the other differences. Along with the life and teachings of the Buddha, one aspect that is highlighted in the writings on Buddhism through the 19th and 20th centuries by both Westerners and Indians is the way Buddhism provided a means of connecting countries, through ideas and beliefs as well as pilgrimage in the past and in the present. As Rene Grousset wrote in 1932, in *In the Footsteps of the Buddha*, 'Buddhism in bringing them (countries of the east) into contact with one another, had created a vast current of humanism, from Ceylon to the furthest isles of the Japanese archipelago'.[1]

DOI: 10.4324/9781003243786-6

A number of articles described the pilgrimage by the Buddhist pilgrims to India in the past,[2] the different pilgrimage spots, their identification in the Buddhist texts and discovery by the archaeologists,[3] a list detailing the geography in the age of the Buddha[4] but the great majority are about Gautama Buddha – biographical details, his teachings and its spread and on the decline of Buddhism in India.[5] Others[6] discuss how the Buddhist links were rediscovered when the texts by the Chinese pilgrims Hiuen Tsang (Xuanzang) and Fa Hien (Faxian) were discovered and translated by European scholars. Fa Hien, writes Harisadhan Mukhopadhyay stayed in Mathura for a month. In his written account one finds that at that time there were at least twenty Buddhist monasteries in that region where almost 3, 000 Buddhist monks lived. Besides there were three stupas dedicated to the close disciples and associates of the Buddha like Ananda, who was famed to have spread Buddhist ideals among women and to the Buddhist texts It was sad, according to the author, that with the passing of time, the Buddhist shrines of worship have been converted into ruins.[7]

Kailash Chandra Sinha as early as 1880, wrote a serialised article on the *Travels of Hiuen Tsang in Bengal*.[8] The historian R.C. Majumdar writing for a literary magazine *Prabashi* discusses the journeys through Asia of many Chinese Buddhist pilgrims, 'who did not attain the fame of Fa Hien, Hiuen Tsang or I Tsing, but they too were motivated by the highest ideals when they made the long and arduous journey to India'.[9]

One favourite theme in many of the essays was the description of how Buddhism became popular in countries outside Buddha's homeland and how the reverence that developed for that great soul could in turn be linked to India. This could be in the form of discussions on the spread of Buddhism as well as on the Buddhists. Satyendranath Tagore included North America and Mexico in the long list of countries where Buddhism spread,[10] while Rabindranath Tagore wrote in *Tattvabodhini Patrika* (1911) about the translation of Asvaghosa's 'Discourse on the Awakening of the Faith in the Mahayana' from Chinese, from the only surviving text.[11] In the periodicals, essays describe Buddhists in different countries of South-East Asia and East Asia, their numbers, forms of worship and ideas and philosophies. Keeping in mind the reader, these articles always focus on similarities or differences with India or they highlight important facts of socio-religious or cultural history. Narendra Dev in his article on *Shyamdesh* (Thailand) describes the Buddhists of Thailand as different from those of India (*Bharat*) or Tibet (*Tibbat*) and they follow the Buddhist rules and conventions of Burma (*Brahmadesha)* and Sri Lanka (*Singhal*). The king is not only the nation's leader, he is also their religious head. There are at least ten thousand Buddhist monasteries (*viharas*) in Thailand and over two lakhs Buddhist monks residing there. The king is the administrator of all these monasteries and the monks are the king's subjects. Western influence has reduced the impact and influence of Buddhism on the daily life of the city people but in the villages Buddhist conventions and even their superstitions reign supreme. For a long time, the art and literature of the country was closely tied up with Buddhism and confined to the *viharas* which naturally meant that art and culture was mainly religious. It is a matter of hope, Dev comments, that today with the spread of education, art and literature is also found to be developing outside the monasteries.[12] He also described the different crafts with Buddhist motifs which were famed products of *Shyamdesh* (Siam).

New pilgrimage

Though travelling for pilgrimage was not new, writing about them by the pilgrims was rare in India; however, some documentation of this pious act has engaged scholars and pilgrims through the ages. Even when travel across seas was forbidden for the Hindus, travel by water to pilgrimage sites was condoned and in fact venerated. With the establishment of the British colonial rule from the mid-18th century, smoother communication networks made travel easier and over the next centuries the purpose of travel changed along with the ease. Pilgrimage to Buddhist sites and writing about them took on a new form in the newly established medium of vernacular periodicals. The newly English-educated elite in Calcutta found the vernacular press a means of expression of their innermost thoughts and values and discovered in it the means of moulding public opinion. The new pilgrimages were not always for religious salvation by the faithful of any particular religion but in a spirit of adventure motivated by a desire for scientific knowledge and a consciousness of the importance of religion beyond esoteric philosophy and vital for the understanding of self and others. In this chapter, I explore the writing of these tourists who were journeying for the pleasure of discovery of the unknown but a missionary zeal for acquiring and disseminating knowledge of a religion towards which they believed the country had done the injustice of forgetting. The deep chasm of difference between religious and secular pilgrimage was removed in this period responding to a changed situation in the intellectual map of India with the rediscovery of Buddhism's birthplace. The 'new' pilgrims from eastern India began intellectual and scholarly pilgrimages to the various sites of Asia, and wrote about their experiences in local languages. Beyond piety their new interest was manifold – understanding the present conditions in different Asian countries, linking them to India's past and documenting the new pilgrimage experience for their countrymen.

Appreciation of art and architecture was also connected with this enterprise as was discovery of Buddhist literary texts in different parts of Asia and writing about the journeys to the different Buddhist sites. For the Indians defying the taboo of crossing the *kala pani* (forbidden oceanic travels abroad)[13] in going to visit the great 'sights' and writing about the impact of Buddhism of 'Indian origin' on the cultures of Asia, there was a distinct sense of national pride. The detailed descriptions probably address the fact that Indians, especially Bengali readers, were not familiar with the Buddhist places of worship. Travelling to Burma once it came under direct British rule became very easy and the visits to the magnificent Buddhist viharas and pagodas form a part of every travellers' tale. Very popular are the descriptions of the Shwe Dagon Pagoda of Burma with its golden crest. Mrinalini Raha describes her visit in 1902 to the pagoda site with a friend, the famous lawyer Namah Shivay Pillay, MA, LLB.

> Since it is a popular tourist spot a number of trams convey the travellers. There is a saying that the Buddha's hair is kept at the Shwe Dagon which is fifteen hands high from the ground. One has to climb a flight of stone steps to arrive at the pagoda. Burmese women can be seen sitting on the steps selling flowers and candles for dedication to the idol . . . Inside there is a gigantic stone Buddha image, in the meditative pose. On either side thousands of candles have been lit and Burmese holding different types of flowers can be seen praying to the Buddha or meditating.[14]

On either side of the Pagoda are Mahabodhi Society and Pagoda Trust office. Besides the main pagoda, there are many more which contain stone images of the Buddha and in one there is the pensive Buddha in a lying position with his hands cradling his head surrounded by his disciples. There is a museum nearby where among other things is a huge bell. After expressing awe at the religiosity of the Burmese, Raha provides other facts of interest to her readers when she writes that the Pagoda is proof of the immortal vigour of the Buddhist religion and the greatness of Buddhist pilgrimage. It is said that in 1858, during the Anglo Burmese war, this Pagoda had acted as a fort, and this story is supported by the existence of the moat around the pagoda very similar to the one surrounding the Fort William in Calcutta. Then Raha expresses a sentiment that is repeated by all the writers who visit these pilgrimage sites:

> I was filled with a deep regret as well as happiness after my visit to Shwe Dagon at the ungratefulness of the Indians and happiness at the deep faith of the Burmese. The birth of the lord Buddha had purified India, revolutionised her faith with his message of equality, yet today with the remorseless passage of time, Buddhism has been banished from India and the lord Buddha is no longer venerated by its people. Yet that Indian holy man is the focus of veneration of crores of men and women in this faraway Burma. The civilized Indians did not appreciate the greatness of the Buddha, yet the uncivilized pay homage to the feet of the same Buddha and achieve their life's fulfilment.[15]

Raha thus reveals here all the prejudices of her race concerning the 'different' Burmese people though she is domiciled there, while she also underlines the awe and gratitude she feels at the devotion of the Burmese. It also salvages her pride in belonging to the country that produced the Buddha with his egalitarian message which the hierarchical Hinduism denies its faithful.

An anonymous writer in *Mahila* some years later, while describing a visit to some Burmese cities, says that a visit to the Buddhist pagoda at Mandalay was compulsory for all visitors. The journey to Mandalay has been described, how it took 10 hours to reach Mandalay and how on the way they could see scattered on the valleys 'hundreds of large and small pagodas as if it was a forest of pagodas.' The author points out that though in Lower Burma, the pagodas are often made of wood, in Upper Burma they are made of bricks and beautifully designed, some with golden crowns[16]

Another traveller, Paresh Chandra Sen, chose Shwe Set Taw (Golden Footprints or Sri-Pad), the less traversed of the four Buddhist pilgrimages in Burma (other three being – Rangoon's Shwe Dagon, Mahamuni temple of Mandalay, Pegan's Ananda temple), for a visit with his companion in 1927 and also includes pictures for his readers. Sarala Debi Chaudhurani, a pioneering woman of Bengal, travelled alone to Burma to attend a Conference in Rangoon and wrote about her travels there. One separate article in the series titled 'Shwe Dagon' is dedicated to the famous Buddhist temple, its connection with Burmese history and description of her visit there with pictorial additions.[17]

Another country where travel invariably included visits to Buddhist pilgrim sites was Sri Lanka. Raja Munindra Deb Ray, associated with the Library Association, travelled in 1927 to Sri Lanka (Singhal Dvip) and provided many pictures of Anuradhapura in the journal *Bharatvarsha*.[18] Manindrabhushan Gupta (trained under Nandalal Bose of Santiniketan) who worked as an art teacher in Ananda College in Sri Lanka in the 1920s,[19] in an article 'Singhaler Chitra' (Portrait of Singhal) prefaced the descriptions of the pilgrimage sites there by myths about how Buddhism spread in Sri Lanka.

Much before Ashoka and 'the king of Singhal Devanampiya Tissa' exchanged gifts and promises to spread the word and faith of the Buddha:

> Buddha arrived in Lanka Dvipa. The ancient text of Mahavamsa says that Buddha set his foot in Singhal many times. Though there is no historical basis for this story, most Sinhalese believe in it. It is said that Buddha prepared the land for the arrival of Mahendra, because he, the Buddha believed that Lanka Dvip would welcome his religion wholeheartedly. From ancient times, the land was overrun by Yakkhas or Yakshas. One day Buddha appeared before them in the sky and created fear in their hearts by ushering in thunder and lightning. When they bowed before him in fear, he pronounced that he would come to save them if they created a sacred spot for him to alight. The yakkhas said that they were willing to leave the whole island to him, hearing which the Buddha alighted from the sky and the rest of the island went up in flames leaving the yakkhas no alternative but to run to the coast for shelter. The Buddha then created a hill island for them towards the east. All the other gods of the Singhal island came to Buddha to be converted to his religion and god Suman who ruled over what is known as the Adam's peak also came to Buddha for his blessings. Buddha gave him a lock of his hair which Suman put in a golden box and created a stupa of precious stones over it . . . The second story of Buddha to the island took place when the Snake god (Nagaraja) whom the original inhabitants of Singhal island worshipped held a gala feast and invited Buddha to it. This arrival of the Buddha was made memorable when he landed on Suman mountain (Adam's Peak) and left his footprints there . . . Even after two and half thousand years today thousands of tourists climb up the mountain to worship the Buddha's footprints there.[20]

During his visit to the Adam's Peak, Gupta points out that the footprints that are visible there on the rocks are claimed to have been created differently by people of different religions. Hindus believe they are the god Vishnu's footprints while Muslims and Christians believe them to be Adam's – the first man who was banished from Heaven by the angels for tasting the forbidden fruit. On important days worshippers of all religions come to this place to pay their respects. Most of the time however Adam's Peak is inaccessible due to inclement weather and fear of wild animals.[21] Gupta gives a beautiful description of the climbing up the mountain in the darkness by pilgrims belonging to different faiths, all chanting the names of their revered gods in perfect harmony. Gupta also describes Mihintal, 8 miles from Anuradhapur, through a forest and skirting the huge lake of Nuwara Wewa, considered to be the memorial of Mahendra, the son of king Ashoka of the Maurya empire, who is considered historically to have brought the Buddhist faith to Sri Lanka. It is said that one of the kings of Anuradhapura spread pieces of cloth along the whole way to Mihintal so that the feet of the pilgrims were not covered in dust. The hill is a thousand feet high and 1840 steps lead to the memorial which the author calls 'steps to heaven'.[22] Gupta also writes that Mihintal was at one time very well administered and all Buddhist kings took pains to ensure that the vihara was well provided for. There were hospitals and community kitchens established as well as good sanitary system for the inhabitants of Mihintal.

Gupta concludes with another miracle story from Mahavamsa describing the miraculous way by which the Bodhi branch was brought to Singhal island. A large golden plate 14 feet in diameter and 8 inches thick was built to hold the branch. King

Asoka took the plate and reached near the Bodhi tree accompanied by soldiers and sages. A mighty festival was taking place and the Bodhi tree was decorated with precious stones, jewels and flags. Beautiful garlands made of brightly coloured flowers were everywhere. The king raised his hands in prayers on eight sides, and then placing the gold plate on a golden stool, he climbed to a high branch of the Bodhi tree where he marked a branch with red marks with a golden pen and is said to have declared that, 'if the tallest branch of the Bodhi tree goes to Lankadvip and if my faith in the Buddha is true then let the branch descend on the golden plate'. As soon as he said these words, the red marked branch separated from the tree and fell on the plate. Asoka cried out in joy at the miracle and all the assembled people echoed his wonder. The Buddhist monks chanted in happiness and even nature seemed to express joy at the miraculous event. Sinhalese royal family members were entrusted with the welfare of the branch during its journey by sea by Asoka and once it reached Sri Lanka, the king Tissa who was waiting at a palace constructed on the shore to await the arrival of the branch, ran out into the sea and accompanied the branch on a chariot which took it to its final destination at Mahamegha garden in Anuradhapura. The moment the tree branch was lowered on to the ground, it is said to have risen to 80 feet and emanated six different coloured lights. Once the lights reached the stars, the roots of the branch along with the golden plate reached into the earth and the tree was feted by man and gods. Rains continued for seven days and when it ceased, the light emanating from the tree became visible.[23]

There are many descriptions of the Buddhist sites in East Asia, China and Japan by the tourists. Though the other religions prevailing there are also discussed, like Confucianism and Shintoism, Buddhist sites are a must visit for all Indians travelling to those countries and a desire to find similarities with worship in India. Benoy Kumar Sarkar travelling in Japan, on his tour of Tokyo, visited a Buddhist monastery, where he finds familiarity in the little shops which line the entrance to any pilgrim spot in India.

> One can buy Japanese pictures, canes, bowls and fans in the shops. Then we spotted two stone figures of Buddhist monks on two sides of a Japanese style gate. It was two storied and made of wood with a large bell hanging next to it . . . Large number of visitors assemble here during Buddha's birth anniversary in the month of *baishak*. Though western influence has come into Japan, not all ancient and medieval elements have been obliterated. No matter how much Japan declares war against superstition, love for Buddha has not been removed from the heart of the Japanese.[24]

While visiting the imperial art museum, Sarkar points out quoting Chamberlain that sculpture remained exclusively in Buddhist hands, at first in those of Korean priests or of descendants of Korean and Chinese craftsmen. It is natural that these images show Indian influence but critics still hesitate as to the share to be attributed to native Japanese style wood and bronze images adorning the temples of Kyoto and Nara which in Sarkar's view may claim a place among the world's masterpieces 'by virtue of their passionate vitality of expression and fidelity to anatomical detail' Yet according to Sarkar, 'the ideal they embodied has not again been reached on Japanese soil since the beginning of Japanese civilization when Buddhism came to Japan from Korea in 552. Her art, education, administration etc all started after that date when from 6th to 9th century, 'Buddhist art in Japan was more or less based on outside influence.'

Sarkar also talks of 'Indian sphere of influence in the whole of Asia at a time when Japanese culture was at its infancy'.[25] Sarkar met a professor in theology, Kinjo Kinje Hirai, at a university in Tokyo who had a theory that 'the yamato spirit in Japan was associated not only with the Chinese civilization but also had elements of Indian and Euro-American culture'. Quoting him, Sarkar writes: 'I had been looking at a Sanskrit English dictionary and suddenly came across the word *yamkoti* as signifying a region as far west and north as Japan is. So, the Hindus knew Japan as Yamkoti which could be possibly a distortion of the word Yamato'.[26] When Sarkar asked him if he had found similarities between Sanskrit and Japanese, Hirai said that he considered the Japanese as 'related to Hindus and descended from them. So long scholars thought that the Japanese were Mongolian or yellow race but I do not agree with them'. Sarkar said that he too had read that some western scholars were disputing the fact that the Japanese were not Mongolian in origin but were descendants of Asian islanders. Hirai told him that in the prehistoric age Japanese were related to Indians. The Japanese got Buddhism in the 6th century from the Koreans and after that their relations with the yellow races of Korea and China increased. But before the 6th century, what was the condition of the Yamato country? Everyone knows that the original inhabitants of Japan were called Aino and their descendants still live in the northern-most islands. The Japanese colonists appeared in the land of the Ainos and then the land of the rising sun came to be known as Yamato, just like Bharat was referred to as Aryasthan or Aryavarta or Aryabhoomi after the arrival of the Aryans there. But where did these foreign settlers come from? Sarkar then asked Professor Hirai if he thought that the Japanese settlers had arrived from India and if Japanese were aware of India in the pre-Buddhist period? Where was the proof that they knew of Hindustan before their contact with Koreans and China? Sarkar reports that Hirai referred to more than one proof – religion was the first proof. When Buddhism came in the 6th century from Korea it could not have been adopted so smoothly if there had been no preexisting religion. The presence of a compatible religion made is easier for the people to accept this religion which did not appear to be a new and alien to the inhabitants. Hirai referred to '*Amanopara*', meaning heaven which was found in the early folklore of Japan and as also referring to a parent's home. In the oldest folktales of Yamato there are references to many Indian stories so a comparative study of Japanese and Indian literature is imperative. Sarkar feels that modern scholars are not very keen on that study of Indo-Japanese exchanges and prefer to study the exchanges between China and Japan. According to Sarkar, Hirai spoke about 'the deep spiritualism of Upanishads, esoteric religion and mysticism' which was already present in Yamatostan. A person called Eninokini had preached semi Buddhist philosophy in that period and there are still some followers of his teachings today. The second proof of connection was language. Japanese was an Aryan language like Greek, Latin, Sanskrit and Persian and did not belong to the Mongolian family – not only in use of words but in grammatical styles as well. Hirai pointed out in a pamphlet called *A Vocabulary of the Japanese and Aryan Languages* that hypothetically compared, it has generally been accepted almost as a truism that the Japanese language belongs to the Ural – Altaig or Turanian family, and the suggestion that Japanese is affiliated to the Indo-European branch would excite laughter. Hirai wrote a brief treatise comparing the Japanese and Indo European grammars, mostly with the Bengali and Assamese pointing out a great similarity between them, and Persian even more so.[27]

Prabodh Chandra Bagchi described his 'pilgrimage' to Koya San from Nara in *Prabashi* where he starts by describing how the priest of the temple started his service with a 'praise song about Shaka-niyorai or the Shaka Tathagata facing westward as symbolising the country of the Lord Tathagata or Buddha'. Bagchi was gratified that the temple which was built for India's beloved but forgotten ideal, has been so well preserved by the Japanese. In this context, he refers to the story of Kobo-Daishi (8–9th century), the Japanese Buddhist monk who established the Shingon school of Buddhism. He travelled to China in his search for the true ideals of Buddhism since he had become disgusted with the existing state of religion in Japan. He had actually wanted to go to India but was only able to reach China where he visited temple after temple in search of the true words of the Buddha, hoping to meet Indian Buddhist monks there. Bagchi believed that imbued with Indian idealism, Kobo Daishi was able to inspire his countrymen to a unique national ideal. It was to pay his tribute to Kobo Daishi that Bagchi visited Koya San.[28]

This voyage that Bagchi made was really an academic pilgrimage as well since he accompanied the Indologist and his teacher Sylvain Levy and Sakaki, professor of Sanskrit at Kiyoto University, in search of manuscripts. Bagchi had been in Japan as part of the fellowship he received to travel to East and South-East Asia in 1922, and work with other Indologists and linguists. The travel account as he pointed out in the beginning was written many years later. In this account, he connects Japanese nationalism with Buddhism when he discusses Prince Shotoku, who as regent guided the minor Empress in the period 593–622. Bagchi writes that Japan then was going through a turmoil and disunity which Shotoku believed, could be changed by creation of a common ideal which would inspire the Japanese and unite them. Buddhism he realised could go a long way to make this idea a reality. There had been an effort to popularise Buddhism in Japan even before this period. In 522, A Chinese Buddhist monk Shiba Tachito, came to Japan via Korea and established a monastery in Yamato Province. But the worship of the Sakya Buddha did not really take off then since the Japanese were suspicious of a foreign religion. Twenty-five years later in 545–552, a Korean feudatory of Kudara on receiving help from the Japanese King sent Buddhist idols and scriptures in gratitude in the hope of cementing stronger ties. When this ploy did not work, he again sent as tribute – around 200 Buddhist images along with architects and masons to set up Buddhist temples. To help the process of establishing Buddhism, two Indian monks were sent from Korea. A Buddhist temple was established in Nani-wa or Osaka due to the enthusiasm of some of the Japanese officials returning from Korea. This was followed by the emergence of Shotoku in Japanese politics. As soon as he came to power, he declared Buddhism as the national religion of Japan and on the seashore the Shi-tenno-ji was constructed along with a school for the monks. Old age homes, health centres and medicine production centres were opened. Since the ships from Korea and China first landed in Osaka, arrangements were made for the residence of the foreign travellers. The temple priests made sure that the hospitality was flawless and that tradition continues in Japan to this day. In the reconstruction of the administration, Shotoku brought in a religious tint and the spiritual development of the citizens was initiated through Buddhism. Since there was no religion which could match Buddhism in its tolerance, Shotoku realised that adopting that religion would help the nation develop strong ties to the monarchy. The process, which took a long time, did witness periodic distortions in the religious development in Japan and reforms became necessary. It was at this juncture that in the end of the 8th century two path-breaking leaders emerged – Dengyo and Ko-bo. They provided the means by which Japan was able to emerge spiritually and nationally strong and powerful.[29]

One article shows an interesting angle of interest of the Indians in understanding variations in Buddhist practices. One Bengali journalist visiting China wanted to witness the consecration of Buddhist monks at a monastery which specialised in monks who had specific marks on their heads. The writer Himangshu Gupta accompanied by a friend who could understand Chinese went to a monastery during a festival in the early hours of the day.[30] After banging on the huge wooden door of the monastery for some time, it was opened by a tall dark clothed figure. The two friends were terrified by the man's appearance as well as his voice and stood petrified unable to speak. Then gathering courage the friend said that they, an Indian from the land of Buddha and a Sri Lankan Buddhist had come to watch the consecration ceremony of the Buddhist monks. Hearing this the ghostly figures ushered the two friends into the hall where there was a large golden image of Sakyamuni at the centre with many smaller images of the Buddhist disciples and Bodhisattvas in the sides. There were three monks who were chanting the scriptures with intermittent striking of the wooden gongs. It was the initiation ceremony of 70 novice monks. In front of the Buddha image, there were small bowls with candles and pieces of charcoal. As the novices came and sat on the mat with their arms on the bench in front the senior monks dipped the charcoal sticks in ink and made twelve marks on their shaven heads. Once that was done for all the seventy novices, their heads were held in a firm grip while another monk held a lit candle in his hand. The chanting of the mantra became louder and louder and then on each novices' head the charcoal was held at the marked spot with the lit candle. The heat made the permanent charcoal marks on the head and then a cold compress was put on the burnt head. Throughout the whole process the novices maintained as silent and still as a corpse. Gupta who was awed and horrified by the ceremony, felt the pain of the novices though they neither moved their lips not distorted their faces. Once their heads were marked, the novices raised their hands and moved away to a nearby garden where they were given oranges to eat since they help in healing. They were now monks and their heads were marked for life. As Gupta writes at the end of the ceremony, 'as the sun rose at the break of dawn, I could detect expressions of pain in some of their faces and all around there was the smell of burning flesh.[31]

Claiming Buddha for India/Asia: a means of recovery from humiliation of a collective national amnesia

One article in 1874 in *Aryadarshan* has claimed for Asia the pride of being the progenitor of four main religions of the world – Hindu, Buddhist, Muslim and Christian – after which they have spread to other parts of the world. 'Majority of the people of Asia are Buddhists', he claims, 'and at one time it held sway in India as well till the untiring efforts of Shankaracharya led to its exodus from India and establishment in other Asian countries'. The anonymous writer of this article speaks of Buddhism as being a part of Hinduism on the whole, though he highlights some of the differences.[32] A large body of literature existing in Bengali discussing various aspects of the Buddha often tries to find links with Hinduism, probably in an effort to establish a claim on the religion which had no followers in India of the 19th–20th century. Articles also expressed national pride when they discussed Indians, specifically Bengalis who spread the word of Buddha and helped with establishment and preservation of the religion in other countries. For the writers, this reiteration seemed to redress some of the humiliation that Indians were faced with when the westerners underlined, through their discovery of Buddhist connections, a disdain at the collective loss of memory by the Indians. An article published in *Manashi o Marmabani* was re-published in *Prabashi* the same year, indicating its importance for contemporary Bengali. It was titled *Role of the Bengali in the Spread of Buddhism* where the author, Biman Behari Majumdar, a history scholar, lists how 'in the period from 6th century to 16th century, Bengalis helped in the spread of Buddhism in China, Tibet, Nepal, Sri Lanka etc, directly or indirectly.[33]

Another article by Haraprasad Sastri in *Sahitya Parishad Patrika* on the 'Buddhist community of Bengal' was re-published in *Prabashi* in 1929 which described how Buddhism was 'swallowed by the Hindu religion . . . when bottled under 700 year Muslim hegemony . . . so Hindus and Muslims too might merge together if bottled under 700 year British colonial rule'.[34] Many years later, pride was visible in the writing of Nirmal Chandra Sinha who wrote how honoured he was when during his visit to Tibet in the 1950s he was asked by a Lama where he was from. On the reply that he was from Kata (the Tibetan for Calcutta), he was surprised by the excitement of the enquiring Lama that he had met a man from the land of Jo-Atisa as Dipankara Srijnana Atisa was referred to in Tibet, where he had come 'to preach the correct doctrine nine hundred years ago and his preaching spread from Tibet into Mongolia'.[35]

Writing for a children's magazine, Nripendra Chandra Bandopadhyay plays his part in the reclamation of Buddha for India. When he writes about Burma, he points out:

> in their features the Burmese look like Chinese and Japanese but in their culture they are akin to Indians. Even the Burmese pagodas owe their artistic origins to India. The Ananda pagoda situated in north Burma is proof of the Indian connection and so are many small pagodas and their ruins lying scattered at different parts of the country. It is true that the Shwe Dagon pagoda of Rangoon does not look like the Indian temples, and it and others like it were influenced by the Sri Lankan pagodas. However, that style too was influenced by India. King Ashoka's son Mahendra spread Buddhism there and from there Buddhism came to Burma...

Highlighting other similarities with India, Bandopadhyay says that just like in our country there are schools (tols) where religious instruction was given, every pagoda in Burma has a children's educational centre. All Burmese children have to have a basic grounding in religion and they all learn to write as well. That is why unlike the millions of illiterate people in India, in Burma everyone can read and write. For some years of their lives the Burmese spend in Brahmacharya till they have a ceremony like the Indian upanayana when they dress like monks and perform rites like begging for food – a common and touching sight on the streets of Burma. Bringing the famous Burmese virtues of hospitality and self grooming habits to the knowledge of the youthful readers of *Ramdhanu,* Bandopadhyay writes that the Burmese are never too busy to spend time between their work to talk to friends and strangers alike or to go to a pagoda to pray to the Buddha for relief from sin and worldly suffering. The Burmese women, beautiful in their bejewelled hair, ears and feet, exquisite in the *tanakha* or sandal powdered faces, gorgeous in their outfits, roam around the city from their home to markets on equal terms with their men but are devoted in the worship of the Buddha.[36]

Sarala Debi Choudhurani, travelling in Burma many years later, ends her travelogue with a *prashasti* or praise verse dedicated to the Lord Buddha where she laments that beauty has vanished from India with the decline of Buddhism and the Hindu temples are no match for the Buddhist pagodas in beauty, nor are the Hindu priests any match for the Buddhist monks in piety and simplicity. The universal values that were so strong in India in the past are now lost there and have to be recognised and retrieved from other countries.[37] This plea by one of India's most discerning and conscious women may be considered to be the essence of India's mission to travel beyond India to discover her real soul. Karuna Mukhopadhyay, writing for the children's magazine *Ramdhanu*, discusses the commonality between countries which pray to Buddha. Though there are no similarities in the food, language, way of life, clothes, social customs, or even in outward appearances between Indians and Burmese, Mukhopadhyay exults when she finds in the Burmese dedication to the Buddha, a link connecting two dissimilar peoples in a family-like bond.

This claim could be established even in appreciation of another country's art and culture. Manindra Bhusan Gupta highlights the Buddhist influence in Chinese art to legitimise his appreciation to his readers and in a sense to make it comprehensible to a lay audience, untrained in Chinese art. To show the popularity of a painter Ku-Kai Chih, Gupta uses a popular story.

> Once the painter Chih was approached for donation to build a Buddhist monastery but his promise to donate one lakh coins was scoffed at by the Buddhist monks as impossible. The angry painter requested for one month's time and locked himself up in his room. When he emerged from it after a month, it was found that he had covered the walls with a brilliant painting of the Buddhist saint Bimalakirti. Soon the news spread and thousands of pilgrims visited his home to pay homage to his creation and their donations helped Chih to fulfil his promise to the monastery.[38]

Gupta says that Chinese painting greatly developed during the Tang dynasty (though he gives wrong dates for the period 618–709 instead of 618–907) when according to him the influence of Buddhism nurtured their imagination and ennobled their literature and painting. In the capital of the Tang dynasty, Luoyang there lived three hundred Buddhist monks and many domiciled Indians who were responsible for the spread of ideas of Indian civilization. Wu Tao Tzu in this period became famous for his portraits of gods and saints through a few strokes of his brush. His most famous painting was the Mahaparinirvana of the Buddha. It is unfortunate that his paintings no longer exist and copies by later painters have been used to piece together his creative genius. The London museum has a copy of this picture where the Buddha lies in salvation while all around are portraits of chaotic grief. One can sense the greatness of the painter even in the copy. He has painted on many Buddhist subjects like, *Sakyamuni, Boddhisattva, Samantabhadra* and *Manjusri.*[39] Gupta contrasts the paintings of this period with later paintings on the basic of the degree of Indian influence. Later painters like Lee Lung Mian during the Sung dynasty also worked on Buddhist subjects but their painting was 'influenced by Zen philosophy. The impact on painting was by ideas which were genuine Chinese. . . Unlike the Tang dynasty when the stress was on forcefulness, Sung painting was gentle and pleasing'.[40]

Rabindranath Tagore was not only one of the leading intellectuals of India but he can be credited with also being the inspiration behind the intellectual movement to revive and spread universalism not only through his writing but actively, 'through the metaphor of pilgrimage'.[41] From the beginning of the First World War, Tagore became worried about the ease with which a country's nationalism could turn aggressive.[42] The only way this danger could be minimised was through discovering a higher nationalism uncontaminated by political or economic greed. Only spiritual or cultural links could provide a long-lasting bond where exchanges were more important than influence. It was this philosophy of cultural and spiritual linkages that were stressed in the popularising mission through the journals. He undertook 'intellectual' and 'scholarly' pilgrimages to the various sites of Asia preceded and followed by many others. For Tagore, at least travels were not prompted 'by any desire for propaganda but fulfilment of a long-time dream to understand the life force of an ancient civilization.' He expressed his solidarity with China in 1924, when he wrote that despite all the storms the country has faced from 'revolutions, invasions, civil war for centuries', the inner strength of the huge population has remained undiminished. 'One should come to the country to pay homage to it in the same way one goes on a pilgrimage.[43]

Tagore like many intellectuals of his time and beyond was fascinated by the Buddha and Buddhism.[44] He wrote essays[45] in which he not only discussed various aspects of Buddha's teachings and philosophy but also creatively incorporated them in his poems, dramas and songs which are immensely popular today.[46] Having made a comparative study of the various religions prevailing in Asia, Tagore came to the conclusion that the 'popular concept in Asia of *Guruship* i.e. raising a man to the level of a God . . . and the practice of repeated chanting of His name for salvation, started from Buddhism'.[47] Tagore also pointed out that during his visits to China and Japan, he felt a connection with the people which was spiritual beyond the physical differences. He regretted that this connection with truth which still flourished in those countries of East Asia was no longer present in India. 'That is why', he wrote, 'these countries are the pilgrimage centres for modern Indians. The eternal identity of Indians is present there'.[48]

Buddhism as the cementing factor in Asianism

As Edwin Arnold, poet and journalist through his *Light of Asia (1879),* (reprinted in different editions many times in its original as well as in translation, read, praised and criticised by many), said in the preface that by depicting the 'life and character' and 'philosophy of that noble hero and reformer, prince Gautama of India, founder of Buddhism' and the conqueror of humanity through love, he has tried to 'appreciate the spirit of Asiatic thoughts' from an Oriental point of view and thereby bring together the east and the west.[49] For most Indians it was the common factor of Buddhism which remained the enduring link between different Asian countries despite the gradual distancing due to evolving historical and political changes. While the writings on the spread of Buddhism in different parts of Asia followed the general outlook of the writers with regard to the different countries, it undoubtedly established a way forward even when the past links were snapped. It was Buddhism that had salvaged India's pride in other Asian countries when in reality India was humiliated by colonial subservience. Promoda Kumar Biswas wrote in *Navya Bharat* in 1912 that Japan still respected India because of their Buddhist links. India is still referred to as 'Tenjiku' (Tianzhu) in Buddhist temples and even churches. It would not be an exaggeration to say that spiritually Japanese men and women consider Indians as divine beings, as descendents of the Lord Buddha. It is indeed gratifying that what Amitabha prophesied to King Suddhodhana, that he did not care for the golden throne since his throne would forever be enshrined in the hearts of men, actually came true. His fellow countrymen Indians are respected by even educated Japanese. Biswas mentions meeting a judge of a district court of Sapporo who told him that from his childhood he had heard his father say, 'Lord Buddha came down from Tenjiku and I used to stare into the sky wondering where that was'. When he grew older and learnt that heavenly Tenjiku was in reality India under British rule he was shocked. He gave his pledge that since it was from that country that their religious leader had given the message of equality so in the time of India's distress the Japanese people would stand by them. .[50]

Kenneth Saunders in *A Pageant of India* treats Indian history as a part of a continuous history of Asia where there is smooth and seamless interweaving of events and facts, from the past as well as the present, from the different Asian countries, especially when he describes Buddha and Buddhism. As he says, the coming of the Buddha was an epoch of the greatest importance to India and to the rest of Asia, and should be studied as the climax of one era and the beginning of another. 'With him, India emerges into history, and becomes the teacher of the Asiatic nations.'[51] Of course, in Saunders writing there is also a constant reference to Christian traditions and establishment of familiarity with western allusions and references like when he writes that 'In (such) insistence on the human values Sakyamuni reminds us of Jesus, and in a certain homely humour and irony, of Socratus. All are practical physicians of the soul – laymen daring to do the work of professional heretics'. Or when he says, 'Buddhism is to Brahmanism what Franciscanism is to medieval Christianity – a simplification and a chastening, a deepening and a humanising. For each embodies in a radiant personality the essence and the true spirit of the old Faith'.[52] Saunders describes the spread of the ideals of Buddhism in different parts of Asia as being 'more stoical and less sure of technique of meditation, yet inspiring kings and scholars to make great efforts' in the south in Ceylon, Burma and Siam. whereas in the north it became 'more emotional and gradually more theistic as the founder became a god, the monk a priest, and the memorial mound a temple.'[53] Despite its long and complex evolution leading to incorporation at times of 'crude superstitions and popular moral practices of the converted', according to Saunders, Buddhism wherever it has been 'true to itself' it has been a 'mighty power for good'.[54]

The argument of the intellectuals of this period was that the cultural pre-eminence that India had established in the other Asian countries in the past through religious, political and culture explorations could be replicated even in the present when the political element would be disregarded and cultural give and take would reinforce connectivity. Thus, on this harmonious ground, a strong network of the countries of Asia would be created, connected by cultural ties and a common historical past. This was a movement in which the cultural leaders of the time would take lead and a mass base would be created by uniting the common people of all the countries of Asia. This united front would be formidable and yet would be free from chauvinism that plagued nationalism. Recently, historian Tansen Sen speaks of Buddhist interactions in the past as creating a 'cosmopolitan world across Asia, where diverse people and objects intermingled'.[55] The ideological movement through the journals, to look beyond boundaries for friendship, was both political and spiritual, nationalistic and universal. Buddhism was one of its tropes which would easily be acceptable in both India and the other countries of Asia as a bonding factor. Today this thought movement could be replicated using similar yet relevant cultural tropes which would unify populations by appealing to universal interests like music, cinema, theatre, art, transnational literature, and even non-confrontational universal socio-religious meetings, fairs and most important of all facilitating movements of population for such events.

In one instance at least, in the past, insularity was overcome and a united effort was made trans-nationally to facilitate preservation of a valuable heritage site. That was the Bodh Gaya case where through the effort of first the Burmese king and then the Maha Bodhi Society set up by Anagarika Dharmapala led to the preservation of the site where Gautama Buddha achieved Nirvana and now it is the place where people from every country come not only for religious pilgrimage but also as a part of heritage tourism. Anagarika Dharmapala's contribution to the establishment of the Mahabodhi Societies in India for the spread of Buddhism makes a fascinating study. That Bengalis venerated Buddhist philosophy intellectually, whether or not they followed its rituals, is amply testified by the very large number of books on the subject and in the cultural impact of Buddhist ideas on Bengali literature and drama. In the public theatre of Calcutta, 'Buddhadev Charita' of Girish Chandra Ghosh ran for many nights at Star, Classic and Unique theatres between 1901 and 1909,[56] and 'Siddhartha' of Amritalal Mitra was popular though to a lesser degree. This realisation that dissemination of shared Asian heritage within all sections of the society brings one back to the eternal question about human knowledge that Xuanzang profoundly asked his teachers in Nalanda many centuries back. This question – 'who would wish to enjoy it alone?', in the words of Amartya Sen, points to a 'foundational issue the relevance of which reaches far beyond Buddhist enlightenment'[57] and may become the main plank on which Asian connectivity could be built up.

Notes

1 Rene Grousset, *In the Footsteps of the Buddha*, translated by Mariette Leon, London: G. Routledge and Sons, 1932, p. ix.
2 Among others, Rabindra Kumar Basu, Gautama Buddha, *Bangalakshmi*, 6(11), 1931, pp. 850–874; Fa Hien er Tirthjatra, *Bharati*, 6(12), 1882, pp. 561–565, 7(2), pp. 65–70, 7(3), p. 112.
3 One example is Bireshwar Goswami, Kushinagar, *Sahitya*, 9(4), 1898, pp. 227–232.
4 Among others, Bimalacharan Laha, Boudhhyajuger Bhugol, *Bharatvarsha*, 20(1)(6), 1932, pp. 955–963.
5 Among others Swami Surananda, Bouddha Dharmamot Utpatti o parinoti, *Bharatvarsha*, 22(1)(6), 1934, pp. 938–939.
6 Bireshwar Goswami, Kushinagar, op. cit., p. 229.
7 Harisadhan Mukhopadhyay, Mathuray Bauddhyadhikar, op. cit., pp. 122–123.
8 Kailash Chandra Sinha, Hiuen Tsang er Bangala Bhraman, *Bharati*, 4(2), 4(3), 4(4), 1880, pp. 67–75, 116–125, 164–171.
9 Romesh Chandra Majumdar, Chindeshiyo Bouddhya Paribrajak, *Prabashi*, 24(1)(6), 1924, pp. 792–795.
10 Satyendranath Tagore, *Bauddha Dharma*, Calcutta: Maha Bodhi book Agency, 1901(2010), pp. 146–151.
11 Rabindranath Tagore, 'Bauddha Dharme Bhaktibad', Reprinted in Rabindranath Tagore, *Buddhadev*, op. cit., pp. 31–50.
12 Narendra Dev, Shyambhumi (Thailand), *Bharatvarsha*, 12(1)(6), 1924, p. 905 (pp.901-10).
13 A debate on this ensued in Committee on Hindu Sea Voyage question and has been collected and published as *The Hindu Sea Voyage Movement in Bengal*, Calcutta: Banerjee Press, 1894.
14 Mrinalini Raha, Bharmadesher Kotha, *Antahpur*, 5(8), 1902, pp. 161–164, 163.
15 Mrinalini Raha, Bharmadesher Kotha, *Antahpur*, 5(8), 1902, pp. 161–164, 163, 164.

16 Anonymous, Amader Bhraman Brittanto: Burmadesh, *Mahila*, 12(10), 1907, 1314 B.Y., p. 259.
17 Sarala Debi, Shwe Dagon, *Bharatvarsha*, 19(1)(2), 1931, pp. 262–268.
18 Kumar Munindra Deb Ray, Singhal Dvip, *Bharatvarsha*, 15(2)(5), 1927, 15(2) (6), 1927, pp. 683–732, 891–924.
19 Gyanendramohon Das, Singhal e Bangali Kaladhyapak Srijukta Manindrabhushan Gupta, *Prabashi*, 26(1)(5), 1926, pp. 767–769.
20 Manindrabhushan Gupta, Singhaler Chitra, *Prabashi*, 34(1)(1), 1934, pp. 28–35.
21 Ibid., p. 30.
22 Ibid., p. 31.
23 Ibid., pp. 33–34.
24 Benoy Kumar Sarkar, Swadhin Ashiar Rajdhani, *Grihastha*, 7(7)(3), 1915, p. 222.
25 Benoy Kumar Sarkar, Swadhin Ashiar Rajdhani, *Grihastha*, 7(7)(4), 1915, p. 338.
26 Ibid., pp. 346–347.
27 Ibid., pp. 348–350.
28 Prabodh Chandra Bagchi, Koya-San er Jatri, *Prabashi*, 27(1)(6), 1931, pp. 840–841.
29 Ibid., pp. 844–847.
30 Himangshu Gupta, Chitrita Sanyasi: Chatushpathi, *Bangasri*, 4(1)(3), 1925, pp. 327–329.
31 Ibid., p. 329.
32 Anonymous. Buddhadev o Tadubhabita Dharma Pranali, *Aryadarshan*, 1(4), 1874, pp. 127–134.
33 Biman Behari Majumdar, Bauddhya dharma Prachare Bangali, reprinted in Kashtipathar, *Prabashi*, 28(1)(3), 1924, pp. 352–355.
34 Haraprasad Sastri, Banglar Bouddhya Samaj, reprinted in Kashti Pathar, *Prabashi*, 29(2) (5), 1929, pp. 679–684.
35 Nirmal Chandra Sinha, *How Chinese Was China's Tibet Region?*, Calcutta: Firma KLM, 1981, p. 19.
36 Nripendra Chandra Bandopadhyay, Burmar kotha, *Ramdhanu*, 1(2), 1927, pp. 90–94.
37 Sarala Debi, Shwe Dagon, *Bharatvarsha*, 20(1)(2), 1932, p. 268.
38 Manindra Bhushan Gupta, Chine Chitrakalar Itihas *Prabashi*, 24(2)(1), 1924, p. 84.
39 Ibid., pp. 85–86.
40 Ibid., p. 87.
41 Sugata Bose, *A Hundred Horizons: The Indian Ocean in the Age of Global Empire*, Delhi: Permanent Black, 2006, pp. 233–271.
42 Rabindranath Tagore, *Nationalism* (1917), Calcutta: Rupa and Company, 1992.
43 Rabindranath Tagore, Chin o Japaner Bhraman Bibaran, *Prabashi*, 24(2) (1), 1924, pp. 89–90.
44 One charming book for children attempts to address an age-old question about the appearance of the Buddha. See Chitra Deb, *Buddhadeb kemon Dekhte chhilen*, Calcutta: Ananda Publishers, 2014.
45 Rabindranath Tagore, *Buddhadev*, Calcutta: Visva Bharati Publishing, 1956 (2012 reprint).
46 Rabindranath Tagore, Poems like *Borobudur, Siam, Sheshtha Bhikkha, Pujarini, Abhisar, Parishodh, Samanya Kshati, Mulyaprapti, Nagarlakshmi, Mastakbikroy, Buddhabhakti,* and plays like *Natir Puja, Chandalika, in Rabindranath Buddhadev O Bouddhasamskriti (Rabindranath, Lord Buddha and Buddhist culture)*, Calcutta: Visva Bharati Publishing, 2003 (2012 reprint).
47 Rabindranath Tagore, Bouddhyadharme Bhaktibad, *Rabindranath Buddhadev o Bouddhasamskriti*, op. cit., pp. 30–31.
48 Rabindranath Tagore, Buddhadev Prasanga, *Rabindranath Buddhadev O Bouddhasamskriti*, op. cit., p. 46.
49 Edwin Arnold, *Light of Asia: Poetical Works of Edwin Arnold*, New York: John W. Lovell Co., 1882, Preface, pp. v–viii.
50 Promoda Kumar Biswas, Japan O Bharater Sambandha, *Nabya Bharat*, 30(6), 1912, pp. 354–355.
51 Kenneth Saunders, *A Pageant of India*, London: Oxford University Press, 1939. Originally Part I of a three part book: A Pageant of Asia: A Study of Three Civilizations, India, China, and Japan (1935).

52 Ibid., p. 40.
53 Ibid., p. 41.
54 Ibid., p. 38.
55 Tansen Sen, *India, China and the World: A Connected History*, Delhi: Oxford University Press, 2018, p. 472.
56 Sankar Bhattacharya, *Bangla Rangalayer Itihasher Upadan (1901–1909)*, Calcutta: West Bengal Natya Academy, 1994, pp. 8–107; 272–274; 373–375.
57 Amartya Sen, *The Argumentative Indian: Writings on Indian History, Culture and Identity*, London: Penguin Books, 2005, pp. 189–190.

7 Nationalist discourse and locating the nation in the world

Most of the articles on Asia, for easy readability, dealt with cultural connections but the writers were quite aware of politics and political history of the countries they were discussing. They never lose sight of their own nationalist context when they are discussing the evolving political situation elsewhere. Sometimes, the affiliations or their sensibilities colour their writing, but most of the time they appear neutral. It is in this apparent conflict that one can locate a thread of sane cosmopolitan weft in the warp of poetic madness of nationalism. The description of Benoy Kumar Sarkar, a traveller and a prolific writer who also contributed articles on Japan in the periodicals, by historian Sumit Sarkar, as 'cosmopolitan, modernist right-wing nationalist whose nationalism incorporated multiple layers: Bengali, Indian and anti-British, cohabiting with western nationalisms and the world',[1] may also describe many other writers of the time.

Control of knowledge empowers and the intended or unintended mission of pen wielding anti-colonialists was to utilise the safety of the vernacular to dissipate this control. Almost as soon as any news was published in the western news agencies, it was translated or transcribed for the local public. Even more effective was the news conveyed by those who were delivering it first-hand. Taking a long-term time profile which included many epochal moments and events occurring in different countries as well as using the views of many different people brings in a variety of expressions yet clarity in the way certain similarities of purpose and motive can be traced. In this chapter, I am dealing only with comments and commentaries on politics and history. These writers are assessing political situations in India and other Asian countries in the colonial context and constantly assessing the feasibilities of linking the colonised countries of the East as a means to empower.

The occupation of Burma by the British in stages through 1826–1886 undoubtedly aroused sympathy in Bengali hearts given their close connections. *Bharati* under the capable editorship of Swarnakumari Devi carried a series of news items and features discussing the changed circumstances after the third Anglo-Burmese war and the occupation of Mandalay, Burma, in 1885 and the creation of the province of Burma next year. Allusions were made to 'might is right' and pointed out that 'if a powerful country preys upon a weak neighbour, then there will be no end to their troubles. The attack of Burma for no real reason by the English reminds us of the story of the tiger who preyed upon the lambs for the trivial reason of dirtying the pond.' Using the pretext of exploitation of the Bombay Trading Company in Burma, the English had attacked and occupied Burma. The report derided this show of force by a so called civilized nation and claimed that the support of the home press like *London Times*,

DOI: 10.4324/9781003243786-7

gave Dufferin the confidence that he could take action with the support of his home country. The refusal of the Trading Company to pay their 23,000/- due to the Burmese King was used by British government as pretext for war but no one was in doubt that the real reason for the war was the economic recession that Britain was facing.[2]

Another editorial in *Bharati,* the same year also conveyed to the readers that though the Burmese King Thibaw was portrayed by the English media as exploitative and bloodthirsty, he was actually a cipher only. It was his minister who was responsible for the killing of the royal family. The king also had no clue about the war and his treacherous minister had told him that the English wanted a treaty with him. The editorial also denied the rumour being circulated in England, that the Burmese wanted the British to annex their country to India. A Burmese political statesman had written in the *Indian Mirror* that the rumour spread by the selfish Englishmen had no basis at all and *The Bombay Gazette* said that maintaining the acquired territories in Burma would prove to be more of a loss than a gain and added tongue in cheek that after all 'it was Indian milch cow who will bear the burden.'[3]

Haricharan Mukhopadhyay discusses these very issues in his article Brahme Engraj[4] (The English in Burma) in *Bharati* in the same year in greater detail. He gives details of the first two Burmese wars and holds Lord Dalhousie's plan of annexing the independent native Indian states as the main motive behind the second war. According to Mukhopadhyay, though the English gained entry into the Burmese commercial scene, despite the presence of an English Resident, it became clear that 'without the permission of the King and his officials, trade (in rice, salt and *shegun/teak* timber) could not be possible since the Burmese King did not care about free trade'.[5] He also wrote about the machinations of the queen Hsinbyumash, one of the consorts of King Mindon Min, in getting Thibaw accepted as the King following the death of King Mindon. All the sons by various consorts of the king were invited to the palace for the choice of a successor, and knowing about the love Thibaw had for her daughter Selinasupaya, she imprisoned the heir apparent Niyonyan (Myingundaing) whom her daughter secretly loved but he escaped to Barrackpore under the protection of the British government. The princess Selinasupaya, having rejected the attentions of Thibaw, became a 'tabind' princess (one who stays unmarried as long as the King is alive) and retired to the monastery (some say that she was killed by Thibaw since she refused his attentions), and Thibaw married her younger sister Supayalat to secure his claims to the throne. Contrary to opinions circulated in the English newspapers, Mukhopadhyay summarily held the Queen mother and Supayalat responsible for the fratricide within the royal family. Thibaw had declared that he had no intention of ascending the throne with the blood of the princes on his hands and he was scared that the news of the terrible massacre might reach the English neighbours and sully his good name. However, his mother and wife were not to be dissuaded and undertook the killings themselves. The prisons were flooded with royal blood and the curses of the princes rang out before they were executed by their jailors. To keep Thibaw distracted loud music was played in the palace. Unfortunately for Thibaw, posterity held him responsible for the heinous crimes and soon he became a puppet in the hands of the powerful women in his family.[6]

The other article by Mukhopadhyay was on the administrative changes that took place in Burma in the post third Anglo Burmese war period. While discussing this, he speaks about the past administrative and judicial system which had been instituted by 'a minister of the King called Manu who was originally a cowherd but by sheer merit became minister'. Mukhopadhyay adds in a postscript that the Burmese books on which he based his essay do not mention whether this Manu was the same as the Indian Manu. He adds that 'the rules of this Manu, like our Manu, guided every aspect of Burmese life. It is not impossible that the Laws of our Manu were translated and popularised in Burma'.[7] This doubt that Mukhopadhyay raised was not there in the writing of N.R. Chakravarti, historian of the Indian diaspora in Burma (*Indian Minority in Burma,* 1971),[8] when he underlined the common concepts of Indian civilisation found in Burma and pointed out the acceptance of traditional Hindu Code of Manu as the prime source of law. In 1886, *Bharati* also discussed the great dilemma before Burma since 'the people of Burma have not been able to accept defeat as easily as their King has'. The author speaks for other Indians that the British government will not be able to silence critics of the Burmese annexation by just announcing that it was for the maintenance of peace. 'Despite all this cry of "dacoit", the British will not be able to declare peace in Burma. But it is worth pondering whether any dacoit, ever in history has had to fight against 15 thousand well equipped soldiers'.[9]

The history of East Asia excited the attention of most people of the world from the middle of the 19th century. The internal history of China and Japan and the connections with British India, especially in connection with the opium trade and wars, conflict between China and Japan over Korea and later Manchuria, and the impact on Asian solidarity are some of the points which are discussed by the writers in the periodicals. Opium addiction in China had a deep impact on the world which, aware of its medicinal qualities, saw in shock what its addictive qualities entailed. *Bharati*'s 1881 article 'Death Trade in China' started the trend of referring to opium addiction as an aspect of colonial exploitation.[10] Ramlal Sarkar who stayed in Burma and China for many years provides a detailed picture of the types of opium that are used as medicinal drugs as well as recreational and the means to make and consume the different varieties. He also gives examples of how bright and talented people he knew in Burma and China met their end in the grip of this narcotic. He linked the opium wars in China to the British imperial policy of ruthlessly removing the local royal resistance to their commercial gain, following up their successful tactics in Asia and Africa. 'Unfortunately', he wrote, 'China in the twentieth century hardly needed foreign coercion to further their opium addiction'.[11]

There is an awareness that China needs to realise her potential strength and build on it to survive. An anonymous writer in *Bharati* in 1880 in discussing the revolutionary power of China writes about two incidents where the Chinese used their 'traditional practices and strategies for success'. 'It is true', the author says, 'that it is difficult to get information about our old neighbour, but luckily two recent books on the subject and newspaper reports have shed light'. Here the reference is to 'Revival of the Warlike Power of China' by Captain Bridge R.N. in the *Fraser's Magazine* (June 1879) and *Central Asia* by C.E. Boulger (London 1879)The author writes that Captain Bridge has tried to explode the general myth that the Chinese were totally against any development and Boulger too has shown that the Chinese have recently reoccupied from the Russians almost the entire eastern Turkestan, which proves that even in the naturally weak portions of their empire, they are trying to rebuild their national strength On the other hand, according to the author, the involvement of the Chinese in the trade with Turkestan has led to loud protestations by the English merchants. But this is only a new manifestation of an old ailment. Ever since the British have found themselves surrounded by Nepal, Bhutan and Tibet which are tributary and allied states of China in the north and Burma in the east, the British have been troubled by Chinese antagonism. They also could not accept the call for ban of opium import demanded by the Chinese emperor since it would hamper East India Company's trade. In the meantime, China was defeated in the Opium war but despite British efforts to establish a European standard ship building factory in Turkestan there has been no softening of attitude on the part of the Chinese. They have bought a number of steamships for war purposes as well as small warships to carry cannons. Different from European iron made ships, these Chinese ships were faster and more durable since they were made of steel. Another difference is that the weapons on these ships are never visible from far so that no incoming ship can destroy them. The author concludes that 'China is not suffering from any geriatric problems, and it remains to be seen how the three great giants of Asia will be able to forge the destinies of their countries'[12] Obviously, this optimism would be proved false when within 15 years the Chinese power of arms on land and on sea would be found to be no match for the Japanese during the war over Korea in 1895, leading to the humiliating treaty of Shimonoseki.

In 1905, an article by Ramlal Sarkar on China's use of indigenous goods connected the Swadeshi movement taking place in Bengal, against the British decision to partition Bengal, with Chinese nationalism. Sarkar writes that there were three reasons why *swadeshi* goods in China were considered to be the only option for the Chinese. Firstly, the Chinese were an independent nation and the government being very conservative was suspicious of foreign goods. Secondly, the Chinese as a race are very proud and had a strong hatred for the uncivilised foreigners. Thirdly, there was Chinese patriotism and feeling of brotherhood for all Chinese people.[13] He then discusses in practical terms which objects in China would in the future be able to retain its '*swadeshi*' elements and which would embrace the foreign-made ones. Writing materials and clothes would possibly remain Chinese-made and there were handlooms in most Chinese homes with women and children engaged in making silk and cotton threads. Sarkar feels ashamed when he compares the rich clothes that Chinese manufacture and wear compared to the average Indian who wears two lengths of cloth only as *dhoti* and *chadar*. The other indigenous products of China are the famous Chinese crockery, leather goods, three types of blankets – red one which is decorative and used like a carpet and blue and white blankets that are worn as protective covering during rains – indigo colour, salt, opium, preserved fruits and paper of three qualities – thick made of papier-mâché used for wrapping, medium and fine one made from tree bark.[14]

In 1894, two empresses of Japan were compared in an article in *Bamabodhini Patrika* as ideal models for Japanese women of the time: one was Empress Jingu who became Regent after her husband's death around AD 200 and another was Empress Haruko of Japan in the 1890s.Jingu was not only beautiful, talented, and deeply religious, she was also an expert in the art of warfare – in fact she is often referred to as the Goddess of war. When she became empress, Japanese were not aware of the existence of China or Korea. One day the queen called on the Mikado and confided to him that a god had sent word to her that there was a kingdom far west of Japan, where the Japanese soldiers could go on board a war ship and they would be successful in bringing back immense loot. The disbelieving King laughed at her saying that both she and her gods were liars. Soon afterwards the rebels in his land imprisoned and killed the King and the Empress took over administration of the land having suppressed the rebels. During her travels she reached Korea and forced the Korean king to surrender to the might of her army[15]

Interestingly, the article was written when China and Japan were locked in a conflict over possession of Korea. China claimed to have a long association with Korea and a treaty between the two super powers had resulted in the sending of China's Yuan Shi Kai as Commissioner to the Korean court, but a local rebellion forced Korea to appeal to both China and Japan for help. Japan sent a larger contingent and this prompted a war between her and Qing China. The author of *Bamabodhini Patrika* continues that Empress Haruko had qualities similar to Jingu Kongo. She is the ideal of the present modern Japanese womanhood. She is inspiring the Japanese to annex Korea and has herself written inspirational martial songs. 'Her aim is to make the Japanese as modern as Europeans and Americans and create a strong nation like Jingu Kongo did in the past.'[16]

In the 1880s, there is a series in *Bharati* which ascribes the 'Foundation of modern development in Japan' to their response to the western incursions from mid-19th century and worry of the Shogun at the 'repeated arrival of the foreign powers'. Even on this occasion, according to the writer, the situation could be gauged correctly by the Japanese Shogun only when a comparison was made with the Chinese situation by the Dutch Factor of Nagasaki who wrote a letter to the Shogun asking him to refrain from political manoeuvres with the European merchants without assessing one's own strength correctly. 'That is why China has lost part of her territory and Canton has been converted into a desert'.[17] In the sequel, Japan's development in different spheres – economic, military, technology, education and language and literature – has been discussed with comparisons with China.[18]

From the mid-19th century, Japan had been attracting interest among the western scholars and travellers regarding the transformation that started in that country and these writings were arriving in India and from being simply an Asian country, Japan emerged as a world power. Different strands of thought prevailing in Japan under the Meiji rule, i.e. de-Asianisation (Datsu – A Ron) of Fukuzawa Yukichi (1885), and the Fenollosa and Hearn-influenced Kakuzo Okakura's *Ideals of the East* (1904) with its opening phrase of 'Asia is one' made an entrance almost immediately in Bengal as well. In fact, even before Okakura visited India, Jyotirindranath Tagore translated Hearn and his different point of view for the journals. But invariably articles on Japan were followed by discussion on China as early as 1880–1881, in same or even successive issues,[19] and proves that they were in fact thought about as belonging to the same larger entity Asia which also included India.

But these ambivalences were removed when Japan began to be celebrated as a super-ordinate power. *Bharati* published a critical translation of Cashel Hoyei's review of a French book *Japan and the Japanese* by Aime Humbert. The author starts with the declaration that the recent unimaginable outcome of the Sino-Japanese war has heralded an epochal change in the history of independent nations in Asia. Many had considered the war between a mighty Chinese empire and a tiny Japan as an unequal military outrage but not anymore since in successive successes, Japan has proved her might. 'The public has now accepted that before a ferocious small lion (Japan) the swaying trunk of the gigantic elephant (China) has become bruised and tormented.' The essay follows Humbert in tracing Japan's rise to power, but at the same time the writer highlights the dilemma that the educated Indian is faced with vis-à-vis the face-off between the two Asian greats. Both the countries are integral parts of Asia and in fact, China is the closer neighbour, and one should feel sympathy for China's loss but every Japanese victory indicates 'the inevitable glory that national unity and perseverance brings while every loss of the conceited, opium addicted, conservative Chinaman of the Heaven Kingdom reflects the shame which his own deeds have created.'[20]

Like the Bharati author above who reminds Indians that 'no one can deny that there can be no hope for any static society in a fast changing world,' Tagore articulates even strongly when he writes in *Nationalism*: When 'we in Asia hypnotised ourselves into the belief that it could never by any possibility be otherwise, Japan rose from her dreams, and in giant strides left centuries of inaction behind, overtaking the present time in its foremost achievement.'[21]

Taraknath Mukhopadhyay won the first prize in the annual essay-writing competition of the Chaitanya Library for his essay 'Rise of Japan' and the long article was serially published in *Navyabharat* in 1906.[22] He recalls an apt remark made by co-passenger in a tram to Kalighat in Calcutta, in the context of the ongoing Russo-Japanese war, that 'previously no one knew anything of Japan beyond Japanese varnish and Japanese prostitutes, and look at her now!!!' What the passer-by meant, of course, was that Japan had come into the radar of intellectuals all over the world ever since she inflicted the defeat on Russia and gained in strength within the shortest time. But Mukhopadhyay argues, there are certain distinctive features that set Japan apart from others. The first advantage that Japan has over other aspiring powers is the fact of 'enduring independence' (*Chira swadhin*) and supreme confidence in maintaining her protection which had been slightly shaken in the mid nineteenth century leading her to take immediate measures to repair. Like all nations who are desirous of increasing strength Japan too concentrated on acquiring firearms from developed nations. But realising the mistake in being too dependent on foreign powers, Japan started developing herself as well by staying informed of all the latest inventions in western countries, strengthening herself through eradication of poverty and generating income, making education universal and most important of all, making all Japanese equal in the eyes of the Emperor by removing all artificial differences[23]

Mukhopadhyay believes that Japan's innovations in these three crucial spheres made her successful – social changes to prepare the citizens for political changes, initiate economic changes in agriculture to improve resources and finally improvement of trade for increase of national wealth.[24]

Jamini Kanta Sen, in his series on 'India's foreign policy' in *Navyabharat* in 1907, brings out an interesting discussion on India's future in Asia where he not only outlines a theory of foreign policy for Indians but also tries to acquaint his fellow readers with the 'realities of Asian politics'.[25] Sen believes that Indians have begun to participate in what he calls a 'social interaction with the world's political powers and intellectuals. Whether it is attending the Stuttgart Conference or the theatrical stage in University of California, Indians are now engaging in an intellectual give and take'.[26] Sen deliberately in this article tries to undermine Japanese rise to power as the source of inspiration for the Indians (in fact, he believes that this widespread adulation for Japan by the Swadeshi movement activists and Swarajists will be ultimately harmful for the development of India's self-reliance[27]). He is writing the article in the context of the Stuttgart Conference, which took place that year, as the means 'to develop self-reliance which will create self confidence that will ultimately bring fruitful interaction with foreign powers on a long-lasting and equal footing'.[28] Virendranath Chattopadhyay, along with Madame Cama and S.R. Rana, attended the Stuttgart Conference of the Second International where they met delegates, including Henry Hyndman, Karl

Liebknecht, Jean Jaurès, Rosa Luxemburg and Ramsay MacDonald, among others. Madame Cama described the devastating effects of a famine that had struck the Indian subcontinent and in her appeal for human rights, equality and for autonomy from Great Britain, she unfurled what she called the 'Flag of Indian Independence'. The other point to note is that Sen seems to be trying to talk about a foreign policy of component parts of India or even that of the people polity separate from the British government. To quote Sen, 'if one could uphold the natural light of India's talent to the world outside, then Bengal, Bihar, Punjab, Gujarat, Maharashtra and Rajputana could possibly have a moral and religious link with the outside world'.[29] In his opinion, what is most important is to understand the nuances of politics and events in the countries which had economic and political strength, moving away from rhetoric of the time and the general viewpoints that are aired in the contemporary writing. The past and present linkages of India with Japan, China, Afghanistan and Persia should be assessed. Initially when China and Japan had locked horns, India was not very attentive towards the conflict, though some had wondered if western uncivilized aggressiveness had impacted Asian ethics. Later it was speculated that the event may not have unmixed results since China may react 'to the bites by the tiny mouse to build a new future'. What China achieved in the last ten years was unthinkable before while the speed with which Japan has been gaining in strength which had initially excited the admiration of Asians was now worrying. Indians studying in Japan have been realising that Japan is not really a friend. They look at Indians with disdain, which according to the author was rather natural since one does not befriend the weak as it serves no purpose. On the contrary the English are quite querulous about the increasing power of the Japanese and the 'Thief and the Drunkard have come to an understanding'. Japan is at present desirous of establishing commercial contacts with English occupied India and 'cordial hugs are being exchanged by two clever peoples.'[30]

He compares the attempt of the Japanese to use British tactics to enter India through the means of religion, through missionary activities and conversions, followed by information gathering, betrayal, gossip and finally penetration. 'There are many Japanese Buddhist missionaries travelling all over India, China, Thailand and Russia', he writes and warns his readers that Indians need to be more aware. He tells a story to illustrate how sharp Japanese eyes are and how closely they scrutinise the Asian map, despite being so many thousand miles away. A Japanese traveller reached the capital of Chittagong hill tracts, Rangamati, on the eastern border. This region which is not too far away from the China border is inhabited by hill people and was in fact not very well controlled by either the English or the Chinese. The traveller came secretly with proper arrangements and provisions to travel into the interior of the region till the British discovered his plans and prohibited his travel. The author finds it amazing that though no Indian, not even a Bengali feels the need to know about the area but the Japanese are willing to travel many miles to gather information[31]

Sen is fearful of an economic invasion of India by Japan and China via the economic treaties with Britain. He says that it might be easier to get freedom from the British ultimately since they are in such small numbers in the country, but if a rejuvenated Japan and China enter India with a lakh of people and set up camp in the heart of India, then the complications that would arise are unimaginable. 'Therefore, it is important that we do not allow Japan to expand commercial relations with India.'[32] Sen also in this discussion brings in a popular view of intellectuals about pan-Islamism between the countries of Afghanistan, Persian and Turkey, which would severely limit the power of Europe. His conclusion was that 'the shrewd Japan' was aware of these discussions. Rumour was rife that Japan would declare Islam as state religion (as written in *The Englishman*) and conversion to Islam would provide for Japan the prefect pretext to interfere in affairs of West Asia. Although Japan is at present tied down by treaties with Europe, both Japan and Europe are aware that they are temporary and not ultimately beneficial to either. In the future, Japan would be interested in expanding within Russia and in the Philippine Islands.[33]

In 1904, Kedarnath Bandopadhyay was in Tiensin/Tianjin in the British sector when the news of the Russo-Japanese war came in and the first reaction was astonishment at the temerity of a small Japanese nation challenging the giant Russians. He testifies that the reaction of his British superiors was one of disbelief at the Japanese audacity and apprehension lest they became involved in the war as 'allies'. Bandopadhyay and his colleague Suresh, while discussing the reason why Japan embarked on the war, concluded that it was based on strength derived from propaganda. It was Japan herself who created an image of a powerful Japan through skilful use pictures of the King Kodo publishing company, twelve years before all other nations started spending millions on preparing their war propaganda machines during the Great War. It was Japan who brought this idea into Asia. Bandopadhyay, who in all his writing attests to the cheerful and industrious nature of the Japanese he meets in China, now describes in awe how the Japanese reacted to the news of their country's war effort. Instead of fear or apprehension as to how their compatriots were faring, the Japanese in China appeared energised in their mission to help the war effort in every way. The geisha entertainers stopped singing romantic songs in their performances in the British sector and only performed songs dedicated to the soldiers fighting on alien soil that they wrote and set tune to themselves.

Bandopadhyay translates one such song which he calls the 'greatest gift to the Japanese nation'.[34]

Discussing the traits of Japanese character in figuring out the mystery of how Japan managed to take the best from the west and yet retain her distinctiveness continued unabated throughout the 20th century. In an article around ten years later, Akinchan Das argues that unlike in other countries which westernised itself to the extent that they lost their distinctive character, Japanese intellectuals identified the family as the real game changer. If the eastern traditional family values could be retained instead of the individuality propounded by the westerners, then the society and the country would be the focus instead of the self. He quotes Count Okuma who said in a speech at the Tokyo Women's University that nothing is as injurious to the proper regulation of a woman's life as the notion that she should have an ideal of her own to pursue. No Japanese woman should accept the western view in this matter as the rule of your life. In the west the husband and wife form a social unit; in Japan father and son constitute the family unit; and the family is the unit of society. That is the ideal Japanese code. Das concludes not only Japanese women, but men too cannot adopt a western outlook without the consent of the King and before the duties to the King and country, self-interest pales into insignificance. Japan belongs to that group of countries where collective rights are the priority, not individual. Two forces that block western style individualism in Japan are royal power and family power and that combination is the secret of Japan's success.[35] Added to these, according to Das, were two other qualities of lack of ceremony and ostentation. Giving the example of Marquis Ito, 'who retired from the highest office in the country with power and wealth' and was able to 'without any difficulty adopt the simple life of a householder without any humiliation or shame', Das quotes Petric Watson (*The Future of Japan*) that 'A Japanese after years in Europe, sits rather uncomfortably on our padded chairs'. Das challenges the Bengali reader to give up being a Babu and return to a simple life following the Japanese policy of *shigatakanai* (what's the use?/it's no use).[36]

A writer in the early 1930s claims that one cannot only talk about a country's past and its ancient glories but must also analyse the present political developments, their economy, industrial endeavours and their aesthetic sense. A nation is known by its way of thinking, its education, military power, literature and art and crafts.[37] Panchugopal Mukhopadhyay defends the title of his article 'Young Japan (Tarun Japan)' after the famous 'Young Italy' saying that the 'similarities between the two countries are not in outward appearances but more notional, in the way in which Italy and Japan are trying to develop and become self-sufficient'. He writes that till recent times, Japan was the butt of world's ridicule and today in naval power Japan stands after one or two of the world's strongest nations. The fame of the Japanese poet Noguchi has transcended the borders of the country and the strength of Japan's textile industry has been causing anxiety to many manufacturing countries. Japan's success, in other words has become highly visible. Mukhopadhyay here refers to the Japanese victory over Russia as a turning point in Japan history and indicates that it was symbolic of Asia's pride. The popular saying that the 'East has been reborn at Port Arthur', is not an exaggeration and the day Japan routed the Russian forces in the war, 'the mist of illusion of the invincible west vanished from eyes of the entire East.' From that day Japan's rebirth started and with it, Asia was reborn as well. Today's Japan has two faces – one which aspires to increase their power through conquest of world and Asian markets which is its demonic and commercial face and the other which is soft and charming like Japanese poetry *hokku* or *haiku*. 'That face is not destructive or acquisitive, it is artistic and creative.'

He discusses both these aspects in the essay. In the context of ongoing Sino-Japanese war, when this article was written, Mukhopadhyay tries to go beyond the question of morality and the calculation of the impact of the war on China, to probe into the reasons for the loss of the promise of friendship that had been promised in the Japanese parliament on 22nd January 1931 by the Foreign minister Baron Shidehara'. Mukhopadhyay says that there is no doubt that the reason for the souring of the harmonious relationship was due to exigencies of trade and business interests. The trade treaty that existed between the two countries ultimately stood in the way of friendship and the declining relations was exacerbated by Manchuria, where a historic relationship developed in the aftermath of the Russo-Japanese war which the Chinese government did not seem to appreciate according to the Japanese.

Another context that Mukhopadhyay highlights in admiration is how Japan grappled with the world economic depression of 1930.The economic leaders of the country concentrated on preservation of wealth instead of risky ventures. Despite difficulties of their own and created by others, the Japanese government did not lose its calm even in the face of this crisis. They have concentrated on trying to retrieve the economic losses and bring back the economic stability.[38] In this article, he also talks about the mass movements in Japan in the third decade of the 20th century – the quest for identity and rights of the Japanese workers under Communist banner 'which was completely new in Japanese history. They involved intellectuals, dramatists, novelists, painters and photographers in their propaganda . . . they were completely against the existing workers organisation in Japan and were violently anti-government in their beliefs and actions'. Mukhopadhyay claims that these activists adopted novel means to attract attention and gives the example of a Yokohama Federated Labour Union leader who climbed on top of a 185-ft chimney to address the workers of the Fuji Gas Spinning Company.[39] He ends with descriptions of the Japanese theatre which was 'a vital part of Japanese life but which was beset with disruptive politics and corruption'.[40] The interest that Mukhopadhyay had in the political situation of Japan and the west is traced through what is generally considered to be outside politics. Japanese literature in his view portrayed an earthquake-like transformation from literature about supermen to the portrayal of ordinary mortals' ever since the tragedy of the earthquake of 1923.Despite the efforts of the classicists, it was this popular literature that held sway in the hearts of the Japanese population, and which flourished under two organisations the Nippon Proletarian Writers Federation and the Nippon Council of Proletarian Artists' Bodies.[41]

Mukhopadhyay concludes that it was indeed a tragedy that 'despite the Indian situation being far worse than Japan economically, no organised effort had been made to collectively address their appalling situation or collectively look for solutions'.[42] Mukhopadhyay gives examples of Japanese writers like Chogu Tokunaga and Tamiki Hoshodar to show how literature can influence politics and can be used in political propaganda. His focus in the three-part series deals with the activities and impact of the socialist and communist movement (*gana andolan*) using literary, art and student organisations and institutions as the mirror.

Japan was of course focus of a lot of writing from the beginning of 20th century, but the politics of many other countries are also discussed. The political and cultural upheaval that occurred in China from the beginning of the 20th century was reflected in the writing of the time in Bengal as well. A republic was formally established on 1st January 1912 following the Xinhai Revolution, which itself began with the Wuchang Uprising on 10th October 1911, successfully overthrowing the Qing dynasty and ending over 2000 years of imperial rule in China. In 1912, Ramlal Sarkar, in his long essay 'Revolution in China', greets the establishment of the Republic as a revolution brought about with the 'life force' of the nation.[43] In the same year in *Bharati*, Sudhangshu Kumar Chowdhury, in 'Republicanism in China' points out that it was the repeated defeat of China by a tiny Japan that made the Chinese conscious about the need to build up their strengths and undo their internal weaknesses by replacing royalty with a Republic.[44]

The anti-imperialist protests on 4 May 1919 had deep social and cultural implications not only for the youth in China but also for all anti-imperialist movements in Asia. A number of articles in the 1920s and 1930s discussed the new awakening in China and how it could be an inspiration for Indians. Prafulla Chandra Roy's 'New China and Bengal' identifies the values which helped China break through the barriers of centuries of superstitions and recover from the humiliating defeat that a westernised Japan had inflicted on her at the end of the previous century. He first mentions the virtues of social equality and religious tolerance of the Chinese. In its past history of three thousand years, the Chinese civilization has no history of untouchability or discrimination to divide the society.' Not even in highest administrative positions is there any appointment except on the on the basis of merit by those who succeed in the public competitive exams. Even an ordinary man to the position of a Mandarin if he had the capability.[45] Secondly, according to Roy, religion in China has never led to any violence or intolerance. 'Since ancient times, they know that there is no connection between outward customs of a religion and the inner spiritual beliefs. Therefore, they are very tolerant in their religious ideas more than any other country in the world.' . . .He then discusses the cultural revolution and the role of the students in the spread of education among the masses through direct interaction and lectures, setting up of night schools for adult education and translation projects of ancient Chinese texts into simple Chinese. 'This youth movement of China', according to Roy, has kept almost 400 periodicals alive, -journals which do not care about politics or religion but only discuss how the general condition of the country can be improved and how the nation's illiteracy can be removed'. He compares with regret the large number of Bengali periodicals which are only concerned about politics, but do not care about developmental programmes for the country that the Chinese periodicals excel in.[46]

The concern for the country's improvement in Roy's opinion is also helped by two other factors. Firstly, that those Chinese who go abroad for higher studies do not return and treat their compatriots as lesser beings like the Indians do and, secondly, that they do not consider any type of work as below their dignity. He concludes by saying that the Chinese youth renaissance unlike in India, was not hollow rhetoric, and their youth were not like young Indians 'submerged in individualistic pleasure and easy consumerism that the west has introduced in India.' He pleaded to his fellow countrymen to 'learn from the Chinese youth that developing one's country and improving the condition of its people is possible following the one's countries own values.'[47]

The discussions on connections between India and China in this period responded to nationalistic impulses within India (as with the studies of the Greater India Society) exemplified in discussions on Indian influences on Chinese religion and culture through Buddhist connections[48] and Indian literature in China,[49] but also expressed sympathy for China in her political problems arising out of imperialistic west and the threat of Japan. They included from very early on expressions of distress regarding opium trade, as Rabindranath Tagore's article in 1881 *Bharati* called 'The Death Trade in China' indicated:

> No one has ever heard before of such a thieving mentality by which the whole race is poisoned for the sake of financial gain . . . China cried out in distress that she wouldn't consume opium but the English merchant tied up her hands and used a cannon to stuff opium into her mouth, and then demanded payment for it. This was the splendid business conducted by the English in China, though that is only a polite way of describing a veritable dacoity which has converted a powerful race into a feeble one.[50]

There are also articles which discuss why the values which had made China powerful in the past could not stand in good stead in the face of aggression from outside. In 1889, an article in *Anjali* highlighted China's greatness in the past and blamed this preoccupation with past glories as the cause for China's gradual decline. The writer whose name was withheld said that for a long time, the world was obsessed with the past. Then, 'Europe, deafened by the monotony of the tune of past glories, turned its face against the past and favoured the present' which led to her rise, 'throwing off the deep dark roots of the past to new life, new science, new literature and religion, society and education adopted the new enlightenment.' Japan and India too followed Europe's footsteps, but only China remained aloof and engulfed in her ancient past. So much so that for a long time, 'no one knew whether China was awake or asleep, dead or alive, conscious or unconscious.' The world hoped that her glorious past would have sustained her and kept her alive but 'but no one approached close enough to check.'[51] The author connected this damning exclusivity and preoccupation with the past to China's present opium addiction that drove her 'Heavenly Middle Kingdom to Hell'.[52]

A scholar and writer, Suniti Kumar Chattopadhyay wrote retrospectively during post-colonial India's friendship attempts with China in the 1950s that 'the close relations between the two great nations, China and India went through periods of alienation and amnesiac forgetfulness but always returned to remembrance their connectivity in order to re-establish physical and mental connections'.[53]

Nationalism in India has from the beginning looked for ideal patriots and statesmen as inspirational rallying points. Mustafa Kemal Pasha, the revolutionary leader and founder of modern Turkey, was one such hero. Besides valourising his victories in the First World War, writing on the Pasha invariably focussed on his modernisation of Turkey into a secular and strong state,[54] and most focussed on the changing status of women under the Republic.[55] In the article 'Turkey's Rise to Modernity and Power under Kamal', Hemendra Prasad Ghosh went beyond that discussion and focussed on the coverage of Turkey by the western press. To contextualise for his readers, in the aftermath of the Non-cooperation-Khilafat movement in India, he starts with the following words, 'At the time when Indian Muslims were embarking on the Khilafat movement and following the freedom struggle in Egypt, a valiant hero emerged in Turkey, Mustafa Kemal Pasha, who reformed Turkish institutions and pledged to bring back its lost glories'.[56] He then brings in an analysis of how western media has demonised Turkey. He links it to the occupation of Smyrna where the fleeing Greeks had taken shelter. For two days of the occupation, there was no indiscipline in the Turk camps but after a fire raged on in the city, there was complete mayhem Smrynians, Armenians, Jews and all those who could not flee from the city, suffered terribly. Needing to blame someone everyone turned against the Turks. *The Times* correspondent wrote, 'the town was given over to fire, pillage and massacre.' It was even said that for the first two days the Turks refrained from arson, looking and murder because the winds were not in their favour. As soon as the winds changed, they let the city burn[57] Quoting figures from *The Times*, Ghosh showed how the western media provided detailed numbers of the Greeks who fled from Athens on American ships, and Reuter is said to have passed the dictum that 'The Turk is unfit to govern anyone but himself'. Ghosh concluded triumphantly that 'it was ultimately proved that the arson in Smyrna was not the work of the Pasha's soldiers but the fleeing Greeks themselves' and that the English who were on the back foot 'after the world condemnation of the Jallianwala Bagh massacre in India' used her media to make the Turks a scapegoat for all their ailments.[58] Ghosh in his three-part article was not only anxious that the British attempt to vilify the Turks be exposed to his countrymen, but also wanted to point out the significance of the achievement of Kemal Ataturk in creation of a modern Turkey, for Indians, in fact for all Asians. As he wrote, 'If Turkey could overcome all her disadvantages and emerge as a modern nation, Asia would have much to gain from it.' Japan had during her growth raised great hope within the Asian heart, but once her development had been achieved, she no longer bothered about the rest of Asia. By overcoming all odds and creating a powerful modern state, Turkey may provide again an inspiration for other countries of Asia. 'The triumph of the democratic spirit of Islam seems to have inspired the Young Turks to emerge from grave difficulties and Kemal Pasha was the embodiment of that movement.'[59]

Idea of 'Greater India' and the *Greater India Society*: a boost to nationalism

The most important development in the psyche of the Indians and in fact all Asians from the middle of the 19th century was a sense of nationalism. In Bengal, the discovery of Indian political and cultural influence in South and South-East Asia through the archaeological and philological discoveries of the French and German scholars invoked a deep pride and nationalistic fervour. India was in no way inferior to their colonisers since they themselves had established a cultural colonisation in many lands of Asia in the past. In the 1920s, a Greater India Society was established in Calcutta where intellectuals tried to popularise the concept of Greater India as a cultural sphere together with the explorations of French archaeologists and writings of French Indologists like Sylvain Levi. The movement's early leaders included the historian R.C. Majumdar, the philologists Suniti Kumar Chatterji and P.C. Bagchi and the historians Phanindranath Bose and Kalidas Nag. Rabindranath Tagore was its ex-officio president as *Purodha* (Chief Priest).

Greater India was a play or variation on the terms Hither India and Further India/Farther India/Ultra India (Hegel spoke about Farther Asia to refer to 'China and Mongols'[60]) that had already gained ground in colonial ideology to denote India and South-East Asia. The term appeared to have been used by some Orientalists not only to challenge the belief in European superiority over the colonised culture but also to highlight the Indo-centrism in South-East Asian language, culture and art through a comparative study of the region. As Tony Ballantyne has shown with reference to the 'Scottish' Orientalists like William Robertson, Alexander Hamilton or Francis Buchanan, 'comparative philology with a heavy Indian focus' was used to suggest 'profound cultural continuities linking south and southeast Asia' but most importantly was a reflection of the British vision of looking at 'both the mainland and island south-east Asia as frontiers of their Indian empire'. This was complemented by accounts from parts of *Further India* by William Marsden, Stamford Raffles and John Crawford discussing words, customs and beliefs that could be traced back to India.[61] However, in general, the use of these terms were by British officials, philologists,[62] geographers[63] and military men[64] stationed at various points of Farther or Further India as well as by intrepid travellers and adventurers[65] seeking to establish or demarcate British colonial jurisdiction or ambition. These accounts, especially the ones which appeared in print in the 19th and early 20th centuries as books or book reviews in English journals and newspapers, attracted much attention among the English-educated Indians.

The term Greater India was already in use by geographers in the 19th century to denote India and South-East Asia and with wider research among both European and Indian scholars, the concept became associated with the theory of Indianisation or Indic influences in Asia. Some of their formulations were inspired by concurrent excavations in Angkor by French archaeologists and by the writings of French Indologist Sylvain Lévi. It was a proof of the nationalist project of the early 20th century, i.e. of appropriating colonial ideology against colonialism, that some Hindu Bengalis of Calcutta started a society to engender greater research as to how Indian culture developed into, what Susan Bayly famously calls, 'supra local civilizing force', 'unabashed(ly) orientalist', yet 'far from deferential in their engagement with British and other understandings of the "Indic", the "Oriental" and the "colonial"' and often 'reformulating theories of languages, history and culture . . . outside the familiar canon of Anglophone Orientalist writings'.[66] According to Bayly, their vision nourished French Indologists, engaged with the Indian diaspora in Asia and Africa and had commonalities with other movements in Asia in 'imagined initiative' in the past and with 'men of action' in the present.[67] What her essay does not include is the range of perspective that these scholars of the Society had, nor how their influence permeated among other intellectuals of the time. In the case of the literary periodicals which try to bring the thought movement to the non-academic masses, it would be expected that nationalist rhetoric in all its exuberance and excess would take precedence over rationality, but very few have taken that easy way out.

Hari Vasudevan and others in a policy document of the Institute of Foreign Policy Studies, Calcutta University, wrote that the ideas of Lévi, Przyluski and other French Indologists were brought to Calcutta's intellectual circle, led by Rabindranath Tagore and Lévi's students, Kalidas Nag and P.C. Bagchi in the 1920s, later joined by Suniti Kumar Chatterji and R.C. Majumdar in the 1930s. They point out that though these scholars, most notably historian Majumdar, were 'exuberant' nationalists referring to 'South East Asian remains as India's own' and even referring to them as 'Indian colonies', but they never 'questioned the role, in the long term, of South East Asian peoples in making their own culture' nor claimed 'dominion' or asserted 'overlordship'.[68]

From 1934, *Journal of the Greater India Society* established a collection of writings on the ideal for posterity, but a glance at the list of contributors shows that it was not really comprehensive. The articles were overwhelmingly academic and mainly historical, archaeological and linguistic. Rabindranath Tagore, despite his enthusiastic support as *Purodha*, did not contribute to it. The term *Greater India* and the notion of an explicit Hindu expansion of ancient South-East Asia have been linked to both Indian nationalism and Hindu nationalism. However, many Indian nationalists, like Jawaharlal Nehru and Rabindranath Tagore, though proud of India as a benign civilisation building influence, stayed away from excessive Greater India advocacy. However, academic writings in the *Journal of the Greater India Society* did have an impact on the non-academic writings which can be seen in a number of essays, both travelogues or otherwise, and often in analyses of cultural and religious aspects of the other Asian countries. Most of these effusive nationalistic expressions of India extending her sphere of influence culturally and religiously consist of small interjections or comments, appearing to be almost involuntary. Swami Jagadishwarananda in 1933, in discussing his trip to Sri Lanka, starts by saying that 'like the pilgrims of the past . . . and following the footsteps of Swami Vivekananada', he had embarked on a discovery of 'Greater Bengal and Greater India in the nearby Singhal, merely 2200 miles from India'.[69] In fact, he refers to it as an 'extension of India as far as race and religion is concerned. Not only is it a part of Greater India but it can be called a colony of greater Bengal'.[70] He refers to the colonisation of Sri Lanka by the Bengali Bijaysena and the creation of Sinhalese language through Ilu which was a mixture of Prakrit, Pali, Sanskrit and the local language. His claim was that the Sri Lankans were quite amenable to and proud of their Bengali descent.[71] He also claims that Singhal was named after Bijaysena's hometown Singhapur or Singur in Hooghly, though locally it was believed that Bijaysena killed a lion (sangha) on his arrival there and that was the origin of the word Singhal. Another evidence is the common use of Bijay as a name in Sri

Lanka. When the swami was in Sri Lanka a play called *Bijay* in Sinhalese had become very popular. He also claimed to find similarities between Singhalese and Bengalis in their dress and behaviour. The women wear sarees in a similar manner and 'when a pregnant woman is about to give birth she is fed a rice pudding (kheer bhaat) very like the Bengali *payesh* and a separate room is designated for child birth in both regions.'[72] The writer refers to both Buddhist associations and the Ram Krishna Missions in Sri Lanka which actively retain Indian connections and he concludes that 'the intelligent reader has realised that in describing Sri Lanka's greatness I have revealed India's greatness'.[73]

Others were translations or representations of academic papers presented at the Greater India Society meetings and lectures and these translations had an educative purpose. Bijon Raj Chattopadhyay and Nihar Ranjan Roy published a paper discussing Indian colonisation in Java, which was read out at Greater India Society meeting. It not only coincided with Rabindranath's visit to South-East Asia in the same year but also followed the publications of his and his companions' travelogues in different literary journals. Chattopadhyay and Roy in this article sublimate Java's history as being a chapter of the glorious history of Greater India and his mention of Tagore's visit as the *Purodha* of Greater India Society somehow limits the larger cosmopolitan strain that Tagore represented.

> 'From ancient times, India had established a colony in Java and till the sixteenth century Indian region and customs, art and literature, politics and kingship spread its hegemonic influence there, so much so that the tiny island was really India in miniature. Centuries later too one can see proof of this everywhere in Java. ...In the past few years Bengali scholars with a focus of highlighting these connections are travelling all over Java, Bali, Champa and Kamboja (Vietnam and Cambodia) and combining their researches with those of the French and the Dutch scholars. It was with this intention that Rabindranath Tagore recently travelled to Java. His poetic soul has been moved by the history of Java and its connections with Indian philosophy and civilization.[74]

But one must remember that in the heyday of nationalism of the 1920s for many cosmopolitanism was limited to looking outwards and nationalism dominated much of their scholarship and endeavour. It was a novel way of serving the nation intellectually, aimed at restoring the honour and prestige of a nation fallen to colonial degradation. P.C. Bagchi justified the role played by the Greater India Society in the Foreword of the *Bulletin of Greater India Society*, in 1927, when he said that

> we Indians, ignore too much that India has played her role *like* the rest of the world *with* the rest of the world. The isolation in which India is living to-day, shut up from the rest of Asia and her general movements, is a forced isolation of her evil days. She has got to break once more the colossal barriers around her and to come in close touch with the outside world on a basis of equality. It is necessary to resuscitate that glorious period of her history, when the missionaries of her civilization went from one end of Asia to the other to lay the foundation of a cultural unity amongst diverse peoples, very different from each other ethnically and linguistically. If religious faith fails to appeal to them anymore, reason will more advantageously take its place. 'Greater India' was an achievement of the glorious

> days of India's history and forms one if its most beautiful chapters. Unlike the rest of the world, India extended her spiritual dominion and founded her cultural colonies through peaceful methods. She has given largely to others without imposing herself on them; she had also received largely from others without having recourse to violence. If it be necessary at all to go back to the past for inspiration or for determining the course which one must choose with due regard to all that is best in one's civilization, if we agree that the past is of no small importance in the formation of a wider outlook of the youth of the country, and if, after all, a true interpretation of the past history of a nation is necessary for vindicating its amour-propre, the 'Greater India Society' will have a justification for its coming into existence.[75]

Yet just ten years later while preparing the 'guidebook' for the 25th session of the Indian Science Congress Association, Bagchi, in his quite comprehensive survey of all educational and research organisations and associations in Calcutta, excluded mention of Greater India Society and its journal.[76]

I must point out that out of the 500 odd articles I have used in this book, unabashed nationalistic writing is rare. There was an awareness that promoting the theory of one-sided Indianisation may serve the purpose of inspiring Bengalis out of their lethargic acceptance of colonial domination, but will arouse deep dissatisfaction and suspicion for India and Indians in south and South-East Asia. Sarala Debi Chowdhurani's travel account proves that she was one of those who was aware that this intense nationalistic portrayal of greater Bengal or Greater India was unacceptable to many in Asia, whether or not she personally approved of it. She speaks about her meeting with two important Burmese professionals in Rangoon who she found out had

> no special attraction towards India . . . Due to the political and financial strife, many Burmese were becoming displeased with the Indians residing in Burma, and they have almost forgotten the debt they owe India regarding their religion and civilization. These facts were not very sweet to hear for the Chairperson of the Hindu Mahasabha, who has arrived with the dreams and news of a Greater India.[77]

Bengal was for obvious reasons the focus of almost all the articles in the journals and to sustain the interest of the Bengali readers, comparisons were drawn with Bengal and Bengali way of life. In fact, in much of the writing, the words 'India' and 'Bengal' are used interchangeably. Biman Behari Majumdar's 'The Role of Bengalis in the Spread of Buddhism'[78] seems rather a departure from the pragmatic approach he has in *History of Indian Political and Social Ideas* written in 1934.[79] In this article which came out in *Manashi o Marmabani* in 1924, Majumdar says that historians of Bengal generally focus on important political events and political actors, whereas it is important to know about the great Buddhist teachers who influenced the spread of Buddhist ideas in other countries of Asia, between 6th and 16th centuries in order to understand essences of Bengali culture and civilisation. He starts with the 'first pride of Bengal, Shilabhadra', the great Buddhist scholar of Nalanda who was the only one who could satisfy the thirst for knowledge that the Chinese pilgrim Hiuen Tsang had. After studying with the 105-year-old scholar for five years, Hiuen Tsang wanted to return to

China but, as Majumdar writes, most of the other scholars of Nalanda were not keen to allow him to

> take the knowledge out of India. However, since the Bengali Brahmin Shilabhadra's heart's desire was to spread Buddhist doctrines outside the country he supported Hiuen Tsang's return. The pupil was able to keep his word to his teacher by bringing about a religious renaissance in his country which led to spread of Buddhism in Japan, Korea, Mongolia etc. It should be a matter of pride that it was a Bengali who was ultimately responsible for the spread of Buddhism to so many countries.[80]

Majumdar then refers to two Bengalis who had been invited to the court of Thi Srong Dentaan, the king of Tibet, for establishing the tenets of Buddhism there. One was the head of Nalanda University, another Bengali like Shilabhadra, Shanta Rakshit. Majumdar writes in pride that 'Bengal has had the honour of providing great teachers in the highest position in the best university of India at that time.' He also connects that fact to the honour that Bengalis receive till date from invitations to impart education all over the world. despite their colonial subjection.[81] In his list of past great teachers among Bengalis, Majumdar also refers to Shanta Rakshit, who was invited to Tibetan court and given the honorific title of Acharya Bodhisattva, and Sarat Chandra Das, who along with other learned pundits of Bengal were invited to Tibet. Another Bengali Atish Dipankar Srigyan too visited Burma and Tibet. Majumdar adds that Bengalis played an important part in the spread of Buddhism in Nepal, Pegan and Sri Lanka as well.

Writing in 1930 about British Malaya, Subimal Chandra Sarkar says that the history of Greater Bengal has not yet been written. When this history unfolds it would reveal new horizons of Bengali bravery and greatness. He requested archaeologists, historians and linguists to apply themselves diligently. There was much scattered proof of Bengali presence in Malay, Sumatra, Java and Bali in historical time and there were still impressions of Bengali characteristics in Malayan language and customs.[82]

Aspiring for a different nationalism: Rabindranath Tagore and his followers

A difference has to be made even within this group of scholars who were motivated by nationalism, trying to bring forth national pride for glories in the past from those who were aware of the pitfalls of such an endeavour and who wanted to temper the pride with a spirit of cosmopolitanism or universalism. Rabindranath Tagore who is acknowledged to be one of the main pillars of the movement was one such individual. What was extraordinary about his effort was that besides being a writer and poet extraordinaire, his actions were greatly important for intra-Asian solidarity, in fact for universal solidarity as well. The very fact that he combined the roles of a pilgrim/traveller with that of an intellectual made him much more acceptable to his readers not only within India but also outside. The accolades he received in the west brought him acceptance in Asia as well. It is interesting that these temperate writings were more available to the readers compared to the academic articles highlighting India's 'colonisation' in the Asian lands via the literary journals and his published works translated into different world languages.[83] Of course, nationalistic pride often became evident even in the Bengali articles in statements of 'cultural domination' or 'civilizing influences by India' in the 'erstwhile barbaric lands of south east Asia' but by and large, these writings spoke about strong local cultures which assimilated Indian features and created a civilisation which was their own.

Many scholars have highlighted Tagore's ideas regarding Asia and universalism important since in the era of nationalism, these contrarian ideas were criticised by even his closest contemporaries and put him through hurt, betrayal and feeling of isolation. Stephen Hay in his book, *Asian Ideas of East and West: Tagore and His Critics in Japan, China and India*,[84] brings into focus how Tagore's ideas on 'East and West and their civilizations' were widely known and warmly debated. What Tagore sometimes called the 'message of India', sometimes the 'voice' of Asia, is therefore significant, both in its own right and because the dramatic way he presented it stimulated educated men in Japan, China and India to articulate their own views on the major issues he raised. As a prism diffracts a single ray of light into the separate bands of colour which comprise it, so Tagore's ideas provoked leading thinkers to make clear just where they stood along, the intellectual spectra of their societies.[85] Hay analysed the writings of 87 Asians – 48 Japanese, 24 Chinese and 15 Indians, to gain 'insight into the structure and movements of thought in the three major countries of Asia during the first half of the 20th century'.[86]

Sugata Bose discusses Tagore's travels eastwards to different countries at various times between 1916 and 1932 in both his book *A Hundred Horizons*[87] and his article, 'Rabindranath Tagore and Asian Universalism', in the publication from Nalanda Srivijaya Centre of Singapore called Tagore's *Asian Voyages: Selected Speeches and Writings on Rabindranath Tagore*.[88] Bose describes Tagore as 'one of the most creative exponents of an Asia sense in the early twentieth century' and quotes Tagore who in a letter to Nirmal Kumari Mahalanobis in 1927 says he 'embarked on a pilgrimage to see the signs of history of India's entry into the universal'.[89] Tagore was not alone on these voyages and was accompanied by many talented men who were also eager to participate in the knowledge pilgrimages he made. Most of these men sent back letters and detailed accounts which were published in different periodicals or daily newspapers or were published as books themselves. Tagore's own travel accounts were also published initially as articles and then later as books. Artist Mukul De accompanied Tagore in 1916, when he travelled by the ship Tosamaru through Rangoon (though he did not land there) to Penang, Singapore, Hong Kong and Kobe (29 May 1916) and then crossed Pacific to North America (7 September 1916). In many of his writings during his travels as well as before and after, Tagore commented on politics and political situations in India and outside – not only commenting on the existing state of affairs but also making accurate predictions. His commitment to cosmopolitanism and nationalism remained with him throughout his life and there was no contradiction between the two.

The year 1916 not only marked Tagore's first travel eastwards, it was in a non-western ship as well. Already close to Japan through his interactions with Okakura, Tagore felt that he was on a journey of knowledge despite his misgivings about the imperialist ambitions of Japan towards Korea and China, on a search for 'World Culture and Universal Man'.[90] The songs he composed on his voyages abroad are testimony to his intense enjoyment of knowing the unknown. On this particular voyage, 'in the midst of a . . . frightening storm in the south China Sea on 21 May 1916, he composed the song *Bhuban jora ashonkhani*', 'asking the Almighty to spread his seat of universality in the individual heart'.[91] At this time, Tagore sent three articles to *Sabuj Patra* – Japan

Jatrir Patra, Japaner Patra and Japaner Kotha – where he wrote about this voyage and it was later compiled into a book called *Japan Jatri.* He was accompanied by Andrews, Pearson and Mukul De. The reason for this interest in Japan was not only cultural but also to pay homage to Japan who, as Tagore wrote among all the countries in Asia, first realised that they have the power to stop the juggernaut that Europe was turning into. The alternative was to perish beneath its wheels. The moment this thought entered their minds, they did not waste a moment and within a few years they were able to emulate Europe's strength[92] Tagore pointed out in this essay in *Sabuj Patra* that the way in which Japan adapted the power of the west was unique. It was not a simple assimilation but one in which the Japanese controlled the changes. In his words,

> If borrowing Europe's weapons were the only means then Afghanistan would not have to worry anymore. What is crucial is to create a mentality for the best use of European goods . . . Thus, we have to admit that Japan did not have to build from scratch her mental makeup was ready to accept the borrowing.[93]

He speaks of two kinds of nations – one mobile and active and the other inert. He put Japan in the former category and India in the latter. He also asked the question how the Japanese could blend their active spirit with the fast-paced modernity. The answer according to Tagore came from the Japanese themselves.

> There is a proverb among the Japanese that they are a mixed race – part Mongolian and . . . part Aryan. In fact, one can see among the Japanese features of both the Mongolians and Indians . . .. If one dressed my friend the painter Taikan in Indian clothes no one would take him to be Japanese. That race which is mixed cannot have a stagnant mind, the different elements within make for mobility and this helps that race to move forward . . .. Most nations deny this racial mixture even at the risk of perpetuating falsehood, but the Japanese have no such false pride . . . Not only that, we may forget that the Japanese are indebted to Indian influence in their paintings but they never deny it . . . since they have converted it from a debt to an asset.[94]

The other asset for Japan, according to the poet, was its small size which lent itself readily to easy assimilation of disparate parts unlike the case of China or India. Tagore also identified similarities between the Bengalis and the Japanese which he points out in this essay. As he also pointed out in his famous essay 'Japan', which he read out during his visit there in 1916, later in the United States during the same year and finally compiled in his book *Nationalism* in 1917, that the truth is that Japan is old and new at the same time. She has her legacy of ancient culture from the East . . . and Japan, the child of Ancient East, has also fearlessly claimed all the gifts of the modern age for herself.'[95]

In 1924, Tagore travelled to Burma, China and Japan and was accompanied by painter Nandalal Bose, Kshitimohan Sen (scholar of Sanskrit and comparative religion) and Kalidas Nag. *Anandabazar Patrika* (ABP) reported that on 28th April, the former Emperor Suang Tang and his private tutor Johnston received Tagore at his residence.[96] Young Chinese actors of the Crescent Moon Society performed his play *Chitra* in English on Tagore's birthday, 8 May 1924, at the Peking Normal University and on this trip, Tagore preached the virtues of close interaction among Asian cultures.

In a lecture to the Chinese students at Hangchow University, he said that 'improvement of transport systems had brought people close, but intimate relations were not being established. There are many obstacles to the unity between China and India but there is a possible path even for that'.[97] Stung by the passage of the Immigration Act of 1924 (sometimes referred to as the Orientals Exclusion Act) in the United States, some of Tagore's admirers even established an Asiatic Association in Shanghai to foster solidarity among all Asians. In the final lecture in China, Tagore said that the reason why the European war had spread worldwide was due to internal reasons, it had not been supplanted from outside. The poison was already within. The situation may be beneficial for Asia, but she must know how much to accept from Europe and what to reject. Till now we have not shown perspicacity in this and in fact China suffers from this the most. She has been imitating western art and culture without restraint. It is true that scientific knowledge comes from the west but science is being used as a destructive weapon . . . the East must restore to the world the attributes of greatness that is almost lost, so that humanity may prove to be greater than totalitarianism.[98] On his way back Tagore stopped at Rangoon where, as reported in ABP, he spoke to a representative of Associated Press, that just as his words of friendship found response in China and Japan, he wanted *maitri* (meaning alliance, friendship or amity) to become the 'eternal truth' for all Asia. ABP pointed out that Tagore had always stressed that Asian values were very different from the western materialistic ideals. From his travels in China and Japan, Tagore had realised that the eastern spiritual values had not been totally destroyed yet. A sense has dawned in Asia that in the near future she will arise from the long-standing inertness and find the ideal truth and new life-force within themselves. All the different nations and civilizations of Asia will unite to pave the way for the welfare of humanity,' he was quoted saying.[99]

In 1927, Suniti Kumar Chattopadhyay, a linguist, and Surendranath Kar, a painter, accompanied Tagore in his visit to South-East Asia and the former left a valuable account of the journey which I have discussed later. Tagore reached Singapore in July 1927 in the steamer *Amboise* and on board he gave a statement to the Associated Press where he said that he was travelling like a 'poor pilgrim' to Indonesia. He was following in the footsteps of the past pilgrims who had travelled to fulfil their thirst for knowledge, truth and compassion and which had brought India greatness. India had in the past 'left her home in the hope of spreading her own realisations and sharing them with her neighbours.' The poet's aim was 'explore' how India stepped out of her geographical limits to overcome her self-restriction, and by travelling there he would, along with his fellow Indians 'use that past knowledge to overcome our penury and pettiness of mind, and strengthen our faith in universalism, truth and generosity.'[100] A very far cry from the arrogance of past 'Indianisation' theories that the Greater India Society was accused of in later years both in the country and in southeast Asia.

(The route he followed was through Malacca 27–29th July, Kuala Lumpur 30 July 1927, Taiping 12–13 August, Penang 13–16 August 1927, Surabaya, Bali and Borobudur, 1927.). A report of the voyage undertaken by Tagore and his associates was given by Suniti Kumar Chatterjee at a lecture at the Mahabodhi Society under the auspices of the Greater India Society and Visva Bharati Patrika on 12 January 1928. The meeting was chaired by the President of Greater India Society Jadunath Sarkar and attended by many distinguished men – German scholar Mann, Ramaprasad Chanda, Banwari Lal Chowdhury, Ardhendu Sekhar Ganguly, Nagendranath Gupta, Kalidas Nag, Padmaraj Jain, Ambikaprasad Vajpeyi, Mohitlal Majumdar and Prafulla

Kumar Sarkar. All the artefacts collected from Java and Bali were displayed, including brass figurines, picture of shadow dance, tapestry painting, embroidered silks, etc. In the lecture, Chatterjee said that the entire expenditure of the voyage that Tagore and his associates undertook in 1927 was borne by the industrialist Ghanshyamdas Birla and another Marwari businessman. Chatterjee then gave details of their trip in Java and Bali and in the end Jadunath Sarkar said that it was important that the ancient ties between India and Greater India be re-established and an exchange of ideas and thoughts initiated.[101] Another news item on 27 June in the same newspaper however contradicts the evidence saying that it was Yugal Kishore Birla and Narayan Das who funded his voyage.[102]

In 1929, Tagore visited Japan and China on the way back from America and Canada. According to a report in *Anandabazar Patrika*, due to ill-treatment by the American immigration, the poet suddenly veered towards Japan. There at a lecture in Asahi theatre, he said that it was not as a philosopher or a teacher but as a poet that he had come to Japan. Poetry is loved universally and difference in language never acts as a barrier. He followed up his lecture by recitation of a number of his poems.[103] Apurba Kumar Chanda, a teacher at Presidency College, who acted as the poet's secretary on this trip later gave a spontaneous description to *Anandabazar Patrika*. Tagore undertook this voyage on the *Naldera* ship along with Professor Arian Williams and Reverend Tucker. In Shanghai, the poet was given a reception by the Chinese which was organised by the Chinese philosopher Hu Shih, poet Tsu Simon, General Chang and Dr Ung. On Tagore's arrival in Japan, Chanda also reports that a reception to the poet was given by the Tagore Society after which he gave a lecture at the Imperial University in Tokyo.

In 1932, Tagore travelled westwards to Iran and Iraq accompanied by his daughter-in-law Pratima Debi, the poet Amiya Kumar Chakrabarty, who was his private secretary, and writer Kedarnath Chattopadhyay.[104] Chakraborty sent news of the details of the poet's engagements there to *Bharatvarsha* which was published as *Parashye Rabindranath*.[105] Unlike the other journeys, this one was done by air. They boarded the plane at Dumdum which was piloted by a Portuguese captain, they reached Jodhpur where the maharaja organised a special tea for the poet. They next day they boarded the flight which took them to Karachi where the local people also organised a reception for the poet. The poet was also warmly received in Jask by the Persian governor and in Bushayar, Kazeran and Shiraz. Chakraborty also reported that the poet was overwhelmed by his visit to the tomb of the world-famous poet Sa'adi. On 23rd April, the poet visited Ispahan and attended two receptions by the royal army and civic municipal authorities before making his way to Teheran on 30th April. There a formal reception was held at a large garden outside the city from where he was ceremoniously conveyed to the home of Asadi where he stayed on the voyage. On 3rd May, Tagore met the Shah of Persia and had a long discussion with him.[106] Kalidas Nag, another ardent admirer and follower of Tagore, also describes this visit. In 1932, the Poet received a personal invitation from the builder of modern Iran, Reza Shah Pehlavi, Tagore then in his seventy-first year, flew to Teheran and to Baghdad and amidst the glorious roses of Iran his birthday was celebrated with banquets and poetic recitals, evoking truly Iranian grace and glamour. The Shah also made gifts of enduring nature to the Poet by sending in his party to Santiniketan the celebrated poet and scholar Poure Daoud, together with rare manuscripts from the Royal Library. Thus, Iran also joined hands with India. And Iran and Iraq were the last foreign countries which the poet could visit in his declining years. The Poet had the satisfaction of seeing firmly established, through the devoted zeal of Professor Tan Yun-San, the China – Bhavana, where a regular cultural exchange between China and India has been established. Scholars and students not only from China, but also from Japan and Java, Siam and Burma, Ceylon, Afghanistan and Iran and far off Palestine, have been visiting the International University of Visva-Bharati.[107]

In his final word on this issue in *Crisis of Civilization* written at the age of 80, Tagore did a survey of sorts of his mental voyage through important strands of civilisation of the west and east, and their mental conflict when they 'disowned with impunity whenever questions of national self-interest were involved'. Praising those countries where governments based on cooperation keep civilisational values alive, unlike those countries which were ruled through exploitation, he lamented at the 'demon of barbarity who . . . has emerged with unconcealed fangs, ready to tear up humanity in an orgy of devastation'. But still positive till the end, Tagore would not 'commit the grievous sin of losing faith in Man' and looked forward to a new dawn from the 'East where the sun rises' when the unvanquished 'Man . . . will . . . win back his lost human heritage'.[108] The Tagore scholar and music exponent, Pramita Mullick pointed out in a lecture that though he changed his ideas on nationalism often from 1905 till the end in 1941, what was constant was his faith in humanity throughout his life. He never lost his positive outlook despite the looming of war clouds, and this can be seen in the fact that none of the songs he composed at that time dealt with the tragedy of war or violence with the sole exception of a song which he composed for the Good Friday celebrations in Santiniketan. Here the direct reference is to the Christ's sacrifice for humanity made through pain and suffering, but the allusion is to military aggression in the contemporary world when His killers have appeared in the present world.[109]

Tagore's associates also describe in their writing Tagore's ideas and actions in reviving what Kalidas Nag, historian and author, called 'inter-Asian relations in modern times'. Nag provides a detailed outline of Tagore's 'interest in Asian affairs' through the years and shows how his abiding interest nurtured by the example of his father's love for China was followed up by actions and inspiring others to follow his goal in his book *The Discovery of Asia*. He not only referred to Debendranath Tagore's interest in Chinese philosophy as well as vivid description of his travel to China in *Tattvabodhini Patrika*, but also touched upon Rabindranath's abiding interests in Chinese history and politics even before he visited East Asia. Tagore's *Gitanjali* was translated into Chinese and Japanese. Nag refers not only to his admiration of Japan but also his 'trenchant criticism of nationalistic chauvinism, which was the cause of the First World War', which he also discussed in his letters to the poet Noguchi (1938). He also discussed Tagore's visit to Burma (he visited thrice in 1916, 1924 and 1927). He writes that Tagore thought that the 'double colonialism' of both British and Indian populations gave the city of Rangoon the most unpleasant form of 'Vanijyalakshmi' (goddess of Commerce). Other than the Shwedagon temple, Tagore did not find anything in the city that was distinctively Burmese. He quoted Tagore as saying: 'This city has not grown like a tree from the soil of the country, it floats like foam on the tides of time.' Rangoon according to Tagore was a 'mere visual acquaintance' but he could not recognise Burma there. . . . 'The city is an abstraction'. (Tagore, 1941 pp. 14, pp. 17–25)[110]

Suniti Kumar Chattopadhyay, often considered to be one of Greater India Society mouthpieces, is at the same time also a loyal follower of Tagore in his blending of the universalist/cosmopolitan spirit with his nationalist concerns and aspirations. Chattopadhyay describes a conversation that the poet had with a French officer Jean Jacques Neuville aboard the ship *Amboise* on their way to Java in 1927. When Neuville asked Tagore if he thought that the Europeans should fear the 'yellow peril' which was considered to be a threat in that period, Tagore's answer revealed a conviction of most Indians in that period:

> Peril indicates a fear of a strong power using their commercial ships, armed soldiers and weapons, their missionary colonial merchants and huge numbers of population preying upon a country who does not want them but has no power to resist. This predatory instinct much like the Old Man of the Sea of the *Arabian Nights* who refuses to let go of his strangle-grip is the creation of the Europeans. It is the means by which Europe is establishing its grip on the whole world and has led to what may be called the white peril. No Asian race has ever done that – recently Japan has been guilty of this in Korea when they tried to imitate Europe. Chinese are a calm and composed race, the only civilized nation who have held the view that the armed forces would always occupy a lower position in society at the level of hired goons and mercenaries. Thus, China wants to follow a system by which they can maintain their traditional values according to their own will and are or dependent on development through greed for foreign goods. But despite all their good intentions the Chinese are being subjected to harassment by foreign powers like England and Japan so naturally they have to retaliate in order to protect themselves. But if China and Japan form an alliance with the restless and powerful Russians then European style peril may be a plausible possibility.[111]

Chattopadhyay added that this was entirely the view of Tagore and he had some differences of opinion on the matter. In 'Dvipamoy Bharat' which was published in *Prabashi* as 19 articles over 1929–1931 and *Javadviper Pothe* in two articles in 1927, Suniti Chattopadhyay goes beyond his assigned role as a follower of Tagore on his journey through South-East Asia and paints a beautiful pen picture of the countries he visited along with a commentary on their history and culture. The travelogue makes very interesting reading and is one of the best travel writings in Bengali.[112] Sugata Bose shows how Chattopadhyay has left a vivid, detailed, and learned travelogue-cum-historical thesis on 'Greater India'.[113] One can only imagine the excitement that the serialised publication of his travelogue created in 1929 and the readers not only toured with Tagore and his companions but also relished Chattopadhyay's comments regarding the connecting links between India and South-East Asia in the past, his astute judgements about the political situation in Asia and the world and his commitment to both nationalism and cosmopolitanism which appear along with his travels. At the outset of the journey, Chattopadhyay laid down the foundation of his research when while standing on the deck waiting for the arrival of Belawan in Sumatra he thought of the 'centuries of linkages between India and South East Asia which had been forgotten in India, Sumatra and Malaya. Only in Java, Thailand and Cambodia is the memory still alive and history text books incorporate that link'.[114] One link that he found very interesting was the fact that the 'Indians in Sumatra were referred to either as "Kling" (meaning Kalinga, while referring to migrants from south India) and "Banggali" meaning from the port of Calcutta in reference to migrants from north India'.[115] 'Indian' in Indonesian generally referred to Indonesians.[116] During his tour of the city of Batavia, Chattopadhyay pointed out that over the past three centuries since 1619, the Dutch have created and developed the city by adding new sectors Weltevreden and Meester Cornelis to the old city of Batavia and acted as the catalyst through which 'Indian artistic influence that was visible in Borobudur, Prambanan changed to a more Malay inspired imaginative, masculine, brusque yet powerful art, which we had the honour to see and appreciate'.[117] Chattopadhyay appreciated the Dutch efforts to compile translations of English, Sanskrit and Dutch literature into Indonesian so that the children in present Indonesia got the opportunity to read world literature. 'We realised that those areas where the light of Indian civilization had not illuminated are no longer under barbarians and this was the effect of the great efforts made by the Dutch'.[118] Though he acknowledged the efforts of the Dutch colonial power, Chattopadhyay was not ready to accept

> the view of some scholars like Bosch working on Indonesian art and culture that instead of the accepted view that Indonesian art developed due to the Indian influence it was the other way round where similarities that were visible between Indonesian art and Nalanda art was due to a counter influence. Some of the Dutch experts contended that it was the Indonesian effort which was at the root of the artistic development there and not Indian influence. But this theory cannot really be accepted.[119]

When the group comprising Rabindranath Tagore, the author, the painter Surendranath Kar and Dhirendranath Burman reached Bangli in Bali to attend the funeral ceremony of a local landlord or raja's relative, it was to a country which followed Hinduism mixed with Tantric Buddhism called *Agama Bali*, and where the Poet Tagore was referred to as the *Mahagoeroe from Voor-India* (meaning great saint from India) . . . . Chattopadhyay was intrigued to notice that during the funeral ceremony, the chanting by the priest presiding over the funeral ceremony were Sanskrit but with distorted pronunciations and interpolations of many Bali words in the language.[120] 'Bali', he points out in another article, 'needs to follow the dictates of the present and open communications with the outside world. In charting out a new path of progress, it would be easier for Bali to seek closeness with those countries which are familiar to the religion and culture of Bali.'[121] Chattopadhyay engaged in this job by showing the Raja who had invited them the way religious rites are performed in India, through mime and explanations of each mantra and movement, lantern shows and picture books. Though the audience listened to his explanations with great attention and asked him many questions, it was the statement by the Raja that astounded Chattopadhyay. The Raja said that despite all the detailed and meaningful rituals one follows, it is in the end only a beautiful performance. The real aim of all the rituals is 'nibbana'. Chattopadhyay was charmed. In that faraway Malay land,' he wrote, 'despite the disjuncture with India, was the kernel of all Indian philosophy, that the pursuit of all worship is the achievement of nirvana or freedom from worldly ties.' When he mentioned his realisation to Tagore, he told Chattopadhyay that the Malay race, are different from Indians, they think differently, despite the fact that certain aspects of Indian religion and culture have adopted or adapted they by and large spectacular in nature. What they have truly achieved is the realisation of the 'the philosophic truth of our civilization' and that is why despite so many obstacles, they have been successful in holding their own civilization intact.[122]That the king was a philosophic man became evident when he handed over to the poet and his companions his book on the excellent practices of religion called *Dharmasushil*. Chattopadhyay recalled in his articles how he was shown great respect since he was a Brahmin from India and was well versed in Sanskrit *slokas*. Once he was caught in a difficult situation and managed to extricate himself from that precarious situation by display of that quality. He had gone to see some old temples in Besakkik in Bali and discovered that the icons were not on display. The local *pamanku* or junior priest offered to provide the tourists from India with the key to the inner chambers as Chattopadhyay was a Brahmin, since they would not generally allow anyone to touch the icons. Sometime later when a senior priest came and raised an uproar for saying that their gods had been insulted, Chattopadhyay offered to recite Sanskrit mantras to pacify the gods. The crowds were charmed and even the priest was forced to withdraw his objections.[123]

Kalidas Nag in *Greater India*, in 1926, made a case for Internationalism through invoking the memories of India's glorious past through tracing

> the influence of the Universal on the history of India, to indicate the landmarks of Internationalism in her national evolution and to point out, by suggestions and implications, if possible, the specific contributions of India to the development of International History. In an age wherein international hatred threatens unfortunately to be the order of the day, such a study may not be without profit, not simply for the transvaluation of historical values but for ascertaining the warning-gesture of the profound Past to our muddling Present.[124]

He traces the landmarks through some symbolic events and values like explosion of the 'splendid isolation theory' that had stuck as the 'tenacious fiction of Indian history' invented according to Nag by both the 'narrow outlook of late Hindu orthodoxy' and the 'early school of occidental philologists'. In his view, India played a symbolic role of 'the Peacemaker of Ancient History' contributing to Internationalism through peace and spiritual unity different from the internationalism of exploitation or the imperialistic internationalism of compulsion of the Phoenicians and Romans, respectively.[125] He stressed the importance of the values of universal tolerance and amity as exemplified in the past through the life and teachings of Buddha who was the incarnate of the 'truth that was burning in the heart of India'. The soul of Asia expressed itself through a history of human thought spread over the continent, the unerring universalism of the Upanishads, the divine cosmopolitanism of the Buddha, Mahavira, preaching Ahimsa, and Lao Tse and Confucius evolving respectively, their grand systems, the Tao-kiao (School of the way) and Ju kiao (school of the Knowers), emphasising the same principles of life non-interference, suppression of ego and purification of the heart. So also in the land of the Iranina cousins of the Indians, the reformation of faith had been started a little earlier by Zoroaster.[126] Writing for a symposium on 'The Role of Internationalism in the Development of Civilization' at a Peace Congress of Lugano in August 1922 which was attended by the master spirits of modern Europe like Romain Rolland, Bertrand Russell, Hermann Hesse and others, Nag traced Indian Internationalism from Boghus Khai inscriptions and connected it to Asian internationalism through the history of ideas.[127] In his view, from the beginning of the Christian era, India started playing her role of internationalism not only through her lofty academic philosophy or through the vigorous propagation of a royal personality, but as a whole people following mysteriously a divine impulse, an ecstatic inspiration to sacrifice the Ego for the All. This grand movement of spiritual conquest, this noble dynamic of cultural imperialism – a legacy of Asoka – soon won for India the inalienable empire over the vast continent, right across Tibet and China to Korea and Japan on the one hand and across Burma and Indo-China to Java and Indonesia on the other, the history of this phenomenal progression has yet to be written. It is full of profound lessons for students of internationalism.[128] It is interesting that though the original long essay was in English, a Bengali translation of the first section by Nihar Ranjan Ray was published in *Prabashi* in 1927 as 'Brihattara Bharat' which concludes with Kalidas Ray's tribute to Asvaghosa's 'Awakening of Faith', as a 'landmark in the history of Indian internationalism'.[129]

In another article where he discusses the contribution of Sylvain Levy to the Science of Indology, he traces the lineage of studies of Greater India to an earlier period to the works of European scholars. In his words, Levi had a 'vision of Indian history and culture not circumscribed by the modern political delimitation of India.' Burnouf and Bergaigne created a grand vision of Magna India which radiates from every page of Levi, who continued the grand traditions of the French school of Indologists, ever expanding the horizon of Indian history. In India he is specially remembered because of he undertook the noble task of training generations of Indian scholars in the science[130]

Ramananda Chattopadhyay in 1925, in *Prabashi* (edited by him), wrote an article on 'Greater India' (*Mahattara* Bharat instead of *Brihat*, indicating great in another meaning, not sense of large), a year before the Society was established in Calcutta. He wrote that in England there was a concept called Greater Britain. In all the countries of the world where the English established colonies, they have made them their own and those areas where which are even now a part of the British empire, those countries comprise Greater Britain. In English great may mean both large as well as sublime so Greater Britain can refer to both immense size as well as the nobility. It is probable that the word refers to larger Britain[131] Chattopadhyay gives the example of the United States to show that this was originally a colony of Britain but gained independence by revolting against them and are 'greater than England in some respects like in producing a statesman like Abraham Lincoln'.[132] Chattopadhyay then talks about the spread of Indian and Greek civilization to other countries in the ancient period, much like the English, French and Spanish civilization. A difference is noticeable between the spread of European civilization in the modern period and spread of Indian Civilization in the ancient period was that European civilization spread in the wake of territorial expansion and wealth acquisition and they practically decimated the native population in the conquered countries or made them totally dependent economically to them. They then proceeded to call these countries 'white man's land'. Unlike England and France who established control over a country and then proceeded to recreate the administration of the conquered country in the lines of London or Paris, no king or emperor of India is recorded to have tried to rule from their capital any occupied land outside their own territory. It is stated by Manu in his Dharmashastra that when a king occupies a land, the administration must be handed over to a scion of the conquered king. Chattopadhyay writes that he has based this thesis on the work on Hindu polity of K.P. Jaiswal, though his work was criticised by another leading scholar of the Greater India Society.[133]

Chattopadhyay wrote in 'Mahattara Bharat' referring to India's influence which spread to Brahmadesha (Burma), Shyam (Thailand), Annam (Vietnam), Cochin, Cambodia etc, and also in Java islands, Bali islands and Sumatra.

> Perhaps some powerful kings or people established colonial settlements or empires in those lands. But they then became one with the land, a part of the local population and as a result of the intermixture of Indians and people of that country a new race had emerged. Their culture and civilization is not truly Indian though one can notice certain influences but one can also notice the dissimilarities.

Ramananda Chattopadhyay also quoted large passages from a speech given by a Chinese professor Liang Chi Chao, during a reception organised in the honour of Rabindranath Tagore's visit there in 1924.He wrote that Chao in his speech agreed with Tagore that India and China were both 'devoted to the cause of universal truth,' and fulfilment of 'destiny of man through cooperation.' He was quoted by Chattopadhyay as saying that, 'We Chinese specially felt the need for leadership from our elder brothers, the people of India,' without 'any self-interest'. What China received from India according to Chao was 'the idea of absolute freedom' meaning a fundamental freedom of mind that enables it to shake off all the fetters of past tradition and habit as well as the present customs of a particular age and a 'spiritual freedom' which casts off the enslaving forces of material existence. According to Chao, China received from India, 'idea of absolute love', meaning a pure love towards all living beings which eliminates all obsessions of jealousy, anger, impatience, disgust and emulation, which expresses itself in deep pity and sympathy for the foolish, the wicked, and the sinful – that absolute love, which recognises the 'inseparability of all beings' longs for.

Chao pointed out that the idea of 'The oneness of myself and all things' was a part of Da Tsang Jen (Buddhist classics) and the teachings in these 7,000 volumes can be summed up in one phrase: To cultivate sympathy and intellect, in order to attain absolute freedom through wisdom and absolute love through pity.[134] Chattopadhyay interpreted Professor Liang Chi Chao's speech to say that China learnt directly or indirectly from India in the fields of music, architecture, painting, sculpture, dramatic literature and performance, writing of poetry and novels, astrology, development of script, prose writing, logic, pedagogy, social customs, etc.

Having followed the Greater India tradition of eulogising Indic influence albeit with a difference by quoting Chao, Chattopadhyay then goes on to show how Tibetan civilisation too is indebted to India as has been revealed by the translation of Sanskrit and Pali texts which have survived there, by Pandit Vishusekhar Sastri in Santiniketan. He also adds that Asian countries were variously influenced by India. Korea was influenced by Indian civilization and Japan was influenced by India partly through Korea, partly through China, and partly directly. Philippines got her ancient script from India. In the Middle East, much of the sandy areas would reveal excavation remains of many sculptures, viharas, temples and manuscripts written in ancient scripts with similarities to Sanskrit. 'These distant lands', he concludes,' were deeply influenced by Indian religion, literature and art.' Indian influence according to Chattopadhyay was also present in south and central Asia, though 'this is denied by many'. That he was aware of new researches which denied Indianisation and focussed on local is evident when he qualifies his past eulogy with the statement that, 'whichever country Indian religion, knowledge, art and culture was carried to, the local people used their own creativity and knowledge to transform them creating a new and at times improved knowledge'.

The above was only the introduction to his real idea of what he considered to be Greater India. It was those areas which were 'Bharatvarsha in heart and spirit' and true Indians were not those who lived in territorial Bharat but were aspirationally western. As he writes,

> Outside the geographical boundary of India there are people who are Indian in heart and soul and . . . they are our relatives, their homes are swadesh (homeland) of spirit, or Greater India (in the sense of large and noble) . . . large because it is huge area and noble because the nobility of spirit there is more than that found in India today.[135]

But Chattopadhyay is not simply lamenting the loss of the great spirit that existed in the past, but urging modern India to embrace that great spirit from outside its boundaries, in order to help its diaspora population in other parts of the world as well as extend help wherever needed.

Kalidas Nag also talked about the 'period of give and take in human history – between Buddhism and Mazdaism, Taoism and Confucianism, Manichaeism and Christianity' and the 'international collaboration' which he and his colleagues hoped to replicate in the Society.[136] This 'internationalism through free economic relations and spiritual exchange' has to be done 'silently by agencies distinctly non-political', and will be far more important than 'the rise and fall of self-centred governments and nationalistic empires'.[137]

Ramesh Chandra Majumdar, was a historian, strongly committed to the Greater India idea, and it was mainly his ultra-nationalistic history project in Bharatiya Bidya Bhavan series that led many later scholars to feel embarrassed while discussing Asian connections leading to the removal of certain and/or content of chapters in history school texts. For example, 'Colonial and Cultural Expansion' in *An Advanced History of India* by R.C. Majumdar, H.C. Raychaudhuri and K.K. Datta, 'Greater India and Spread of Indian Culture' in D.N. Kundra's book of India School Certificate Examinations in different states was replaced by 'India's Cultural Contacts with the Asian Countries' in Ram Sharan Sharma's *Ancient India History* textbook. Majumdar's non-academic writing like his short travelogue 'Letter from Abroad' published in *Bharatvarsha* in 1931 has shades of both his acute awareness of his Indianisation project and his enjoyment in the distinctiveness of the place he is visiting. He writes from the Shiva temple grounds situated at Fanrang which he reminds his readers was a 'historic city named Pandurangbhoomi by our forefathers'. An accomplished writer, Majumdar describes the city of Saigon, wittily dismisses the discomforts of the train and boat ride to visit Nhatrang, the temple at Po Nagar, highlighting the cultural linkages with India in the past and present. Unlike his academic writings which appear like a litany of one-sided giving of civilising influences to inert countries receiving culture, here is the vibrant story of a traveller overcoming travel woes to study a temple as a historical monument of the ancient kingdom of Champa. Majumdar's description of the scenic beauty of the ocean with the mountains in the background in Nhatrang is almost lyrical, though every part of his journey to Po Nagar appears fraught with snags, accidents and frustrating delays, which he describes in vivid details.[138] Of course, Majumdar cannot but revert to being a proud Indian, but this time it's not only because of past glories but also for a contemporary pride when he comes across a young Annamese who was an admirer of Gandhi. To quote Majumdar, 'I felt very proud to realise the depth of respect that the Annami youth had for Mahatma Gandhi, as a true patriot at par with Sun

Yat Sen who was also deeply revered'.[139] In his autobiography *Jiboner Smritidipe*, Majumdar doesn't, as much as one would have expected, deliberate on Greater India but is rather pragmatic about how he decides to learn French and Dutch since he had made up his mind to work on the Indian diaspora in South-East Asia and most of his sources would be in those languages. To further his research, he was granted funds and leave for ten months to travel in Europe and Asia in 1928. After travelling extensively in England, France, Italy, Germany, Belgium, etc., he reached Java and Bali where he was deeply impressed by the beauty of the country and the architecture. It is true he was primarily interested in locating the Hindu diaspora in those countries as well as Champa (Vietnam), Cambodia, Malaya and Thailand and exploring the temples in those countries, but like in his travelogue he described his experience in meeting new people during his travels.[140]

Presumably, all intellectuals are products of the past and in that sense, it might be doing an injustice to brand all the members of the Greater India Society as aggressively nationalistic. Even if some of them wrote about Indianisation or Indic influences in South-East and East Asia, it was not as if they were unaware of it being firmly in the past, however golden it might have seemed to be. Other than inspiring pride in themselves, the Indian writers of the Greater India Society showed a more inquisitiveness with regard to links and connections in the past between the different countries of Asia. S.R. Sharma in *India as I See Her* wrote that 'India and Asia are members one of another, not only geographically and racially, but also culturally'. The contrast between the Indian and the Trans Indian movements shows that the number of pious trans-Indian pilgrims who came to India was smaller than that of the Indians who went to China and the Far Eastern countries. 'In South East Asia, as is well known, a Greater India grew up as a consequence of these contacts (or rather connexions) through several centuries'. . . .Sharma also writes that the Graeco Roman names: 'Serindia for Central Asian region', and 'India extra Gangem' for India's eastern neighbours and 'Indonesia' for the island countries of South East Asia 'are significant pointers.' He also suggests that 'Indo-China (in its wider connotation)' is more comprehensively 'suggestive of the meeting of the two biggest countries of Asia whose names are compounded in that meaningful term.'[141]

K.M. Panikkar's 'interest' in South-East Asian history and its future grew 'naturally' out of his study of Indian history. As he writes in his autobiography Cambodia, Siam, Java, Malaya and other countries were once 'subject to Indian cultural influence.' He not only visited the countries he read about but became invested in their future through the Pacific Relations Conference. In 1943, they were mostly under Japanese influence, and if they reverted to European control after the Japanese were expelled it would be 'detrimental to Indian independence.' He therefore worked 'for a post-war settlement which would free these countries from colonialism.' This conviction led to his book, *The Future of South East Asia*[142]

> The future of South East Asia could not be divorced from India and the security of countries like Burma, Siam and Malaya had to be linked with India if their independence was to be guaranteed against interference by other powers, ... if the Europeans tried to maintain their imperialist hold on these countries after the War it would lead to serious unrest, consequently these countries should be co-ordinated with India's. The history of post war events more or less confirms my thesis and I consider this somewhat gratifying.[143]

Notes

1 Sumit Sarkar in Introduction of Satadru Sen, *Benoy Kumar Sarkar: Restoring the Nation to the World*, Delhi: Routledge India, 2015.
2 Mr. Politician,Burma Yuddha, Rajnoitik Alochana, *Bharati*, 9(8), 1885, pp. 396–397.
3 Brajendranath Bandopadhyay, Brahmarajyer Swadhinata lop, Rajnoitik Alochona, *Bharati*, 9(10), 1885. p. 483.
4 Haricharan Mukhopadhyay, Brahme Engraj, *Bharati*, 9(12), 1885, pp. 578–585.
5 Ibid., pp. 581–582.
6 Ibid., pp. 583–585.
7 Ibid., p. 585.
8 N.R. Chakravarti, *The Indian Minority in Burma: The Rise and Decline of an Immigrant Community*, London: Oxford University Press, 1971, p. 2.
9 Brajendranath Bandopadhyay, Brahma Rajye Bishom Birambana, Rajnoitik Alochona, *Bharati*, 10(5–6), 1886, p. 367.
10 Anon., Chinaye Moroner Byabshay, 5(2), *Bharati*, 1881, pp. 93–100.
11 Ramlal Sarkar, Chindeshe Chandushebon, *Prabashi*, 4(5), 1904, pp. 272–277.
12 Anon., Chiner Samgramik Shakti, *Bharati*, 4(5), 1880, pp. 246–248.
13 Ramlal Sarkar, Chindeshe Swadeshi, *Prabashi*, 6(4), 1906, pp. 192–200.
14 Ramlal Sarkar, Chindeshe Swadeshi, op. cit., pp. 198–200.
15 Anon., Japan- Samraggi Dvay (the two empresses of Japan), *Bamabodhini Patrika*, 5(3) (363), p. 363.
16 Ibid., p. 364.
17 *Bharati*, 5(2), 1881, pp. 72–73.
18 *Bharati*, 5(3), 1881, pp. 122–133.
19 *Bharati*, vol. 4, 1880 and vol. 5, 1881.
20 Anon., Japan o Japani, *Bharati*, 20(4), 1896, pp. 214–225.
21 Tagore, *Nationalism*, op. cit., p. 17.
22 Taraknath Mukhopadhyay, Japaner Abhyudoy, *Nabyabharat*, (1–5), 24(1), 24(2), 24(4), 24(5), 24(7), 1906, pp. 11–27; 100–123; 169–179; 229–235; 344–358.
23 Taraknath Mukhopadhyay, Japaner Abhyudoy, *Nabyabharat*, 24(1), 1906, pp. 11–14.
24 Ibid.
25 Jamini Kanta Sen, Bharater Bohirrashtra Neeti (1–3), *Nabyabharat*, 25(7), 1907, pp. 337–351; 25(9), 1907, 497–504; 25(12), 1907, pp. 639–643.
26 Jamini Kanta Sen, Bharater Bohirrashtra Neeti (1), *Nabyabharat*, 25(7), 1907, pp. 342–343.
27 Ibid., p. 449.
28 Ibid., p. 344.
29 Ibid.
30 Ibid., pp. 347–348.
31 Ibid., pp. 448–449.
32 Ibid., p. 350.
33 Ibid., p. 503.
34 Kedarnath Bandopadhyay, Chiner Smriti, *Bharatvarsha*, 19(1)(6), 1931, pp. 957–960.
35 Akinchan Das, Japani Jatir Bishesotto, *Nabyabharat*, 33(10), 1915, pp. 627–628.
36 Ibid., pp. 629–630.
37 Panchugopal Mukhopadhay, Tarun Japan, *Bharatvarsha*, 20(1), 1932, pp. 157–158.
38 Panchugopal Mukhopadhay, Tarun Japan, *Bharatvarsha*, 20(1)(5), 1932, pp. 678–679.
39 Ibid., pp. 682–683.
40 Ibid.
41 Julius Moritzen, Current Trends in Japanese Literature, *Books Abroad*, 7(1), 1933, pp. 8–11. doi:10.2307/40073634 accessed on 06.08.19.
42 Panchugopal Mukhopadhay, Tarun Japan, *Bharatvarsha*, op. cit., p. 864.
43 Ramlal Sarkar, Chine Rashtrabiplab, *Prabashi*, 9 issues between 12(1)(2); 12 (2)(6), 1912. pp. 155, 289, 366, 491, 590/12, 259, 251, 364.
44 Sudhangshu Kumar Chowdhury, Chine Prajatantra, *Bharati*, 36(8), 1912, pp. 821–826.
45 Prafulla Chandra Roy, Navya Chin o Bangala, *Prabashi*, 29(2)(1), 1929, p. 81.
46 Ibid., pp. 83–84.

47 Ibid., pp. 90–91.
48 Kailash Nath Sinha, Hiuen Tsang er Bangla Bhraman, *Bharati*, 4(2), 1880; Ramlal Sarkar, Chine Dharma Charcha, *Prabashi* 7(12).
49 Prabhat Kumar Mukhopadhyay, Chine Bharatiya Sahitya, *Prabashi*, 25(2)(5), 1930; Prabhat Kumar Mukhopadhyay and Sudhamoyee Debi, Chine Hindu Sahitya, (Hindu Literature in China), *Bichitra*, 1&2, 1927–28 (details in Bibliography).
50 Editorial, Chine Moroner Byabshay, *Bharati*, 5(2), 1881, pp. 93–100.
51 Anonymous, Chin-Porachinporotar porinam, *Anjali*, 1(1), April 1989, pp. 40–42.
52 Ibid., p. 42.
53 Suniti Kumar Chattopadhyay, Chin o Bharat: Bharater Opor Prachin Chiner Prabhab (India and China: The Influence of Ancient China over India), Baridbaran Ghosh, ed., *Ogranthito Suniti Kumar* (Unpublished Suniti Kumar), Calcutta: Deep Prakashan, 2009, pp. 717–730.
54 Including an editorial in a children's magazine, Turashka o Mustafa Kemal Pasha, *Ramdhanu*, 1(11), 1927, pp. 560–567.
55 Hemendranath Dutta, Turashker Ramani, *Bharat Mahila*, 4(8), 1908, pp. 97–101 on status of Turkish women before the Republic and Monomohan Ghosh, Turk Shadharon Tantre Narir Mukti, *Bichitra*, 2(2)(5), 1928, pp. 722–732 on the freedom of women under the Turkish Republic.
56 Hemendra Prasad Ghosh, Turkir Joy, *Mashik Basumati*, 1(2) (1), 1922, p. 82. There were two others on Turkey by the same author, Turkeyr Kotha, *Mashik Basumati*, 1(2)(2), 1922, pp. 257–263, Turkir Punarabhyudoy o Bartoman Shamasya, *Mashik Basumati*, 1(2)(3), 1922, pp. 295–300.
57 Ibid., pp. 82–83.
58 Ibid.
59 Hemendra Prasad Ghosh, Turkir Joy, *Mashik Basumati*, 1(2)(2), 1922, pp. 262–263.
60 Georg W.F. Hegel, *The Philosophy of History*, Ontario: Batoche Books, 2001, p. 129.
61 Tony Ballantyne, *Orientalism and Race: Aryanism in British Empire*, New York: Palgrave Macmillan, 2002, pp. 33–35.
62 Capt C.J.F.S. Forbes, *Further India: A Fragment and Other Essays*, London: W.H. Allen & Co., 1881.
63 Samuel Augustus Mitchell, *Hindoostan and Farther India*, 1864, https://en.wikipedia.org/wiki/Greater_India#/media/File:1864_Mitchell_Map_of_India,_Tibet,_China_and_Southeast_Asia_-_Geographicus_-_India-mitchell-1864.jpg, accessed on 14.07.20.
64 Among others, Major Gen. Robert Ogden Tyler, *Memoirs and Journal of Two Months Travel in British and Farther India*, Philadelphia: J. B. Lippcott, 1878; Frank Vincent, *The Land of the White Elephant, Sights and Scenes in Southeast Asia, A Personal Narrative of Travel and Adventure in Farther India Embracing the Countries of Burma, Siam, Cambodia and Cochin China (1871–72)*, New York: Harper and Brothers, 1874; Major Gen A. Ruxton Macmahon, *Far Cathay and Farther India*, London: Hurst & Blackett, 1893 on the border politics between Burma and China; Samuel M. Zwemer and Arthur Judson Brown, *The Nearer and Farther East: Outline Studies of Moslem Lands and of Siam, Burma & Korea*, New York: The Macmillan Company, 1908.
65 Among others, Mary Lovina Cort, *The Heart of Farther India*, New York: Anson D.F. Randolph & Co., 1886 on her stay in Thailand (Siam) for two years; Katherine Neville Fleeson, *Laos Folk-Lore of Farther India*, New York: Fleming H. Revell & Co., 1899.
66 Susan Bayly, p. 706.
67 Ibid., p. 708.
68 Hari Vasudevan, Bhaskar Chakravarty, Lakshmi Subramanian, Bishnupriya Basak, and Suchandra Ghosh, India South East Asia Cultural Interactions: The Challenge of a Common "Heritage" Enterprise, *Report of the Indian Foreign Policy Studies Special Group*, Calcutta: Calcutta University Press, year not mentioned, pp. 3–4.
69 Swami Jagadishwarananda, Singhaler Kotha, *Mashik Basumati*, 12(1)(6), 1933, p. 972.
70 Ibid., p. 973.
71 Ibid., p. 975.
72 Ibid., p. 976.
73 Swami Jagadishwarananda, Singhaler Kotha, *Mashik Basumati*, 12(2)(3), 1933, p. 373.
74 Bijon Raj Chattopadhyay and Nihar Ranjan Roy, Javadvipe Bhatatiya Upanibesh, *Prabashi*, 27(1)(6), 1927, pp. 812–813.

75 Prabodh Chandra Bagchi, India and China, *Greater India Society Bulletin No. 2*, Calcutta, Jan–Feb. 1927, Foreword, p. 1.
76 P.C. Bagchi, ed., *Second City of the Empire*, Calcutta: Indian Science Congress Association Publishing, 1938.
77 Sarala Debi Chowdhurani, Rangoon, *Bharatvarsha*, 19(2)(4), 1931, pp. 610–611.
78 Biman Behari Majumdar, Bouddhya Dharma Prachare Bangali, *Manashi o Marmabani*, 16(1)(4), 1924, pp. 323–327.
79 Biman Behari Majumdar, *History of Indian Social and Political Ideas: From Rammohan to Dayananda*, Calcutta: Firma KLM Pvt Ltd., 1996 (1934).
80 Biman Behari Majumdar, Bouddhya Dharma Prachare Bangali, op. cit., pp. 323–325.
81 Ibid., p. 324.
82 Subimal Chandra Sarkar, Malayer Pathe, *Bangalakshmi*, 6(5), 1930, p. 355.
83 Not only in India and Asia, Shobharani Hui refers in a travelogue to factory workers in a small German town discussing *Ghare Baire* which had apparently sold more copies in translation there than in India, Germany Bhraman, *Prabashi*, 1938, 38(2)(6), p. 876.
84 Stephen N. Hay, *Asian Ideas of East and West: Tagore and His Critics in Japan, China and India*, Bombay: Oxford University Press, 1970, https://archive.org/details/asianideasof east00step/page/11/mode/1up, accessed on 21.02.20.
85 Ibid., p. 11.
86 Ibid.
87 Sugata Bose, *A Hundred Horizons: The Indian Ocean in the Age of Global Empire*, Delhi: Permanent Black, 2006.
88 Sugata Bose, Rabindranath Tagore and Asian Universalism, in *Tagore's Asian Voyages: Selected Speeches and Writings on Rabindranath Tagore*, Nalanda – Srivijaya Centre, Institute of Southeast Asian Studies, Singapore, 2011. http://research.gold.ac.uk/209 08/23/Rabindranath%20Tagore%20and%20Asian%20Universalism.pdf, accessed on 30.07.19.
89 Quoted in Sugata Bose, Rabindranath Tagore and Asian Universalism, op. cit., p. 10.
90 E.P. Thompson, Introduction to Rabindranath Tagore's *Nationalism*, Calcutta: Rupa Paperback, 1991 ed. (first published in 1917), p. 4.
91 Sugata Bose in *Tagore: The World Voyager*, translation of Rabindranath Tagore's songs, Delhi: Random House, 2013, p. 15.
92 Rabindranath Tagore, Japaner Kotha, *Sabuj Patra*, 4(1), 1917, p. 42.
93 Ibid., p. 43.
94 Ibid., pp. 45–46.
95 Rabindranath Tagore, *Nationalism*, Calcutta: Rupa and Co (paperbacks), 1991, p. 20.
96 *Anandabazar Patrika*, 7th June 1924, *Rabindra Prasanga: Anandabazar Patrika, 13th March 1922–21st March 1932*, vol. I, ed. Chittaranjan Bandopadhyay, Calcutta: Ananda Publishers, 1993, p. 499.
97 ABP, 11the June, 1924, *Rabindra Prasanga*, op. cit., p. 499.
98 ABP, 19th June, 1924, ibid., pp. 499–500.
99 ABP, 15th July 1924, ibid., p. 500.
100 ABP 15th July, 1927, *Rabindra Prasanga*, op. cit., pp. 521–522.
101 ABP, 13th January 1928, *Rabindra Prasanga*, op. cit., pp. 534–536.
102 ABP, 27th June 1927, *Rabindra Prasanga*, op. cit., p. 520.
103 ABP, 25th April 1929, *Rabindra Prasanga*, op. cit., pp. 542–543.
104 Ibid.
105 Amiya Kumar Chakraborty, Parashye Rabindranath, *Bharatvarsha*, 19(2)(6), 1932, pp. 983–986.
106 Ibid., pp. 985–986.
107 Kalidas Nag, *The Discovery of Asia*, Calcutta: The Institute of Asian African Relations, 1957, pp. 9–10.
108 Rabindranath Tagore, *Crisis in Civilization*, Calcutta: Visva Bharati, 2000 (1941), pp. 11–23.
109 *Ekdin jara merechhilo tare giye, rajar dohai diye, e juge tara jonmo niyechhe aji, mandire tara eshechhe bhakta shaji, ghatak shoinye daki, 'Maro' uthe hanki* ', Rabindranath Tagore, *Gitabitan*, Calcutta: Visva Bharati Publishing, 1985.

(Once those who assassinated Him, in the name of the king, have appeared again now, disguised as devotees in prayer; Turning to their soldiers, the killers scream 'Kill' in loud command) Translation mine.

110 Ibid., p. 162.
111 Suniti Kumar Chattopadhyay, *Dvipamoy Bharat*, Calcutta: Book Company Limited, 1940.
112 Suniti Kumar Chattopadhyay, Dvipamoy Bharat, *Prabashi*, vols. 29–31, 1929–31.
113 Sugata Bose, *A Hundred Horizons: The Indian Ocean in the Age of Global Empire*, Delhi: Permanent Black, 2006, pp. 246–247.
114 Suniti Kumar Chattopadhyay, Dvipamoy Bharat, *Prabashi*, 29(2)(3), 1929, pp. 388–389.
115 Ibid., p. 326.
116 Suniti Kumar Chattopadhyay, Dvipamoy Bharat, *Prabashi*, 29(2)(4), 1929, p. 578.
117 Ibid., p. 583.
118 Ibid., p. 585.
119 Ibid., p. 586.
120 Suniti Kumar Chattopadhyay, Dvipamoy Bharat, op. cit., *Prabashi*, 30(1)(2), 1930, p. 272.
121 Suniti Kumar Chattopadhyay, Dvipamoy Bharat, op. cit., *Prabashi*, 30(1)(4), 1930, p. 578.
122 Ibid., p. 579.
123 Suniti Kumar Chattopadhyay, Dvipamoy Bharat, op. cit., *Prabashi*, 30(1)(5), 1930, pp. 738–739.
124 Kalidas Nag, *Greater India (Greater India Society Bulletin No. 1)*, 1926, Calcutta: Scholar Select, p. 3.
125 Ibid., pp. 4–5.
126 Ibid., p. 10.
127 Ibid., p. 44.
128 Kalidas Nag, *Greater India*, op. cit., p. 20.
129 Kalidas Nag, Brihattara Bharat (Translated by Nihar Ranjan Ray), *Prabashi*, 26(2)(2), 1927, pp. 285–298.
130 Kalidas Nag, Sylvain Levi and the Science of Indology, *The Journal of the Greater India Society*, 3(1) 1936, pp. 3–13.
131 Ramananda Chattopadhyay, Mahattara Bharat, *Prabashi*, 25(1)(1), 1925, pp. 119–124.
132 Ibid., p. 119.
133 Ramananda Chattopadhyay, Mahattara Bharat, op. cit., p. 120.
134 Ramananda Chattopadhyay, Mahattara Bharat, op. cit., p. 121.
135 Ramananda Chattopadhyay, Mahattara Bharat, op. cit., pp. 123–124.
136 Kalidas Nag, *Greater India*, op. cit., p. 20.
137 Ibid., pp. 23–24.
138 Ramesh Chandra Majumdar, Prabasher Patra, *Bharatvarsha*, 19(1)(5), 1931, pp. 697–702.
139 Ibid., p. 703.
140 Ramesh Chandra Majumdar, *Jiboner Smritidipe*, Calcutta: General Printers and Publishers Pvt Ltd., 1978, pp. 63–69.
141 S.R. Sharma, *India as I See Her*, Agra: Agarwal Educational Publishers, 1956, pp. 137–138.
142 K.M. Panikkar, *The Future of South East Asia (An Indian View)*, New York: The Macmillan Company, 1943.
143 K.M. Panikkar, *An Autobiography*, transl from the Malayalam by K. Krishnamurthy, Madras: Oxford University Press, 1977, pp. 182–183.

8 United Asia

Hope and disillusion

'Asia Is Awakening ... the day of Asia's regeneration has come', George Sherwood Eddy (1871–1963) wrote in 1907. He was a leading American Protestant missionary, administrator, educator and traveller, who linked and financed networks of intellectuals across the globe, especially Christian leaders in Asia and the Middle East. He writes,

> Japan is already awake, China is rousing herself from the sleep of centuries, Korea is being reconstructed, the Philippines are being educated, Persia is in the throes of the birth pangs of liberty and Turkey's reconstruction will affect the Mahomeddan population of Asia. Even Thibet, the hermit nation is opening her doors for the first time in history; and India – with her great past and her yet greater future is awakening ... the vast continent of Asia is awakening....[1]

A maverick evangelist, closely associated with the YMCA movement in Asia for almost half a century, Eddy combined both cultural imperialism (leading to a verbal conflict with Swami Vivekananda on his voyage back from the Parliament of Religions) and a sensitivity to local ideas and movements[2]; Eddy's writings provide an outsider's view of the Asian consciousness and ideas of positivity circulating at the time. With the Swadeshi movement spreading its patriotic mantra throughout India and outside, intellectual outreach outside the territorial limits of the countries of Asia enriched the hope for a United Asia.

T.A. Keenleyside (1982) referred to this as being initiated by Japan and then becoming popular in all Asian lands, as a 'sense of solidarity to counter the omnipresent colonial manacles'.[3] Ashis Nandy, in an article in 1998, spoke about the idea of Asia emerging as an artefact of Asian reaction to Western colonialism.[4] In a recent anthology of Greater India articles, Prasenjit Duara, in the introduction to the volume, brings out the role of the journal *New Asia* in furthering Sun Yat Sen's idea of great Asianism in 1925 at the same time as the Greater India Society in Calcutta was bringing out the India–Asia linkages.[5] However, this consciousness was present among the other Asian intellectuals much before that time. Keshab Chandra Sen and Swami Vivekananda explored the power of Asian spirituality and intellectuals like Kakuzo Okakura (Ideals of the East in 1904) and Rabindranath Tagore (Nationalism in 1918) among others were committed to playing a role in leading Asia to a new and more just world while strengthening their own solidarity. Okakura identifying India as 'the holy land of our (the Japanese) sacred memories'[6] felt the need to call upon the peoples of all Asia to explore the 'secret energy' of thought, science, poetry and art of Asia, and then aim to protect and restore 'Asiatic

DOI: 10.4324/9781003243786-8

modes'.[7] Modern scholars like Birendra Prasad in 1979 (Indian Nationalism and Asia) explored this 'cult of Asianism'.[8] Prasenjit Duara in 2001 spoke of an 'alternative discourse of civilization' which was not western, and Sugata Bose (2006) in *A Hundred Horizons* argues, citing examples of sea voyages of Curzon, Tagore, Gandhi and other unknown merchants, labourers, soldiers and pilgrims, for an 'extra-territorial and universalist anti-colonialism that co-existed and contended with territorial nationalism'.[9]

One question that arose in this hope of uniting Asia is whether being united and being one was the same. When Okakura talked about 'Asia being One', he meant a cultural similarity as being most important for unification.[10] Benoy Kumar Sarkar, on the other hand, brought out this very disparity as being the reason why Asia could not be united. In his words: 'the word Asian unity is mere words in the contemporary period.' In the ancient period, though there was no unity of language, yet there was unity of literature, feeling, ideals, knowledge and science, arts, and rituals. In the modern period however, 'the *mool* (italics mine) mantra of all Asians come from outside Asia.' In literature, philosophy, science, and art, idealism and inspiration comes from Europe and America, which makes the idea of Asia being one, false. 'Asia is Many', according to Sarkar though Europe and America are really one because English language acts as the binding force.[11]

Hope of pan-Asianism among Asian intellectuals

In much of the writing, unity of Asia is a familiar theme, explored variously with varied motivations in a varied manner. A magazine coming out from Mymansingh district of Bengal, *Arati*, published in 1906 an article called the 'Rise of Asia',[12] in which the anonymous writer spoke about the excitement created in the Asian world with the victory of Japan over Russia but also spoke about the need for individual nations to build up their own strength with help and inspiration from the developed nations and strive to keep the signs of Asia's rise, intact. Everywhere there is restlessness against unrestricted state authority and an overwhelming urge to attain the citizen's natural rights and identities. Everywhere there is rise of national consciousness and faith in own power and strength among the nations of the East. There is a conscious demand in the Asian countries for establishment of modern rule and the Asian continent can no longer be considered to be the model of traditionalism.[13] The article, which the author acknowledges is an adaptation of an essay published in *Indian Review*, cites examples of China, Persia, Afghanistan and India to illustrate his point. He says that in the aftermath of the Russo-Japanese war China brushed aside centuries of lethargy and conservatism and started 'roaring like a tiger awakened from sleep'. A large number of Chinese have become keen to acquire education at the Japanese educational institutions, and on their return are demanding a popular, welfare oriented administrative system. Persia too like China is trying to become industrious and powerful in the Japanese mode. Along with Islamic education, Chemistry, Physics, History and Foreign languages are being taught there. The political powers of Afghanistan too have not been able to ignore these changes, and the Amir has set up an advisory committee of 42 headed by Sardar Nasirullah Khan, to formulate rules for governance in accordance with new hopes and new ideals[14] The author satirically points out that even though these three countries that have not received the benefits of English education nor read the works of Mill or Burke have still taken cognizance of the demands of their intellectuals and the new hopes and desires of the people. So why shouldn't India?

Another strange way of introducing the point of Asian solidarity was visible in an article in *Bharati* where the death of the Japanese Emperor Meiji apparently united the whole of Asia in grief. A similar sentiment can be identified through a different style when Jadunath Sarkar who was educated in Japan writes in 1912 that just as glass is able to reflect light from one direction to others, the Mikado was able to 'diffuse the light of western civilization not only within Japan but to the whole of Asia.' This illumination that Japan got has 'also enabled China to wake up from her deep slumber'. and has also reached India and Persia. The emperor Meiji whose passing he mourned, was in his words 'a noble soul under whose inspiration fallen Asia has been reborn'.[15]

A more widely known advocate of Asian unity, with his staunch anti-colonial, yet restrained nationalistic ideal of Asian cosmopolitanism, Rabindranath Tagore, emerged after winning international laurels in 1913, as the 'spokesperson of the East' and a 'symbol of spiritual wisdom of the east'.[16] *Anandabazar Patrika* reported that in Manila a reporter of a Chinese newspaper while covering the news of Tagore's travels in South-East Asia commented that 'where he goes, his white beard is the centre of Pan-Asianism'.[17] Kalidas Nag in a letter from aboard the *S.S. Ethiopia* in 1924, while accompanying Rabindranath Tagore to China, reflects that this invitation extended to the poet was a reminder of past connections. Just like the moonlight shining on the river Bhagirathi, India's life-flow flooded East Asia and nourished her for centuries in the past'. For a century, this life force had been ignored and now had been revived by the invitation extended to India's poet-saint by the most ancient country of Eastern Asia, China, during their time of historical crisis to hear from his mouth about the eternal values of India.[18] But more importantly, Nag discusses how a ship exhibits a cosmos in miniature and proves the possibility of Asians uniting: The ship which was carrying the World poet and others had many Chinese and Japanese passengers who were returning to their countries from the west and though majority spoke in German or French, there seemed to be a common language of the heart which made for easy friendship. 'This was' according to Nag, 'quite unlike the imperceptible yet all-pervading white-black colour barrier in west bound ships. Despite the presence of people of different races on board we never felt any racial distinctions among us.' He talks in colourful terms about the different people travelling, a Muslim merchant speaking chaste Urdu were travelling to Thailand on business, an Armenian family was travelling to Java and a Japanese Buddhist monk despite his world travels proudly proclaimed his Japanese smile and Japanese tongue on his way back to his country. 'It was as if all the people on board were linked by their Asianism which attracted all of us to each other and was a source of awe and happiness to me.'[19] Nag made the acquaintance of a middle-aged Chinese who had a business of war supplies and was engaged for the past 22 years with Sun Yat Sen's army in Canton. He had been in Europe, recuperating from an injury and was now returning to China. What that farsighted man told Nag was significant. He said that, having travelled the world, he had realised that the 'land from Suez Canal to the Pacific Ocean can be called one country' since despite differences, Asian people are one. This is because their soul force is the same and though there is disparity with the west there is a unity among Asians.[20] This Chinese soldier also said that the modern Chinese do not realise what they are losing with their new-found love for violence, which is destroying their traditional life force. From Rangoon via Penang, Kuala Lumpur and Singapore, Tagore and Nag then embarked on the Japanese ship *Atsuta Maru* on their way to China. There were many Japanese and Chinese passengers on board. The Japanese youths were mostly returning from Germany and they were polite and friendly towards Indians. But they were rather disparaging about the Chinese. One of the Japanese students said that, just like the English and the French, the Chinese and Japanese could never be united.[21] Nag wondered why despite long historical as well as religious, literary and artistic linkages between the two countries, they were so alienated from each other. Nag concludes, listening to all the different opinions, that 'the word Asia that we use in writing all the time, is really a fictitious creation, a philosophy, we have not yet comprehended it in its true colours and variations'.[22]

Despite the aim of Indian nationalist intellectuals who were aware of an Asian entity to reinterpret the idea, imported from the west towards a new notion of Asianness, it was 'the contention of Asia's spiritual wealth that would gild Asia's escutcheon anew'.[23] It was an attempt to raise the continent's self-esteem to Asia as well to Europe. India's image in East Asia and those countries which were as yet proudly uncolonised and un-westernised, was sullied by her supposed lack of opposition to western domination and the representation in the form of Indian diaspora in those countries. Jadunath Sarkar speaks of his encounter with Japanese conception of India while studying and working in Japan. Though India still commands respect as the land of Buddha's birth, it was not universal. When he visited a Buddhist temple along with some Japanese friends, they were treated with great respect and many elderly men and women in the temple said that meeting him was going one step closer to Heaven for them. Sarkar explained that it was actually an allusion to an old reference when India used to be referred by the Japanese as *Tenjiku* or Heaven and Indians as *Tenjikujin* or people living in Heaven. 'Things changed after the Japanese victory in the Russo-Japanese war', Sarkar wrote, 'Japanese no longer venerate India as Heaven and she is now slightingly referred to as Indo. Before, when I walked in the streets of Japan, people would politely call me Indo San but soon I became only Indo'. Sarkar believes that knowledge about the troubles in India started coming in during the Swadeshi movement and this knowledge destroyed the old 'mystery' that surrounded India. It was tragic for Sarkar that 'even ten-year old Japanese girls know about the degraded condition of India ... and the Japanese consider themselves so superior that they have started referring to Indians as "negroes"'.[24]

Buddhist linkages in Asia were often probed in the journals as a means of considering a long-lasting unity. Many, including Rabindranath Tagore, considered the study and practice of Buddhism in Japan important in providing mental strength to the race and worth emulating. Prabodh Chandra Bagchi in *The Cosmopolitan* in 1926 describes the study of Buddhism in Japan as being impartial, comprehensive and of the highest quality, pursued in nine universities where out of 10 journals and 30 monthly magazines of the different Buddhist sects, only a few are in English like *Young East* and *East Buddhist*, the rest are in Japanese.[25] An allegorical story by Nripendra Krishna Chattopadhyay speaks of how the faith of non-violence preached by Buddha reached into the heart of the most violent blood thirsty Japanese hunter through the sacrifice of his flower-like two daughters who inspired by Buddha's teachings wanted to save their father and make him realise his wrongdoing.[26] Phanindra Nath Bose in an article in *Prabashi* traces the linkages that Buddhism has created in Asia through translation and re-translation of Buddhist texts. 'Buddhism connected Indians, Chinese, Tibetans, Mongolians, Koreans and Japanese in a single bond'.[27] Ramesh Chandra

Majumdar too in *Prabashi* draws similar linkages through descriptions of travels of Chinese Buddhist pilgrims. He writes that, in those days the journey between India and China was not easy. Overcoming a lot of constraints and difficulties twenty five committed pilgrims managed to reach their destination and the rest succumbed to the hazards of the travel. That these men ignored physical discomfort in the burning desire for spiritual knowledge makes it important for posterity to honour the memories of these intrepid travellers. 'Unlike Fa-Hien, Hiuen Tsang, and I-Tsing some of them did not gain fame, but their efforts are memorable nonetheless.[28] In this context, he discusses the lives and contributions of Prakashmati (Yuen chao), Sri Dev (Tou Hi), Chang Min, Mahayan Pradip (Tang Cheng Teng), Sanghavarma, Tang Kwang, Song chi, and Pragyadev (U Hing), among others.

An Asian nation's triumph symbolised the end of western hegemony as well as Asia's awakening. Thanks to its new status, Japan became a major source of inspiration for Indian nationalists. In 1885, Jatindranath Mitra writing in the years following the First World War analyses the Japanese rise saying that when the East was rendered hopeless and despondent, Japan rose on the horizon and challenged Russia and defeated her in her own weapons. Thus the theory that was propounded by the European scientists that the weak East exists to serve the stronger brother West had fallen through. What has been proved instead is that with equal facilities and environment, superiority of one nation over others vanishes.[29]

Showing solidarity for Asians during the movement around the Immigration Act of 1924, including the Asian Exclusion Act in the United States, an article called 'Asia's Distress in America' by Sarat Mukherjee in *Bangabani* pointed out that no western country has been sympathetic towards the Asians. 'The Westerners do not want that the Easterners come to their lands and establish a majority which would undermine their superiority'.[30] The reason for this hatred according to Mukherjee is that the Asians prefer to retain their inherited traditions and practices even when they make the west their home. He cites the example of the Japanese in California where they form a majority in the population compared to the local Americans. Since the Japanese school students use their mother tongue for all subjects, the American schools have been forced to appoint Japanese teachers, thus transforming the schools into veritable Japanese institutions. This was offensive to the Americans. Mukherjee says the case of the Chinese and Hindus there was the same, though he is rather scathing of Indian immigrants into the western countries saying that they do not adapt well and maintain their dirty and unhealthy habits. The Japanese and Chinese are better workers than Indians, willing to and able to work better with lesser pay than Americans which again makes the latter wary. Indians, in Mukherjee's view, only excite disgust since they live in squalid conditions and are not able to work as hard as others. Mukherjee ends with the plea that it is high time that the American fear of joint action by Asians be made true. It was feared that Japan may excite 50 crores Chinese and 30 crores Indians to action. It is true that if Japan ever succeeds in doing so their power will be greatly enhanced. But it is doubtful if that will ever be possible. India has not been able to unite her people and China too has not been able to rise above its internal conflicts. Mukherjee thought that though the whites may unite against Asians, the latter will not be able to forget their own differences. Only subjection is the unifying force which may bring unity.[31]

The one thing that emerged in this period was the notion that Japan had earned the right to mentor Asia and Japanese example needed to be followed by other Asian nations. But the question that often arose was how! What was the secret formula which enabled them to negotiate the delicate line between adopting western modernity yet keeping their own identity and tradition intact. In a previous work,[32] I have assessed how Japan was visualised in non-academic writings of travellers and analysts who discussed her rise to super-power-hood. But doubts appeared when Japan used her power as an aggressor against the east rather than a facilitator of a pan-Asian solidarity which was reflected in some of the writing. What there was no doubt about was the quest for finding the sources of strength within Japanese character and tradition and why Japan abused her moral leadership over Asia. Rabindranath Tagore's initial euphoria and his later indictment of Japanese aggression were important markers for the others who wavered between admiration for Japan and sorrowful commiseration for Korea and China – the victims of Japan's aggression in the second and third decades of the 20th century.

Analysis of Japan's success was initiated by the western scholars who were horrified and amazed at its meteoric rise and these writings were undoubtedly read by Indians. What is interesting is that only a select few are translated for their readers and this selection process is interesting. Jyotirindranath Tagore's translation of the writing of the French writer Felicien Challaye[33] and Lafcadio Hearn's ideas via Challaye's writings[34] were published in *Bharati* in 1908, within three years of the publication of the book *Le Japan Moderne*, which was an interesting deviation from the other translations. I juxtapose these writings with Rabindranath Tagore's ideas in *Japan Jatri* or *A Traveller to Japan*,[35] first published in *Sabuj Patra* in 1925–1926 and later compiled in a book, where he traces Japan's success to certain inalienable values and tries to resolve the dichotomy between his early admiration and later disappointment. Even earlier in 1881, one notices in *Bharati* an article written without mentioning authorship (may well have been the work of Jyotirindranath or his sister Swarnakumari Debi, who was the editor then), on the historical analysis of Japan's rise to a modern nation, with Meiji Restoration as the catalyst of change for modernity. Changes in administrative system, army, innovations in the legal system, etc. were discussed to show how they ushered in a new ability and a new desire to 'deal' with the west.[36] This article is different from the translations in the sense that it contains far more independent input. There are small asides in the narrative that bring in the eastern solidarity. For example, while discussing the army, the writer says that few among the Japanese can equal the English sailors in physical strength. They are smaller in build and get tired easily when handling the cannons. That is why they need to be replaced more frequently than the English sailors. Despite all that, their courage and enthusiasm for war is in no way inferior to that of the Europeans.[37]

The choice of the writings in French by Challaye for translation by Jyotirindranath Tagore is interesting since the travelogue and essay are written by a westerner but with a non-western outlook. Challaye's reasons for writing the book as translated by Tagore was to show what the prevalent view of Japan's assimilation of western ideas was. Some Japanese intellectuals believed in the idea of western civilizational superiority, so they embarked on a process of adoption of western ideas. However, modern Japan is a combination of traditional practices and modern western adaptations. This creates inadvertent incongruences because of which Europeans in their arrogance, call modern Japan as 'Europe's copy, but not a good one'. Challaye on the other hand realized that Japanese were self conscious about their difference with westerners so they only reveal their outward changes 'in case they are considered to be primitive'.

To understand the real Japan one must adopt a different approach strategy which was to study Japan through the Japanese way.[38] Application of this strategy to write about Japan meant that it was not only a descriptive format but choosing to describe everything he finds strange to western eyes, as 'belonging to Japanese culture, way of life and eastern values'. For example, when he describes the Japanese houses made of wood and paper, he points out that they are uniform and differences in status and wealth are much less evident here than in the west. Every individual has the duty to not distinguish themselves from others but to maintain uniformity. All Japanese respect this ideal which is inspired by Buddhism. Besides, for them, aesthetics of simplicity are of greater importance than any display of ostentatious and conspicuous living. When Challaye returned to the west after absorbing the beauty of the Japanese home, they realize how much of the Japanese ideas and ideals have seeped in unconsciously. The large European style house seem like ugly barracks or jails.[39] This aesthetics of simplicity is also discussed by other Indian writers in the journals, as being unique even by Asian standards. Challaye says that the Japanese values which are passed on to the younger generation at home and in school are 'the religion of nationalism, homage to the Mikado, worship of ancestors, respect for parents or grandparents, selflessness, and loyalty, maintaining a smiling and poised countenance, courage and dedication and love for nature'[40] He also discussed their virtues of 'cleanliness, decency and good nature, which are very ancient national virtues, expressed through their customs and behaviour'.[41] The writer also distinguishes 'eastern' politeness as far more egalitarian, despite Japan being a hierarchical society compared to that of a western democracy. It was the genuineness rather than formality in politeness that the writer refers to – the warmth shown at the end of every business transaction, exchange of small gifts even after a lunch in a restaurant or a purchase in a shop or in the deep respect and affection they show to their elders. Tagore quotes Challaye as saying that Japanese politeness sometimes takes the form of a spiritual self discipline and self control when they avert giving pain to others by revealing their injury or pain openly. There is great courage in this self discipline, that is expressed when they smile through their pain and grief, even when talking of death of their loved ones. The source of this spiritual equanimity lay in their faith in patriotism, love for nature and sensitivity to humour, charity and tolerance, according to Tagore.[42] In conclusion he writes, It is evident that the Japanese have retained in modern Japan, those aspects of their ancient civilization that they consider important, significant and close to their heart. The daily habits, home, furniture, food, clothing, emotions, values, conventions, amusements, art and culture and religion – all that which is connected to the personal life of the modern Japanese has been retained according to their past practices. The heart of European civilization does not attract them in the least. In their eyes European culture is far inferior to theirs – it is unsophisticated and non-spiritual and not worthy of emulation.[43] The secret of Japan's success being Japan's own values rather than western comes from his narrative on the life and thoughts of Lafcardio Hearn, who 'brought about the unity of the highest values of European civilization with those of the Japanese to create a blending of the two for an ideal world civilization'.[44] Hearn also identifies certain distinctive qualities in Japanese life and belief, which has led them to success. There is an ever-changing quality in the Japanese way of life which Hearn finds from Japanese nature – the seasons, flowers and fruits change and even mountains and rivers seem to change due to their volcanic nature. The Buddhist saying that the world is restless and changing seems to be a part of the Japanese belief as well. They consider this life as only a temporary resting place in the eternal journey. The simple way of life they prefer is connected to their love of freedom and this simplicity is the cornerstone of their success story. In Hearn's view, 'the Easterners are more controlled than us, more tolerant and more productive. They will possibly upstage us in the battle of life'.[45]

Another Tagore, Rabindranath, wrote in 1932 that

> life in Asia has become restless and self-assertive. The reason is, in spite of the unremitting pressure of Europe she has completely lost her true hold upon Asia's mind. Once, exploited and beaten Asia acknowledged Europe as in every way superior to herself. Today from one end to the other of Asia there is no longer any feeling of respect for Europe, and even fear in their mutual dealings is fast losing its force.[46]

In his view, this loss of respect for the west had revived the old unity in Asia. He recalled a mythical era when 'the whole of eastern Asia from Burma to Japan was united with India in the closest tie of friendship, the only natural tie which can exist between nations'. Asia was then organically united: 'There was a living communication of hearts, a nervous system evolved through which messages ran between us about the deepest needs of humanity'. Asia's mythical past was opposed in every way to the European political system that was founded on nation states geared to compete with each other. Tagore's ideal was to revive this Asia, united in its burgeoning cultures and spiritual traditions. Wearing the halo of the first Asian recipient of the Nobel Prize, the poet had from the second decade set to work on his pan-Asianist ideals, by travelling extensively in the continent, reinforcing friendly relations between India, China, South-East Asian countries and Japan. His trip to China culminated in the creation of an Asian association in Shanghai, the first concrete success of his ideal of a united Asian culture. A few years later, he established Santiniketan, a university for higher studies on Asia. In 1916, a special correspondent of *Manchester Guardian* wrote that Rabindranath Tagore was in Tokyo where he was very cordially received which 'has a significance more than literary and more than personal, for it is one of the may indications of the growing intimacy between Japan and India and of the evolution of a new Asia awakening to a consciousness of unity'.[47]

Rabindranath felt the need to apply an 'eastern outlook' to analyse the qualities of the Japanese, though he does not believe that these values are only applicable to Asians. He talks about universal human ideals which must be perfected by maintaining the distinctiveness of each country but accepting the truth that there are great qualities in all.[48] But the 'eastern outlook' is distinct because 'in the East, we are conscious through all individual things of the infinity which embraces them'.[49] *Japan Jatri* is written by Rabindranath in the form of a diary when he travels to Japan in 1916. Even before his arrival at Kobe, on board the *Tosamaru*, Rabindranath started his analysis of reasons of Japanese success. He writes that 'the eastern mind of the Japanese has received training for active work from the westerners but has retained the executive control. This gives me hope that Japan will be able to combine western action with eastern feeling'.[50] He expresses this binary through describing Japanese men and women. Japanese men have become transformed into office-goers in western clothes. They no longer have their own identity but have joined the 'office of the world which is same everywhere', while their women maintain their Japanese identity through their clothing, despite the fact that they are visible outside their homes.

> They alone comprise the Japanese home, the Japanese nation and do not belong to the office. I have heard from some that Japanese women do not get respect from men here. I do not know if it is true but there is a respect that is inalienable, it comes from within. The women here in Japanese dress have undertaken to preserve Japan's self-respect.[51]

Rabindranath compares the Bengalis with Japanese as the only Indians who have the malleability of mind to embrace the new because of 'mixed racial blood in the Bengali veins and because the geographical position of Bengal has separated her from the Indian mainland'.[52]

Rabindranath considers the quality of calm, tranquillity that he finds typical of the Japanese their source of strength.

> There are crowds on the streets but no noise. It is as if the people here do not know how to shout and even children in Japan do not cry . . . They do not fritter away their life-strength in useless and loud fracas. This peacefulness and tolerance of mind and body is a part of their national endeavour. They are self-controlled in sadness and grief, pain and excitement. Most foreigners find the Japanese inscrutable.[53]

Rabindranath also sees this restraint in their literature and culture. The ability to convey ideas and emotions through minimum expression indicates an immense capability of imagination, ability to understand through a series of pictures expressed in a few words, eliminating the need for superlative emotional expression which characterises Indian poetry and songs. He writes that the Japanese poetry show pictures, they do not sing. The restraint and tranquillity in expression and emotion is not unbalanced by the heart's boisterous unrest. 'I think that Japan has a deep identity which is thrift or austerity.[54] Even in the tea ceremony, Rabindranath noticed the same introspection. It is evident that the aesthetic sense of the Japanese is a source of great strength and worship. Ostentatious luxury only expends resource and weakens but pure aesthetics preserves a mind from the material demands. That is why within the Japanese mind one can see a unity of vigour and sense of beauty.[55]

For Tagore, the takeaway from Japan was not the modern western qualities of 'their factories, their industriousness, their wealth and their power' but 'the creative human strength' which is revealed below 'the disguise of modernity'. 'It is not pride, power or ostentation, it is worship.' Power desires to flaunt itself so tries to create imposing structures which will make all cower before it but worship respects the greatness beyond self, so its creation is beautiful and pure, not merely large and numerous.[56] In his address to the Indian community in Japan, he says that by identifying these 'characteristic truths in the Japanese race', he wanted to create an impact on their minds and souls[57] and while addressing students there, he claimed that his knowledge would help Asiatics to gain their 'rights of sovereignty in a higher world than theirs, – in the spiritual world'.[58]

The opposition that Rabindranath Tagore faced from some Japanese students created an outrage among his admirers in Calcutta but Tagore rising above the sycophancy of his supporters said at a lecture at the Calcutta University Institute that, instead of humiliation, he felt happiness in Japan because he 'found a ray of hope and a way forward'. India should not be side-tracked by unimportant things and her 'sole aim should be to proclaim the faith of Asia in the language of Asia since that is superior to the power of the state or economy'.[59] In Tagore's view, the whole of Eastern Asia 'from Burma to Japan was united with India in the closest tie of friendship, the only natural tie which can exist between nations. There was a living communication of hearts'. Japan had succeeded in fulfilling Asian destiny by 'coming out first in the East'. Now she must provide Asia with the 'hidden fire which is needed for all works of creation' which will ultimately 'illuminate the whole world'.[60]

Tagore earned the reputation of an ambassador of universalism despite his vigorous anti-colonial stance and through his travelling in Asia, the connections were explored more than ever in modern times. U Tuk Kyi, a Burmese MLA who presided over a reception given to the poet during his visit in 1924 there said, 'We greet you in the name of that universal culture which you have promoted with admirable devotion and singleness of aim . . . We greet you as representing the rebirth of Asia'.[61] Tagore considered his visits to these Asian countries as part of a pilgrimage to understand the 'eastern spirit and values' which could provide a universalist and humanist touch to nationalism, thereby cleansing it of excessive aggression which he considered as harmful as western imperialism. Already in his previous visit to Burma in 1916, he visited Rangoon as a guest of barrister P.C. Sen and celebrated his 56th birthday by a visit to the Shwe Dagon pagoda where he felt that 'unlike the commercial capital Rangoon which had no real Burmese flavour, the pagoda revealed the real Burmese self'.[62]

On his visit in Bali in 1924, Rabindranath expressed effusively his pleasure at finding cultural similarities between India and Bali during the *jatra*/drama performance which he attended during the funeral ceremony at the home of Hida Anake Agoeng Bagoess Djelantik, the landlord of Karangasem. That it was reciprocated by some at least in that country was proved when the local king of Karangasem was thrilled to have the company of the poet on that important occasion and in the words of Sunitikumar Chattopadhyay who documented the poet's visit there: 'in order to demonstrate the age old closeness between Bali and India the raja recited some Sanskrit *slokas* and some random geographical and mythological names'. Chattopadhyay found this amusing since for the major part of the journey from the ceremony place to the raja's home where the poet was being escorted to had been spent in silence since the two did not know each other's own language and the state languages were different in India (English) and Bali (Dutch). Again when the poet was about to enter the home of the local king, the traditional link between India and Bali was highlighted by some Brahmin priests who gave a performance of reciting Sanskrit *slokas* in musical notes as welcome to the honoured guest.[63]

Pan-Asian Associations and Asian Federation (within and outside Asia)

Pan-Asiatic forums and conventions were from the beginning of the century considered important in intellectual exchanges, which were deemed important for further growth by citizens and rulers alike. The claim for the first ever international convention in Asia was held by the Convention of the World's Student Christian Federation, held in Tokyo in 1907 where 500 delegates representing 25 countries attended. As an outcome of the convention, a book on Japan and India was written by G.S. Eddy who was a part of the delegation from India. He writes that receptions were given to the Conference by Count Okuma, Baron Goto, Viscount Hayashi, the minister of Foreign Affairs and by the leading citizens of Tokyo and the Mayor. The delegates from India, after visiting the principal cities of Japan, went up into the beautiful mountains at Nikko, and saw snowfall for the first time in their lives. 'Many were the lessons learnt and many are the memories of gratitude for the great hospitality of the Japanese and the splendid receptions given to the delegates from all parts of Asia and Europe'.[64] The intellectual effervescence around the idea of Asia soon gave rise to a grand design of political mobilisation at continental level. During the 1920s, progressive leaders of the Indian National Congress participated in various pan-Asian conferences: Baku Conference in 1920, the first pan-Asian Conference at Nagasaki in 1926 and the pan-Asian Conference at Shanghai. The Congress of Oppressed Nations held in Brussels in 1927 assumed special importance. This assembly aimed at consolidating various liberation movements and struggles against imperialism. The first direct contact between Asian nationalist militants was established and Nehru felt that most Asian countries evinced a strong desire for closer ties. In the 1930s, nationalists of the Indian Congress took the initiative to organise various pan-Asian summits, such as the Asian Conference on Education at Benaras in December 1930, the Asian Conference on Women in Lahore in January 1931 and the pan-Asian Labour Conference in Colombo in May 1934. At the same time, Nehru took unofficial diplomatic trips to Myanmar and Malaysia in 1937 and to Sri Lanka and China in 1939. Nehru's visit to Beijing forged the Indian ideal of close cooperation with China against the Japanese aggressor. India's sympathy for China had, in fact, strengthened with the increasing disappointment with Japan's expansionism. Japan's attack on Korea in 1910–1911 and the 21 ultimatums delivered to China altered to a great extent the admiration for Japan prevailing among a section of the Indian intelligentsia. The archipelago, which till 1920 was a role model in the eyes of a section of Indian nationalists, was accused of having succumbed to imperialist temptations imbibed from the west.

Soon after the First World War, the ideal of Asian solidarity evolved into plans of regional integration. The idea of an Asian Federation then became very much in vogue among the Indian intelligentsia. In 1928, the Congress got ready to organise the first session of the Pan-Asian Federation to be held in 1930. K.M. Pannikar, who in 1926 had made Paris his headquarters as a journalist writing in renowned journals like *Europe, Europe Nouvella* and *Literaire*, referring to it as the 'most cosmopolitan' capital in the world, refers to a number of joint efforts by political exiles there for fighting for freedom in their countries. He joined the Hindustan Samaj there, which under the secretaryship of Prabodh Chandra Bagchi welcomed him to 'learn something about the freedom movements of far eastern countries like Indo-China and Java'.[65] He became close friends with the leader of the Indo-Chinese Freedom Party, Duong van Giao and Mono Nutu of Java. In his words: 'We took to each other like brothers from the first. We used to meet daily and discuss political subjects, specially the future of Asia and what could be done immediately to better it'. Possibly desiring to strengthen intra-Asian connections, Gio responded to an 'invitation from Jawaharlal Nehru (to attend) ... the Calcutta Congress in 1928. Later he took part in the liberation movement of Indo-China and was imprisoned several times'.[66] However, the Civil Disobedience Movement launched by the Congress made it impossible to organise such a conference. Nevertheless, the enthusiasm of Indian nationalists for an idea of an Asian Federation did not die down, more so as it fitted in logically with the liberation of the nations of the continent. Indeed, it was felt that if the Asian countries stood united, independence would come faster. However, the concept of an Asian federation fluctuated greatly. In August 1940, Nehru invoked a potential Eastern Federation, bringing together China, India, Myanmar, Sri Lanka and Afghanistan. A few months later he enlarged this regional plan to include Nepal, Thailand, Malaysia and China, as well as any interested Asian nations. Whatever the scenario, the Federation was not to be seen as a block or an alliance based on any logic of alignment. Nehru, who remained faithful to the thinking of Tagore and Vivekananda, conceived this plan as a cause of renaissance of the spirit of Asian civilisation. The Asian federation, in its substance, was the expression of an ideal model of international relations.[67]

Asian ties were most expediently expressed through the associations set up outside Asia through which how Asian nationalism could be fostered were discussed using the various tools and strategies suggested by nationalists of different Asian countries. Panikkar not only refers to the Hindustan Samaj in Paris which was the haunt of all Asians visiting or studying there but also writes about the Oriental Society he helped to set up. Besides Duong Van Giao of Vietnam and Mono Nutu, a Communist leader of Java, Prion Mantri of Siam (Thailand) and Chin of Kuomintang Party from China, and Ali Bey of Azerbaijan were his friends and associates of Oriental Society. Chin was Oriental Society's President, Panikkar was its Vice-President and Duong its Secretary. Nearly thirty people from Indo-China and Java belonged to this Society. Their object was to correct the false propaganda often appearing in European newspapers about the countries of the East and to represent the countries in the various European conferences. Some of them used to gather every evening in the Domago coffee house and exchange news from the far east. Chin used to talk about China; Mono Nutu about Java; while Duong was abreast of developments in most countries. It was at one of these discussions that Panikkar met Mohammed Hatta who later became a leader of the freedom struggle in Java[68] These discussions reflected not only a need to know about other Asian countries, their condition and politics but also to create a positive image in the world's eyes regarding these nationalist movements. He refers to a World Peace Conference that he attended in 1926, as an Indian delegate, since it was essential for them to go there and speak about the politics of the Orient. A body of representatives from each Asian country was elected. Pannikkar as the leader of the delegation, in consultation with Duong, prepared a paper for circulation at the Conference on the need for a proclamation of independence by Asian countries. The paper though drafted by him bore the signatures of the entire delegation. They argued that the British rule in India was responsible for mortgaging the freedom of Asia and as long as Britain's empire in Asia continued, world peace would be in danger and the freedom of other Asian countries thus depended on India's own independence. Panikkar wrote that, no one in those days appreciated the international significance of the Indian claim to independence. Only when a group of advocates for freedom from several Asian countries seized on this point did the major newspapers of Europe realise that the Indian claim had important implications elsewhere.[69]

K.P.S. Menon talks about a similar association in Oxford, the Oxford Majlis, which he calls a 'forum for letting off steam', which produced a number of revolutionaries and where they 'made vehement speeches which we thought patriotic and which the British thought seditious'. During his term as President of the Majlis, Rabindranath Tagore visited Oxford. 'With his long beard, flowing robes and silvery voice, he looked like a being from another planet'.[70] M.C. Chagla, was also President of the Oxford Majlis and invited guests like Bertrand Russell after his China visit and Sarojini Naidu to speak there.[71] A bilateral association between India and Japan has been referred to by Benoy Kumar Sarkar, which he came across during his visit to Japan in 1915. This

Indo-Japanese Association had many prominent members of the Japanese society and was mainly concerned with promotion of Japanese trade with India. According to Sarkar, the father of modern Japan Count Okuma was the President of the Association. Since, India had no position in the world except as a part of the British empire, the Japanese discussed with the British any India related issue. The offensive and defensive alliance that the Japanese made with the British made it liable for them to provide all kinds of help to the British if there was any offensive on India by a foreign power. Also, if Britain announced war against any Asian power then Japan would follow suit. It was on these grounds that when Britain declared war on Germany, Japan attacked the German protectorate of China. The Objectives of the Association were 'to promote intimate relations between Japan and Indian countries (British India, Netherlands India, Strait Settlements, Siam, French Indo China etc.).' The work of the Association were (1) To study commercial, industrial, scientific and religious topics relating to the above-mentioned countries. (2) to afford facilities for traffic and communication between the respective countries, and for the investigation and study of things Indian and Japanese. Experts on Buddhist literature, Dr Buniu Nanniyo, Professor Takakusu and Professor Anesaki were all members of this Association[72] Sarkar argues that in the years following the defeat of Russia by Japan, though Indians were impressed by the rise of Japanese power, they did not feel close to them. With the shift of the balance of power during the beginning of the war, and the closure of import of German and Austrian commerce which had a beneficial impact on the Swadeshi enterprise in India, Japan found a golden opportunity. As he wrote:

> What Japan was finding difficult to achieve on their own was made possible by the world war . . . while the Europeans were killing each other in the war, Japan was able to build up an industrial and commercial empire in Asia. I notice in 1915, a new interest in Japan regarding India.[73]

Kshitish Chandra Bandopadhyay says that while he was in Japan, Manila was declared to be a Commonwealth by America with the promise of full independence in ten years. 'Many of us Indians met and celebrated the occasion and we even sent our heart-felt congratulations to Dr. Manuel L.Quezon, the first elected President'.[74]

Kalidas Nag spoke about an Asian Congress which was organised in Baku in 1920 by the newly established Soviet Government. 'A big university of Oriental Studies' was also set up in 'Moscow, where many promising scholars from India and other countries of Asia have been working'.[75] Sunitikumar Chattopadhyay in 1939 refers to the four-day annual conference of Indian and Sinhalese Students Association at Berlin.' Rabindranath Tagore's former secretary Amiya Chakraborty came from Oxford to preside over the Conference. The Asian students, though few in number were offered hospitality by local Berliners at the Dom hotel. The Nazi government of Germany extended cooperation for the Conference which was attended on the first day by foreign students at Berlin university and some Indian sympathizers among the Germans. Sudhir Sen, pursuing higher studies in economic theory presented his paper in German for the comprehension of the German students present. Amiya Chakraborty presented an address on internationalism and unity among races. On behalf of the university and the Germans, a young student in uniform spoke welcomed the Asian students and spoke about Nazi ideals. The support that the German government extended to the Asian students was unprecedented especially by British standards[76]

While discussing the historical background to the Bandung Conference, Roeslan Abdulgani refers to its prehistory in and outside Indonesia, namely the Bierville Conference of 1926, Brussels Conference of 1927 and the writings of Bung Karno. In France, Indonesian students like Bung Hattam Nazir Pamontjak, Achmad Subardjo, Arnold Mononutu, Gatot Tarumihardja and Abdul Manaf were active in developing a spirit of solidarity of Asia and Africa and in Bierville Congress in 1926, Bung Hatta as the leader of the Indonesian delegation, together with the young Duong Van Giao from Annam (Indo China), the young Toptchybachy from Azerbaijan (Soviet Asia), the young Tung Meau from China and the young K.M. Panikkar from India issued the 'Joint Manifesto' which, inter alia, called upon Europe to 'Liberate the spirit of Asia and you will have peace, not a peace imposed by the sword, but a peace based on good will. The spirit of Asia is essentially pacific'. The same spirit and attitude were also borne by the young men of Indonesia under Bung Hatta's leadership to Brussels. At that Congress, an international organisation called the 'League against Imperialism, against Colonial Oppression and for National Independence' was being formed. Besides Hatta, Jawaharlal Nehru of India, Liau representing China, Hafiz Rahman Bey from Egypt and Senghor from Senegal were also present. In the words of Abdulghani:

> they were all in the grip of the same impassioned spirit and they all spoke with the same reverberating voice. That is, the spirit and the voice of their peoples, who were colonised, oppressed, humiliated . . . but . . . not only the groans to which they gave voice, they also aroused the spirit of nationalism and patriotism.[77]

In this context, Abdulghani also refers to Bung Karno's article, 'Indonesianism and Pan-Asianism' where he spoke of the importance of the consciousness of solidarity among the nations of Asia who were fighting for independence. He specifically stressed the importance of the struggles of Sun Yat Sen in China (1911), Kemal Ataturk in Turkey (1912), Mahatma Gandhi in India (1919) and Zagul Pasha in Egypt (1924). According to Abdulghani, Bung Karno was convinced that the spirit of Pan Asianism was 'sure to be able to live and arise' in the spirit of Indonesian nationalism because according to him 'there was unity of lot'. And this unity of lot was sure to 'create unity of attitude and unity of feeling'.[78] After his release from prison in 1931, Karno's eloquence in public meetings was expressed in the following words:

> 'when the Liong-Sai Dragon of China works together with the Nandi cow of India, with the Sphinx of Egypt and Peacock of Burma, with the White Elephant of Siam, with the Hydra of Vietnam, with the Tiger of Philippines and with the Bantera Bull of Indonesia, then it is certain that international colonialism will be smashed to bits.[79]

Role of women in Asian unity

A change in the mindset of Indians was taking place with greater interaction with the outside world. This clarity of vision was more visible among those who settled even for a short period outside the home country. Kedarnath Bandopadhyay wrote in *Bharati* in 1903 that the reason why some countries were more advanced than others was because in those countries women had a significant role in the life of the people:

in the workplace, duty and grace; in courage and destruction; in wealth and beauty; proficient in education, art or literature. They are not mere helpmates of men, but *samakakkha sahakari* co-workers at par'.[80]

The All Asian Women's Conference which was held in 1931 was an important landmark in Asian connectivity and unity for women. A recent research on the Conference by Sumita Mukherjee (2017)[81] describes it as 'pan Asian feminist organisation' under the 'leadership' of Indian women. One year before it was held in 1930, Sita Debi in *Bangalakshmi* discusses the importance of the Conference for Asian women in general and Indian women in particular. She speaks about a notice from the Convenors of All Asian Women's Conference to be held the next year (1931) which was printed in an issue of *Bangalakshmi* along with an 'excellent reply to the invitation by the Persian national women's organisation'. (Presumably, Patriotic Women's Association was established by Eskandari.) This notice was a circular invitation to the All Asia Women's Conference which was issued by Indian women suggesting dates in January signed by 14 Indian women, including Sarojini Naidu, Muthulakshmi Reddi, Rajkumari Amrit Kaur, Lady Abdul Quadir, Lakshmibai Rajwade and Rustomji Faridoonji, who were all members of the All India women's conference and were well known social activists in India. The dates for the AAWC were chosen so that it could sit between the two Pan-Pacific Women's conferences planned for Hawaii in August 1930 and China 1932. It was also planned to immediately follow the All-India Women's conference meeting in the same month and location (Lahore) to help with issues of organisation and the availability of India delegates.[82] Sita Debi in her article in *Bangalakshmi* also refers to a letter by the Java women's association in which they express appreciation 'to the organisers for trying to bring all the scattered women's groups to a common platform to fight for equal rights, and . . . this endeavour will help us to understand the women's movements in other countries'.[83] She refers to an article in *Lahore Tribune* on the forthcoming conference where she says that the author has said many significant things. She quotes from it what she considers important motives of the organisers.

> In the last 50 years all over the world women's movement is being organised and in many countries women have had to fight hard to free themselves from the slavery to men . . . India too is no longer a silent spectator . . . If women are allowed the full physical, mental and moral development then the whole of mankind will benefit. Today or tomorrow they will achieve this anyhow, therefore opposing their initiative now would be useless and only aggravate confrontation between the sexes.

A cautionary note was also added in the essay that women's empowerment did not mean doing away with the social rules which safeguard the family. Sita Debi says quoting from the article that:

> in Europe and America this problem (breakdown of social rules through excessive individualism) looms large, therefore women of Egypt, Turkey, Japan and India may benefit from the western experience. The Asian women's conference which would through circumspection and prudent judgement chart the way ahead.

She calls upon Bengali women to participate in the conference, saying that, 'we have a duty not only to ourselves but also to the eastern civilization as well as to the world.'

Intermixing with women from different races makes the world easier to comprehend and exchange of views improves mental capacities. She hoped that similar conferences would be held in Bengal in future and that should be the aim of the different women's organisations here. Bengali women are not backward in intellect or capabilities compared to other Indians but social restrictions imposed on them have prevented them from taking an active part in social service or women's empowerment movements. The financial input that was necessary in organising the conference taking place in Punjab, appeared quite formidable but would not be a deterrent for a conference held in Calcutta. The amount of money that had been spent at the Calcutta Congress had become quite legendary and it was Sita Debi's intention to ensure that in organising Asian women's conference in Calcutta it was not money but a volunteer corp of sincere educated workers that was of utmost importance. Every aspect of the Conference would be organised by women from welcoming the delegates at the conference, hospitality, decoration of the stage, maintenance of order and discipline, and even maintaining traffic mobility. Her dream was to organise an international women's conference in Bengal in 1932, so planned to start organising it early so that other nations had ample time for preparation.[84]

In the next issue of *Bangalakshmi,* another appeal was made by the honorary organising secretary, Rani Lakshmibai Rajwade, as the Asian Conference approached that more women were requested to join as volunteers paying a minimum entry fee of Rs. 10. Besides, she also appealed for one-time special donations. Financial support was necessary not only for the conference but also for stay, food and travel allowance of the delegates from different countries. Unfortunately, the railway authorities had announced that they were unable to provide concessions which meant that travelling budget exceeded the estimates. The Hony Secretary appealed to the local zamindars and estate owners for financial aid. The Conference organisers received assurances from Palestine, Syria, Sri Lanka, Burma, Baluchistan, Nepal, Persia, Japan and Java that they would send delegates and the participants from New Zealand and the United States had already arrived. There were negotiations going on with Thailand, Georgia, Afghanistan, China, Indo-China, Iraq and Turkey regarding their delegations. The organisers of the welcome committees in Calcutta, Bombay and Karachi were Indira Devi Chowdhurani, Faiyaz Taiyabji and Homi Mehta. The donations and membership fees were to be sent to M.E. Cousins in Lahore.[85] In the words of a modern researcher 'The All Asian Women's conference is an example of the agency of non-western women in the interwar period in setting up their own transnational network, shifting the centre away from the metropole.' Though the AAWC brought together women from all over the world and not only Asia, 'to articulate the concerns and visions of marginalised voices' yet there was hardly 'any lasting impact.' The fact that the 1931 AAWC was not the start of a series of meeting for Asian women was because the participants were unable to provide a 'sustainable definition of Asian womanhood' and pan-Asian objectives were 'overridden by domestic concerns.'[86]

The same issue of *Bangalakshmi,* also refers to another all Asian women's meet being held in the United States. It was the All Asian Association of University Women held at Michigan, in which there were participants from China, Japan, Korea, the Philippines, Turkey and India. The Secretary and Treasurer of the organisation was Kumari Janaki Ammal.[87]

Importance of diaspora in internationalism: another 'Greater India'

With the spread of an Indian diaspora around the world, interactions between Asians became very visible in the west on the one hand, while, on the other hand, in Asian countries, interaction with the local people helped to establish personal bonds far outweighing the importance of connections between nations. In the latter case, as fellow sufferers of colonialism, patriotic exchanges through joint forums of Asian nations undoubtedly helped pan-Asianism. This was what Benoy Kumar Sarkar called the Greater India, 'Indians outside of India', who have contributed to the widening of India's horizon and consciousness of Asia and the world to the value of India and Indians. He considered that Greater India was a unit of enlarged experiences and thought compelling discoveries. One of them was that people and their problems were much the same, Indians through the power of self-consciousness could find solutions within India as well. The other achievement of Greater India was breaking down the isolation of country and making the world conscious about the potential of Indians. The message of Greater India, he concluded, was the 'equality of the East and the West'.[88]

The lives and activities of ex-patriot Indians form a part of all discussions on Asia. Their success abroad is proudly described along with their patriotic feelings and sense of hospitality towards their fellow countrymen. Mrinalini Raha in *Antahpur* tries to capture the interest of her readers by mentioning names of some of the Bengalis who have settled in Burma and who held important position. P.C. Sen, Jotish Ranjan Das, lawyers Debendra Nath Palit, MA, BL, Babu Kunjabehari Bandopadhyay (whose hospitality is well known to all Bengali expatriates in Burma) and Aghorenath Chattopadhyay. She also refers to a number of social clubs established by Bengalis in Burma – social club, dramatic club and a Durgabari established by Bengalis from Chittagong where Durga puja is celebrated every year. A friend of hers had gone to see a Bengali play 'Harish Chandra' performed at Rangoon Victoria Hall and exclaimed that the audience was almost cent percent Bengali and she felt as if she was in Calcutta. Raha concluded that,' Rangoon for the young Bengalis was a new Brindavan, a pilgrimage where one can overcome the pangs of *samsara* easily'. In Burma, there is not much initiative for higher education, so the domiciled Bengalis set up their own schools, like the Indian Seminary set up by Jashodananda Sen in 1900. There was an engineering school but no medical education.[89] Another writer in 1907, describing travels in the cities of Burma, refers with gratitude to the hospitality of their hosts in the different cities and their qualities. In Mandalay it was the leading lawyer Satish Chandra Mukherjee and his family who were the gracious hosts of the writer along with the hospitality of others like Basanta Halder and his wife (whom he/she referred to as mother) in Pinmana, Dr Nakurchandra Bandopadhyay and his son Surendranath in Taunggyi all his co-religionist Brahmos.[90] Subimal Chandra Sarkar during his travel to Penang in 1930 too discussed the domiciled Indians there. There were people who had migrated there from the different states of India and who lived in different environments and experienced different situations. While discussing the economic condition there, he pointed out that due to the loss of market of tin and rubber, a crisis situation has occurred in the Malaya Straits just like in Java and Ceylon. This has resulted in widespread unemployment. Majority of the labourers of the rubber plantations are Indians – Tamilians and Malabaris. Among the tin labourers Indians comprise one-third. Even though the import of fresh Indian and Chinese labourers have been stopped the existing people are facing a crisis.[91] Very early on in the 20th century,

M.K. Gandhi realised the importance of setting up strong diaspora in different parts of the world and accused the Bengalis of

> lack of enthusiasm to leave the land of their forefathers and settle in other countries instead of facing humiliation for acquiring petty government jobs. This ennui is due to their lack of distrust of colonialism and refusal to travel to and settle in other countries.[92]

Gandhi here makes the case for South Africa in the article he writes for *Bharati* which was translated into Bengali for its readers, whereby migration of educated Indians from Bengal would strengthen the hands of the Indian diaspora already present there. There was from the beginning of the 20th century a similar attempt to make Bengalis follow other Indians to travel and settle abroad in other Asian countries like Japan. Ashutosh Deb not only discusses the importance of travelling abroad for education but also gives the example of Japan where a cheaper yet successful alternative may be availed by Indians looking for higher education.[93] Deb also provides as inspiration a list of Indians who have successfully travelled to Japan on a shoestring budget, yet who have achieved industrial education and training and who have successfully returned to start businesses or get profitable jobs. K.V. Kulkarni got some donation from the Maharaja of Kolhapur and went to Japan in 1897 and after getting the Koja Kushi Degree from the Tokyo Imperial University returned in 1900 to a successful career here. G.S. Paranjapee who went as his personal assistant also studied at Tokyo's Industrial College and returned in 1900. From Bengal, Ramakanto Roy went to Tokyo Imperial University to study coal mining and after getting the diploma, worked at Matsui Coal company for a year. G.S. Saligram of Kolhapur first learnt Japanese language on reaching Japan and then studied chemical industry in Higher Technological School, becoming the only Indian to graduate from that school. He returned in 1901 and was employed by Messers Gadgil and Co. in the manufacture of perfumes. According to Deb, Saligram had the intention of giving the English Lavender and French Eau de cologne a run for their money with an authentic Indian brand. P.D. Tambat from Jalgaon apprenticed at a match factory in Japan. In 1900, two Sikh youths from Rawalpindi – Puran Singh (Tokyo Medical College) and Damodar Singh (electrical engineering) also returned after successfully qualifying in the exams. Deb also refers to Sarojendra Guha who went to study soap making in Japan and on his return set up a soap factory in Mymensingh.[94]

In 1929, Satish Ranjan Khastagir provided a list and pen picture of Bengali diaspora in Sri Lanka. Nanigopal Mukhopadhyay, an electrical engineer, was the first to reach Sri Lanka in 1919, and settled in Colombo with his family. He passed engineering from the Bombay Jubilee Technical Institute. Ajarnath Ghosh, BA, the grandson of Jadunath Ghosh, editor of *Bengalee* and *Hindu Patriot,* was the principal of Anirudh College of Nawalapitiya town near Kandi. Ghosh has been living in Sri Lanka for the last nine years and serving the college creditably. Debkinkar Mukhopadhyay, BE (Sheffield) AMIEE, has been serving from 1923 the Colombo government technical college as a professor. He has also achieved fame as an actor. He was married to the daughter (Daya Devi) of an old lawyer of Rangoon High Court, Kunjabehari Bandopadhyay. He then speaks of Hemendranath Mukhopadhyay, the Telegraph inspector. He came to Colombo at a young age, six years ago. He passed London Matrik as well as city and guild's telegraph exams by his own efforts and managed to find a job in the government's telegraph division. Mukhopadhyay is also an aficionado of music and literature. Bhupesh Chandra Dasgupta, MRCP (Ireland) and VPH (London), was the Health Officer of Kalutara after living in different cities of Sri Lanka for six years. He belonged to the famous Das family of Telibagh and was married to Aswini Kumar Sen of Dhaka. Sen had recently returned from a visit to America where he was sent by the Sri Lankan government as a Rockfeller fellow to research on public health. Dr Prabhatchandra Sarbadhikari, who was teaching at the university college was going to represent Ceylon at the Fifth International Botanical Conference in London as well as the ninth horticultural conference. Before that in 1927, he participated in the Empire University Congress, British Association of Science and Paris Science Academy as the representative from Sri Lanka. Nalinaksha Basu, BSc from Edinburgh, was the government railway engineer of Ceylon. He was a brilliant student of Edinburgh and was placed in the first place in Mathematics and Civil Engineering. In 1927, he arrived in Sri Lanka, and worked in Anuradhapura. All those who visit the place to look at the Buddhist relics, remark on the hospitality skills of Basu.[95] There are many more instances of descriptions and lists of Indians working and settling in the various countries of Asia, making a point to the readers of the simplicity and efficacy of travelling and working in hitherto unknown regions of the east.

Descriptions of Indian diaspora in western countries had an added significance in the 20th century. Cosmopolitanism and a sense of homecoming and familiarity were probably the main motivation for writing about Indians staying in the Asian countries and a broadening of regional identities is noticeable since not only Bengalis are referred to but also Indians in general. In the case of writings on the west, nationalism plays a larger role with a focus on pan-Asianism from the second decade of the 20th century. Benoy Kumar Sarkar's writing played an important role in pan-Asianism in the context of the Asian diaspora in America.[96] In 'Americanisation from the view point of Young Asia', based on lectures delivered at the University of Pittsburgh in July 1918, he speaks about the 'Asian factor' in America which despite its lack of 'formidable magnitude' was attacked by a prohibitive stop on immigration. He is also vocal about the discrimination against Asian immigrants (Chinese, Japanese and Hindus) vis-à-vis the European immigrants. As he puts it, on the one hand the patriotic Americanizers have been trying their best to abolish their 'race lines' from European immigrant colonies but on the other hand, American behaviour towards Asian immigrants has been the very antithesis of this attitude. It was a slow systematic ostracism, localisation, persecution and torture from the beginning to the end.[97] He adds that 'young Asia is fully conscious of the situation, and has been preparing itself to contribute to the grand cosmic evolution from its own angle of vision'.[98]

Sunitikumar Chattopadhyay in *Pashchimer Jatri* (Travels to the West) gives vivid and detailed descriptions of Asian encounters with the west while travelling in Berlin, Brussels, Paris, London and Venice. Not only the people, his writing also becomes for his readers a window into International Exhibitions and Museums which most travellers do not give detailed accounts of.[99] He ends his article with a new twist on the concept of Greater India:

> I was most surprised at how these uneducated or half educated Muslims from the remote villages of Hooghly settled gradually in central and southern America and helped to establish a Greater India there . . . a large number of Bengali Muslims are engaged in trade in silk fabrics, shawls, chikan embroidery, and garments . .

. between Panama and Costa Rica, Nicaragua, Honduras, Salvador, Guatemala, Mexico and extending to southern Colombia, Venezuela, Ecuador, and Peru . . . they trade in Japanese silk and are fluent in Spanish.'[100]

The Indians Abroad Bulletin published for the Imperial Indian Citizenship Association, Bombay, was also published in a shortened version in *The Modern Review*. This Bulletin published in 1923, in vivid detail the Indian question in Kenya and Jehangir Bomanjee Petit on behalf of the secretariat of the Association, very clearly delineated 'the Indian position on the issue' and to 'reassure the Kenya Indians and the public of India of the sympathy and support of the Imperial government in the present plight of Kenya Indians'. While declaring its solidarity with the British rule, the Association urged the 'Imperial and Indian government will do anything to secure the rights of citizenship to Indians in Kenya and to protect their lives and property in the events of these threats (of bloodshed)'.[101] In the case of Fiji, C.F. Andrews published in Bulletin No. 7, in the same year, the Report of Florence Garnham who provided graphic descriptions of the hardships of the Indian indentured labour in Fiji, though the previous report in 1918 by MacNeil and Chamanlal had claimed that 'the advantages under the indenture system outweigh the disadvantages' and their recommendation that the moral problem of depression be solved by sending more women from India was proved fallacious by the Garnham Report. Andrews referred to the Report that he and Pearson had submitted to the Viceroy in 1916, thereby leading to the Abolition of Indenture Act, 1916, but which was not immediately implemented. In 1920, when Florence Garnham, who was urged by Andrews himself to submit a report along with Burton's book *Fiji of To-day*, proved beyond doubt the evils of indentured labour that all Indian labourers in the plantations were granted freedom. But the evils of deprivation continued specially since most of the returned labour were rejected by the Indian society due to social constraints. The fact that the news of the Indian diaspora was reported widely and printed and reprinted in Indian publications was indicative that despite social bans, nationalism demanded redressal of suffering of Indian diaspora. As Andrews pointed out, Mahatma Gandhi, Annie Beasant, Lokmanya Tilak, Pandit Madan Mohan Malavia, and many other leaders, took up the indentured question as a primary national concern and the whole country rang with indignant voices at this betrayal of India, in refusing to close down altogether the indentured labour, after a solemn promise had been given.[102] The role of the press in presenting the condition and demands of the Indian diaspora is also seen in autobiographies of editors and journalists[103] in various research works on diaspora-owned newspapers like *Rangoon Mail* owned by Ramesh R. Caterham.[104]

Disillusion of the hope of pan-Asianism

Admiration for Japan which was so pervasive in the articles from the turn of the century turned quickly to foreboding within a decade. The sympathy for the brave Japanese warrior who sacrificed himself to ensure his country's success, seen in poems in *Bharati*, by Swarnakumari Debi[105] and others at the beginning of the century soon turned to horror when the might of Japan was used to attack other Asian countries instead of leading them to unified resistance against the western onslaught, as had been hoped. Rabindranath Tagore who had been so inspired by the Japanese qualities of success wrote a letter to C.F. Andrews in 1914,

> I am almost sure Japan has eyes upon India. She is hungry – she is munching Corea, she has fastened her teeth upon China and it will be an evil day for India when Japan will have her opportunity . . . Japan is the youngest disciple of Europe – she has no soul – she is all science – and she has no sentiment to spare for other people than her own . . . Japan is Asia and Europe combined – so we shall have a monster whose teeth are European and whose apparatus of digestion is Asiatic.[106]

Jatindranath Mitra in his book called *A Lost Nation* blamed the failure of an united Asian opposition to the European retaliation towards what they considered to be 'yellow peril' to be a blunder. Mitra believed that this peril 'was a combination of Japan and China with India, Arabia and Persia in the wings, which no amount of arms or European diplomacy could meet'. Unfortunately, according to him, a 'Pan Asiatic fear' or rather phobia of united action 'led the nations of the West to seek friendship with Japan, kindle a civil war in China and to divide and partition Africa and Persia among themselves'.[107]

One wonders if the dreams for a united Asia or a pan-Asian unity could have materialised for any length of time when nationalism was the need of the hour. In the drive to give precedence to nationalism, anti-colonial or otherwise, in the first half of the 20th century, all other aspirations were sacrificed. Complications arose also from the conflict between nationalisms of the different nations, and reflection of these debates can be inferred from the contemporary writing. If Japanese aggression in Korea and China was being criticised, Indian glorification of her colonisation even if only culturally or civilisationally was disliked in the South-East Asian countries. Chinese search for 'lost territories' was another aspect where pan-Asianism faltered.

In 1909, Sureshchandra Bandopadhyay in an essay 'Religion of Japan', published in *Prabashi*, wrote that those who have followed the events in Japan, Korea and Manchuria during the past two years will not take long to realise that Japan undertook the war to swallow Korea and establish an area of influence on Manchuria with a view to occupying her gradually. This and only this, was the reason for the Russo Japanese war. Allowing Russia to remain close to Korea was hampering Japan's agenda in Korea and preventing her from looting her resources . . . Her selfishness, in using another country's wealth for the improvement of one's own country may be harmful for the victim but for Japan it was beneficial. Whether such an action was justifiable is debatable but there is no doubt that it was Japanese nationalism that was the motive. Though living in Japan, Bandopadhyay warns Indians not to be blinded or overawed by their admiration for Japan. Japan had already cast her covetous eyes over India and the fact that many Indians are using Japanese goods as almost like Indian goods while rejecting European goods as foreign may soon be fooled into exploitation. He concludes that, If the chance came, Japanese will not hesitate to plunge a knife into the heart of India if it suited her purpose'.[108]

Even before that Japan's aggression on China as a result of ambitions in Korea has been referred to in *Japan Jatri* by Rabindranath as 'creating an painful incongruence in the Japanese spirit of selflessness by a display of pride and power'.[109] Occupation of Korea in 1910 and the First World War worried Tagore so much that in his lecture tours, he faced the ire of the Japanese students while campaigning against the ideology of aggressive nationalism in which he saw the roots of the World War. *Nationalism*[110] was published in 1917 which was an open indictment against 'the political civilization which has sprung up from the soil of Europe and is overrunning the whole world' since it is 'scientific, and not human'. As Rabindranath said in the speech to the Indian community in Japan in April 1925

> it was here that I first saw the Nation, in all its naked ugliness, whose spirit we Orientals have borrowed from the West.... I heartily deplored the fact that she (Japan), with her code of honour, her ideal of perfection and her belief in the need for grace in everyday life, could yet become infected with this epidemic of selfishness and with the boastfulness of egotism.[111]

One can also see this censure in the student leader in Burma Ko Nu, though a devout Buddhist (writing about Buddhist philosophy and Sanghas for the Kamala lectures of Calcutta University in 1961), along with his associates at the Rangoon University, Aung San, Kyaw Nyein, Thein Pe, Ko Ohn and M.A. Raschid, admired Japan for its defiance of western imperialism but disapproved of the aggression towards China, an Asian land.[112] Tagore's associations with Japan now had to be more aggressively cultural. Internationalism rather than nationalism was stressed. Tagore's missionary travels abroad were partly aided by the climate of internationalism prevailing after the end of the First World War and formation of League of Nations and partly due to the positive developments in Asia like the establishment of the Republic of Turkey by Kamal Ataturk (1923) whom Tagore admired and the anti-imperialist struggle in Indonesia (1926).[113] But in 1938, Tagore could not accept the justification by the Japanese poet Noguchi, of Japan's attack on China, and replied that 'Japan does not yet understand the inner strength of China. At the present moment China has much greater moral strength than Japan and they should in the near future erase the painful memories and recreate a pure Asia', as reported in *Bharatvarsha.*[114]

A recent scholar, Isabelle Saint Mezard, in her book *Eastward Bound: India's New Positioning in Asia*, speaks of the impact of upholding Buddhist links as ultimately being detrimental to future peace prospects. She says that unlike India's somewhat patronizing attitude vis-à-vis south east Asia, it considered China as its 'alter ego.' Not only did the Greater India proponents consider China as a great civilization whom they greatly admired but also cherished the long relationship that had been shared between the two great civilizations in the past. They highlighted the 'role of Buddhist missionaries in establishing close ties between the two countries' and considered the ancient India China relations as based on 'Buddhist connection.' , According to Saint Mezard the argument was that it was India who 'extended its influence to China and not the opposite ' through the spread of Buddhism, bringing 'the spiritual homogeneity and cultural unity of the(Asian) continent.'[115] Isabelle Saint Mezard, however, finds ominous reflection of this on future developments since the Greater India theory 'established an intellectual environment that was fairly loaded with underlying meanings.' It was as she puts it, 'faithfully exploited by the Hindu nationalist group' some of whom 'dreamt of forming a pan-Buddhist block comprising of Japan, India, Tibet, Thailand, Sri Lanka, Cambodia, Java, China, and Myanmar.'[116]

From the 1930s, India seems to have joined the rest of powerful Asia in talking about herself vis-à-vis the Asian superpowers China and Japan. The question remains if this is only a nationalistic retaliation against colonialism or was it also a response to Asian ambitions of Greater China and Greater Japan? Corollary to this was of course the realisation among intellectuals that these ambitions nascent or overt were obstacles to a united Asia. Prabodh Chandra Bagchi's article in 1931 in *Bichitra* addresses this question. He writes: that,

> for some time we are hearing of the possibility of a union among the eastern races. Of the powers of the east, China, Japan and India take priority. As races these three countries have no semblance of unity – since Japanese are of Mongolian stock and have no racial similarity with China. The Chinese too have racial differences with Indians. The languages of the three countries are different. . . . There are differences in the various religious beliefs existing in the three countries . . . Yet there is an underlying unity among these races . . . the unity is spiritual. This spiritualism has travelled from India to Japan and China. But though Japan has achieved success in harmonizing between tradition and modernity, China has not been able to do so . . .. Internal disharmony has disrupted the spirituality there and impacted cultural growth. Thus, like India, China too has to start her development from scratch. One wonders if China will be able to keep her traditions intact in this new growth, since she looks westward. That was evident when they rejected the words of Rabindranath and claimed that modern China does not need ancient spiritualism, which they claim is a shadowy mysticism. Western scientific knowledge which they claim is more lucid is the basis of Chinese national development now. Whether the knowledge of spiritualism which tied the countries of the east from ancient times, will be the bond which will bind them now and forever, despite dissident views, is a question which only future can answer.[117]

Prasenjit Duara links pan-Asianism to the development of an alternative conception of civilisation which was centred around the concept of Asia. Although it was a conception that the Japanese distinctly inherited from the Europeans only in the nineteenth century, it became 'a powerful, if changing, spatial representation in relation to which Japanese identity came to be repeatedly made and remade.'[118] Discussing the role of Okakura Tenshin in this context, Duara writes that his Asian civilisation 'entailed a deep familiarity with European modes of constructing the idea of civilization'. Okakura was aware of differences between Asian 'civilizations but he believed that 'they all differed from the Western Civilization in principle – in their promotion of peace and beauty.' Okakura saw Japan as the 'exhibition hall' of all of these Asian civilizations but did not advocate what would become a general idea in the aftermath of the Russo-Japanese war which was that Japan become the leader of an Asian Federation because 'it could harmonise the best of Asian civilization with that of Civilization'. Rather he urged the various Asian nations to look within their common traditions to produce an 'alternative to the aggressive and dominating Civilization of the West.'[119]

Pan-Asianism in China, according to Prasenjit Duara, was in the context of a civilisational discourse which changed from being invoked by the western countries as a 'signifier to justify their conquest as a civilizing mission' to a post–First World War alternative formulation connected to an 'ideational or spiritual quality of culture' against the 'materialism and destructiveness of Western civilization'. In Duara's words, 'the philosophy of Spengler and Toynbee reflected the world as a newly unified theatre of history', and his insistence in seeing Europe as just a 'bit-part of the history of humanity' suited those nations who used a similar language to call for a nationalism which was 'genetically linked to a universalism greater than itself, just as globalism itself came to be figured through the language of nationalism.[120] In the case of China, Duara writes: the 'new civilization discourse and its links to pan-Asianism', has been overlooked now 'because of its association with Japanese imperialism.' But between 1911 and 1945, the 'discourse of Eastern civilization – whether as superior to Western Civilization or as necessary to redeem the latter' was active in China as 'an intellectual, cultural and social movement.' His opinion is that there is an ambivalence in the ideas though between the nationalists who 'sought to conflate the civilization with the territorial nation', while spiritually the formulation of civilisation 'tended to seek a universal sphere of application, viewing the national boundaries as artificial walls'. Duara shows that the 'modern intellectual construction of civilization tended towards the conflation, whereas the more popular, social movements tended to view civilization more transnationally'.[121] Tansen Sen, while describing exhaustively pan-Asianism and renewed connections in Asia, shows how despite efforts of many to 'underscore the peaceful and harmonious nature of intra-Asian interactions before European colonization', 'internal political changes, and other realities of the colonial period' hampered the 'rhetoric of friendship and bonding', 'discourse of India-China oneness, and renewal of Buddhist connections with the failure of Pan Asianism'.[122]

The 'lost territories' ideas that lay at the root of Chinese ambitions fired the youngsters as K.P.S. Menon testifies to in his book *Many Worlds*. His daughter Kunja was studying at Ginling College, Chengtu, China, in 1943–1944 and provided an insight into the minds of the younger generations. She pointed out that at a poll held by the YWCA and the New Life Movement, majority of the girl students expressed their ambition for healthy marriage and family of four children and 'have a hand in the restoration of all 'lost territory' including Korea, Indo-China and Burma, which were formerly dependencies of China.[123]

Manomohon Ghosh in his book *China's Conflict with India and the Soviet Union* outlines in the first chapter not only the revival of contact between China and other Asian countries, including India, but also the political aims of Chinese statesmen to create a Federation of Asian states. Ghosh points out that the success of the October Revolution which had a deep impact on the youth of China led the University of Peking to invite John Dewey and Bertrand Russell to inspire the students with the real intention to wean them away from Communism. Russell spoke about the need to form an 'Asiatic bloc to save the peace of the world . . . in the interest of mankind'. Ghosh pointed out that though Russell's advice was not very acceptable to the youth Chinese, some of the leaders of the Chinese community invited Rabindranath Tagore in the hope that he might bring with him the wisdom of India to give a more profitable direction to their young compatriots'. Tagore was invited by Sun Yat Sen to Canton as 'not only a writer but a rare worker in the field of endeavour wherein lies the seeds of man's future welfare and spiritual triumphs'. Unfortunately as Ghosh explains for the young Chinese students, that appeared to be of lesser importance than fighting for their country's freedom from the domination of foreign Powers which reduced it practically to vassalage by their right of extra-territoriality, dictated tariff and control of customs they were not very much interested in(an) Asiatic bloc.[124] Though Tagore did not go to Canton finally whether discouraged by the British authorities or due to the fact that his invitation was from the North which was under a different government, Ghosh points out, the speech he gave in the garden house of Cursun Chang, a Chinese philosopher, raised hackles among some. Tagore expressing his love and admiration for the Chinese people said that, 'Age after age in Asia, great dreamers have made the world sweet with showers of their love.' And that Asia is again waiting for such dreamers to come and carry on the work not of fighting, not of profit-making, but of establishing bonds of 'spiritual relationship'. Ghosh believed that some interested parties thought that they discovered in this reply an aim of creating 'a Pan-Asian, movement which might hurt their interests which is why they criticised his views[125] Ghosh also points out that those students led by Hu Shih initially considered Tagore to be conservative and a traditionalist, later a detailed meeting with Hu Shih was able to dispel the prejudice. That melted the opposition of the young men of Peking and the informal talks held at the National University were 'a marvellous success. Tagore told them that he was travelling to explore the message of Asia; not as an individual Indian, but as a representative of Asia. The great unity which he was thinking of was not an Asian Federation or Co-prosperity, but a 'Cultural Unity.'[126]

The fluctuating faith for united Asia in intellectuals in Asia was a response to the changing circumstances in volatile times. With the horrors of Second World War unfolding from the end of the third decade, Indian intellectuals wildly wavered between anti-colonial commitments in the cause of Indian national movement and wonder at Japan's temerity to confront the devil in their own game. The alternative experiment undertaken by the great Bengali hero, Netaji Subhas Chandra Bose, of escaping from under the eyes of the British spies and forging a new and formidable site of power with the help of the enemies of the colonial masters of India totally stunned Bengalis and Indians and energised them as never before.[127] In others too sometimes more subtly, cosmopolitanism was the real nationalism when anti-colonial sentiments led them to take strong and controversial actions. The stand taken by the Indian lawyer Radha Binode Pal during the International Military Tribunal for the Far East or Tokyo Trials (1946) when he 'absolved all the accused of all charges' becoming a dissenting judge muddied the waters even more since anti-imperialist tone of his dissention seemed to absolve Japan of aggression against other Asian nations that was being talked about till then. In a recently published book, Partha Chatterjee marks out the main dissenting points of Pal as refusal to accept 'aggressive war as criminal in international law as it existed before World War II' and challenging the move to make 'conspiracy' to wage war a crime under international law since it was not so in non-Anglo-American nations. Pal's argument that Japan's aggressive actions from 1928 were according to 'standard practices adopted by sovereign states for their self-preservation' was according to Chatterjee coming from 'mainstream anti-imperialist nationalism that was beginning to be voiced in international forums by leaders from countries colonised'.[128]

Notes

1 G.S. Eddy, *Japan and India*, Calcutta: Student Volunteer Movement of India and Ceylon, 1910, pp. 108–109.
2 R. Nutt, G. Sherwood Eddy and the Attitudes of Protestants in the United States toward Global Mission, *Church History*, 66(3), 1997, 502–521. www.jstor.org/stable/3169454, accessed on 17.08.20.
3 T.A. Keenleyside, Nationalist Indian Attitudes towards Asia: A Troublesome Legacy for Post-Independence Foreign Policy, *Pacific Affairs*, 55(2), Summer 1982, p. 201.
4 Ashis Nandy, A New Cosmopolitanism: Towards a Dialogue of Asian Civilizations, in Kuan-Hsing Chen, ed., *Trajectories: Inter-Asia Cultural Studies*, London: Routledge, 1998, p. 145.

5 Prasenjit Duara in foreword to Kwa Chong Guan, ed., *Early South East Asia Viewed from India: An Anthology of Articles from Journal of Greater India Society*, Manohar: New Delhi, 2013, p. viii.
6 Kakuzo Okakura, *The Ideals of the East with Special Reference to the Art of Japan*, New York: E.P. Dutton and Co., 1904, p. 212, http://www.sacred-texts.com/shi/ioe/index.htm, accessed on 16.08.19.
7 Ibid., pp. 240–241.
8 Stolte Carolien and Fischer-Tine Harald, Imagining Asia in India: Nationalism and Internationalism (ca. 1905–1940), *Comparative Studies in Society and History*, 54(1), 2012, pp. 65–92.
9 Sugata Bose, *A Hundred Horizons: The Indian Ocean in the Age of Global Empires*, Delhi: Permanent Black, 2006, p. 275.
10 Kakuzo Okakura, op. cit.
11 Benoy Kumar Sarkar, Swadhin Asiar Rajdhani, *Grihastha*, 7(7)(3), 1915, p. 209.
12 Sri Swadeshi, Asiar Jagaran, *Arati*, 6(9), 1906, pp. 241–246.
13 Ibid., p. 241.
14 Ibid., p. 243.
15 Jadunath Sarkar, Mikado, *Bharati*, 36(6), 1912, pp. 660–669.
16 Pankaj Mishra, *From the Ruins of Empire: The Revolt against the West and the Remaking of Asia*, London: Penguin Books, 2013, pp. 226–227.
17 ABP 14th October 1927, *Rabindra Prasanga: Anandabazar Patrika 13th March 1922–21st March 1932*, vol. I, ed. Chittaranjan Bandopadhyay, Calcutta: Ananda Publishers, 1993, p. 528.
18 Kalidas Nag, Puber Chithi (Letters from the East), *Bangabani*, 3(1)(4), 1924, p. 517.
19 Ibid., p. 518.
20 Ibid.
21 Kalidas Nag, Puber Chithi (Letters from the East), *Bangabani*, 3(2)(1), 1924, pp. 43–44.
22 Ibid., p. 44.
23 Isabelle Saint-Mezard, *Eastward Bound: India's New Positioning in Asia*, Delhi: Manohar, 2006, p. 176.
24 Jadunath Sarkar, Bharater Shahit Japaner Sambandha, *Bharati*, 36(2), 1912, pp. 125–132.
25 Probodh Chandra Bagchi, The Study of Buddhism in Japan, *The Cosmopolitan*, 1, January, 1928, pp. 44–46.
26 Nripendra Krishna Chattopadhyay, Kirti Kahani: Japaner Duti Meye, Chatushpathi, *Bangasree*, 1(2)(4), 1933, p. 528.
27 Phanindranath Bose, Budhhadharmer Itihasher Digdarshan, *Prabashi*, 25(2)(3), 1925, pp. 343-354
28 Ramesh Chandra Majumdar, Chindeshiya Bouddha Paribrajak, Kashti Pathar, *Prabashi*, 24(1)(6), 1924, pp. 792–795.
29 Jatindranath Mitra, *A Lost Nation*, Calcutta: J.N. Mitra, no date, p. 72.
30 Sarat Mukherjee, Americay Asiar Durdasha, *Bangabani*, 3(2)(1), 1924, pp. 55–56.
31 Ibid., p. 59
32 Sarvani Gooptu, Japan and Asian Destiny: India's Intellectual Journey through Contemporary Periodicals, 1880s–1930s, in Ishita Banerjee-Dube and Sarvani Gooptu, eds., *On Modern Indian Sensibilities: Culture, Politics, History*, London: Routledge, 2018, pp. 198–216.
33 Jyotirindranath Tagore, Adhunik Japan: Felician Shaal er Phorashi Hoite (Modern Japan from the French Writing of Felician Shaal), *Bharati*, 32(1)(2)(3)(4)(5)(6), 1908.
34 Jyotirindranath Tagore, Lafcadio Hearn er Japan Chitra: Felicia Shaal er Phorashi hoite (Portrait of Japan by Lafcadio Hearn: From the French Writing of Felicia Shaal), *Bharati*, 32(7)(8)(9)(10), 1908.
35 Rabindranath Tagore, *Japan Jatri*, Kolkata: Visva Bharati Patrika, 2015, reprint (first published serially in *Sabuj Patra*).
36 Anonymous (possibly by the Editor, Swarnakumari Debi), Japaner Bartoman Unnatir Mool Pattan, *Bharati*, 5(2), 1881, pp. 70–77 and Japaner Bartoman Unnati *Bharati*, 5(6), pp. 122–133.
37 Ibid., p. 126.

38 Jyotirindranath Tagore, Adhunik Japan: Felician Shaal er Phorashi Hoite, *Bharati*, 32(1), 1908, pp. 20–21.
39 Ibid., pp. 24–25.
40 Ibid., p. 87.
41 Jyotirindranath Tagore, Adhunik Japan, op. cit., p. 133.
42 Ibid., p. 135.
43 Jyotirindranath Tagore, Adhunik Japan, *Bharati*, 32(6), op. cit., p. 267.
44 Jyotirindranath Tagore, *Lafcardio Hearner Japan Chitra: Felician Shaal er Phorashi Hoite* opcit,*Bharati*, 32(10), 1908, p.306
45 Ibid., p. 307.
46 Rabindranath Tagore, Asia's Response to the Call of the New Age, *The Modern Review*, LIL(4), October 1932, p. 370.
47 Rabindranath Tagore, *Japan Jatri*, op. cit., appendix, p. 174.
48 Rabindranath Tagore, To the Indian Community in Japan, *Japan Jatri*, op. cit., p. 117.
49 Rabindranath Tagore, *Japan Jatri*, op. cit., appendix, p. 175.
50 Rabindranath Tagore, *Japan Jatri*, op. cit.., p. 44.
51 Ibid., p. 72.
52 Rabindranath Tagore, *Japan Jatri*, op. cit.., p. 103.
53 Rabindranath Tagore, *Japan Jatri*, op. cit.., pp. 73–74.
54 Ibid., p. 76.
55 Ibid., p. 80.
56 Rabindranath Tagore, *Japan Jatri*, op. cit.., p. 90.
57 Rabindranath Tagore, 'To the Indian Community in Japan', *Japan Jatri*, p. 120.
58 Rabindranath Tagore, *The Soul of the East*, first published in *Vishwabharati Quarterly*, April 1925, and reprinted in *Japan Jatri*, op. cit.., p. 132.
59 Rabindranath Tagore, Chin o Japaner Bhraman Bibaran, *Prabashi*, 24(2)(1), 1924, pp. 100–101.
60 Tagore, *Nationalism*, op. cit.., p. 46.
61 Quoted in Prasanta Kumar Pal, *Rabijibani*, Vol. IX, Calcutta: Ananda Publishers, 2012 (2003), p. 61.
62 Prasanta Kumar Pal, *Rabijibani*, Vol. VII, Calcutta: Ananda Publishers, 2013 (1997), p. 173.
63 Suniti Kumar Chattopadhyay, Dvipamoy Bharat, *Prabashi*, 30(1)(3), p. 413.
64 G.S. Eddy, Japan and India, Calcutta: Student Volunteer Movement of India and Ceylon, 1910 (not clear), p. 3.
65 K.M. Panikkar, *An Autobiography*, translation from the Malayalam by K. Krishnamurthy, Madras: Oxford University Press, 1977, p. 60.
66 Ibid., p. 62.
67 Prasenjit Duara, The Discourse of Civilization and Pan-Asianism, op. cit.., p. 105 pp. 178–932.
68 K.M. Panikkar, *An Autobiography*, op. cit.., pp. 62–63.
69 Ibid., pp. 63–64.
70 K.P.S. Menon, *Many Worlds: An Autobiography*, London: Oxford University Press, 1965, p. 54.
71 M.C. Chagla, *Roses in December: An Autobiography*, Bombay: Bharatiya Vidya Bhawan, 1973, pp. 42–44.
72 Benoy Kumar Sarkar, Swadhin Asiar Rajdhani, *Grihastha*, 7(7)(3), 1915, p. 216.
73 Ibid., p. 217.
74 Kshitish Chandra Bandopadhyay, Philippine e Bangali Porjyotok, *Bharatvarsha*, 26(2)(3), 1938, p. 454.
75 Kalidas Nag, *The Discovery of Asia*, Calcutta: The Institute of Asian African Relations, 1957, p. 17.
76 Sunitikumar Chattopadhyay, Pashchimer Jatri, *Bharatvarsha*, 24(2)(1), 1939, pp. 127–128.
77 Abdulgani, Roeslan, *The Bandung Connection: The Asia-Africa Conference in Bandung in 1955*, translated by Molly Bondan, Singapore: Gunung Agung, 1981, pp. 9–11.
78 Ibid., pp. 9–10.
79 Quoted in ibid., p. 10.
80 Kedarnath Bandopadhyay, Chin Prabashir Patra (2), *Bharati*, 28(1), 1904, pp. 46–61.

81 Sumita Mukherjee, The All-Asian Women's Conference 1931: Indian Women and Their Leadership of a Pan-Asian Feminist Organisation, *Women's History Review*, 26(3), 2017, pp. 363–381.
82 Ibid., p. 367.
83 Sita Debi, Desher Kaaje Banglar Meye, *Bangalakshmi*, 6(1), 1930, pp. 68–71.
84 Sita Debi, ibid., pp. 69–71.
85 Asian Women's Conference, Nanakotha, *Bangalakshmi*, 6(2), 1930, p. 155.
86 Sumita Mukherjee, The All-Asian Women's Conference 1931, op. cit.., p. 376.
87 Nikhil Asia, Vishwavidyalay Maihla Sangha, Ghore Baire, *Bangalakshmi*, 6(2), 1930, p. 270.
88 Benoy Kumar Sarkar, *The Futurism of Young Asia and Other Essays on the Relations between East and the West*, Berlin: Julius Springer, 1922, pp. 359–361.
89 Mrinalini Raha, Bharmadesher Kotha, *Antahpur*, 5(8), 1902, p. 163.
90 Anon, Amader Bhraman Brittanto: Burmadesh, *Mahila*, 12(10), 1907, pp. 261–263.
91 Subimal Chandra Sarkar, Malayer Pathe, *Bangalakshmi*, 6(5), 1930, p. 352.
92 M.K. Gandhi, Dakshinafricay Bharatuponibesh, *Bharati*, 26(1), 1902, pp. 137–142.
93 Ashutosh Deb, Bharatbashir Japane Shilposikhsha, *Bharati*, 26(5), 1902, pp. 483–486.
94 Ashutosh Deb, Japane Bharatiya Chhatra, *Bharati*, 26(5), 1902, pp. 893–903.
95 Satish Ranjan Khastagir, Singhal Prabashi Bangali, *Prabashi*, 29(2)(4), 1929, pp. 490–496.
96 Benoy Sarkar, The Americanisation from the Point of View of Young Asia, in Banesvar Das, ed., *The Social and Economic Ideas of Benoy Kumar Sarkar*, Calcutta: Chuckervartty Chatterjee and Co., 1939, pp. 315–336.
97 Ibid., p. 328.
98 Ibid., p. 336.
99 Sunitikumar Chattopadhyay, Pashchimer Jatri, *Bharatvarsha*, 24(2)(1), 24 (2)(2), 24(2)(4), 24(2)(5), 1936, pp. 120–130; 246–256; 585–593; 796–809.
100 Sunitikumar Chattopadhyay, Pashchimer Jatri, *Bharatvarsha*, 24(2)(5), 1936, p. 838.
101 *Indians Abroad*, *Bulletin no 1-Kenya*, Bombay: S. Bose for the Imperial Indian Citizenship Association, Jan 1923, pp. 2–3.
102 C.F. Andrews, Introduction, *Indians Abroad – Fiji*, Bulletin No. 7, Bombay: S. Bose for the Imperial Indian Citizenship Association, August 1923, p. 2.
103 Nripendra Chandra Banerji, *At the Cross Roads*, Calcutta: Jijnasa, 1950.
104 Su Lin Lewis, Print Culture and the New Maritime Frontier in Rangoon and Penang, *Moussons*, 17/2011, pp. 127–144, http://journals.openedition.org/moussons/583, accessed on 09.12.19.
105 Swarna Kumari Debi, Japani Bir (a poem), *Bharati*, 27(8), 1903, pp. 725–727.
106 Letter from Tagore to Andrews, quoted in Prashanta Kumar Paul, *Rabijibani (A Biography of Rabindranath Tagore)*, *Volume VII (1914–1920)*, Calcutta: Ananda Publishers, 2002 (1997), p. 105.
107 Jatindranath Mitra, *A Lost Nation*, Calcutta: J.N. Mitra, no date, pp. 84–88.
108 Suresh Chandra Bandopadhyay, Japaner Dharma, *Prabashi*, 9(4), 1909, pp. 231–234.
109 Ibid., p. 91.
110 Tagore, *Nationalism*, op. cit.., p. 24.
111 Rabindranath Tagore, To the Indian Community in Japan, *Japan Jatri*, op. cit.., p. 118.
112 Richard Butwell, *U Nu of Burma*, Stanford: Stanford University Press, 1963, p. 19.
113 Sabyasachi Bhattacharya, *Rabindranath Tagore: An Interpretation*, New Delhi : Penguin/Viking, 2011, p. 133.
114 Japan o Rabindranath, Samayiki, *Bharatvarsha*, 26th year, Vol. I, 1345 (1938), pp. 790–791.
115 Isabelle Saint-Mezard, *Eastward Bound: India's New Positioning in Asia*, Delhi: Manohar, 2006, p. 184.
116 Ibid.
117 Prabodh Chandra Bagchi, Bharat o Chin-Japan, *Bichitra*, 4(2)(5), 1931, pp. 583–585.
118 Prasenjit Duara, The Discourse of Civilization and Pan-Asianism, *Journal of World History*, 12(1), Spring 2001, p. 109.
119 Ibid., pp. 109–110.
120 Prasenjit Duara, The Discourse of Civilization and Pan-Asianism, op. cit.., p. 105.
121 Ibid., pp. 112–113.

122 Tansen Sen, *India, China and the World: A Connected History*, Delhi: Oxford University Press, 2018, pp. 293–376.
123 K.P.S. Menon, *Many Worlds: An Autobiography*, London: Oxford University Press, 1965, p. 191.
124 Manomohan Ghosh, *China's Conflict with India and the Soviet Union*, Calcutta: The World Press, 1969, pp. 48–51.
125 Ibid., p. 52.
126 Ibid., pp. 55–56.
127 Details in Netaji Collected works and in Sugata Bose (2011), *His Majesty's Opponent: Subhas Chandra Bose and India's Struggle against Empire*, Delhi: Penguin Random House.
128 Partha Chatterjee, *I Am the People: Reflections on Popular Sovereignty Today*, Ranikhet: Permanent Black, 2020, pp. 6–24.

9 Institutionalising dreams

Tagore, Bose and Nehru

Three dreamers of universalism tried to put it into action through building of temporary or permanent institutions, for the new nation-state they envisaged, in accordance with ideal principles. Rabindranath Tagore was undoubtedly a great motivator and inspiration behind the intellectual movement of wanting to know about Asia and being identified as an Asian, even though, as I have shown, he too was the receiver of a tradition of cosmopolitan and universalist ideas. Two others encompassed their dreams of cosmopolitan, anti-colonial nationalism into a nation-state of their dreams, one whose dream never materialised and the other who took charge. One was Netaji Subhas Chandra Bose, in the Provisional Free India government that he set up outside colonised India in an Asian country, and the other was Jawaharlal Nehru, whose cosmopolitan world view combined with deep nationalistic ideas not only encompasses all his writings throughout his life but who was able to bring them to fruition through the First Asian Relations Conference, which he convened in early 1947, and the non-alignment movement he initiated. In this final chapter, I have tried to make a tally of how the ideas of cosmopolitanism and nationalism impacted these individuals, who tried in three ways to crystallise the abstract intellectual movement. Obviously, a movement of ideas which has not been discussed so long except only partially in the context of other ideas, must have imploded itself, but have left imprints for posterity.

Rabindranath Tagore and the Visva Bharati experiment

Rabindranath Tagore not only inspired a whole generation to break free from inward-looking shackles of nationalism but also tried to bring his dream of universalism to fruition through an educational and institutional model of Visva Bharati. This model was inspired through a systematic knowledge gathered both personally and through others and by a system of inviting scholars from different countries of Asia and the world for exchange of knowledge and views. It is doubtful whether this experiment which he incorporated into the university education system was ever replicated anywhere else in the country. The nucleus of this was the school set up by Tagore on his father's estate near Bolpur. Started with three teachers, Reba Chand, Jagadananda Roy and Shibdhan Vidyarnab, apart from Rabindranath and Brahmabandhab, and students, Rathindranath Tagore, Gourgobinda Gupta, Premkumar Gupta and Ashok Kumar Gupta, it set on its own path soon with the departure of Brahmabandhab.

Rabindranath Tagore can truthfully be called a universal man at least as far as his ideas as expressed in innumerable writing and speeches went and in the way his presence was celebrated and memories of his visit institutionalised in different countries.

DOI: 10.4324/9781003243786-9

I have already discussed in some detail his travels to various countries in Asia and here I would like to see how through different means these visits were reciprocated. While staying at the American embassy, Okakura met Sister Nivedita who organised a party at the consulate to introduce Okakura to her Indian friends, specially the Tagores. Okakura and Nivedita then visited Santiniketan and thereby started a fruitful and deep friendship between India and Japan.[1] Tagore's biographer Prashanta Kumar Pal writes that the 'Tagore household moved closer to Okakura than the other way round'. They discovered in Okakura's lifestyle, the ideal of the beautiful yet simple Japanese life philosophy which attracted them very much. As a result, the decor and furniture in Jorasanko changed immensely. Having come close to Abanindranath and Gaganendranath Tagore, Okakura on his return to Japan sent two Japanese artists to India – Taikan Yokoyama and Hishida Sunso – whose painting style influenced the modern Bengali art. Kusumoto San, an architect, and Sanosan, who was an expert in Jio Jitsu, were then sent to Rabindranath's school at Santiniketan. Their expertise was not limited to Santiniketan and Kusumoto taught at Taraknath Palit's Bengal Technical Institute and the Artisan School in Tripura.[2] Many testify to Rabindranath Tagore's admiration for the founder of Judo, Jigoro Sano, whom he visited during his trip to Japan and subsequently Shinzo Tagagaki came to Santiniketan on the invitation of Tagore.[3] Tagore was conscious about the need for acquiring accurate knowledge about other countries at all times and this he achieved through his friends, contacts and admirers all over the world. He contacted Rikhang N. Kimura who studied Sanskrit and Pali in Chittagong and then Oriental Studies in Calcutta University before pursuing research in Asiatic Society under Haraprasad Sastri, asking him to be his translator for the duration of his travel in Japan but before that 'to make necessary preparations'. As he wrote in his letter to Kimura, 'I want to know Japan in the outward manifestation of its modern life and in the spirit of its traditional past. I also want to follow the traces of ancient India and have some idea of your literature if possible'.[4] In 1924, *Anandabazar Patrika* published news that a 64-year-old baby Chu Chen Tan was born in China on 8 May. The occasion was commemorated by the Crescent Moon Society in Peking where it was decided that this birthday celebration would be an annual feature. Rabindranath Tagore was on his Asian journey. The Peking Union Medical College auditorium was packed with people waiting to wish Rabindranath Tagore on his new Chinese name given by the famous Chinese philosopher Hu Shih Hu and Liang Chi Chao. In ancient Chinese, India is referred to as Chu and Rabi as Chen and Indra as Tan, hence Chu Chen Tan for Rabindranath of India. Tagore's play *Chitra* was read on the occasion.[5] Two years later, another birthday was celebrated in Tokyo, Japan, in 1927 where Tachibana and Rashbehari Bose spoke on various facets of the poet's life.[6]

The principles that prompted the foundation of Visva Bharati University were so unique that during the stone-laying ceremony in 1918, as Rathindranath, the poet's son wrote in his diary, on that day Rabindranath gave a short lecture on the aims and purposes of Visva Bharati, and people were so overwhelmed that 'about ten thousand rupees of donation was promised on the spot'.[7] Tagore said in his speech:

> A veritable Diwali has illuminated the world of learning. When every race raises the glow so that the illumination mingles with others' then the festival will be complete . . . It has already been proved that *Bharat* has used her intellect to ponder on the different problems of the world and find solutions to them. That education which, helps to reveal real truth to the Indians and through them to the

> world, will be most appropriate at this time. The education which teaches through repetition or replication is not genuine and can be done by machines . . . The real field of knowledge in education is where knowledge is innovative. The real work of a university is to create knowledge and its secondary work is to disseminate that knowledge. It will be necessary for our university to invite those intellectuals who by their innovativeness and diligence are involved in research, discovery and creation of knowledge. Where ever these intellectuals meet, knowledge will bloom there naturally and eternally and it is in the shores of that emerging stream that a true university will be set up. It will not be a fake replica of a foreign university . . . Every country's education is connected to their own traditions and lifestyles. . . . Our new universities are not built on indigenous roots but hang like parasites on alien trees branches . . . I want to name our ideal university Visva Bharati.[8]

This was not a university in the sense of a European university but 'a true university . . . more like what we had in ancient Nalanda, an educational colony which will be in direct touch with all the requirements of the modern man'. Visva Bharati was established on 23 December 1918 and became functional six months later from 3 July. On that occasion Rabindranath gave a speech in which he proclaimed the 'real motive' of 'true education' to be not for providing education for a better lifestyle but 'to a higher end which had not yet revealed itself to Indians'.[9] Tagore's biographer Prasanta Kumar Pal has mentioned a booklet, *A Centre of Indian Culture*, where Tagore outlined what the ideal of education in India should be:

> Each race has the duty to keep alight its own lamp of intellect to play its part in the illumination of the world. ...He who has no light is unfortunate enough, but utterly miserable is he who, having it, has been deprived of it, or has forgotten all about it. India has proved that it has its own mind, which has deeply thought and felt and tried to solve, in the light of its own knowledge, the problems of existence. The education of India is to enable this mind of India to find out truth, to make this truth its own wherever found and to give expression to it in such a manner as only it can. In order to carry this out, first of all the mind of India has to be concentrated and made conscious of itself and then only can it accept education from its teachers in a right spirit, judge it by its own standard and make use of it by its own creative power. The next point is that, in education, the most important factor must be the inspiring atmosphere of creative activity. And therefore the primary function of our University should be the constructive work of knowledge. ... Education can only become natural and wholesome when it is the direct fruit of a living and growing knowledge. The last point is that our education should be in full touch with our complete life, economical, intellectual aesthetic, social and spiritual; and our educational institutions should be in the very heart of our society, connected with it by the living bonds of varied co-operations.[10]

This booklet was changed and expanded into another one during his tour of Europe and America, called *The Appeal for an International University*. Sarvepalli Radhakrishnan, philosopher and the second Indian President, definitely thought that Visva Bharati was an 'international university where the whole world has become a single nest', where the students imparted a 'background of internationalism' and helped to 'realise the true character of our interlinked humanity'.[11] It was not that everyone was supportive in the university venture. The example of historian Jadunath Sarkar comes foremost to mind. After formulation of the Constitution, Tagore then tried to acquire permission from different leading academics for joining the Governing Body of the university. He approached Dr Jadunath Sarkar to give his consent to become a member along with Dr Jagadish Chandra Bose and Pramatha Chowdhury. While the latter two sent their consent to the appeal, Jadunath Sarkar refused citing two reasons. One reason was that Sarkar lived too far away in Cuttack for attending to day-to-day issues regarding the university and the second reason was that in his view Santiniketan as a school was better where the students' mind and body were developed in a good and healthy manner, after which they could join some ordinary college and attain ordinary education which would make them fit to join the multitude. But a university was a different thing for Sarkar. He believed that it was necessary to have highly qualified teachers in all subjects, as well as students trained in receiving intellectual discipline and exact knowledge to pursue higher research and education, and a leader with moral and educational integrity. By that standard, the students of Bolpur did not receive that preliminary education, on the contrary, they have learnt to hate exact knowledge and intellectual discipline, 'considering their teachers and guardians to be heartless enemies of universalism and mock them as fraudulent scholars.' He therefore declined the proposal of Tagore, though he was willing to attend a lecture or history symposium organised there[12] Tagore was very disheartened by what he considered a betrayal by his erstwhile friend whose scholarship he admired very much. In a letter to Prasanta Chandra Mahalanabis, he confided his sense of loss at the lack of support by Sarkar but accepted the rejection saying that his name would be struck off from the Constitution. However, Tagore's biographer Paul writes that since the Constitution had already been printed, Sarkar's name could not be removed.[13]

From the beginning, Tagore had wanted his Visva Bharati to live up to its name where scholars and talented people from different parts of India, Asia and the world would converge and impart their knowledge to the students. This ideal was for him an extension of the policy which had led him to invite many scholars from outside India to the school in Santiniketan. Besides Okakura's visit in 1902, I have previously discussed the presence of painters Taikan Yokoyama and Hisisda Sunso, architect Kusumoto San, and martial arts specialist Sanosan at Santiniketan. Another young Buddhist monk Yoshinori Hori, or Sri Chidananda, who had accompanied Okakura to India from Japan, was sent by Okakura to Santiniketan to learn Sanskrit. Tagore was very pleased that his plan of making Santiniketan the cauldron of a mixture of Asian culture was bearing fruit. As was evident in his letters to his followers and admirers, Tagore did not leave any stone unturned to make Hori feel at home. He made sure that his food was served by the students of the school and that he was taught English along with Sanskrit. A plan was being made that a student trained in Sanskrit and Tibetan should be sent along with Hori to various monasteries in China and Japan to collect or copy manuscripts in Bengali and Devanagari. But the plan fell through because Hori inexplicably left Santiniketan and went on a tour of India with a Japanese visitor Ito. As Sister Nivedita wrote in a letter to Mrs Macleod, 'On the journey, he scratched his finger in a railway carriage somewhere in the Panjaub, and the wound turned to lockjaw, and then, on the way from Lahore to Calcutta, he died'.[14]Among the many scholars and visitors to Visva Bharati, *Anandabazar Patrika* highlights some special ones. On 16th October 1928, a Chinese poet Tse Mon Hu visited Santiniketan,[15] while on 10th December 1929, a Chinese monk travelled to Santiniketan on foot to study

Persian, Sanskrit and Buddhist philosophy.[16] The Cheena Bhavan set up as a joint initiative between Indian and Chinese intellectuals became the new site of scholarly interaction and visits by Buddhist monks and political leaders such as Chiang Kai Shek, Nehru and Zhou Enlai as discussed exhaustively by Tansen Sen recently.[17]

Discussing the influence of Visva Bharati and Sri Niketan and its affiliated organisations, Nripendranath Banerji, in his autobiography written in 1950, had commented that 'in free India, Visva Bharati may well grow to be the nucleus of a university connecting India, the Far East, and the Near East, and the Western Hemisphere in one golden chain of an inter-fused and interlocked cultural assimilation',[18] but like all the other inter-Asian experiments, the golden period dimmed over the years, especially after his death. But till 1941 at least all the famous visitors to India wanted to be a part of its creative process. Rabindranath in his letters mentions the gift of a beautiful Batik cloth made for the members of Java's royal family[19] which he brought back. What was extraordinary was not simply the gracious acceptance of gift but as proof of his deep appreciation he popularised the making of batik cloth so much so that batik on cloth and leather became a local handicraft in Santiniketan. The same is noticeable in the dance form emerging from Santiniketan, to complement Rabindra sangeet. It was a fine and sensitive amalgamation of dance forms, classical and folk of not only Indian origin but also from the countries of South and South-East Asia. There were a number of foreign students who knew different dance styles from Malaysia, Vietnam and Java and they were all associated with the dance movement of Tagore. Sometimes troupes from Visva Bharati also travelled to other countries to perform dance dramas. *Anandabazar Patrika* in 1934 published serially over April and May news that Rabindranath Tagore was invited by some leading citizens of Colombo to accompany some artists and students of Santiniketan. On 4th May before his departure, Tagore said that most of the students of Ceylon were educated abroad and wanted to know India intimately because India and Ceylon were like the entangled roots of a tree. 'Just as a tree is destroyed when it is pulled out by its roots and replaced in a pot, the separation (of India and Ceylon) has adversely affected the original art and culture'.[20] Santidev Ghosh who accompanied him mentions performance of *Shaapmochon* in Sri Lanka in 1938 which was praised in the *Ceylon Daily News*.[21]

Santiniketan welcomed Chinese poet and scholar Tsu Simo, a professor of Peking University who was inspired by Tagore when he had visited China. According to Tsu, the ancient Sino-Indian cultural and spiritual contact had been revived by Tagore's visit. Most Chinese had been unaware of India, and Tagore's personality impressed everyone so much that they wanted to renew the contact between the two civilisations. To keep the memory of Tagore's visit fresh, a society had been set up in China called Crescent Moon Society. Anath Nath Basu gave detailed descriptions of how Kalabhavan was decorated for the visit of the Chinese scholar and how Tsu addressed the students after enjoying a cultural programme organised by Dinendra Nath Tagore.[22] On 14th December 1932, to commemorate the centuries-long friendship ties between Japan and India, a function was organised by the Japanese Ambassador Hara where Rabindranath Tagore and the Japanese Sculptor Kosetsu Nosu were invited to speak in the presence of many eminent personalities – Manmathanath Mukhopadhyay, Bhandarkar, Gaganendranath Tagore, Abanindranath Tagore and Suniti Kumar Chattopadhyay.

Tagore's greatest fear was that the Asian bond would be hampered and the dream of the Asiatic League would fall through nationalistic aggressions. That is why even the unsympathetic reception that the poet received from the young radicals in both countries, China and Japan, did not deter him from either artistically incorporating Japanese styles of dance in his dance dramas or hoping that both countries would realise the potential power of each. His commitment to universalism, 'albeit with a twist' as Sugata Bose points out compared to the universalist claims of Europe,[23] was not necessarily a harking back to the past and was one of the many differences he had with MK Gandhi whom he also greatly admired as a leader as Amartya Sen points out.[24] It was not only nostalgia but a positive experiment with a view to looking to the future as words of his popular song indicated, '*Give and take, unite and be united*'.[25]

Netaji Subhas Chandra Bose's free India provisional government in Asia

Subhas Chandra Bose, Indian nationalist and cosmopolitan, whose life 'encapsulated the contradictions of global history',[26] frequently visited Europe as a student and later during his career as a politician, he was in close touch with nationalist leaders of different countries of Asia and Europe there – yet he chose to proclaim his Provisional Government of Azad Hind, in Asia. Bose declared on 21st October in 1943, at a speech at Syonan (Singapore), that

> for the first time in recent history, Indians abroad have . . . been politically roused and united in one organisation. They are not only thinking and feeling in tune with their countrymen at home, but are also marching in step with them, along the path of freedom . . . Now that the dawn of freedom is at hand, it is the duty of the Indian people to set up a provisional government of their own, and launch the last struggle under the banner of that Government . . . After the British and their allies are overthrown and until a permanent national Government of Azad Hind is set up on Indian soil, the provisional Government will administer the affairs of the country in trust for the Indian people.[27]

Bose had plans to lead the Indian National Army of which he was the Supreme Commander – an exciting plan to enter India from outside and jointly with an aroused Indian population to remove the British from their seat of power. With the slogan of *Chalo Delhi*, the INA would then replace the British government in a smooth transition with an already working Indian government in Asia.

Bose identified two areas which would work as positives for his plan – one was contacting the Indian diaspora in Asia along with the Indian army prisoners of war in South-East Asia overrun by the Japanese, and the second was challenging the British government in their most vulnerable spot as the Great Revolt had proved more than 80 years ago, which was the British Indian Army, famed all over the world for their unquestioned loyalty. That Bose was constantly grappling with the changing politics of Asia and Europe despite his unswerving focus on the fight for Indian's freedom is seen in his writings, speeches and broadcasts. Like the writers I have discussed in the book, Bose followed closely and analysed keenly the struggle unfolding in Asia in the 1930s. In 1937, in 'Japan's Role in the Far East' published first in the journal *Modern Review*, Bose analysed in minute details the prelude to Japan's aggression on China. Through a 'scientific examination of the internal economy of Japan', Bose tried to find reasons why Japan made imperialist demands on her neighbour, China, whose 'vastness, potential richness, and the internal weakness' made her a tempting target but whose 'national honour and self-interest' stood in the way of accepting the 'political and economic suzerainty' of Japan.[28] As Sugata Bose in *His Majesty's Opponent* points out, Subhas Chandra Bose made a 'remarkably dispassionate analysis of the power relations in East Asia' though in the end he feels that Subhas conceded that Japan 'had done great things for herself and for Asia' and admired Japan for 'her stance against the Western imperialist powers' but towards the end of the article, Subhas revealed 'where his sympathies lay'.[29] Not only was he against Japan's imperialistic moves, but he also brings in the same logic that many others in the Bengali periodicals use with regard to the China–Japan rivalry. Subhas Bose writes: could not all this (referring to the 'great things' like 'shattering white man's prestige in the Far East', putting 'western imperialist powers on the defensive', and maintaining her 'self-respect as an Asiatic race') have been achieved without imperialism . . . with humiliating another proud and cultured Asian race?,[30] thus bringing in the reference to glorious relations that India–China shared in the ancient past. For Subhas Chandra Bose, celebrating Japan's victory in Singapore through his first Azad Hind Radio broadcast in 1942, it meant 'collapse of the British empire, the end of the iniquitous regime . . . the most diabolical enemy of freedom and the most formidable obstacle to progress'.[31] For Bose, the end of the British Empire would mean freedom not only for India but all of Asia. In the next broadcast on 13th March 1942, titled 'Burmese Freedom', Bose exults in the swift collapse of military bases of Britain's imperialistic allies in East Asia. The Japanese capture of Rangoon has revived the hopes of freedom of the Burmese.[32] He was ecstatic that he could be present in Burma at the time of the declaration of her independence on 1st August 1943 and rejoiced at complete independence of the Philippines on 14th October 1943. Bose wanted to separate India's Asian consciousness from enslavement by the British when he points out that the British intrigue has mischievously created discord not only within Indians but also between Indians and Asians. They have been convinced that their frontiers lie where the British need them to be 'on the Suez Canal and in Hong Kong . . . Libyan Desert and France . . . The Indians understand that they have no enemy outside the Indian frontier'.[33] All these events as well as the Quit India Movement occurring in India convinced Bose that he had to reach the East, as close as possible to India, and after a perilous sea journey reached Sabang in Sumatra in 1943. For a year from his escape from house-arrest in 1941, Bose relentlessly pursued ways and means to foster Indian independence movement in Europe before he returned to Asia taking up the responsibility of leadership against imperialism in South-East Asia. Bose reached Singapore in July 1943 and spent the next few months in touring Malaya, Thailand, Indo-China and Burma in preparation of involving the large numbers of Indian civilians residing in South-East Asia. The Provisional government he set up came about just months later.

As the press statement in August 1943 pointed out, Bose had come to the conclusion that with the suppression of the Quit India Movement in India, the responsibility of the Indian freedom fighters in South-East Asia towards the leaders of the freedom movement in India was twofold. Military help and support would be provided by the INA and moral support by the Provisional Government of Free India. It was very important at that crucial juncture, according to him, to establish strong connections between Indians in India and Indians abroad. As was announced in the Singapore Radio, not only the large number of Indians living in South-East Asia was keen on the Provisional government but also Bose established contacts with the Premier Pibul

Songgram of Thailand and Chief of State, Dr Ba Maw, of Burma to ensure their support.[34]

Having made full preparations, Bose then launched the military and political apparatus of the freedom movement of the Independence League in East Asia distinguishing it from all other diaspora-based organisations by removing the limitations of a 'mere propaganda organ' – the Indian National Army and the Provisional government. He underlines in pointing out the significance of the Provisional government through thorough historical research on the previous provisional governments set up by the Irish (1916), Czechs (1917) and the Turks under Mustapha Kemal in Anatolia (1927), combining it with his intimate knowledge of the Indian political circumstances. In his words,

> the Provisional government of Azad Hind will not be like a normal peace-time government . . . it will be a fighting organisation . . . to launch and conduct the last war against the British and their allies in India. Consequently only such departments will be run by the government as will be necessary . . . When the Provisional government is transferred to Indian soil, it will assume the functions of a normal government operating in its own territory.[35]

On declaration of war against the British, the Head of State, Prime Minister and Minister of War and Foreign Affairs announced that the government, besides its primary function of conducting war, would 'undertake to administer the liberate territories during the transition period only' and would 'continue to function till the last Englishman is driven out of India'.[36] The Provisional Government was recognised by Japan (23 Oct), Burma (24 Oct), Germany and the Philippines (30 Oct), Nationalist China and Manchukuo (1 Nov), Italy (19 Nov) and Croatia (27 Dec). The headquarters were then shifted to Rangoon in February 1944 and the INA began its doomed march. After the failure of the campaign and defeat by the British Indian forces there followed the tragic accident that befell the Supreme Commander Bose, and the Red Fort trials of the INA officers, Shah Nawaz, Dhillon and Sahgal. Among the ten charges directed against them, one was on the Provisional Government. Details of the functioning of the government were given among others by S.A Ayer, the propaganda minister of Azad Hind government who deposed before the General Court Martial that 2,32,562 persons had sworn allegiance to the government in Malaya alone by June 1944. This statement was not questioned by the prosecution and the documents placed before the court proved the operations of the government through the Army, its badges and emblems and territorial possessions in Andaman and Nicobar Islands handed over by Japan and the Ziawadi estate in Burma and Manipur by Parmanand, corroborated by statements made by Dinanath, Lt. Shiv Singh and Captain R.M. Irshad. The resources of the government were financed by Azad Hind Bank, and the impressive details of transactions were deposed to the Court by one of its Directors, Dinanath. Finally, the deposition of Renzo Sawada proved that the appointment of T. Hachiya as Minister in Rangoon in 1945 and the circumstances under which the war was waged with an organised Government and an organised Army, the Court could not judge that continuation of war by the INA under the Provisional Government was not an offence.[37]

Jawaharlal Nehru and the Asian Relations Conference, 1947

Nationalist and Indian political leader, Jawaharlal Nehru's commitment to universalism and cosmopolitanism is widely known, though here I will only refer to the

Conference he organised in 1947, just before the declaration of Independence, to further Asian connections. In the welcome address, the Chairman of the Reception Committee, Shri Ram, in welcoming his guests thought that it was apt that India had been chosen as the venue of the conference since it had been the 'meeting ground . . . of different cultures and has made her own unique contribution in synthesising seemingly antagonistic cultures'.[38] Jawaharlal Nehru, on the other hand, considered India's contribution in initiating the Conference as only coincidental. The response was 'not merely (due) to that call from us but some deeper urge'.[39] According to Jayantanuj Bandopadhyay, Nehru's words in his inaugural address, that 'in order to have one world, we must also, in Asia, think of the countries of Asia cooperating together for that larger ideal' was merely giving concrete expression to a long felt idealistic aspiration of the Indian national movement.[40] Yet Nehru tried to allay some fears which he said had arisen abroad, 'that this was some kind of a Pan Asian movement directed against Europe and America. We have no designs against anybody; ours is the great design of promoting peace and progress all over the world'.[41] These quotations state in summary Nehru's beliefs.

From the end of the First World War, the Indian National Congress talked, year after year, almost without interruption of the need for an 'Asiatic Federation'. In 1928, the Congress resolved that 'India should develop contacts with other countries and peoples who also suffer under imperialism and desire to combat it' and directed its Working Committee to convene 'the first Session of a Pan-Asiatic Federation in 1930 in India'. In the following year, Jawaharlal Nehru, as President of the Congress, spoke eloquently of the past glories of all Asian nations, now in a state of humiliation and subjection under western nations, not only in the realm of thought but also in military and political spheres. 'We have forgotten', he said, 'that for millennia the legions of Asia overran Europe and modern Europe itself largely consists of the descendants of these invaders from Asia'; however, Nehru asserted, 'with some confidence that Asia, and even India, will play a determining part in future world policy'.[42] In a letter to his sister in 1939, Nehru observed that the future relations between India and China visualised by him was one approximating merger. In 1942, the Congress resolved that 'the freedom of India must be a symbol of and prelude to the freedom of all other Asiatic nations under foreign domination. Burma, Malaya, Indo-China, the Dutch Indies, Iran and Iraq must also attain their complete freedom'.

In 1927, Nehru attended the Brussel Congress against Colonial Oppression and Imperialism as the representative of the Indian National Congress, where another Indian Virendranath Chattopadhyay took an active part in its organisation and was its general secretary. On Jawaharlal Nehru's participation at the Congress, Sarvepalli Gopal writes that it was a 'turning point in Jawaharlal's mental development'. The Brussel congress was attended by what Gopal calls a 'a medley group' comprising of 'European communists, trade unionists, and pacifist nationalists from Asia, Africa and Latin America, and secret service agents – with many delegates doubling the roles.'[43] In a statement to the press, Nehru emphasised 'the common element in the struggle against imperialism in various parts of the world' and reminded the people that 'the fabric of imperialism looked imposing and appeared to hold together, but any rent in it would automatically lead to its total destruction'. 'Indian nationalism', according to Nehru, 'was based on the most intense internationalism, just as the problem of Indian freedom was a world problem'.[44] According to S. Gopal, Nehru drafted a joint declaration of Indian and Chinese delegations, which bears the marks of an outlook which was to remain unchanged for over 30 years. Friendship with China was the core of his pan-Asian feeling. The declaration, in line with the prevalent attitude of cultural nationalism in India and its stress on the ancient civilisations of the East, recalled the close cultural ties between the peoples of India and China for over 3,000 years and blamed the British for fostering ill will against India in China by utilising Indian mercenary troops 'in support of British capitalist brigandage. It was therefore, urgent and essential that the Indian people should be educated regarding China and British imperialism'. This statement of Nehru in the Draft Declaration was very similar in vocabulary in the articles on China written in the period in the Bengali journals and must therefore have been in the minds of nationalist Asians globally. Gopal points out that despite the important role India commanded at the Conference, Nehru did not take an active role in the drafting of the manifesto at the end of the Conference nor in the activities of the League which was set up to facilitate interaction among the Asian nationalists. There was some talk of forming an Asian Federation, but many others dissented considering it premature.[45] This concern about the condition of Asia continued to remain important to Jawaharlal in the next decade. Gopal writes in the volume 1 of his three-volume biography of Jawaharlal Nehru that after the war, Nehru's direct concern was the question whether the old imperialist powers – the British in Burma and Malaya, the Dutch in Indonesia and the French in Indo-China – would be able to restore their former dominance. Gopal believed that Jawaharlal was keen that the Asian countries should help each other. He welcomed the idea of an Asian conference which had been suggested by Aung San of Burma.[46] Jawaharlal wanted to visit Burma, Malaya and Indonesia to meet the nationalist leaders of these countries, plan cooperative endeavour and inquire into the conditions of the Indians settled there. He was also concerned about the conditions of the INA officers and leaders who had been imprisoned, but he was not given permission to visit the countries. He was allowed to visit Singapore under the supervision of Lord Mountbatten, but he showed his individuality regarding his sympathy for the INA soldiers judiciously.[47]

The Asian Relations Conference, notwithstanding its limitation, may be considered to be the progeny of intellectual movement that was going on throughout the first half of twentieth century and perhaps the progenitor of his non-aligned movement. For some decades, at least Asian camaraderie appeared successful and later changed situations and focus of the constituent countries inhibited its progression. However, today, when the focus is back on Asia during the 'Asian Century', a look back at the intellectual exercises made by an uncoordinated yet intellectually unified group for the unity and development of the Asian community may be worthwhile. Jawaharlal Nehru considered the occasion of the Conference as an important watershed time for Asia. It was in his words, 'the end of an era' and 'the threshold of a new period of history'.[48] The genesis of the convening of the Asian Relations Conference can be traced in the announcement by Nehru of his desire to have a meeting of Asian minds in 1945, when in a special interview to the correspondent of *Manchester Guardian* and *The Hindu*, B. Shiva Rao, he said that an Asian Conference could be helpful to the understanding of Asia's problems and to the promotion of cooperation among Asian peoples. Thereafter on his return from a tour of South-East Asia in March 1946, he announced that some leaders like Aung San had expressed their desire to attend an Asian Conference. As he said in a message he sent through his emissary team led by U. Kyaw Myint, he had no doubt that the Conference would be guided in the task before it 'by a new consciousness of the oneness of Asia' and also by 'the supreme necessity on the part of all countries of Asia to stand together in weal and woe.[49] As Birendra Prasad has shown, the newly formed Indian Council for World Affairs with 600 members and a journal *India Quarterly* expressed their intention of undertaking the onerous task of organising the Conference in India. Once the decision to hold the Conference had been made, the team of organisers met in April 1946 and decided that the Conference would be an 'unofficial' and 'cultural' one and that 'its main object would be to exchange ideas regarding the common problems which all Asian countries had to face in the post-war era' 'round table groups' would study the problems on the basis of 'data papers' prepared in advance by specialists.[50] It had initially been thought that it would be ideal if the agenda for discussion could be fixed by a committee comprising members from different Asian countries, but the plan could not be put into action due to difficulties in communication in the short planning period. After some deliberations, five main topics were decided on – national movements for freedom, migration and racial problems, economic development and social services, cultural problems and women's problems. The working committee was comprised of Pandit Jawaharlal Nehru as Chairman with Hannah Sen, Dr P.S. Lokanathan, N. Santharam, B. Shiva Rao, D.G. Mulerkar, Dr Zakir Hussain, Dr I.H. Qureshi and Secretary Dr A. Appadorai. Later Sir S.S. Bhatnagar, Dr P.P. Pillai, Hansa Mehta, K.L. Punjabi, Pandit H.N. Kunzru, Sheikh Hashmatullah Koreshi, R. Masani and K. Shiva Rao were co-opted in. It had been decided that the invitations would be sent to organisations similar to the Indian Council of World Affairs to send 16 delegates from cultural associations and institutions from Asia, to individual scholars to supplement the representation from public associations, and four observers from the government of each Asian country. Observers were also invited from institutions of non-Asian countries like Australia, New Zealand, Britain, the United States and the Soviet Union. Responses to the invitations came in from the end of 1946 and the final count of delegates was 142 from 27 countries besides India. The delegates who had come to deliberate on the various issues were not in official government capacities and so could have a people-to-people dialogue without restrictions on their freedom of speech, yet as the organisers believed, 'such agreements or understanding as may be reached here, even if only informal, and not legally binding on the Governments, will not command any less weight with the Governments and peoples of the participating countries'.[51]

The opening Plenary session met at 5 p.m. on 23rd March at Purana Qila where a distinguished gathering of delegates, observers and guests as well as foreign diplomatic officials and visitors on tickets who numbered more than ten thousand met. A large map of Asia had been specially prepared for the occasion by the Council of Scientific and Industrial Research and flags of all participating Asian countries added to the picturesqueness of the occasion.[52] The audience was addressed by the Chairman of the Reception Committee, Sir Shri Ram. The Round Table groups and the Group plenary sessions met from 24th March to 2nd April and the final plenary session met again at the Purana Qila on 2nd April.

In his inaugural speech, besides stressing peace and Asia's refusal to be 'pawns' and 'playthings' in an 'atomic age', Nehru talked about ideal of 'one world' and 'world federation' like that of the UNO, but where Asia will play an important role. The Asian Relations Conference was important according to him because 'in a small measure it represents this bringing together of the countries of Asia. Whatever it may achieve, the mere fact of its taking place is itself of historic significance'.[53] Nehru obviously had high hopes of the success of his dream of international amity and peace since in planning the conference, he had forsaken any stress on too detailed discussion of internal politics of the countries. He admitted that it was important to study common problems, but hoped that a permanent Asian Institute would arise out of the Conference where scholars and students could discuss it. The conference would not seek to promote any 'narrow nationalism'. As he said in his speech 'Nationalism has a place in each country and should be fostered, but it must not be allowed to become aggressive and come in the way of international development'.[54]

Kalidas Nag prepared a detailed Memorandum on the literary, artistic and cultural collaboration of the Asian nations:

> that India should be the first to invite and to be the venue of the Asian Relations Conference is a fact of tremendous historical significance. Interested foreign propaganda has always tried to prove that Indian people and civilization grew in 'splendid isolation'. Yet, from the earliest phase of her documented history India was in constant touch with all the principal currents, racial and cultural, of Asia. . . . The complicated pattern of Asiatic culture was admirably represented in the first Asian Relations Conference in New Delhi. Over 200 delegates, representing about 30 nations of Asia, met in a most friendly atmosphere in spite of differences of political, economic and social outlook . . . . Pandit Jawaharlal Nehru, with rare tact and patience, controlled the situation . . . (his) sound statesmanship . . . and the towering personality of Srimati Sarojini Naidu, the chairman, worked miracle; and they piloted the vessel of the Conference through troubled waters to the haven of human fellowship and collaboration.[55]

To Nag, the presence of the delegates from the different parts of Asia, traversing long distances and navigating difficult routes, was a triumph of the Asian spirit and the crowning moment of the Conference came when Mahatma Gandhi greeted the delegates in the final session personally and delivered 'his profound message of Ahimsa', thereby placing the symbol of the Triratna – Truth, Non-Violence and Amity, 'on the superb dome of the Asian Relations Organisation'.[56] It is true that the lack of presence of the Far East Asian representatives from Japan and Communist China prevented the fullest success for the Conference, but the speech of Nobo Sambo, the leader of the Mongolian delegation, struck a chord when he said that the Conference

> proved to the world that Asians are determined not only to maintain peace and harmony, but to free the peoples of Asia and other parts of the world. It is the right time for the Asians to get together to make determined effort to conquer the world by Love and Truth . . . Asia is rising from a great slumber to lead the world, through the true path, to fight side by side with, the oppressed peoples for their cherished goal of Independence and to throw aside foreign influence.[57]

The Korean delegation which arrived at the last minute presented a set of dolls to Prime Minister Nehru and was very warmly lauded. The Chinese delegation was led by Cheng Yin-fun and the members were Wen Yuan-ning, who was a member of Legislative Yuan and editor of *T'ien Hsia*; Mao Yee-hang of the Democratic Socialist Party; G.K. Yeh of Chinese Foreign Office, who was an observer; Han Hin-wu, Vice Minister of Education; Wang Sing-kung, Professor of Sun Yat-sen University, who spoke on educational problems of south China; Dr D.H. Lew; Yi yun Chen, editor of *Women's Echo*; and Marjorie Chen and Dr Wei Chug-tsao, who were secretaries. Tan Yun-shan was also present representing Cheena Bhavan of Visva Bharati. The Chinese delegation invited all the participants to attend the Asian Conference to be held in China in 1949. The Malayan delegation which contained many members were vociferously against the proposed Malayan union, the new constitution being concocted in London' . . . which contained seeds of disunion, because the chief sponsors were the British planters and mercantile syndicates who had monopolized the economic resources of Malaya. The natural reaction of the Asian communities was hostile to the so called Malaya Union.[58] The leader of the Philippino delegation was Prof Ananstacio de Castro, who was Governor of LA Union and member of the Academy of Foreign Affairs, and some of the prominent members in the delegation were Paz Policarpio Mendez, Professor of English, University of Santo Tomas, and editor of *Women's Home Journal* and *Women's World*; Professor Mauro Mendez, also of the University of Santo Tomas and editor of several newspapers; Manuel S. Enverga, a lawyer; and Joe A Carpio, a leading economist.

The Indonesian delegates who attended the Conference during the most crucial phase of their fight for freedom received tremendous ovation. Their leader Dr Abu Hanifah, a member of the Indonesian Parliament, published a joint statement with Dr Tran Van Luan, the Vietnam delegation leader, for 'concerted action by Asian nations to prevent colonialism from re-establishing its position as suppressors of Asian peoples.[59]

Nag did not find the delegations from Cochin China, Cambodia and Laos as impressive as the three energetic Viet Nam delegates though the Siamese delegation was ably led by Phya Anuman Rachathon. Nag also wrote that the Burmese delegates were unanimous in their conviction that Burma which had suffered most in the last World war must gain her full independence in the near future.[60] Despite the declaration of boycott of the Asian Relations Conference by the Pakistanis, Nag was surprised to discover so many distinguished men and women leaders from Islamic Asia, attending the Conference. Turkey sent as observer H. Kocaman, and Arab League too sent Tauqiudin-el-Soleh as observer, and only Egypt sent both a delegate Mustafa Momin and observers Havai Idrees of Women's Union and Kareema El Sayid of Social Reform Association.

The Asian Relations Conference held at New Delhi between 23 March 23 and 2 April 1947 decided to discuss some of the major problems of Asia under the following heads: national movements for freedom, racial problems and colour bar, migration inside and outside Asia, transition from colonial to national economy, agricultural reconstruction and industrial economy, agricultural reconstruction and industrial development, labour problems and social services, cultural problems, status of women and women's movements.[61] Nag mentioned a few achievements of the Delhi Conference like the naming of the central body as the Asian Relations organisation and fixing of the location of the A.R.O provisionally in a temporary building 'Travancore House' on the Canning Road. It was decided that the original members of the A.R.O should be the nations who participated in the first Asian relations Conference, But any other nation, big or small, free or unfree, who would be ready to co-operate with and to accept the purposes and principles of our charter of Fundamental Rights would be permitted to join as members after due formalities of application and procedures of election.[62]

A source book was written at this Conference for ready reference – stating the essential facts concerning Asian countries in relation to the general political and economic development of the rest of the world by – H. Venkatasubbaiah,[63] and Fredrick James, who lived in India for 25 years, worked at Tata Group from 1941, and was one of the founders of the Indian Institute of International Affairs, submitted a paper called a Note on the Agenda of the Asian Relations Conference.

It was a matter of debate how much the ARC was influenced by the Greater India concepts. That Jawaharlal Nehru was influenced by the Greater India movement though the concept never figured as an official reference in the Indian National Congress was not denied by K.M. Panikkar. He said that 'like many other Indian nationalists, he (Nehru) believed that . . . the vision of India as the mother of all Asian civilizations' and 'in the post war context, India was necessarily the pivot of south east Asia's economic development, political emancipation and strategic stability'.[64] R.C. Majumdar pursued his Greater India agenda at the Asian Relations Conference in March–April 1947 when he said that

> any plan for the future relation between India, as an independent nation, on one hand, and Indo-China and Indonesia on the other must be based on a clear comprehension of the relations that subsisted between them in the past. It would be hardly any exaggeration to say that the earliest civilisation of Burma, Siam, Malay Peninsula, Cambodia, Annam and neighbouring regions in the interior as well as Java, Bali and other islands in the archipelago was deeply influenced by India and to a large extent directly introduced from this country.

In order to establish this claim, he outlined some facts as providing 'unimpeachable evidence' in the form of 'earliest records in these countries' in 'Indian language and Indian script'; influence of Indian philosophy and literature and vocabulary in Java and Bali; 'Indian characteristics' in architecture and sculpture in Java, Burma and Indo China, 'despite gradual modification'; influence in social customs and law books. Majumdar claimed that stating these facts were a means for 'promotion of cultural relations between India and all these countries, but also in drawing up schemes for the development of education, art, and architecture in each of them'. Only 'accurate and detailed knowledge of past history' of a country can create the 'consciousness of a great nation' and be a 'splendid asset from which they can freely draw for building up their future'.[65]

One failure of the Asian Relations Conference of 1947 was the absence of delegates from Japan and Communist China. As Nag writes, though in the interwar period Japan dominated all the Asian Relation Conferences taking place then, they were unrepresented at the first Inter-Asian Relation Conference' and this led to dissension among the delegates who felt that Japan could have been represented by pacifists like Dr. Kagawa, or from among the Japanese Buddhist community. Nag points out that though invitations had been sent, there was no response from post war Japan.[66]

All apparent failures have an inherent thread of success and it is by discussing threadbare so-called failures of Indian history that we can hope to tide over overarching dissensions within the country and without through locating amity and connections. One unifying symbol in the world today is the greatest Indian, Mahatma Gandhi, and in most of Asia and Africa, his name remains connected with freedom, peace and non-violence, so much so that many claimed his influence despite veering away from his principles (U Nu, and Aung San Suu Chi of Burma, African nationalist leaders like Kenneth Kaunda of Zambia, Kwame Nkrumah of Ghana and Nelson Mandela of Africa,[67] Julius Nyerere of Tanzania, and a number of environmental activists and leaders like Petra Kelly as well as anti-nuclear armaments campaigners). A Chinese intellectual Carsun Chang, who hosted Rabindranath Tagore during his visit there and was forced to flee in 1949 from China and take shelter in Nehruvian India, has dedicated a section of his book *China and Gandhian India*, where he compares Gandhi with Confucius,[68] thereby laying claims for the Chinese who 'much appreciated' him. Buddhism too remains the other connecting force as any trip to Buddhist sites in India today, Sarnath or Bodh Gaya, will prove. Tagore's dream of India becoming the ocean of *mahamilan* or the great unity seems a reality there. His vision of 'Freedom not only from external bondages, but from those of slumberous inaction and disbelief in one's inner power'[69] was in tune with that of many cosmopolitan-nationalists which were concomitant with the nationalists dream of freedom with a higher cosmopolitan ideal.

Notes

1 Prashanta Kumar Paul, *Rabijibani*, vol. 5 (1901–1907), Calcutta: Ananda Publishers, 2001(1990), pp. 54–61.
2 Prashanta Kumar Paul, Rabijibani, op. cit., p. 61.
3 Murli K. Menon, Nippon-shio of Rabindranath Tagore, http://bengalbee.com/the-nippon-shio-of-rabindranath-tagore/, accessed on 19.04.20.
4 Letter from Rabindranath Tagore to Kimura, Prashanta Kumar Paul, *Rabijibani* op. cit., p. 60.
5 *Ananda Bazar Patrika* (1993), 7 June 1924, Chittaranjan Bandopadhyay ed. *Rabindra Prasanga: Anandabazar Patrika, 13th March 1922–21st March 1932*, vol. I, Calcutta: Ananda Publishers, p. 5.
6 Ibid., p. 7.
7 Prashanta Kumar Paul, *Rabijibani*, op. cit., vol. VII, p. 373.
8 Translation mine, ibid., p. 373.
9 Ibid., p. 429.
10 Rabindranath Tagore, A Centre of Indian Culture, http://tagoreweb.in/Render/ShowContent.aspx?ct=Essays&bi, accessed on 28.2.20.
11 Sarvepalli Radhakrishnan, *Rabindranath Tagore: A Centenary*, Delhi: Sahitya Akademy, 1992, p. xxiii.
12 Prashanta Kumar Paul, *Rabijibani*, op. cit., vol. VIII, p. 205.
13 Ibid.
14 Quoted in Prashanta Kumar Paul, *Rabijibani*, op. cit., vol. 5, p. 77.
15 *Ananda Bazar Patrika*, 16th October 1928, *Rabindra Prasanga: Anandabazar Patrika 13th March 1922–21st March 1932*, op. cit., vol. I, p. 108.
16 *Ananda Bazar Patrika*, 10th December 1929, ibid., p. 110.
17 Tansen Sen, *India, China and the World: A Connected History*, Delhi: Oxford University Press, 2018, pp. 306–320.
18 Nripendra Chandra Banerji, *At the Cross Roads, 1885–1846*, Calcutta: Jignasa, 1974 (1950), p. 248.
19 Rabindranath Tagore (1927/2010), *Letters from Java: Rabindranath Tagore's Tour of South East Asia 1927*, op. cit., p. 115.
20 Chittaranjan Bandopadhyay (1996), *Rabindra Prasanga: Anandabazar Patrika*, op. cit., vol. 3, pp. 313–314.
21 Santidev Ghosh, *Jiboner Dhrubatara*, Calcutta: Ananda Publishers, 1996, pp. 141–143.
22 Anath Nath Basu, Santiniketan e Chainik Sudhi Su Simor Abhyarthana, *Prabashi*, 28(2), 1928, p. 386.
23 Sugata Bose, *A Hundred Horizons: The Indian Ocean in the Age of Global Empire*, New Delhi: Permanent Black, 2006, p. 268.

24 Amartya Sen, *The Argumentative Indian: Writings on Indian Culture, History and Identity*, London: Penguin Books, 2005, p. 92.
25 Rabindranath Tagore, *Dibe ar nibe, milabe milibe, jabe na phire, Ei Bharater Mahamanaber Sagoro teere*. Traditions exchanged, racial barriers removed, No one returns empty-handed from this vast expanse of the great mankind, http://www.geetabitan.com/lyrics/rs-h/hey-mor-chitto-punyo-english-translation.html, accessed on 28.2.2020.
26 Sugata Bose, *His Majesty's Opponent: Subhas Chandra Bose and India's Struggle against Europe*, Delhi: Penguin Random House, 2013 (2011).
27 Subhas Chandra Bose, Proclamation of the Provisional Government of Azad Hind, in Sisir Kumar Bose and Sugata Bose, eds., *The Essential Writings of Netaji Subhas Chandra Bose*, Delhi: OUP, 2009 (1997), p. 298.
28 Subhas Chandra Bose, Japan's Role in the Far East, in Sisir Kumar Bose and Sugata Bose, eds., *The Essential Writings of Netaji Subhas Chandra Bose*, Delhi: OUP, 2009 (1997), pp. 175–190.
29 Sugata Bose, His Majesty's Opponent, Subhas Chandra Bose and India's Struggle against Empire, p. 122.
30 Subhas Chandra Bose, Japan's Role in the Far East, op. cit., p. 190.
31 Subhas Chandra Bose, Fall of Singapore First Broadcast 19 Feb 1941, in Sisir K. Bose and Sugata Bose, eds., *Azad Hind: Writings and Speeches 1941–1943*, Netaji Collected Works, vol. 11, Ranikhet: Permanent Black, 2002, pp. 67–68.
32 Subhas Chandra Bose, Burmese Freedom, ibid., p. 71.
33 Ibid., p. 72.
34 Subhas Chandra Bose, *Chalo Delhi: Writings and Speeches 1943–1945*, in Sisir Kr. Bose and Sugata Bose, eds., Netaji Collected Works, vol. 11, Ranikhet: Permanent Black, 2007, pp. 77–78.
35 Subhas Chandra Bose, *Chalo Delhi: Writings and Speeches 1943–1945*, in Sisir Kr. Bose and Sugata Bose, eds., Netaji Collected Works, vol. 11, Ranikhet: Permanent Black, 2007, pp. 114–120.
36 Subhas Chandra Bose, *Chalo Delhi*, op. cit., p. 133.
37 R.P. Singh, *Rediscovering Bose and Indian National Army*, New Delhi: Manas Publications, 2010, pp. 269–278.
38 Ibid., p. 18.
39 Jawaharlal Nehru, Asian Relations, op. cit., p. 21.
40 Jayanatanuja Bandopadhyaya, *The Making of India's Foreign Policy: Determinants, Institutions, Processes and Personalities*, Delhi: Allied Publishers, pp. 75–76.
41 Jawaharlal Nehru, Asian Relations, op. cit., p. 24.
42 Jawaharlal Nehru, *Presidential Address to the INC in Lahore in December 1929*, reprinted in India and the World, London: George Allen & Unwin, 1936, pp. 13–38.
43 Gopal, Sarvepalli. Jawaharlal Nehru: Europe 1926–1927, *Indian Literature*, 48(1) (219), 2004, pp. 61–74. *JSTOR*, www.jstor.org/stable/23341426, accessed on 12.02.20.
44 Ibid., p. 65.
45 Ibid., p. 70.
46 Sarvepalli Gopal, *Jawaharlal Nehru: A Biography, Vol. I (1889–1947)*, Delhi: Oxford University Press, 2015(1975), p. 308.
47 Ibid., pp. 309–312
48 Jawaharlal Nehru, Inaugural Address, *Asian Relations: Report of the Proceedings and Documentation of the First Asian Relations Conference New Delhi, March–April 1947*, Delhi: Asian Relations Organisation, 1948, p. 21.
49 Asian Relations, op. cit., p. 38.
50 Asian Relations, op. cit., p. 3.
51 Shri Ram, Welcome Address, Asian Relations, op. cit., p. 17.
52 Ibid., p. 13.
53 Ibid., p. 25.
54 Ibid., p. 26.
55 Kalidas Nag, *Discovery of Asia*, Calcutta: The Institute of Asian African Relations, 1957, pp. 5–7.
56 Ibid., pp. 7–8.
57 Kalidas Nag, Discovery of Asia, op. cit., p. 21.

58 Ibid., p. 25.
59 Kalidas Nag, op. cit., pp. 28–29.
60 Ibid., pp. 33–35.
61 Ibid., p. 79.
62 Ibid., pp. 83–84.
63 H. Venkatasubbiah, *Asia in the Modern World*, New Delhi: Asian Relations Conference, Indian Council of World Affairs, 1947.
64 Isabelle Saint-Mezard, *Eastward Bound: India's New Positioning in Asia*, Delhi: Manohar, 2006, pp. 184–185.
65 R.C. Majumdar, *Cultural Problems of India and Indonesia, Asian Relations Conference March–April 1947*, Delhi: Indian Council of World Affairs, pp. 1–3.
66 Kalidas Nag, Discovery of Asia, op. cit., p. 20.
67 B.R. Nanda, *In Search of Gandhi: Essays and Reflections*, Delhi: Oxford University Press, 2002, p. 61.
68 Carsun Chang, *China and Gandhian India*, Calcutta: The Book Company, 1956, p. 275.
69 Rabindranath Tagore, Asia's Response to the Call of the New Age, *The Modern Review*, LII (4)(310), 1932, pp. 370–371.

Bibliography

Abdulgani, Roeslan, *The Bandung Connection: The Asia- Africa Conference in Bandung in 1955*, Translated by Molly Bondan, Singapore: Gunung Agung, 1981.

Appiah, Kwame Anthony, *Cosmopolitanism: Ethics in a World of Strangers*, New York: W.W. Norton, 2006.

Aries, Philippe, *Centuries of Childhood: A Social History of Family Life*, Translated from French by Robert Baldick, New York: Alfred A. Knopf, 1962.

Arnold, Edwin, *Asian Relations: Report of the Proceedings and Documentation of the First Asian Relations Conference New Delhi, March-April 1947*, Delhi: Asian Relations Organisation, 1948.

Astarita, Claudia and Lim, Yves-Heng, eds., *China and India in Asia: Paving the Way for a New Balance of Power*, New York: Nova Science Pub., 2012.

Auslin, Michael R., *The End of the Asian Century: War, Stagnation and the Risks to the World's Most Dynamic Region*, New Haven: Yale University Press, 2017.

Ayyub, Abu Sayeed, *Modernism and Tagore*, Translated by Amitava Ray, Calcutta: Sahitya Academy, 1995.

Ba, U., *My Burma: The Autobiography of a President*, Montana: Literary Licensing, 2011, p. 38.

Bagchi, P.C., *India and China*, Greater India Society Bulletin no 2, Calcutta: Greater India Society, Jan–Feb 1927, Foreword, p. 1.

Bagchi, P.C., *India and China: A Thousand Years of Cultural Relations*, Calcutta: Saraswat Library, 1981.

Bagchi, P.C., ed., *Second City of the Empire*, Calcutta: Indian Science Congress Association pub., 1938.

Ballantyne, Tony, *Orientalism and Race: Aryanism in the British Empire*, New York: Palgrave Macmillan, 2002.

Banerjee, Anil Chandra, *Annexation of Burma*, Calcutta: A. Mukherjee and Bros, 1944.

Banerjee, Bibhuti Bhusan, Moroner Donka Baje, *Bibhuti Racanabali*, Vol 9, Calcutta: Mitra and Ghosh Pvt Ltd, 9th ed., 1998.

Banerjee, Bijoy Kumar, *Japani Rananeeti*, Calcutta: Satabdi Sahitya Mandir, n.d.

Banerjee, Brojendra Nath, *Bangla Samayik Patra (1818–1868)*, Calcutta: Bangiya Sahitya Parishad, 1935.

Banerjee, Chittaranjan Ed., *Rabindra Prasanga: Anandabazar Patrika 22nd Mar 1932-31st Dec 1941*, Vol 3, Kolkata: Ananda Publishers Private Ltd, 1996.

Banerji, Nripendra Chandra, *At the Crossroads 1885–1946: Autobiography*, Calcutta: Jignasa, 1974 (1950). https://archive.org/details/atcrossroads188500bane accessed on 19.02.20.

Barns, Margarita, *The Indian Press: A History of the Growth of Public Opinion in India*, London: George Allen & Unwin Ltd., 1940.

Basu, Prasenjit K., *Asia Reborn: A Continent Rises from the Ravages of Colonialism and War to a New Dynamism*, Delhi: Aleph Book Company, 2017.

Bayly, Christopher and Tim, Harper, *Forgotten Armies: Britain's Asian Empire and the War with Japan*, London: Penguin Books, 2005 (Allen Lane 2004).
Bayly, Susan, Imagining 'Greater India': French and Indic Visions of Colonialism in the Indic Mode, *Modern Asian Studies*, 38(3), July 2004, pp. 703–744.
Bhattacharya, Sabyasachi, *Rabindranath Tagore: An Interpretation*, New Delhi: Penguin/ Viking, 2011.
Bhattacharya, Sabyasachi, *The Defining Moments in Bengal, 1920–1947*, New Delhi: Oxford University Press, 2014.
Bhattacharya, S.K., *Story of Indian Art*, Delhi: Atma Ram & Sons, 1966.
Blair, Hamish, *India: The Eleventh Hour*, London: The Chawton Pub, Co. Ltd, 1934.
Blyth, Robert J., *India, Eastern Africa and the Middle East, 1858–1947*, Hampshire: Palgrave Macmillan, 2003.
Bonea, Amelia, *The News of Empire: Telegraphy, Journalism and the Politics of Reporting in Colonial India c.1830–1900*, New Delhi: Oxford University Press, 2016.
Bose, Buddhadeva, *An Acre of Green Grass: A Review of Modern Bengali Literature*, Calcutta: Orient Longmans Ltd., 1948.
Bose, Nemai Sadhan, *Racism, Struggle for Equality and Indian Nationalism*, Calcutta: Firma KLM Private Limited, 1981.
Bose, Pramatha Nath, *A History of Hindu Civilization during British Rule*, Vol III, Intellectual condition, Calcutta: W. Newman & Co., 1896.
Bose, Pramatha Nath, *The Illusions of New India,* Calcutta: W. Newman & Co., 1916.
Bose, P.N and Moreno, H.W.B, *A Hundred Years of the Bengali Press, Being a History of the Bengali Newspapers from Inception to the Present Day*, Calcutta: Central Press, 1920.
Bose, Subhas Chandra Bose, Chalo Delhi: Writings and Speeches, 1943–1945, in Sisir Kumar Bose and Sugata Bose (eds.), *Netaji Collected Works*, Vol 12, Ranikhet: Permanent Black, 2007.
Bose, Sugata, *A Hundred Horizons: The Indian Ocean in the Age of Global Empire*, New Delhi: Permanent Black, 2006.
Bose, Sugata, *His Majesty's Opponents: Subhas Chandra Bose and India's Struggle against Empire*, Delhi: Penguin, 2011a.
Bose, Sugata, Rabindranath Tagore and Asian Universalism, in *Tagore's Asian Voyages: Selected Speeches and Writings on Rabindranath Tagore*, Nalanda: Srivijaya Centre, Institute of Southeast Asian Studies, Singapore, 2011b, pp. 10–11.
Bose, Sugata and Manjapra, Kris (eds.), *Cosmopolitan Thought Zones: South Asia and the Global Circulation of Ideas*, London: Palgrave Macmillan, 2010.
Brekenridge, Carol A., Pollock, Sheldon, Bhaba, Homi K., and Chakraborty, Dipesh (eds.), *Cosmopolitanism*, Durham/London: Duke University Press, 2002.
Breuilly, John, *Nationalism and the State*, Manchester: Manchester University Press, 1982.
Brodrick, Alan Houghton, *Beyond the Burma Border*, London: Hutchinson and Co. 1944.
Brown, Garette Wallace and Held, David, *The Cosmopolitanism Reader*, Cambridge: Polity Press, 2010.
Cady, John F., *South East Asia: Its Historical Development*, Delhi: Surjeet Publications, 4th ed., 2014.
Chagla, M.C., *Roses in December: An Autobiography*, Bombay :Bharatiya Vidya Bhawan, 1973.
Chakraborty, Dipesh, *Provincializing Europe: Post Colonial Thought and Historical Difference*, Princeton, NJ: Princeton University Press, 2000.
Chakraborty, Dipesh, *Habitations of Modernity: Essays in the Wake of Subaltern Studies*, Delhi: Permanent Black, 2002 (Rpr 2006).
Chakravarti, N.R., *The Indian Minority in Burma: The Rise and Decline of an Immigrant Community*, London: Oxford University Press, 1971.
Chakravarti, P.C., *India-China Relations*, Calcutta: Firma K.L. Mukhopadhyay, 1961.
Chatterjee, Partha, *Nationalist Thought and the Colonial World: A Derivative Discourse*, London: Zed Books, 1986.

Chatterjee, Partha, *Nation and Its Fragments: Colonial and Postcolonial Histories*, Delhi: Oxford University Press, 1994.

Chatterjee, Partha, *I am the People: Reflections on Popular Sovereignty Today*, Ranikhet: Permanent Black, 2020.

Chatterjee, Suniti Kumar, *Agranthito Suniti Kumar*, Baridbaran Ghosh (ed.), Calcutta: Deep Prakashani, 2009.

Chaudhuri, Nirad Chandra, *Atmaghati Bangali*, Calcutta: Mitra and Ghosh, 1988.

Chavan, R.S., *Nationalism in Asia*, Delhi: Sterling Pub., 1973.

Cheah, Pheng and Robbins, Bruce (eds.), *Cosmopolitics: Thinking and Feeling Beyond Nation: Cross-Disciplinary Essays on Cultural and National Identities*, Columbia: Camdin House, 1996.

Chen, Kuan-Hsing (ed.), *Trajectories: Inter-Asia Cultural Studies*, London: Routledge, 1998.

Chirol, Valentine, *The Occident and the Orient: Lectures on the Harris Foundation, 1924*, Chicago, IL: The University of Chicago Press, 1924.

Choudhuri, Indra Nath (ed.), *Tagore's Vision of the Contemporary World*, New Delhi: Har-Anand Publications, 2016.

Christie, Clive J., *Southeast Asia in the Twentieth Century*, London/New York: I.B. Tauris Publishers, 1998.

Christie, Clive J., *Ideology and Revolution in Southeast Asia 1900–1980: Political Ideas of the Anti-Colonial Era*, Richmond, Surrey: Curzon Press, 2001.

Cohen, Paul A and Goldman, Merle (eds.), *Ideas across Cultures: Essays in Chinese Thought in Honor of Benjamin I. Schwartz*, Cambridge, MA: Harvard University Press, 1990.

Collins, Michael, *Empire, Nationalism and the Post Colonial World: Rabindranath Tagore's Writings on History, Politics and Society*, London: Routledge, 2014.

Cressey, George B., *Asia's Lands and Peoples: A Geography of One Third the Earth and Two-Third Its People*, New York: Mc Graw Hill Book Co., 1951.

Dass, Baneswar (ed.), *The Economic and Social Ideas of Benoy Sarkar*, Calcutta: Chuckervartty Chatterjee and Company Limited, 1939.

De Bary, Wm.Theodore and Embree, Ainslie T. (eds.), *Approaches to Asian Civilizations*, New York: Columbia University Press, 1964.

Dieckhoff, Alain, and Jaffrelot, Christophe (eds.), *Revisiting Nationalism: Theories and Processes*, London: Hurst and Company, 2005.

Donnison, F.S.V, *Public Administration in Burma: A Study of Development during British Connexion*, London & New York: Royal Institute of International Affairs, 1956.

Dua, R.P., *The Impact of the Russo-Japanese (1905)* War *on Indian Politics*, Delhi: S. Chand and Co., 1966.

Duara, Prasenjit, Foreword (ed.) Kwa Chong Guan, *Early South East Asia Viewed from India: An Anthology of Articles from Journal of Greater India Society*, New Delhi: Manohar, 2013.

Eddy G.S, *Japan and India, Calcutta: Student Volunteer Movement of India and Ceylon*, 1910.

Edwardes, Michael, *Asia in the European Age, 1498-1955*, Bombay: Asia Publishing House, 1990.

Embree, Ainslie T., *Imagining India: Essays on Indian History*, Mark Juergensmeyer (ed.), New Delhi: Oxford University Press, 1989.

Emmer, P.C. (ed.), *India and Indonesia from the 1920s to the 1950s: The Origins of Planning*, Vol. I, Leiden: E.J. Brill, 1987.

Fleming, Peter, *The Siege at Peking*, London: Rupert Hart-Davis, 1959.

Garcia-Moreno, Laura, and Pfeiffer Peter, C. (eds.), *Text and Nation: Cross-disciplinary Essays on Cultural and National Identities*, Columbia, USA: Camden House, 1996.

Gedement, Francois, *The New Asian Renaissance: from Colonialism to the Post Cold War*, Translated by Elisabeth, J. P. Arcell, London: Routledge, 1997.

Gellner, Ernest, *Nationalism*, London: Weidenfeld & Nicolson, 1997.

Ghosh, Aurobindo, *The Significance of Indian Art*, Bombay: Sri Aurobindo Circle, 1947.

Ghosh, Benoy, *Selections from English Periodicals of 19th Century Bengal, Vol VIII: 1875-80*, Calcutta: Papyrus, 1981.

Ghosh, Benoy, *Samayikpatre Banglar Samajchitra, Part I: Sanvad Prabhakar*, Calcutta: Prakash bhavan, 2015 (1962).

Ghosh, Manomohan, *China's Conflict with India and The Soviet Union*, Calcutta: The World Press Private Ltd., 1969.

Ghosh, Santidev, *Java o Balir Nrityageet*, Calcutta: Vishwa Bharati Granthanbibhag, 1994(1952).

Ghosh, Santidev, *Jiboner Dhrubatara*, Calcutta: Ananda Publishers Pvt Limited, 1996.

Ghosh, Sisir Kumar (ed.), *Faith of a Historian: Selections from Arnold Toynbee*, Bombay: Bharatiya Vidya Bhawan, 1967.

Gopal, Sarvepalli. "Jawaharlal Nehru: Europe 1926–1927." *Indian Literature*, vol. 48, no. 1 2004 (2019), pp. 61–74. JSTOR, www.jstor.org/stable/23341426 accessed 12 Feb. 2020.

Gordon East, W., Spate, O.H.K, and Fisher, Charles A. (ed.), *The Changing Map of Asia: A Political Geography*, London: Methuen and Company. Ltd., 1950.

Grousset, Rene, *Sum of History*, Essex: Town Bridge Publications, 1931 (1946).

Grousset, Rene, *In the Footsteps of the Buddha*, Translated by Mariette Leon, London: G. Routledge and Sons, 1932.

Guha, Ramachandra, *Democrats and Dissenters*, Gurgaon: Penguin Books, 2016.

Gupta, Manindra Bhushan, *Singhaler Shilpa o Sabhyata*, Calcutta: Vishwa Bharati Granthanbibhar, 2000 (1953).

Gupta, Nagendranath, *Reflections and Reminiscences*, Delhi: Hind Kitabs Ltd., 1947.

Hahn, Emily, *China Only Yesterday: 1850–1950*, London: Weidenfeld and Nicolson, 1963.

Havell, E.B, *Ideals of Indian Art*, London: John Murray, 1920 (1911),

Hay, Denys, *Europe: The Emergence of an Idea*, Edinburgh: Edinburgh University Press, 1968.

Hay, Stephen N., *Asian Ideas of East and West: Tagore and His Critics in Japan, China and India*, Bombay: Oxford University Press, 1970.

Heesterman, Chaudhuri, Dharma, Kumar, *India and Indonesia: General Perspectives Comparative History of India and Indonesia*, Vol IV, London: E.J.Brill, 1989.

Herbert, Jean, *An Introduction to Asia*, Translated by Manu Banerji, London: George Allen and Unwin Ltd., 1965.

James, Fredrick, *A Note on the Agenda of the Asian Conference*, Delhi: Indian Council of World Affairs, 1947.

Karl, Jaspers, *The Origin and Goal of History*, New Haven and London: Yale University Press, 1965 new ed., 1953.

Kahin, George McTurnan, *The Asian-African Conference Bandung, Indonesia, April, 1955*, Ithaca, NY/Cornell University Press, 1956.

Keay, John, *Empire's End: A History of the Far East from High Colonialism to Hongkong*, New York: Scribner, 1997.

Keay, John, *China: A History*, London: Harper Press, 2009.

Keenleyside, T.A., Prelude to Power: The Meaning of Non-Alignment Before Indian Independence, *Pacific Affairs*, 53(3), 1980, pp.461–483.

Kesavapany, K., Mani, A., Ramasamy, P., *Rising India and Indian Communities in East Asia*, Singapore: Institute of Southeast Asian Studies, n.d.

Lach Donald, F., *Asia in the Making of Europe*, Vol I, The Century of Discovery Book One, Chicago, IL: The University of Chicago Press, 1965.

Lach Donald, F., *Asia in the Making of Europe*, Vol II, A Century of Wonder, Chicago, IL: The University of Chicago Press, 1970.

Lal, Chaman (ed.), *India and Japan: Friends of Fourteen Centuries,* Ambala: Tribune Press, 1959.

Laskar, Bruno, *Peoples of Southeast Asia*, New York: Alfred A Knopf, 1944.

Lattimore, Owen, *The Situation in Asia*, Boston, MA: Little, Brown and Company, 1950.

Leifer, Michael (ed.), *Asian Nationalism*, London: Routledge, 2000.

Levi, Werner, *Free India in Asia*, Minneapolis, MN: University of Minnesota Press, 1952.

Long, Rev. J, *A Descriptive Catalogue of Bengali Works*, Calcutta: Sanders, Cones and Co., 1855.

Lovell, Julia, *The Opium War: Drugs, Dreams and the Making of China*, London: Picador, 2011.

Majumdar, J.K. (ed.), *Indian Speeches and Documents on British Rule 1821–1918*, Calcutta: Longmans, Green and Co. Ltd, 1937.

Majumdar, R.C., *Jiboner Smritideepe*, Calcutta: General Printers and Publishers, 1978.

Majumdar R.C., *Cultural Problems of India and Indonesia, Asian Relations Conference March April 1947*, Delhi: Indian Council of World Affairs.

McCallum, J.A. "The Asian Relations Conference." *The Australian Quarterly*, 19(2), 1947, pp. 13–17. JSTOR, www.jstor.org/stable/20631455 accessed 6 Feb. 2020.

Menon, K.P.S, *Many Worlds: An Autobiography*, London: Oxford University Press, 1965.

Mishra, Pankaj, *From the Ruins of Empire: The Revolt against the West and the Remaking of Asia*, London: Penguin Books, 2013.

Mitra, Jatindranath, *A Lost Nation*, Calcutta: J.N. Mitra, n.d.

Mitra, S.N., *Indian Problems*, London: John Murray, 1908. (Introduction by George Birdwood).

Mitter, Partha, *Indian Art*, Oxford: Oxford University Press, 2001.

Mukherjee, Meenakshi, *An Indian for All Seasons: The Many Lives of R.C. Dutt*, Delhi: Penguin Books, 2009.

Mukherjee, Sumita, The All-Asian Women's Conference 1931: Indian Women and Their Leadership of a Pan-Asian Feminist Organisation, *Women's History Review*, 26(3), 2017, pp. 363–381.

Myint-U, Thant, *The Making of Modern Burma*, Cambridge: Cambridge University Press, 2001

Myint-U, Thant, *Where China Meets India: Burma and the New Crossroads of Asia*, London: Faber and Faber, 2011.

Nag, Kalidas, *Discovery of Asia*, Calcutta: The Institute of Asian African Relations, 1957.

Natarajan, J. *History of Indian Journalism: Part II of the Report of the Press Commission*, New Delhi: Publications Division GOI- M.I&B, 2017(1955).

Okakura, Kakuzo, *The Ideals of the East with Special Reference to the Art of Japan*, New York: E.P. Dutton and Co., 1904.

O'Malley, Andrew, *The Making of the Modern Child: Children's Literature and Childhood in the Late 18th Century*, New York: Routledge, 2003.

Otis, Andrew, *Hicky's Bengal Gazette: The Untold Story of India's First Newspaper*, Chennai: Tranquebar, 2018.

Ozkirimli, Umut, *Theories of Nationalism: A Critical Introduction*, Hampshire/London: Macmillan Press, 2000.

Pal, Bipin Chandra, *The Spirit of Indian Nationalism*, London: Hind Nationalist Agency, 1910.

Pal, Bipin Chandra, *The Soul of India: A Constructive Study of Indian Thoughts and Ideals*, Calcutta: Choudhury and Choudhury, 1911.

Pal, Prasanta Kumar, *Rabijibani: A biography of Rabindranath Tagore*, Vols I–XII, Calcutta: Ananda Publishers Private Limited, 2002(1997).

Panikkar, K.M., *The Future of South East Asia (An Indian View)*, New York: The Macmillan Co., 1943.

Panikkar, K.M., *An Autobiography*, Translated from the Malayalam by K. Krishnamurthy, Madras: Oxford University Press, 1977.

Perry, F.W., *Order of Battle of Divisions Part 5B, Indian Army Divisions*, Newport: Ray Westlake Military Books, 1993.

Peterson, A.D.C., *The Far East: A Social Geography*, London: Gerald Duckworth and Co., 1949.

Prasad, Birendra, *Indian Nationalism and Asia (1900–1947)*, Delhi: B.R. Publishing Corporation, 1979(1952).

Radha, Kumar, *The History of Doing: An Illustrated Account of Movements for Women's Rights and Feminism in India, 1800-1990*, Delhi: Zubaan, 1993.
Radhakrishnan, Sarvepalli, *Rabindranath Tagore: A Centenary*, Delhi: Sahitya Akademy, 1992.
Rai, Lala Lajpat, *An Interpretation and a History of the Nationalist Movement* (First pub.1916), Delhi: Srishti Books Distributors 2016 (reprint).
Ray, Bharati, *Early Feminists of Colonial India: Sarala Devi Chaudhurani and Rokeya Sakhawat Hossain*, Delhi: Oxford University Press, 2002a.
Ray, Bharati (ed.), *Nari o Paribar: Bamabodhini Patrika*, Calcutta: Ananda Publishers, 2002b.
Ray, Bharati (ed.), *Prabashi te Naari (1901–1947)*, Calcutta: Ananda Publishers, 2016.
Raychaudhuri, Tapan, *Perceptions, Emotions and Sensibilities: Essays in India's Colonial and Post Colonial Experiences*, Delhi: Oxford University Press, 1999.
Robin, Jeffrey (ed.), *Asia: The Winning of Independence*, London: Macmillan Education, 1981.
Robinson, Kathryn (ed.), *Asian and Pacific Cosmopolitans: Self and Subject in Motion*, Hampshire/New York: Palgrave Macmillan, 2007.
Romulo, Carlos P., *The Meaning of Bandung*, Chapel Hill, NC: University of North Carolina Press, 1956.
Rovisco, Maria andNowicka, Magdalena (eds.), *The Ashgate Research Companion to Cosmopolitanism*, Surrey: Ashgate Publishers, 2011.
Roy, Rammohan, *Selected Works of Raja Rammohan Roy*, Delhi: Publications Division, 1958.
Roy, Rammohan, Kalidas Nag and Debajyoti Burman (eds.), *English Works of Raja Rammohan Roy, Part IV*, Calcutta: Sadharon Brahmo Samaj, 1947.
Roy, Supriya (ed.), *Letters from Java: Rabindranath Tagore's Tour of South East Asia 1927*, Translated by Indira Devi Chaudhurani and Supriya Roy, Calcutta: Vishva Bharati Pub., 2010.
Saaler, Sven and Szpilman, Christopher W.A. (eds.), *Pan Asianism: A Documentary History*, Vol I (1850–1920) and II (1920-present), Latham: Rowman and Littlefield Pub. Ltd., 2011.
Saint-Mezard Isabelle, *Eastward Bound: India's New Positioning in Asia*, Delhi: Manohar, 2006.
Sarkar, Sumit, *Modern Times: India 1880s to 1950s*, Ranikhet: Permanent Black, 2014.
Sastri, Haraprasad and Sukumar Sen (eds.), *Rachana Samagra, 1853–1931*, Calcutta: W.B. State School Book Society, 1981.
Saunders, Kenneth, *Whither Asia?: A Study of Three Leaders*, New York: The Macmillan Company, 1933.
Saunders, Kenneth, *A Pageant of India*, London: Oxford University Press, 1939.
Sen, Abhijit and Ray Ujjal, *Pother Kotha: Shatabdir Shondhikkhone Bangamohilar Brahman*, Calcutta: Stree, 1999.
Sen, Amartya, *The Argumentative Indian: Writings on Indian History, Culture and Identity*, London: Penguin Books, 2005.
Sen, Anikendra, Datta, Devangshu, Roy, Nilanjana S. (eds.), *Patriots, Poets and Prisoners: Ramananda Chatterjee's The Modern Review*, Noida: Harper Collins India, 2016.
Sen, Dinesh Chandra, *Brihat Banga*, Vol 1 (First pub.1935), Kolkata: Dey's Publishing, 1993.
Sen, N.C., *A Peep into Burma Politics (1917–1942)*, Allahabad: Kitabistan, 1945.
Sen, N.C., China as Viewed by two Early Bengali Travellers: The Travel Accounts of Indumadhav Mullick and Benoy Kumar Sarkar, *China Report*, 43(4), 2007, pp. 465–484.
Sen, Satadru, *Benoy Kumar Sarkar: Restoring the Nation to the World*, Delhi: Routledge India, 2015.
Sen, Simonti, *Travels to Europe: Self and Other in Bengali Travel Narratives, 1870–1910*, Delhi: Orient Longman, 2005.
Sen, Tansen, *India, China and the World: A Connected History*, Delhi: Oxford University Press, 2018.
Sen, Tansen and Tsui, Brian (eds.), *Beyond Pan-Asianism: Connecting China and India, 1840s and 1960s*, Delhi: Oxford University Press, 2021, pp. 1–2.
Sengoopta, Chandok, *The Rays before Satyajit: Creativity and Modernity in Colonial India*, New York: Oxford University Press, 2016.

Sengupta, Pallab (ed.), *India's Vernacular Journalism: A Journey of Two Centuries*, Calcutta: Setu Prakashani, 2019.
Sharan, Shankar, *Fifty Years after the Asian Relations Conference*, Delhi: Tibetan Parliamentary and Policy Research, 2000 (1997).
Sharma, S.R., *India As I See Her*, Agra: Agarwal Educational Publishers, 1956.
Shih, Chih-yu, Singh, Swaran, Marwah, Reena (eds.), *On China By India: From Civilization to Nation-State*, New York: Cambria Press, 2012.
Shilotri, Prabhaker S., *Indo-Aryan Thought and Culture and Their Bearing on Present Day Problems in India: An Argument from the Standpoint of a Native of that Country*, New York: The Evening Post Job Printing Office, 1918.
Sidhu, Waheguru Pal Singh and Yuan Jing-dong (eds.), *China and India: Cooperation or Conflict?*, London: Lynne Rienner Pub., 2003.
Singh, Uma Shankar and Das, Parimal Kumar (eds.), *Indians in South East Asia*, Delhi: Sterling Publishers, 1982.
Sinha, Nirmal Chandra, *How Chinese was China's Tibet region?*, Calcutta: Firma KLM (P) Limited, 1981.
Smith, Anthony D., *National Identity*, London: Penguin Books, 1991.
Smith, Anthony D., *Nations and Nationalism in a Global era*, Cambridge UK: Polity Press, 1995.
Spencer Minocher, K., *Education in India and Japan*, Bombay: Vaibhav Press, 1918.
Suu, Kyi and Aung San, *Burma and India, Some Aspects of Intellectual Life under Colonialism*, Shimla: IIAS, 1990.
Swami, Sambuddhananda, *Swami Vivekananda on Himself*, Calcutta: Swami Vivekananda Centenary, 1959.
Tagore, Rabindranath, *Java Jatrir Patra*, Calcutta: Vishwabharati Granthanbibhag, 1985a (1929).
Tagore, Rabindranath, *Parashya Jatri*, Calcutta: Visva Bharati Patrika, 1985b (1963).
Tagore, Rabindranath, *Nationalism*, Calcutta: Rupa and Company, 1992 (1917).
Tagore, Rabindranath, *Crisis in Civilization*, Calcutta: Visva Bharati, 2000 (1941).
Tagore, Rabindranath, *Kalantor* (first pub in 1937), Calcutta: Vishwabharati Granthanbibhag, 2002 Reprint.
Tagore, Rabindranath, *Rabindranath Buddhadev o Bouddhasamskriti*, Calcutta: Vishwabharati Pub., 2003a (2012 reprt).
Tagore, Rabindranath, *Rabindranath Omnibus*, Vols I–IV, Calcutta: Rupa, 2003b.
Tagore, Rabindranath, *Buddhadev*, Calcutta: Vishwabharati Pub., 2012 (1956).
Tagore, Rabindranath, *Japan Jatri*, Calcutta: Visva Bharati, 2013 (1919).
Tagore, Satyendranath, *Bauddha Dharma*, Calcutta: Maha Bodhi Book Agency, 1901 (2010).
Tarling, Nicholas, *The Fall of Imperial Britain in South East Asia*, Singapore: Oxford University Press, 1993.
Tarling, Nicholas, *Nationalism in Southeast Asia: 'If People Are with Us'*, London/New York: Routledge, Curzon, 2004.
Temple, Sir Richard, *Progress of India, Japan and China in the Century*, London: The Linscott Publishing Company, 1900.
Thakur, Vineet, An Asian Drama: The Asian Relations Conference, 1947, *The International History Review*, 41(3), 2019, pp. 673–695.
Thompson, Edward, *Rabindranath Tagore: Poet and Dramatist*, London: Oxford University Press, 1926.
Tilman, Robert O., *Man, State, and Society in Contemporary Southeast Asia*, New York/London: Praeger Pub., 1969.
Tipton, Frank B., *The Rise of Asia: Economics, Society and Politics in Contemporary Asia*, London: Macmillan Press, 1998.
Townsend, Meredith, *Asia and Europe: Studies Presenting the Conclusions Formed by the Author in a Long Life Devoted to the Subject of the Relation Between Asia and Europe*, New York: G.P. Putnam's Sons, 1901.

Venkatasubbiah, H., *Asia in the Modern World*, New Delhi: Asian Relations Conference, Indian Council of World Affairs, 1947.

Wilson, Dick, *Asia Awakens: A Continent in Transition*, London: Weidenfeld and Nicolson, 1970.

Zachman, Urs Mattias (ed.), *Asia after Versailles: Asian Perspectives on the Paris Peace Conference and the Interwar Order 1919–1933*, Edinburgh: Edinburgh University Press, 2017.

Zaidi, A.M. (ed.), *Congress Presidential Addresses* Vol I 1885–1900, Vol II 1901–1911 (1986), vol III 1912-1920 (1986), vol IV 1921–1939 (1988), New Delhi: Indian Institute of Applied Political Research Pub Division, 1985.

English Periodicals consulted for articles on Asia

The Indian World: Vols 2–5.
The Modern Review: Vols 1-CXXXXII.

Selected articles on Asia in Bengali periodicals:

Aitihasik Chitra

Bandopadhyay, Brojendranath, Chiner Utsab (The Festivals of China).

Alochana

Anon, China Darshanik Mahatma (The Noble Chinese Philosopher), 2, 1885, pp. 300–315.

Dutta, Umesh Chandra, Samajgati o Tahar Parinam (Social Mobility and Its Impact), 1, 1884, pp. 15–22.

Sen, Brajendranath, Bilat Pratyagata Bangali (The England returned Bengali), 2, 1885, pp. 99–109.

Anjali

Anon, Chin-Parachinparatar Parinam (The Result of Traditionalism in China), 1(1), 1898, pp. 40–22.

Antahpur

Raha, Mrinalini, Brahmadesher Kotha (Tales of Burma), 5(8), Agrahayan 1309, pp. 161–164.

Anusandhan

Anon, Chindiger Achar Byabohar (The Customs and Practices of the Chinese), 5(2), 1891, pp. 524–528.

Anon, Chindiger Bibaha Padhyati (The Marriage Customs of the Chinese), 5(23), 1892, pp. 546–550.

Lahiri, Durgadas, Introduction, 1(1), 1887, pp. 1–2.

Arati

Swadeshi, Sri, Asiar Jagaran (The Rise of Asia), 6(9), 1906, pp. 241–246.

Aryadarshan

Anon, Peking hoite Canton porjonto-Othobak on Irish Bhraman Karir Brittanto (From Peking to Canton–or Description of an Irish Traveller), 6(2), 1880, pp. 75–79.
Editor, Swajatiprem o Swadeshanurag (Love for Country and Its People), 3(7), 1876, pp. 306–313.
Sourindra, Sri, Sangeet Pathik (i) (The Music Traveller), 1(1), 1874a, pp. 51–54.
Sourindra, Sri, Sangeet Pathik (ii), 1(3), 1874b, pp. 134–142.
Sourindra, Sri, Sangeet Pathik (iii), 1(4), 1874c, pp. 192–199.
Sourindra, Sri, Sangeet Pathik (iv), 1(6), 1874d, pp. 295–300.
Sourindra, Sri, Sangeet Pathik (v), 1(7), 1874e, pp. 343–346.
Sourindra, Sri, Sangeet Pathik (vi), 1(9), 1874f, pp. 434–439.

Bamabodhini Patrika

Anon, Chin Kahini (i) (Tales of China), 5(2)(344), 1869a, pp. 148–150.
Anon, Chin kahini (ii), 5(2)(346), 1869b, pp. 200–201.
Anon, Chin kahini (iii), 5(2)(348), 1869c, pp. 274–275.
Anon, Chin Samrater Prarthona (Prayer by the Chinese Emperor), 5(3)(360), 1869d, pp. 274–275.
Anon, Japan (A Poem), 5(3)(362), 1869e, pp. 338–339.
Anon, Japan Samragiidwoy (The Two Japanese Empresses), 5(3)(363), 1869f, pp. 363–364.
Anon, Japane Korpur Briksha (The Camphor Tree in Japan), 5(2)(341), 1869g, pp. 43–45.
Anon, Singhaler Kotokguli Achar Byabahar (Some Customs of Singhal), 5(3)(362), 1869h, pp. 334–337.
Anon, Brahma Mahila (The Women of Burma), 2(6)(393), 1870a, pp. 213–216.
Anon, Parashyer Prachin Bibaran (The Past in Persia), 2(6)(82), 1870b, pp. 14–17.
Anon, Chindeshiyo Strijati (Chinese Women), 3(54), 1887, pp. 678–680.
Anon, Korea Pradesher Mahila (Women in Korea), 5(3)(361), 1895, pp. 313–314.
Bose, Abala, Japane Strishiksha o Amader Kartabya (Women's Education in Japan and Our Duty), 10(4)(53), 1915, pp. 174–180.

Bangabani

Bandopadhyay, Basudeb, Prachye Gupta Sandhani (The Search for Secret of the East), 4(1)(5), 1925, pp. 636–638.
Kimura, R., Japaner Shamajik Pratha (Social Customs in Japan), 2(2)(1), 1923, pp. 29–33.
Kimura, R., Japaner Shamajik Pratha (ii), 2(2)(2), 1923a, pp. 167–171.
Kimura, R., Japaner Shamajik Pratha (iii), 2(2)(4), 1923b, pp. 500–505.
Kimura, R., Japaner Shamajik Pratha (iv), 3(1)(3), 1924, pp. 317–324.
Mukherjee, Sarat, Americay Asiar Durdasha (The Dilemma of Asia in America), 3(2)(1), 1924a, pp. 55–60.
Mukherjee, Sarat, Nabin Turashka (Young Turkey), 3(2)(3), 1924b, pp. 329–332.
Mukhopadhyay, Surendranath, Asikar Masamuye o Japani Tarabari (A Japanese Story), 2(2)(2), 1923, pp. 218–226.
Nag, Kalidas, Puber Chithi (Letters from the East), 3(1)(4), 1924a, pp. 517–520.
Nag, Kalidas, Puber Chithi (ii), 3(2)(1), 1924b, pp. 41–46.
Tagore, Rabindranath, Rangoon Bangla Sahitya Sanmelanite Kobi Sambordhona Upalakkhye Rabindranather Abhibhashon (Rabindranath Tagore's Speech at the Rangoon Literature Festival), 3(1)(4), 1924, pp. 514–526.

Banga Lakshmi

Debi, Sita, Parashyer Naari (Women of Persia), 6(5), 1930, pp. 387–391.
Sarkar, Subimalchandra, Malayer Pothe (On the Way to Malaya), 6(5), 1930, pp. 351–355.

Bangasree

Bandopadhyay, Bibhutibhushan, (Bichitra Jagat) Micronesiar ogyato onchol (The Unknown Regions of Micronesia), 3(2)(6), 1935a, pp. 835–840.
Bandopadhyay, Bibhutibhushan, (Bichitra Jagat) Prithibir Bishalotomo Aronyerpothe (On the World's Highest Mountainous Roads), 4(1)(3), 1935b, pp. 402–407.
Bandopadhyay, Bibhutibhushan, (Bichitra Jagat) Asiar nodipothe (The Riverways of Asia), 4(1)(5), 1936a, pp. 695–700.
Bandopadhyay, Bibhutibhushan, (Bichitra Jagat) Bharat somudrer ekti dvip (An Island on the Indian Ocean), 4(1)(6), 1936b, pp. 803–808.
Bandopadhyay, Bibhutibhushan, (Bichitra Jagat) Jabadviper Agneyogiri 'Bromo' (The Volcano Bromo of Java) 4(1)(1), 1936c, pp. 33–38.
Chakraborty, Shibram, (Bichitra Jagat) Machher Deshe Japan (Japan the Land of Fish), 3(1)(2), 1934, pp. 193–196.
Chattopadhyay, Nripendra Krishna, Durgampather Jatri (Ferdinand Magellan) (The intrepid traveller), 4(2)(3), 1936a, pp. 324–329.
Chattopadhyay, Prabhat, Tibbot o Chiner Shimanaye (On the Borders of Tibet and China), 4(2)(5), 1936b, pp. 630–637.
Mukhopadhyay, Sarat Chandra, Kongphutje Ba Confucius, 3(1)(6), 1936, pp. 709–711.

Bharat Mahila

Dutta, Hemendranath, Turashker Ramani (Women of Turkey), 4(8), 1908a, pp. 171–174.
Dutta, Sarajubala, Chiner Porolokgota Maharani (The Departed Empress of China), 4(8), 1908b, pp. 188–192.
Dutta, Sarajubala, Japan–Mahilarsamajik Obostha (The Social Condition/Position of Japanese Women), 4(12), 1908c, pp. 273–276.
Dutta, Sarajubala, Japaner Mahila Vishwavidyalaya (Women's University of Japan), 4(5), 1908d, pp. 97–101.
Dutta, Sarajubala, Uta Imai, 4(2), 1908e, pp. 45–47.
Ghosh, Kalimohon, Japaner Grihadharma Neeti (The Internal Policy of Japan), 8(2), 1912a, pp. 38–40.
Ghosh, Kalimohon, Turashker Samrajya (The Turkish Empire) 8(8), 1912b, pp. 250–252.
Roy, Ashutosh, Chindeshiyo Ramanigoner Bibaron (Women of China: A Description), 6(10), 1910, pp. 318–319.
Roy, Ganapati, Japane Strijatir Ritiniti (Women's Position in Japan), 6(2), 1910a, pp. 318–319.
Roy, Ganapati, Japane Strijatir Ritiniti (ii), 6(3), 1910b, pp. 85–87.
Sen, Rabindranath, Eto Narisuker Porinoy (The Marriage of Eto–Narisuke: A Japanese Story), 8(1), 1912, pp. 340–342.
Takeda, Hariprabha, Bangamahilar Japanjatra (i) (A Bengali Woman's Journey to Japan), 8(8), 1912, pp. 252–256.
Takeda, Hariprabha, Bangamahilar Japanjatra (ii), 9(3), 1913a, pp. 82–88.
Takeda, Hariprabha, Bangamahilar Japanjatra (iii), 9(4), 1913b, pp. 109–113.

Bharati o Balak

Anon, Japane Phool Binyash (Art of Flower Decorations in Japan), 2(16), 1892, pp. 108–109.
Mukhopadhyay, Harishadhan, Brahma Desher Achar Byabohar (Social Customs of Burma), 2(10), 1886, pp. 67–76.

Bharati

Anon, Chiner Sangramik Shakti (The Military Power of China), 4(5), 1880, pp. 246–250.

Anon, Chiney Moroner Byabshay (The Death Trade in China), 5(2), 1881a, pp. 93–100.
Anon, Japane Bartoman Unnati (Rise of Japan), 5(3), 1881b, pp. 122–133.
Anon, Japaner Bartoman Unnatir Mul Pattan (The Roots of the Present Success of Japan), 5(2), 1881c, pp. 70–77.
Anon, Japan o Japani (Japan and the Japanese) (translation of book by M. Aime Humbert from French work by Mrs Cashel Hoey (ed.) W.H. Bates), 20(4), 1896b, pp. 214–225.
Anon, Brahme Natpuja (worship of Nat in Burma), 24(10), 1900, pp. 922–927.
Anon, Bharatbashir Japane Shilpashiksha (Industrial Training of Indians in Japan), 26(5), 1902a, pp. 483–486.
Anon, Japane Bharatiya Chhatra (Indian Students in Japan), 26(9), 1902b, pp. 893–903.
Bandopadhyay, Kedarnath, Chin Prabashir Patra (Letter from Japan), 27(12), 1903, pp. 1186–1193.
Bandopadhyay, Kedarnath, Chin Prabashir Patra (ii), 28(1), 1904, pp. 46–61.
Bandopadhyay, Charuchandra, Chin Deshe (In China), 29(4), 1905, pp. 306–316.
Bandopadhyay, Gouranganath, Meyeder Shiksha (Women's Education), 45(10), 1921a, pp. 909–916.
Bandopadhyay, Suresh Chandra, Japane Nababarsha (New Year in Japan), 37(1), 1913, pp. 33–4.
Bandopadhyay, Suresh Chandra, Japani Shraddhabashar (Funeral Customs in Japan), 45(10), 1921b, pp. 961–964.
Bhattacharya, Surendranath, Prince Ito, 33(8), 1909, pp. 447–450.
Bhattacharya, Surendranath, Japaner Aino Jati (The Aino Tribe of Japan), 36(2), 1912, pp. 205–207.
Birbal, Amra o Tomra (Us and You), 26(4), 1902, pp. 405–408.
Bose, Santosh Kumar, Chin Kusum (Poetry) (Flowers of China), 34(2), 1910, p. 133.
Chakraborty, Jnanendranath, Chin Ramanir Prempatra (Love Letters of a Chinese Woman), 37(11), 1913a, pp. 1194–1198.
Chakraborty, Jnanendranath, Chin Ramanir Prempatra (ii), 37(12), 1913b, pp. 1291–1297.
Dalal, Kalachand, Brahmadesher Bouddhya Mandir (The Buddhist Temples in Burma), 35(5), 1911a, pp. 443–446.
Dalal, Kalachand, Brahmadesher Ramani (Women in Burma), 35(8), 1911b, pp. 751–756.
Das, Bhupendranath, Chank-Wayng Pagoda, 37(8), 1913, pp. 892–894.
Deb, Ashutosh, Japane Bharatiya (Indians in Japan), 26(12), 1902, pp. 893–903.
Debi, Swarnakumari, Japani Bir (Poem) (The Brave Japanese), 27(8), 1903, pp. 725–727.
Dharmananda, Mahabharati, Mahatashaisha, 1901, pp. 246–258.
Dutta, Satyendranath, Chiner Kobita (Chinese Poetry), 33(11), 1909, pp. 630–631.
Dutta, Satyendranath, Nididyasan (Based on a Japanese Play), 36(7), 1912, pp. 724–731.
Fischer, W.H., Chiner Naba Abhyudoy (The New Rise of China), 50(4), 1924, pp. 581–585.
Hori, Shitoku, Japaner Shanatan Adarsha (The Traditional Ideal of Japan), 27(1), 1903, pp. 90–94.
Mitra, Kalipada, Madhya Asiar Bouddhya Shilpakala (The Buddhist Art of Central Asia), 42(12), 1918, pp 927–938.
Mukhopadhyay, Harichan, Brahme Ingraj (The English in Burma), 9(12), 1885, pp. 578–585.
Mukhopadhyay, Harichan, Brahmadesher Achar Byabohar (The Customs of the Burmese), 10(2), 1886, pp. 67–76.
Mukhopadhyay, Nibaran Chandra, Malay Dwippunje Hindu Dhormer Bistar (The Spread of Hinduism in the Islands of Malaya), 6(11), 1882, pp. 517–521.
Roy, Ashutosh, Chindesher Dharma (Religion in China), 36(10), 1912a, pp. 1014–1017.
Roy, Ashutosh, Chindesher Dharma (ii), 36(11), 1912b, pp. 1118–1123.
Roy, Dinendra Kumar, Chinergolpo (Tales of China), 17(7), 1893a, pp. 405–418.
Roy, Dinendra Kumar, Shyam o Shyamer Abhyantarin Abostha (Shyam and Her Internal Condition), 17(11), 1893b, pp. 680–684.

Roy, Dinendra Kumar, Shyamer Raj Antahpur (The Royal Household of Shyam, Thailand), 17(12), 1893c, pp. 720–724.

Roy, Ganapati, Japane Shiksha (Education in Japan), 34(5), 1910, pp. 374–378.

Roy, Ganapati, Malay Upadvipe Hindubhasha o Sahitya (Hindu Civilization in Malaya Islands) 35(5), 1911, pp. 443–446.

Sarkar, Jadunath, Japaner Abhyudoy (Shiksha) (The Rise of Japan-Education), 30(11), 1906a, pp. 1050–1070.

Sarkar, Jadunath, Japaner Rajniti (Politics in Japan), 30(2), 1906b, pp. 176–207.

Sarkar, Jadunath, Japaner Shilpa o Banijya (Japan's Industry and Trade), 30(5), 1906c, pp. 454–472.

Sarkar, Jadunath, Nippon Samaj (The Nippon Society), 31(3), 1907, pp. 200–212.

Sarkar, Jadunath, Japane Bhikkhuk (The Japanese Monk), 34(1), 1910a, pp. 29–32.

Sarkar, Jadunath, Japaner Khela (Sports in Japan), 34(11), 1910b, pp. 905–910.

Sarkar, Jadunath, Japaner Shahar (Cities in Japan), 34(7), 1910c, pp. 567–575.

Sarkar, Jadunath, Japaner Shahar (ii), 34(8), 1910d, pp.627–633.

Sarkar, Jadunath, Japaner Shongbad Patra (Newspapers in Japan), 34(10), 1910e, pp. 870–874.

Sarkar, Jadunath, Prabashi Japaner Sabha Smiti (The Diaspora Associations in Japan), 34(3), 1910f, pp. 212–216.

Sarkar, Jadunath, Prabashi Japaner Sabha Smiti (ii), 34(4), 1910g, pp. 300–303.

Sarkar, Jadunath, Japane Snanagar (The Bathing Houses in Japan), 35(4), 1911a, pp. 322–327.

Sarkar, Jadunath, Japaner Atithi Satkar (Japanese Hospitality), 35(3), 1911b, pp. 231–237.

Sarkar, Jadunath, Japaner Dharma (Religion in Japan), 35(6), 1911c, pp. 512–519.

Sarkar, Jadunath, Japaner Dharma (ii), 35(8), 1911d, pp. 751–756.

Sarkar, Jadunath, Japaner Sena o Noubibhag (Army and Navy in Japan) 35(11), 1911e, pp. 1061–1070.

Sarkar, Jadunath, Japani Akriti Prakriti (Japanese Customs), 35(1), 1911f, pp. 41–49.

Sarkar, Jadunath, Bharatersahit Japaner Shambandha (Relations between India and Japan), 36(2), 1912a, pp. 125–132.

Sarkar, Jadunath, Bharatersahit Japaner Shambandha (ii), 36(4), 1912b, pp. 434–440.

Sarkar, Jadunath, Japaner Rail o Tram (Railways and Trams in Japan), 36(11), 1912c, pp. 1131–1138.

Sarkar, Jadunath, Mikado, 36(2), 1912d, pp. 660–669.

Sarkar, Jadunath, Japaner Shiksha o Banijya (Education and Trade in Japan), 38(2), 1914, pp. 145–151.

Sen, Premadananda, Brahmaprabashir Patra (Letter From a Resident of Burma), 31(4–5), 1907, pp. 430–439.

Sinha, Kailash Chandra, Hiuen Tsanger Bangla Bhraman (Travels in Bengal), 4(2), 1880a, pp. 67–75.

Sinha, Kailash Chandra, Hiuen Tsanger Bangla Bhraman (ii), 4(3), 1880b, pp. 117–125.

Sinha, Kailash Chandra, Hiuen Tsanger Bangla Bhraman (iii), 4(4), 1880c, pp. 164–171.

Sudhangshu, Chine Prajatantra (Republic in China) 36(8), 1912, pp. 821–826.

Tagore, Dwijendranath, Fa Hien er Tirthajatra (Fa Hien's Pilgrimage), 6(12), 1882, pp. 561–565.

Tagore, Dwijendranath, Fa Hien er Tirthajatra (ii), 7(2), 1883a, pp. 65–70.

Tagore, Dwijendranath, Fa Hien er Tirthajatra (iii), 7(3), 1883b, pp. 105–112.

Tagore, Satyendra Nath, Rajnaitik Alochona: Burma (Political Discussion on Burma), 9(11), 1885, p. 531.

Tagore, Jyotirindranath, Adhunik Japan: Parichhad o Acharbyabahar (Modern Japan: Dress and Customs), 32(2), 1908a, pp. 84–89.

Tagore, Jyotirindranath, Adhunik Japan (ii), 32(3), 1908b, pp. 133–140.

Tagore, Jyotirindranath, Adhunik Japan (iii), 32(4), 1908c, pp. 175–179.

Tagore, Jyotirindranath, Adhunik Japan (iv), 32(5), 1908d, pp. 217–273.

Tagore, Jyotirindranath, Adhunik Japan (v), 32(6), 1908e, pp. 267–273.

Tagore, Jyotirindranath, Ekjon Bahiskriter Dainik Lipi (Farashi theke) (Daily Writing by an Exile: from the French Original), 32(12), 1908f, pp. 579–583.
Tagore, Jyotirindranath, Lafcardio Hearner Japan Chitra (The Picture of Japan by Lafcardio Hearn), 32(7), 1908g, pp. 304–309.
Tagore, Jyotirindranath, Lafcardio Hearner Japan Chitra (ii), 32(8), 1908h, pp. 355–358.
Tagore, Jyotirindranath, Lafcardio Hearner Japan Chitra (iii), 32(9), 1908i, pp. 419–424.
Tagore, Jyotirindranath, Lafcardio Hearner Japan Chitra (iv), 32(10), 1908j, pp. 461–467.
Tagore, Jyotirindranath, Cochin Chine Bhraman (Travel in Cochin China), 33(6), 1909a, pp. 299–303.
Tagore, Jyotirindranath, Cochin Chin (Cochin China), 33(8), 1909b, pp. 435–437.
Tagore, Jyotirindranath, Cochin Chin (ii), 33(9), 1909c, pp. 520–522.
Tagore, Jyotirindranath, Cochin Chin (iii), 33(10), 1909d, pp. 557–558.
Tagore, Jyotirindranath, Cochin Chin (iv), 33(11), 1909e, pp. 628–630.
Tagore, Jyotirindranath, Cochin Chin (v), 33(12), 1909f, pp. 695–700.
Tagore, Jyotirindranath, Ekjon Bahiskriter Dainik Lipi (Farashi theke) (ii), 33(1), 1909g, pp. 28–35.
Tagore, Jyotirindranath, Javadvipe (In Java Islands), 34(1), 1910a, pp. 49–51.
Tagore, Jyotirindranath, Javadvipe (ii), 34(3), 1910b, pp. 220–221.
Tagore, Jyotirindranath, Javadvipe (iii), 34(4), 1910c, pp. 303–307.
Tagore, Jyotirindranath, Javadvipe (iii), 34(5), 1910d, pp. 421–426.
Tagore, Jyotirindranath, Javadvipe (iv), 34(6), 1910e, pp. 494–497.
Tagore, Jyotirindranath, Javadvipe (v), 34(7), 1910f, pp. 575–576.
Tagore, Jyotirindranath, Javadvipe (vi), 34(8), 1910g, pp. 676–678.
Tagore, Jyotirindranath, Asiaic o Europeo Sabhyata (Civilizations of Asia and Europe), 38(9), 1914, pp. 863–868.
Vidyabhushan, Amulyacharan, Bharatbarsher Upanibesh (The Colonies of India), 44(3), 1920, pp. 235–239.

Bharatvarsha

Anon and Anon., Prabasher Patra, Champa Rajya (The Kingdom of Champa), 19(1)(5), 1931, p. 735.
Bajpei, Gajanand, Mahastresthi Mitsui (The Great Nobleman Mitsui), 26(1)(4), 1938, pp. 544–548.
Bandopadhyay, Kshitish Chandra, Chine Dashyuder Haate (In the Hands of Chinese Dacoits), 26(1)(2), 1938a, pp. 261–265.
Bandopadhyay, Kshitish Chandra, Phillippine e Bangali Porjotok (A Bengali Traveller in Philippines), 26(1)(5), 1938b, pp. 747–751.
Bandopadhyay, Nityanarayan, Aden 21(1)(2), 1933a, pp. 225–237.
Bandopadhyay, Nityanarayan, Cairo, 21(1)(4), 1933b, pp. 516–535.
Baypei, Gajanand, Mahashashti Mitsui, 26(1)(4), 1938, pp. 44–548.
Bose, Bharat Kumar, Iraq, 19(2)(6), 1932a, pp. 964–973.
Bose, Bharat Kumar, Manchuria 19(2)(5), 1932b, pp. 697–707.
Chattopadhyay, Bijonraj, Malay o Shyamrajya 11(2)(1), 1923, pp. 27–31.
Chattopadhyay, Hemanta, Borneo Dvipbashider Kotha (Tales of Borneo Islanders), 15(1)(2), 1927a, pp. 315–326.
Chattopadhyay, Hemanta, British Borneor Aranyabashider Kotha (Tales of Forest Dwellers of British Borneo), 15(1)(1), 1927b, pp. 933–941.
Chattopadhyay, Hemanta, Cambodia, 15(2)(4), 1927c, pp. 571–584.
Chattopadhyay, Sunit Kumar, Paschimer Jatri (Traveller to the West), 24(2)(1), 1936a, pp. 120–150.

Chattopadhyay, Sunit Kumar, Paschimer Jatri (ii), 24(2)(2), 1936b, pp. 246–256.
Chattopadhyay, Sunit Kumar, Paschimer Jatri (iii), 24(2)(4), 1936c, pp. 585–593.
Chattopadhyay, Sunit Kumar, Paschimer Jatri (iv), 24(2)(5), 1936d, pp. 796–809.
Chowdhurani, Sarala Devi, Burma Yatra (On the Way to Burma), 19(1)(5), 1931a, pp. 772–782.
Chowdhurani, Sarala Devi, Rangoon, 19(2)(4), 1931b, pp. 604–613.
Chowdhurani, Sarala Devi, Shwe Dagon, 20(1)(2), 1932, pp. 260–268.
Dev, Narendra, Annam, 11(1)(1), 1923a, pp. 121–136.
Dev, Narendra, Prachya o Pratichya, Japan (West and East in Japan), 11(1)(5), 1923b, pp. 763–780.
Dev, Narendra, Philippine, 12(1)(3), 1924a, pp. 444–460.
Dev, Narendra, Philippine (ii), 13(1)(4), 1924b, pp. 584–599.
Dev, Narendra, Purba Bharater Dvipabali (The Islands of Eastern India), 12(1)(1), 1924c, pp. 113–138.
Dev, Narendra, Purba Bharater Dvipabali (ii), 12(1)(2), 1924d, pp. 276–290.
Dev, Narendra, Shyam Bhoomi (The Land of Shyam), 12(1)(5), 1924e, pp. 761–773.
Dev, Narendra, Shyam Bhoomi (ii), 12(1)(6), 1924f, pp. 901–910.
Editorial, Parashye Rabindranath (Rabindranath in Persia), 19(2)(6), 1932, pp. 983–986.
Ghosh, Hemendra Prasad, Juddha Kshetre (On the War Front), 7(2)(1), 1919, pp. 53–60.
Gupta, Keshab Chandra, Malay Jati (The Malay Race), 24(2)(1), 1936a, pp. 84–91.
Gupta, Keshab Chandra, Malay Jati (ii), 24(2)(2), 1936b, pp. 270–275.
Gupta, Keshab Chandra, Malay Jati (iii), 24(2)(3), 1936c, pp. 459–461.
Gupta, Keshab Chandra, Malay Jati (iv), 24(2)(4), 1936d, pp. 608–616.
Gupta, Keshab Chandra, Malay Jati (v), 24(2)(5), 1936e, pp. 83–793.
Gupta, Keshab Chandra, Malay Jati (vi), 24(2)(6), 1936f, pp. 934–942.
Majumdar, Ramesh Chandra, Prabasher Patra Champarajya (Letters of a Traveller to Champa Kingdom), 19(1)(5), 1931, pp. 697–705.
Mitra, Ganesh Chandra, Brahma Prabasher Chitra (Pictures of Domicile in Burma), 14(1)(1), 1927a, pp. 75–86.
Mitra, Ganesh Chandra, Brahma Prabasher Chitra (ii), 15(1)(3), 1927b, pp. 447–453.
Mitra, Nibaran Chandra, Yuddhe Bangali (Bengalis at War), 12(2)(5), 1925, pp. 667–670.
Mukhopadhyay, Girindra Chandra, Chiner Kotha (Story of China), 25(1)(2), 1937a, pp. 296–308.
Mukhopadhyay, Girindra Chandra, Japan, 25(1)(3), 1937b, pp. 473–475.
Mukhopadhyay, Girindra Chandra, Japan (ii), 25(1)(4), 1937c, pp. 611–613.
Mukhopadhyay, Girindra Chandra, Japan (iii), 25(1)(6), 1937d, pp. 908–911.
Mukhopadhyay, Girindra Chandra, Japan (iv), 25(2)(1), 1937e, pp. 94–99.
Mukhopadhyay, Girindra Chandra, Japan (v), 25(2)(2), 1937f, pp. 223–228.
Mukhopadhyay, Girindra Chandra, Japan (vi), 25(2)(5), 1937g, pp. 740–743.
Narendra, Arab 11(1)(2), 1923, pp. 265–271.
Nath Ghosh, Birendra, Sarat Chandra Das, 17(2)(1), 1929, pp. 158–162.
Ray, Kumar Munindra Dev, Singhal Dwip (Sri Lanka), 15(2)(5), 1928a, pp. 683–732.
Ray, Kumar Munindra Dev, Singhal Dwip (ii), 15(2)(6), 1928b, pp. 811–824.
Roy, Ashutosh, Juddhabandir Atmakahani (The Autobiography of a War Prisoner), 7(1)(6), 1919a, pp. 782–785.
Roy, Ashutosh, Juddhabandir Atmakahani (ii), 7(2)(2), 1919b, pp. 194–197.
Roy, Ashutosh, Juddhabandir Atmakahani (iii), 7(2)(4), 1919c, pp. 509–514.
Roy, Hemandralal, Afghanistan, 21(2)(4), 1933a, pp. 538–551.
Roy, Hemandralal, Afghanistan (ii), 21(2)(6), 1934b, pp. 842–851.
Roy, Hemandralal, Afghanistan (iii), 22(1)(2), 1934c, pp. 258–269.
Roy, Satyaranjan, Brahmadesher Kotha (Tales of Burma), 1(4), 1913, pp. 527–529.
Sarkar, Himangshu Bhushan, Dvipamoy Bharat o Bharatiya Sabhyata (Indian Civilization in Insulindia), 25(1)(6), 1937, pp. 825–829.

Sen, Jamini Kanta, Chainik Chitrakalar Chhayapath (In the Shadowy Paths of Chinese Art), 26(1)(4), 1938, pp. 579–587.
Sen, Paresh Chandra, Machhagirir Padamule (Pagodar Deshe) (In the Land of Pagodas: At the Feet of Machha Mountains), 15(1)(5), 1927a, pp. 781–793.
Sen, Paresh Chandra, Sri Pad Darshan: Shweset, Tirthe o Pothe (Offering prayers at Sri Pad: Shweset, Pilgrimage and on the road), 15(2)(2), 1927b, pp. 238–249.
Sen, Paresh Chandra, Sri Pad Darshan: Shweset, Tirthe o Pothe (ii), 16(2)(4), 1928, pp. 530–531.
Sen, Paresh Chandra, Sri Pad Darshan: Shweset, Tirthe o Pothe (iii), 17(1)(2), 1929, pp. 267–271.
Sinha, Jadunath, Bibdha Prasanga: Bishwamanab (Universal Man), 17(2)(1), 1929, pp. 88–94.
Sorcar, P.C., Japaner Pothe (On the Way to Japan) 25(1)(4), 1937a, pp. 582–590.
Sorcar, P.C., Japaner Pothe (ii), 25(1)(5), 1937b, pp. 692–698.
Sorcar, P.C., Japaner Pothe (iii), 25(2)(1), 1937c, pp. 62–69.
Sorcar, P.C., Japaner Pothe (iv), 26(1)(1), 1938a, pp. 65–73.
Sorcar, P.C., Japaner Pothe (v), 26(1)(5), 1938b, pp. 677–684.
Tagore, Rabindranath, Chin o Japan 12(1)(3), 1924, pp. 423–426.

Bhramar

Anon, Bange Pathak Sankhya (The Readers in Bengal), 2(1), 1875, pp. 2–4.

Bichitra

Bagchi, Prabodh Chandra, Bharat o Chin–Japan (India and China–Japan), 4(2)(5), 1931, pp. 583–585.
Bandopadhyay, Bibhuti Bhushan, Bishwa Prakriti: Borniyo Dviper Palli Anchal (World Nature: The Countryside of Bali Island), 10(1)(2), 1936, pp. 163–168.
Bandopadhyay, Kedarnath, Chiner Smriti (Memories of China), 6(2)(6), 1933, pp. 732–737.
Bhopwmick, Panchanan, Brahma Prabashi Bangali (Ex-patriot Bengalis in Burma), 10(1)(5), 1936, pp. 601–604.
Bose, Himangshu Kumar, Brahmadesher Prakritik Soundarya (The Natural Beauty of Burma), 2(2)(6), 1929a, pp. 954–959.
Bose, Himangshu Kumar, Tibboti Lamader Anusthanik Nach (Bibidha Sangraha) (The Ceremonial Dances of the Lamas of Tibet), 2(2)(6), 1929b, pp. 957–960.
Ghosh, Monomohon, Turk Sadharontantre Narir Mukti (Women's Emancipation under the Turkish Republic), 2(2)(5), 1928, pp. 722–732.
Ghosh, Rabindranarayan, Prachyer Parichoy (Knowledge of the East) 7(2)(1), 1933, pp. 19–23.
Ghosh, Santidev, Sinhale Rabindranath (Rabindranath in Sri Lanka), 8(1)(5), 1934, pp. 654–669.
Kar, Surendranath, Balir Kotha (Tales of Bali), 2(2)(3), 1928, pp. 353–360.
Mukhopadhyay, Prabhat Kumar and Debi, Sudhamoyee, Chine Hindu Sahitya (Hindu Literature in China), 1(2)(2), 1927a, pp. 238–245.
Mukhopadhyay, Prabhat Kumar and Debi, Sudhamoyee, Chine Hindu Sahitya (ii), 1(2)(3), 1927b, pp. 414–421.
Mukhopadhyay, Prabhat Kumar and Debi, Sudhamoyee, Chine Hindu Sahitya (iii), 1(2)(4), 1927c, pp. 566–571.
Mukhopadhyay, Prabhat Kumar and Debi, Sudhamoyee, Chine Hindu Sahitya (Hindu Literature in China), 2(2)(2), 1928a, pp. 250–255.
Mukhopadhyay, Prabhat Kumar and Debi, Sudhamoyee, Chine Hindu Sahitya (ii), 2(2)(3), 1928b, pp. 338–342.

Mukhopadhyay, Prabhat Kumar and Debi, Sudhamoyee, Chine Hindu Sahitya (iv), 1(2)(5), 1928c, pp. 686–691.
Mukhopadhyay, Prabhat Kumar and Debi, Sudhamoyee, Chine Hindu Sahitya (v), 2(1)(1), 1928d, pp. 795–800.
Mukhopadhyay, Prabhat Kumar and Debi, Sudhamoyee, Chine Hindu Sahitya (vi), 2(1)(2), 1928e, pp. 260–267.
Mukhopadhyay, Prabhat Kumar and Debi, Sudhamoyee, Chine Hindu Sahitya (vii), 2(1)(3), 1928f, pp. 386–391.
Mukhopadhyay, Prabhat Kumar and Debi, Sudhamoyee, Korea 0 Japaner Hindu Sahitya (Hindu Literature in, Korea and Japan), 2(1)(6), 1928g, pp. 897–901.
Mukhopadhyay, Sailakumar, Sikkim o Tibet E Baro Din (Twelve Days in Tibet), 10(1)(4), 1936a, p. 48.
Mukhopadhyay, Sailakumar, Sikkim o Tibet E Baro Din (ii) 10(1)(5), 1936b, pp. 548–553.
Mukhopadhyay, Sailakumar, Sikkim o Tibet E Baro Din (iii), 10(1)(6), 1936c, pp. 693–698.
Sen Sharma, Manilal, Shilpi Manindra Bhushan Gupta o Tar Chitrakala (The Artistic Style of Painter Manindra Bhusan Gupta), 7(1)(4), 1933, pp. 477–487.
Sorcar, P.C., Japan o Japani (Japan and Japanese), 11(1)(4), 1937, pp. 488–494.

Grihastha

Maitreya, Upendranath, Chine Shishu Shiksha (Children's Education in China), 8(8)(2), 1916, pp. 122–128.
Sarkar, Benoy Kumar, Asiar Manchester (The Manchester of Asia), 7(7)(5), 1915a, pp. 411–425.
Sarkar, Benoy Kumar, Cheena Kobider Prakriti Nishtha (The Love for Nature of the Chinese Poets), 7(7)(11), 1915b, pp. 977–981.
Sarkar, Benoy Kumar, Eksaptahe Ardhek Japan (Half a Week in Japan), 7(7)(2), 1915c, pp. 167–189.
Sarkar, Benoy Kumar, Po-chaier Binawali (The Flautist of Po-Chai), 7(7)(11), 1915d, pp. 1030–1035.
Sarkar, Benoy Kumar, Swadhan Asiar Rajdhani (The Capital of Independent Asia), 7(7)(3), 1915e, pp. 209–235.
Sarkar, Benoy Kumar, Swadhan Asiar Rajhdani (ii), 7(7)(4), 1915f, pp. 332–350.
Sarkar, Benoy Kumar, Sanskrita Bouddhya Sahityer Cheena Onubad (Chinese Translation of Buddhist Literature in Sanskrit), 8(8)(1), 1916, pp. 17–21.
Sarkar, Benoy Kumar, Chhatrer Porjyoton- China kobitar Bonganubad (The Journey of a Student, Bengali translation of a Chinese poem), 8(8)(11), 1917, pp. 893–894.
Sarkar, Ramlal, Chine Hindur Prabhab (The Influence of Hindus in China), 4(4)(8), 1913, pp. 489–497.

Janmabhoomi

Bandopadhyay, Durgadas, Amar Jiban Charit (My Life Story), 1(7), 1891a, pp. 365–371.
Bandopadhyay, Durgadas, Amar Jiban Charit (ii), 1(8), 1891b, pp. 462–471.
Bhattacharya, Surendranath, Jih Pener Japan Desh (In Jih Pen's Country-Japan), 22(7), 1914, pp. 241–245.
Mitra, Pramatha Nath, Japaner Abhyudoy (The Rise of Japan), 15(11), 1907a, pp. 425–434.
Mitra, Pramatha Nath, Japaner Abhyudoy (ii), 15(12), 1907b, pp. 463–473.
Sanyal, Ajit Prasad, Chin Chitra (A Picture of China), 11(9), 1902, pp. 334–341.

Mahila

Anon, Amader Bhrahman Brittanto (Descriptions of Our Travel), 12(9), 1907a, pp. 233–234.

Anon, Amdesh Bhraman Brittanto (ii), 12(10), 1907b, pp, 258–267.
Anon, Brahma Deshe Stri Swadhinata (Women's Freedom in Burma), 12(8), 1907c, pp. 196–200.
Anon, Burma Deshiyo Ramani o Bibidha Bishoy (Burmese Women and Other Things), 12(11), 1907d, pp. 284–293.
Anon, Rangoon, 13(2), 1907e, pp. 40–43.
Anon, Rangoon (ii), 13(3), 1907f, pp. 45–79.
Anon, Rangoon (iii), 13(4), 1907g, pp. 106–109.
Anon, Rangoon Hoite Kolkata (Rangoon to Calcutta), 13(5), 1907h, pp. 127–132.
Anon, Tangu Nogor Gomon (Travel to Tangu Town), 12(12), 1907i, pp. 310–314.
Anon, Tangu o Fiyu Nogor (Tangu and Fiyu Towns), 13(1), 1907j, pp. 17–20.

Manashi

Bandopadhyay, Brojendranath, Chine Bibaha Pratha (Wedding Rituals in China), 1(12), 1909, pp. 566–577.
Nath Ghosh, Manmatha, Japane Stricharitra (Women in Japan), 1(2), 1908a, pp. 93–96.
Nath Ghosh, Manmatha, Japane Stricharitra (ii), 1(6), 1908b, pp. 252–255.
Nath Ghosh, Manmatha, Japane Bibaha (Marriage in Japan), 3(9), 1911a, pp. 599–603.
Nath Ghosh, Manmatha, Japane Bibaha (ii), 4(2), 1911b, pp. 112–115.
Nath Ghosh, Manmatha, Japane Dharma Biswas (Religious Beliefs in Japan), 4(6), 1912a, pp. 366–371.
Nath Ghosh, Manmatha, Japaner Dharma (Religion in Japan), 5(2), 1912b, pp. 134–136.
Nath Ghosh, Manmatha, Japaner Dharma (ii), 5(4), 1913, pp. 289–295.
Roy, Ganapati, Japaner Stri Jatir Itihash (History of Women in Japan), 2(12), 1910, pp. 732–739.

Manashi o Marmabani

Abani, Kumar De, Japaner "Robin Hood" Mitsuru Tushama (Mitsuru Tushama-the Robin Hood of Japan) 19(1)(2), 1926, pp. 111–118.
Abani, Kumar De, Chine Bideshi Samashya (The Problem of Foreigners in China), 20(1)(2), 1927, pp. 163–168.
Bose, Phanindranath, Shyamdeshe Hindurajya (Hinduism in Shyamdesh/Thailand), 12(1)(5), 1920, pp. 478–480.
Majumdar, Nalini Kanta, Jakkha ba Lamar Desh (In the Land of the Yakshas or Lamas), 17(1)(1), 1924, pp. 2–7.
Mitra, Purna Chandra, Mesopotamia, 11(2)(5), 1919, pp. 526–529.
Roy, Kinnaresh, Mog Muluker 'Phungi' (The Phungis of the Land of the Mogs), 13(1)(2), 1920, pp. 161–167.
Roy, Krishna Behari for Sitanath Bhatta, Kut-Juddhe Turki Haste Bandi Bangalir Atmakahani (Autobiography of a Bengali Imprisoned by Turks in the Kut War), 11(2)(2), 1919, pp. 121–125.
Roy, Sris Chandra, Bibhinna Jatir Antyeshti Pratha (Funeral Rites of Different Races), 12(1)(1), 1919a, pp. 81–90.
Roy, Sris Chandra, Bibhinna Jatir Antyeshti Pratha (ii), 12(1)(2), 1919b, pp. 175–186.
Roy, Sris Chandra, Bibhinna Jatir Antyeshti Pratha (iii), 12(1)(3), 1919c, pp. 312–319.
Roy, Sris Chandra, Bibhinna Jatir Antyeshti Pratha (iv), 12(1)(5), 1919d, pp. 480–486.
Sen, Gour Hari, Japaner Bhabishyat (Baideshiki) (The Future of Japan), 12(2)(4), 1920, pp. 387–389.

Masik Basumati

Anon, Chiner Prachir (The Chinese Wall), 1(2)(6), 1922, p. 717.

Debi, Aparna, Japane Ki Dekhlam (What I Saw in Japan), 12(2)(5), 1933, pp. 703–710.
Ghosh, Hemendra Prasad, Turkir Joy (The Victory of Turkey), 1(2)(1), 1922a, pp. 81–89.
Ghosh, Hemendra Prasad, Turkir Kotha (Tales of Turkey), 1(2)(2), 1922b, p. 257.
Ghosh, Hemendra Prasad, Turkir Punarabhydoy o Bartaman Samasya (The Revival of Turkey and the Present Problems), 1(2)(3), 1922c, pp. 295–300.
Ghosh, Sarojnath, Japani Nartaki (The Japanese Dancer), 2(2)(1), 1923, pp. 82–89.
Ghosh, Sarojnath, Chin (China), 6(1)(3), 1927, pp. 438–456.
Harisadhan, Ghoshal, Chine Bharater Chintadhara (Indian Thought in China), 6(1)(4), 1927, pp. 543–545.
Jagyadishwarananda, Swami, Singhaler Kotha (Tales of Sri Lanka), 12(1)(6), 1933a, pp. 972–986.
Jagyadishwarananda, Swami, Singhaler Kotha (ii), 12(2)(1), 1933b, pp. 95–100.
Jagyadishwarananda, Swami, Singhaler Kotha (iii), 12(2)(3), 1933c, pp. 368–376.
Jaminikant Sen, Chainik Chhitrakalay Bharatiya Oisharjya (Indian Treasures in Chinese Art), 14(2)(3), 1935, pp. 480–488.
Roy, Dinendrakumar, Chiner Jaladasyuder Bombete Giri (The Exploits of the Chinese Sea Pirates), 9(1)(3), 1930, pp. 524–533.
Sadananda, Swami, Brihittara Bharater Devdevi (The Gods and Goddesses of Greater India), 14(2)(4), 1935, pp. 502–508.
Sarkar, Girindranath, Brahma Prabashe Sarat Chandra (Sarat Chandra in Burmese Exile), 16(2)(6), 1937, pp. 913–917.

Nabajiban

Ta Pra, Cha, Singhal Yatra (ii), 1(2), 1884a, pp. 86–92.
Ta Pra, Cha, Singhal Yatra (iii), 1(3), 1884b, pp. 150–157.
Ta Pra, Cha, Singhal Yatra (iv), 1(5), 1884c, pp. 273–280.
Ta Pra, Cha, Singhal Yatra (v), 1(7), 1884d, pp. 405–410.
Ta Pra, Cha (Taraprasad Chattopadhyay?), Singhal Yatra (Travel to Sri Lanka), 1(1), 1884e, pp. 26–34.

Nabya Bharat

Basu, Prasad, Javadvipe Kabibhasha (Poetic Language in Java), 23(5), 1905, pp. 232–241.
Biswas, Promoda Kumar, Japan o Bharater Sambandhya (Japan-India Links), 30(6), 1912, pp. 352–358.
Das, Akinchan, Japani Jatir Bisheshotto (Characteristics of the Japanese Race), 33(10), 1915, pp. 627–631.
Das, Sarat Ch., Tibboter Pothe (On the Way to Tibet), 19(8), 1901, pp. 425–433.
Majumdar, Durjoy Ch., Japani Adarsha (Japanese Ideal), 23(3), 1905, pp. 148–151.
Mukhopadhyay, Taraknath, Japaner Abhyudoy (Rise of Japan), 24(1), 1906a, pp. 11–27.
Mukhopadhyay, Taraknath, Japaner Abhyudoy (ii), 24(2), 1906b, pp. 100–123.
Mukhopadhyay, Taraknath, Japaner Abhyudoy (iii), 24(4), 1906c, pp. 176–179.
Mukhopadhyay, Taraknath, Japaner Abhyudoy (iv), 24(5), 1906d, pp. 229–235.
Mukhopadhyay, Taraknath, Japaner Abhyudoy (v), 24(7), 1906e, pp. 344–358.
Sarkar, Ramlal, Chindeshe Santan Churi (Child Theft in China-novel), 22(3), 1904, pp. 161–165, (ii) 22(5), 1904, 242–248;(iii), 22(7), 1904, 398–381; (iv), 22(10), 1904, 529-534; (v), 23(3), 1905, 140–145; (vi), 23(4), 1905, 200-207; (v), 23(6), 1905, 302–311; (vi), 23(8), 1905, 434-; (vii), 23(10), 1905, 509–523; (viii), 23(11), 1905, 600–607; (ix) 23(12), 1905, 664-668;(x) 24(2), 1906, 75-92.
Sen, Jamini Kanta, Bharater Bohir Rashtra Neeti (India's Foreign Policy), 25(7), 1907a, pp. 337–351.

Sen, Jamini Kanta, Bharater Bohir Rashtra Neeti (ii), 25(9), 1907b, pp. 497–504.
Sen, Jamini Kanta, Bharater Bohir Rashtra Neeti (iii), 25(12), 1907c, pp. 639–643.
Sen, Sasankamohan, Europe o Asia (Poem), 24(4), 1906, pp. 207–210.

Prabashi

'A', Japane Dharmotshaho (Religious Inspiration in Japan), 9(8), 1909, pp. 613–614.
Anon, Antortajik Nari Sammelan (International Women's Conference), 22(2)(5), 1922, pp. 682–683.
Bandopadhyay, Suresh Chandra, Japaner Dharma (Religion in Japan), 9(4), 1909, pp. 231–234.
Bandopadhyay, Suresh Chandra, Satchollish Ronin (The 47th Ronin), 11(2)(5), 1911a, pp. 420–474.
Bandopadhyay, Suresh Chandra, Satchollish Ronin (ii), 11(1)(5), 1911b, pp. 474–478.
Bandopadhyay, Suresh Chandra, Satchollish Ronin (iii), 11(1)(6), 1911c, pp. 634–639.
Bandopadhyay, Suresh Chandra, Satchollish Ronin (iv), 11(2)(1), 1911d, pp. 38–40.
Bandopadhyay, Suresh Chandra, Satchollish Ronin (v), 11(2)(2), 1911e, pp. 174–179.
Bandopadhyay, Suresh Chandra , Satchollish Ronin (vi), 11(2)(3), 1911f, pp. 237–240.
Bandopadhyay, Suresh Chandra, Satchollish Ronin (vii), 11(2)(4), 1911g, pp. 341–347.
Bandopadhyay, Suresh Chandra, Mikado Mutsuhito 12(1)(5), 1912, pp. 542–546.
Bandopadhyay, Suresh Chandra, Japan Utsab o Anusthan (Ceremonial Rules in Japan), 14(1)(1), 1914, pp. 59–68.
Bhattacharya, Narendranath, Brahmabalika o Tahar Pronoy kahiniKahani (The Love Story of a Burmese Girl), 2(12), 1902, pp. 419–423.
Bhowmick, Bijoy Kumar, Bagdad 23(1)(1), 1923, pp. 47–58.
Bose, Phanindranath, Champarajye Hindu Upanibesh (Hindu Colonisation in Champa), 26(1)(3), 1926, pp. 565–568.
Chattopadhyay, Hemanta, Manchuria, Mongolia o Tibboter Naari (Women of Manchuria, Mongolia and Tibet) 22(2)(2), 1922, pp. 210–215.
Chattopadhyay, Shanta, Boro Budur 14(2)(4), 1914, pp. 397–402.
Chattopadhyay, Suniti Kumar, Javadviper Pothe (On the Way to Java), 27(1)(5), 1927a, pp. 671–681.
Chattopadhyay, Suniti Kumar, Javadviper Pothe (ii), 27(1)(6), 1927b, pp. 833–847.
Chattopadhyay, Suniti Kumar, Dvipamoy Bharat (Insulindia/Islands of India), 29(2)(3), 1929a, pp. 388–400.
Chattopadhyay, Suniti Kumar, Dvipamoy Bharat (ii), 29(2)(4), 1929b, pp. 578–588.
Chattopadhyay, Suniti Kumar, Dvipamoy Bharat (iii), 29(2)(5), 1929c, pp. 727–735.
Chattopadhyay, Suniti Kumar, Dvipamoy Bharat (iii), 29(2)(6), 1929d, pp. 857–871.
Chattopadhyay, Suniti Kumar, Dvipamoy Bharat (iv), 30(1)(1), 1930a, pp. 97–108.
Chattopadhyay, Suniti Kumar, Dvipamoy Bharat (v), 30(1)(2), 1930b, pp. 265–277.
Chattopadhyay, Suniti Kumar, Dvipamoy Bharat (vi), 30(1)(3), 1930c, pp. 408–420.
Chattopadhyay, Suniti Kumar, Dvipamoy Bharat (vii), 30(1)(4), 1930d, pp. 577–589.
Chattopadhyay, Suniti Kumar, Dvipamoy Bharat (viii), 30(1)(5), 1930e, pp. 735–745.
Chattopadhyay, Suniti Kumar, Dvipamoy Bharat (ix), 30(1)(6), 1930f, pp. 878–887.
Chattopadhyay, Suniti Kumar, Dvipamoy Bharat (x), 30(2)(1), 1930g, pp. 85–97.
Chattopadhyay, Suniti Kumar, Dvipamoy Bharat (xi), 30(2)(2), 1930h, pp. 244–251.
Chattopadhyay, Suniti Kumar, Dvipamoy Bharat (xii), 30(2)(3), 1930i, pp. 358–368.
Chattopadhyay, Suniti Kumar, Dvipamoy Bharat (xiii), 30(2)(4), 1930j, pp. 530–538.
Chattopadhyay, Suniti Kumar, Dvipamoy Bharat (xiv), 31(1)(1), 1931a, pp. 81–91.
Chattopadhyay, Suniti Kumar, Dvipamoy Bharat (xv), 31(1)(3), 1931b, pp. 355–367.
Chattopadhyay, Suniti Kumar, Dvipamoy Bharat (xvi), 31(1)(4), 1931c, pp. 537–547.
Chattopadhyay, Suniti Kumar, Dvipamoy Bharat (xvii), 31(1)(5), 1931d, pp. 709–723.
Chattopadhyay, Suniti Kumar, Dvipamoy Bharat (xviii), 31(1)(6), 1931e, pp. 815–831.

Chowdhury, Hemada Kanta, Lankay Bouddha Bihar (The Buddhist Viharas in Sri Lanka), 10(2)(1), 1910, pp. 4–12.
Das, Pannalal, Chin Juddhe Dafadar Harinarayan Basu (At the War in China), 30(2)(3), 1930, pp. 314–320.
Das, Suresh Chandra, Javadviper Nrityakala (The Art of Dance in Java), 25(2)(4), 1925, pp. 523–524.
Debi, Hemlata, Japane Bhaktibader Guru (The Preceptors of Japanese Bhakti Movement), 10(2)(4), 1910a, pp. 456–460.
Debi, Hemlata, Japane Bhaktibader Guru (ii), 10(6), 1910b, pp. 549–553.
Debi, Hemlata, Japane Bhaktibader Guru (iii), 11(1)(5), 1911a, pp. 474–478.
Debi, Hemlata, Japane Bhaktibader Guru (iv), 11(1)(6), 1911b, pp. 634–639.
Debi, Hemlata, Japane Bhaktibader Guru (v), 11(2)(1), 1911c, pp. 38–40.
Debi, Hemlata, Japane Bhaktibader Guru (vi), 11(2)(2), 1911d, pp. 174–178.
Debi, Hemlata, Japane Bhaktibader Guru (vii), 11(2)(3), 1911e, pp. 237–240.
Debi, Hemlata, Japane Bhaktibader Guru (viii), 11(2)(4), 1911f, pp. 341–347.
Gangopadhyay, Manilal, Chin Desher Kaji (The Qazi of China), 9(11), 1909, pp. 925–933.
Gangopadhyay, Manilal, Rin Shodh (Repayment of Loan-Inspired by a Japanese Story), 12(1)(5) 1912, pp. 504–510.
Ghoshal, Haripada, Chine Prakriti Puja (Nature Worship in China), 25(1)(3), 1925a, pp. 363–366.
Ghoshal, Haripada, Confucius, 25(2)(6), 1925b, pp. 745–748.
Gupta, Manindra Bhushan, Chine Chitrakalar Itihas (The History of Art in China), 24(2)(1), 1924, pp. 81–89.
Gupta, ManindraBhushan, Singhaler Chitra (A Picture of Sri Lanka), 34(1)(1), 1934, pp. 28–35.
Harkara, Dak, Antortajik Nari Sanmelan (International Women's Conference), 21(2)(2), 1921, pp. 202–206.
Hemandralal Roy, Shyam-Rajya, (In the Shyam/Thai Kingdom), 24(2)(1), 1924, pp. 65–73.
Lahiri, Kumudnath, Brahmer Naba Borshotav (The New Year in Burma), 10(6), 1910a, pp. 536–538.
Lahiri, Kumudnath, Burma – Samalochona (Burma – An Analysis), 10(3), 1910b, pp. 536–538.
Majumdar, Akshoy Kumar, Bangali o Japani (Bengalis and Japanese), 5(4), 1905, pp. 207–209.
Majumdar, Bijoy Chandra, Bahir Bharat (Outer India), 11(2)(5), 1911, pp. 425–430.
Majumdar, Ramesh Chandra, Chindeshiya Bouddha Paribrajak (A Chinese Buddhist Traveller), 24(1)(6), 1924, pp. 792–795.
Mohan Das, Gyanendra, Singhale Bangali Kala Adhyapak Srijukta Manindra Bhushan Gupta (A Bengali Art Lecturer in Singhal/Sri Lanka), 26(1)(5), 1926, pp. 767–769.
Mukhopadhyay, Prabhat Kumar, Chine Bharatiya Sahitya (Indian Literature in China), 25(2)(5), 1925, pp. 619–623.
Mukhopadhyay, Prabhat Kumar, Kung Fu Tsu (Translated from Chinese), 26(1)(1), 1926, pp. 102–105.
Nag, Kalidas, Brihattara Bharat (Greater India), 26(2)(2), 1927, pp. 285–208.
Roy, Prafulla Chandra, Nabya Chin o Bangla (Modern China and Bengal), 29(2)(1), 1929, pp. 80–91.
Roy, Ramakanta, Japan Prabashir Patra (Letters from Abroad in Japan), 1(4), 1901, pp. 160–163.
Sanyal, Brojo Sundor, Japane Strishiksha (Women's Education in Japan), 8(8), 1908, pp. 435–440.
Sarkar, Girindranath, Brahmadeshe Bangali (Bengalis in Burma), 1(8–9), 1901, pp. 347–350.
Sarkar, Girindranath, Brahma Prabashe (poem)(Abroad in Burma), 2(10–11), 1902, pp. 384–385.
Sarkar, Ramlal, Chindeshe Basantotsab (Spring Festival in China), 4(2), 1904a, pp. 81–83.
Sarkar, Ramlal, Chindeshe Chandu Sheban (Opium Addiction in China), 4(5), 1904b, pp. 272–277.

Sarkar, Ramlal, Sir Robert Hart o Chiner Sashan Sanskar (Sir Robert Hart and Administration of China), 4(9), 1904c, pp. 482–488.
Sarkar, Ramlal, Chin Rajkarmacharigoner Biswasghatokota (The Treachery of the Chinese Officials), 5(10), 1905a, pp. 613–620.
Sarkar, Ramlal, Chindeshe Natyabhinoy (Theatre Performances in China), 5(3), 1905b, pp. 143–147.
Sarkar, Ramlal, Chindeshe Yamraj (Yama, the God of Death in China), 5(5), 1905c, pp. 277–283.
Sarkar, Ramlal, Chindeshe Swadeshi (Swadeshi in China), 6(4), 1906a, pp. 192–200.
Sarkar, Ramlal, Japani Adarsha o Chin Jatir Shiksha Sanskar (Education Reforms on the Japanese Model in China), 6(9), 1906b, pp. 493–498.
Sarkar, Ramlal, Peking Rajpuri (The Royal Palace in Peking), 6(12), 1906c, pp. 662–675.
Sarkar, Ramlal, Chin-Brahma Simanter Ashobhyo Jati (The Uncivilized Tribes of the China-Burma Border), 11(2)(6), 1911, pp. 542–552.
Sarkar, Ramlal, Chin-Brahma Simanter Ashobhyo Jati (ii), 12(1)(3), 1912a, pp. 289–297.
Sarkar, Ramlal, Chin-Brahma Simanter Ashobhyo Jati (iii), 12(1)(4), 1912b, pp. 366–380.
Sarkar, Ramlal, Chin-Brahma Simanter Ashobhyo Jati (iv), 12(1)(5), 1912c, pp. 491–497.
Sarkar, Ramlal, Chin-Brahma Simanter Ashobhyo Jati (v), 12(2)(1), 1912d, pp. 12–25.
Sarkar, Ramlal, Chin-Brahma Simanter Ashobhyo Jati (vi), 12(2)(2), 1912e, pp. 151–160.
Sarkar, Ramlal, Chin-Brahma Simanter Ashobhyo Jati (vii), 12(2)(3), 1912f, pp. 251–260.
Sarkar, Ramlal, Chin-Brahma Simanter Ashobhyo Jati (viii), 12(2)(4), 1912g, pp. 364–370.
Sarkar, Ramlal, Chin-Brahma Simanter Ashobhyo Jati (ix), 12(2)(5), 1912h, pp. 448–484.
Sarkar, Ramlal, Chin-Brahma Simanter Ashobhyo Jati (x), 12(2)(6), 1912i, pp. 568–578.
Satish Ranjan Khastagir, Singhal Prabashi Bangali (A Bengali at Sri Lanka), 29(2)(4), 1929, pp. 490–496.
Sharma, Paresh Chandra, ShyamrajyeFarashiDoutyo (A French Envoy at Shyam Kingdom), 23(1)(1), 1923, pp. 90–99.
Som, Nagendra Chandra, Balidvip (Dharma o Upasana)(Religion and Worship in Bali Island), 4(2), 1904, pp. 73–80.
Tagore, Rabindranath, Vishwabodh (Internationalism), 9(11), 1909, pp. 889–898.
Tagore, Jyotirindranath, Shyamrajye Bhraman (Trans. of Travels in Thailand from *Le review*) 10(6), 1910, pp. 546–549.
Tagore, Rabindranath, Chin o Japan Bhraman Bibaran (Description of My Tour in China and Japan), 24(2)(1), 1924, pp. 792–795.

Pradip

Anon, Japan, 2(9), 1899, pp. 304–308.
Anon, Chin Prasanga (About China), 7(1), 1904, pp. 26–32.
Bhattacharya, Bisweshar, Japani Ramani (Japanese Women), 8(7), 1905, pp. 262–265.
Lahiri, Sisir Chandra, Japaner "Ainu", 8(3), 1905, pp. 106–115.
Maitreya, Akshoy Kumar, Bali Dwiper Hindurajya (The Hindu Kingdom of Bali), 2(5), 1899, pp. 201–205.

Purnima

Anon, Brahmadesher Bibaran (Descriptions of Burma), 3(3), 1895a, pp. 92–96.
Anon, Brahmadesher Bibaran (ii), 3(4), 1895b, pp. 119–127.
Anon, Brahmadesher Bibaran (iii), 3(5), 1895c, pp. 157–159.
Anon, Brahmadesher Bibaran (iv), 3(6–7), 1895d, pp. 205–208.
Anon, Brahmadesher Bibaran (v), 3(10), 1895e, pp. 289–294.
Anon, Brahmadesher Bibaran (vi), 3(11–12), 1895f, pp. 332–338.

Chattopadhyay, Bishanupada, Rush-Japan Samar Upalokhye (On the Russo-Japanese War), 12(1), 1904, pp. 12–30.
Ghosh, Ananda Gopal, Chiner Bibaran (Descriptions of China), 3(8), 1895, pp. 215–244.

Ramdhanu

Anon, Turashka o Mustapha Kemal Pasha, 1(11), 1927, pp. 560–567.
Anon, Japan Kobe Jaglo (When Did Japan Rise), 2(3), 1928, pp. 145–149.
Anon, Jave ba Javadvip (Java or the Island of Java), 6(2), 1932, pp. 95–101.
Bandopadhyay, Atul Chandra, Bangali Jahaj o Banglar Samudra Banijya (Bengali Ships and Bengal's Sea-trade), 10(7), 1937, pp. 352–357.
Bandopadhyay, Birajkumar, Ascharya Prachir (The Wonderful Wall), 5(1), 1931, pp. 28–30.
Bandopadhyay, Nripendra Chandra, Burmar Kotha (Tales of Burma), 1(1), 1927a, p. 48.
Bandopadhyay, Nripendra Chandra, Burmar Kotha (ii), 1(2), 1927b, pp. 90–94.
Bandopadhyay, Nripendra Chandra, Burmar Kotha (iii), 1(3), 1927c, pp. 115–118.
Bhattacharjya, Kshitindranarayan, Japan Desher Chellemeye (Boys and Girls of Japan), 3(5), 1930, pp. 212–219.
Bhattacharjya, Kshitindranarayan, Madhya Asiar Moru prantore (On the Deserts of Central Asia), 8(9), 1935, pp. 430–438.
Bhattacharya, Manoranjan, Shyam Desh, 6(1), 1932, pp. 48–52.
Chainik, Sri, Tomader Chhoto Cheena Bhayera (Your Little Chinese Brothers), 2(2), 1928, pp. 75–79.
Chowdhury, Subinoy Roy, Deng mo-Chi, 10(7), 1937, pp. 352–357.
Dhar, Dhirendralal, Balidvip, 6(6), 1933, pp. 289–291.
Dhar, Dhirendralal, Nanking Fronte (On the Nanking Front), 11(5), 1938, pp. 292–296.
Editorial, Parasya Shekal o Ekal (Persia Yesterday and Today), 2(4), 1929, pp. 189–195.
Gopal, Satya, Dr Chiranjeeber Adventure, 8(9), 1935, pp. 438–445.
Jagatmohan Sen, Japan! Japan! , 9(11), 1936, pp. 550–560.
Mukhopadhyay, Karuna, Mih Thun Pyoye 11(6), 1938, pp. 361–366.
Mukhopadhyay, Prabhat Kumar, Kajir Bichar (The Qazi's Justice), 1(1), 1927, pp. 33–42.
Roy, Kalidas, Japani Golpo (Stories of Japan), 10(11), 1937, pp. 649–653.
SantiAich, Ekti Japani KahiniKahani (A Japanese Story), 6(6), 1933, pp. 305–306.
Sen, Bimal, Chiner Chhatra Samaj (The Student Community of China), 1(7), 1927, pp. 351–355.

Sadhana

Anon, Japan, 2(12), 1899, p. 547-incomplete.
Chakraborty, Rukmini Kanta, Singhal Bhraman (Travel in Sri Lanka), 2, 1892–93, pp. 46–50.
Gupta, Umesh Chandra, Singhal Lanka o Sumbhadesh, 2(12), 1899, pp. 558–564.

Sahitya

Das, Saratchandra, Japaner Pratham Upanyash (The First Novel of Japan), 8(2), 1897, pp. 90–96.
Gupta, Nagendranath, Bibidha Misc (on Chinese Saint), 3(7), 1892, pp. 361–366.
Paribrajak, Japaner Patra (Letter from Japan), 8(3), 1897, pp. 139–143.
Paribrajak, Japaner Patra (ii), 9(9), 1898, pp. 544–558.
Roy, Dinendra Kumar, Parashyer Garhasthya o Rajakiya Pratha (The Internal and Royal System of Persia), 4(10), 1873, pp. 749–755.
Tagore, Jyotirindranath, Ingraj-borjito Bharatbarsha (India Without the English), 15(4), 1904a, pp. 219–226.
Tagore, Jyotirindranath, Ingraj-borjito Bharatbarsha (ii), 15(5), 1904b, pp. 285–291.

Tagore, Jyotirindranath, Ingraj-borjito Bharatbarsha (iii), 15(6), 1904c, pp. 339–345.
Tagore, Jyotirindranath, Ingraj-borjito Bharatbarsha (iv), 15(8), 1904d, pp. 478–482.
Tagore, Jyotirindranath, Ingraj-borjito Bharatbarsha (v), 15(10), 1904e, pp. 620–623.

Sakha

Gupta, Biharilal, Chiner Kotha (Tales of China), 5(4), 1887, pp. 39–63.
Roy, Upendrakishore, Chiner Golpo (Stories of China), 4(1), 1886, pp. 10–15.

Sandesh

Anon, Japani Devata (The Japanese God), 1(4), 1913, pp. 109–113.
Anon, Banger Samudra Dekha-Japani Golpo (Frog's Vision of the Sea: A Japanese Story), 3(4), 1915a, pp. 93–94.
Anon, Chineder Kotha (Tales of Chinese), 3(2), 1915b, pp. 54–56.
Anon, Chindesher Kotha (Story about China), 3(10), 1915c, pp. 314–318.
Anon, Chiner Pachire (Chinese Wall), 8(3), 1920a, pp. 82–87.
Anon, Debata Janen (Chinese Story), 8(8), 1920b, pp. 247–25.
Anon, Lohir Pahara (Chinese Story), 8(3), 1920c, pp. 213–217.
Chakraborty, Punyalata, Pratigyar Daye (Arab Story), 7(12), 1919, pp. 333–335.
Debi, Jyotirmoyee, Dushtu Genumu (Naughty Genumu), 8(2), 1920, pp. 40–44.
Mukul, Ch. De, Fujiyama, 5(10), 1917a, pp. 302–304.
Mukul, Ch. De, Japaner Kotha (Descriptions of Japan), 5(9), 1917b, pp. 265–268.
Mukul, Ch. De, Raban Rajardeshe (In the Land of King Ravana), 5(11), 1917c, pp. 333–334.
Mukul, Ch. De, Raban Rajardeshe (ii), 5(12), 1917d, pp. 367–368.
Mukul, Ch. De, Aschrjyo Chabi (Japanese Story), 6(4), 1918a, pp. 113–116.
Mukul, Ch. De, Wang (Chinese Story), 6(6), 1918b, pp. 162–164.
Ray, Kuladaranjan, Andha Lo Saw (Chinese Folk Tale), 8(9), 1920, pp. 264–27.
Roy, Kularanjan, Rustom o Sohrab, 3(9), 1915a, pp. 258–260.
Roy, Kularanjan, Rustom o Sohrab (ii), 3(10), 1915b, pp. 297–301.

Sabuj Patra

Tagore, Rabindranath, Japaner Kotha (Description of Japan), 4(1), 1917, pp. 45–52.

Index

For Product Safety Concerns and Information please contact our EU representative GPSR@taylorandfrancis.com Taylor & Francis Verlag GmbH, Kaufingerstraße 24, 80331 München, Germany